GRAPHIC JOURNALING

MOH'D BILBEISI, RA

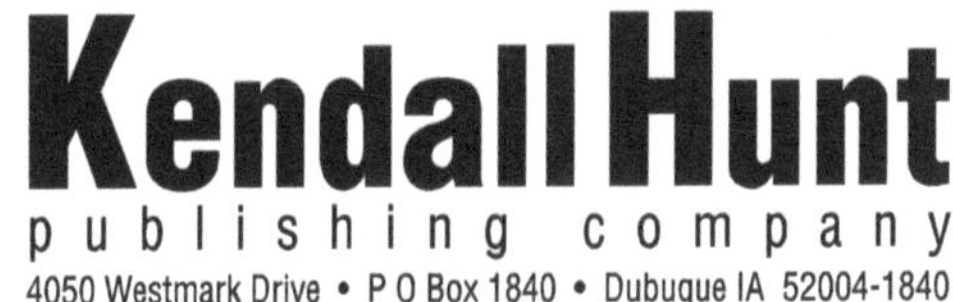

ISBN 978-0-7575-6262-4

Printed in the United States of America
10 9 8 7 6 5 4

Cover images created by the author.

dedication

This book was made possible through the boundless generosity and support of many dedicated individuals - my students, colleagues and friends, who donated their effort, time, and journal pages to this project. I would like to thank Oklahoma State University School of Architecture for allowing me the opportunity to pursue this project and for providing me with the necessary support. I also would like to acknowledge my friends and mentors, Inad Bilbeisi, Prof. John Bryant, Prof. David Hanser, Prof. Nigel Jones, Prof. Paul Laseau, Prof. Steve O'Hara, and Prof. Andy Urich for their encouragement and helpful advice. I especially want to thank Prof. Suzanne Bilbeisi for editing this book.

This book is dedicated to my wife and travel partner Suzanne, who has spent years keeping me out of trouble, to my wonderful son Moraad, to my parents, and to my students throughout the world.

preface

There is no denying the importance of keeping a journal. It is important to spend time reflecting upon the experiences that we encounter throughout our lives. Robert Gruden, in his book *The Grace of Great Things*, refers to this as self-knowledge ... "our unique ability to reflect on the past and the future." Spending the time to draw a few lines within a blank sketchbook to analyze and imagine should inspire and develop within each of us a meaningful state of awareness to last a lifetime. We live in a Post-Modern age where our experiences are fast-paced and our cognition of these experiences is very rapid. More often than not this cognition is processed after the fact, which nullifies and sterilizes the effect. A graphic journal is the antithesis of such phenomena - it tends to stop time so as to entice us to meaningfully absorb and instantaneously reflect upon the experience in real time. This is how we mature as individuals and designers.

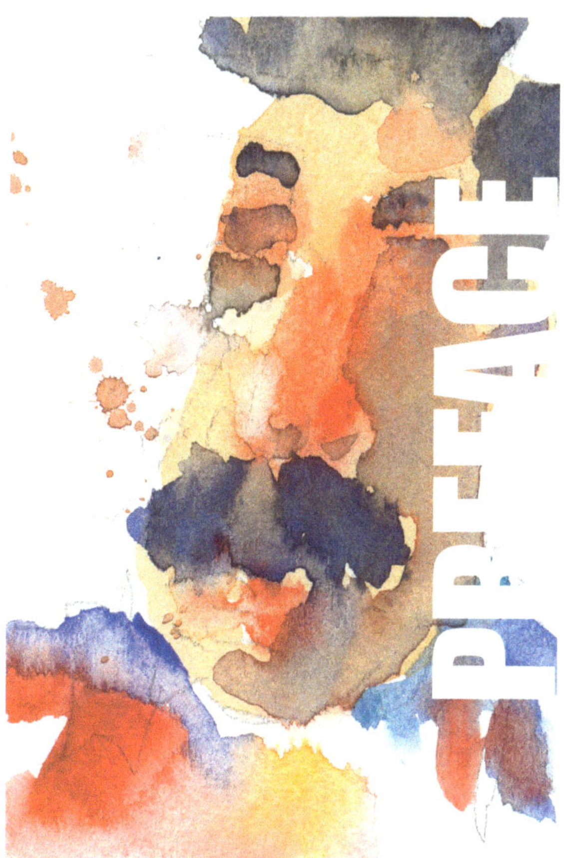

This book is a summary of more than 15 years of teaching students the art of generating ideas and graphically communicating their ideas. Throughout these years, I have come to the conclusion that great ideas are generated by individuals who are operating at a very high level of awareness of the world around them and highly reflective upon their own personal experiences. Of course, I can not prove this statement scientifically... it is my opinion!

This book is not a recipe for producing great graphic journals. Rather, it is intended as a celebration of the work of many individuals who view the world as a series of lines to be scribed by their pens and pencils while trying to comprehend why things are the way they are! The journaling paradigms/case studies were carefully selected from a wide gamut of submissions to illustrate different issues associated with intent, compositional aspects, and technique.

I have personally kept and maintained a graphic journal for more than twenty-five years. My work exhibits varying degrees of success, and a fair share of utter failure at times. My first attempts were meager, the subsequent were better! If anything, this indicates that keeping a graphic journal is a journey and a quest for a perfection that might not be attained; however, it is the journey that matters. **Pack your supplies and go!**

000 - CONTENTS

the topics within this book

table of contents

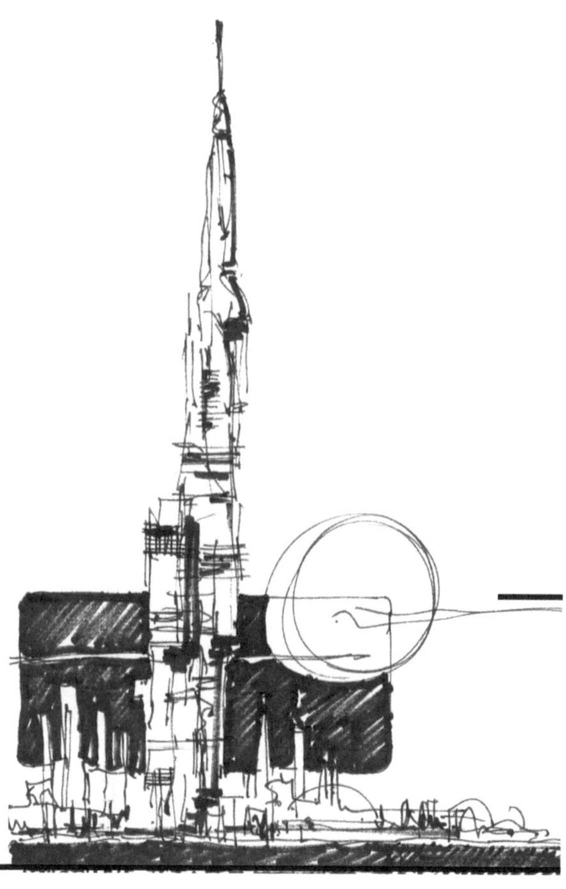

Fig. 000-1 Study for a skyscraper, Moh'd Bilbeisi, Ink and marker on paper.

00 - INTRODUCTION
what this book is about

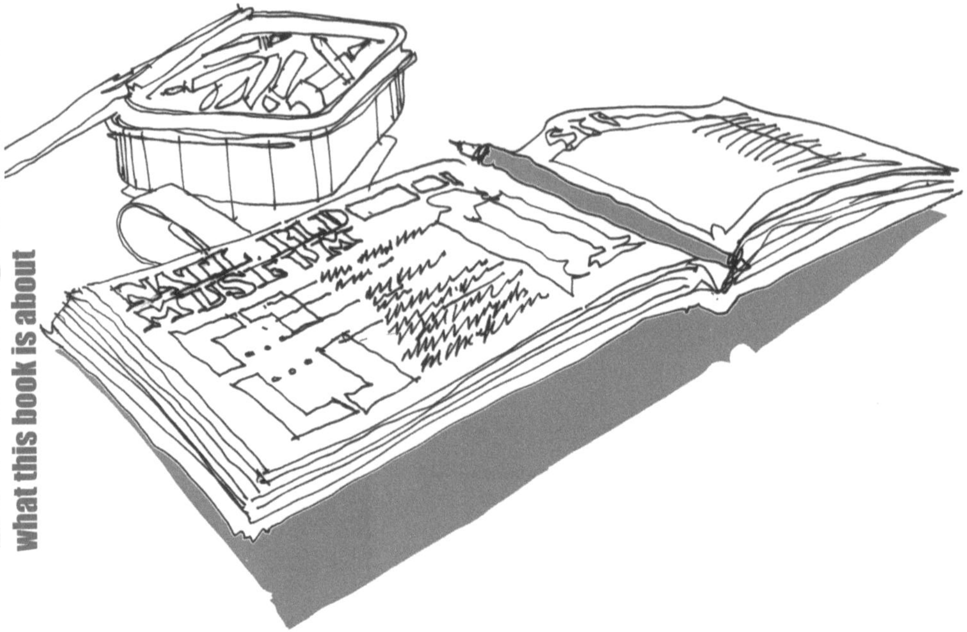

Prior to discussing the virtues of graphic journaling and attempting to de-mystify and divulge its secrets, please note that it is not my intention in any way to downplay other techniques and strategies nor endorse one graphic medium or product over another. I will be as factual and unbiased as possible, so as to allow the reader to become aware of the attributes and eccentricities associated with the world of artistic and architectural representation and graphic/drawing supplies.

In terms of methodology, this book is not a report nor a recipe about the subject of journaling. This book is a personal testimony of what a graphic journal is, what its possibilities and benefits are, and how it can be conducive to a person's development.

Over the course of ten years, I have collected hundreds of diverse examples from students, academicians, and professionals. This collection contains a rather colorful palette of styles and techniques; my hope is simply to promote this wonderful design habit!

I came to the United States of America as an international student to study architecture. Learning about architectural history - in English - was not as easy as I thought; I soon realized that I could remember more about the buildings by quickly sketching the slides shown on the big screen. The brief time period that the professor showed the slide on the projection screen ensured a honing of my abilities to sketch at lightning speed, only recording the most important aspects of the image.

My class notes became a mélange of the written word and the drawn image. In the beginning, the pages turned into a complete disaster... chaos and poor page composition. This led me, ultimately through necessity, to devise a master page composition that was more conducive to this image/word combination. That is when I started to favor the landscape page format over the portrait.

When color was the topic of the slide, it was faster for me to annotate the slide with the name of the color instead of taking the time to color the drawing on the page. I did, however, color the drawings when I went back to my desk with colored pencils if I had the time. My fondness for bright colors and my penchant for speed led me to watercolors, and I never stopped using them.

During my third year in architecture school, I discovered the architect, **Le Corbusier**. This is when I lost interest in sleep and would rather spend my free time reading about this fascinating individual's life and work. He subsequently became my hero. I learned that Le Corbusier kept a journal and used a fountain pen (Parker 51 to be exact), as well as graphite and colored pencils when working in his journal. Further investigations led me to the fact that most of the influential designers throughout history had maintained a journal in one form or another.

Who were these individuals interested in self-development through graphic journaling? **Leonardo Da Vinci, Michelangelo, Rembrandt, Goya, El Greco, Isaac Newton, Darwin, Thomas Edison, Albert Einstein, Vincent Van Gogh, Pablo Picasso, Joseph Turner, Cezanne, John Singer Sargent, Lawrence of Arabia, Norman Foster, Richard Rogers, Renzo Piano, Carlo Scarpa, Le Corbusier, Richard Sapper, Laurie Olin, Frank Gehry, Zaha Hadid, and Santiago Calatrava**, to name a few.

Since 1986 I have maintained a graphic journal. My shelves are lined with these journals and I still return to them to review what I drew and wrote many years earlier. These recordings and thoughts help me make decisions today. This is why I continue to use a graphic journal.

Periodically I conduct regional, national, and international field study courses that explore the complex relationship between humans, the natural environment, and architecture in various conditions. I teach my students the art of graphic journaling, to help them mature as designers and as individuals. The majority of the work included in this book is from these students' journals as well as my own. I have also included the work of practicing architects and that of others in academia, in the hopes of showing a wider gamut of graphic journaling.

Please note that the journal entries included are stylistically diverse. They all, however, share a single goal which is to more thoroughly understand the world around us.

Moh'd Bilbeisi

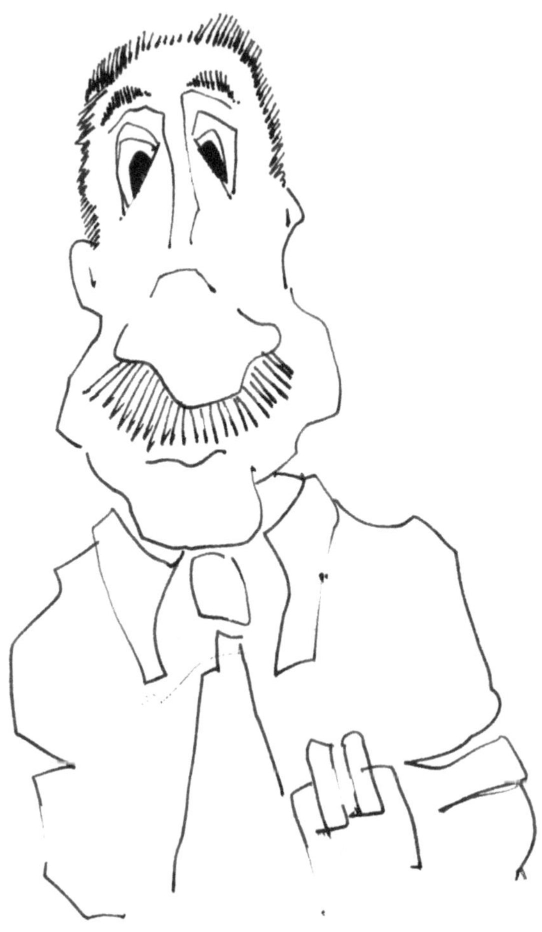

01 - KEEPING A JOURNAL

is it a lot of work?

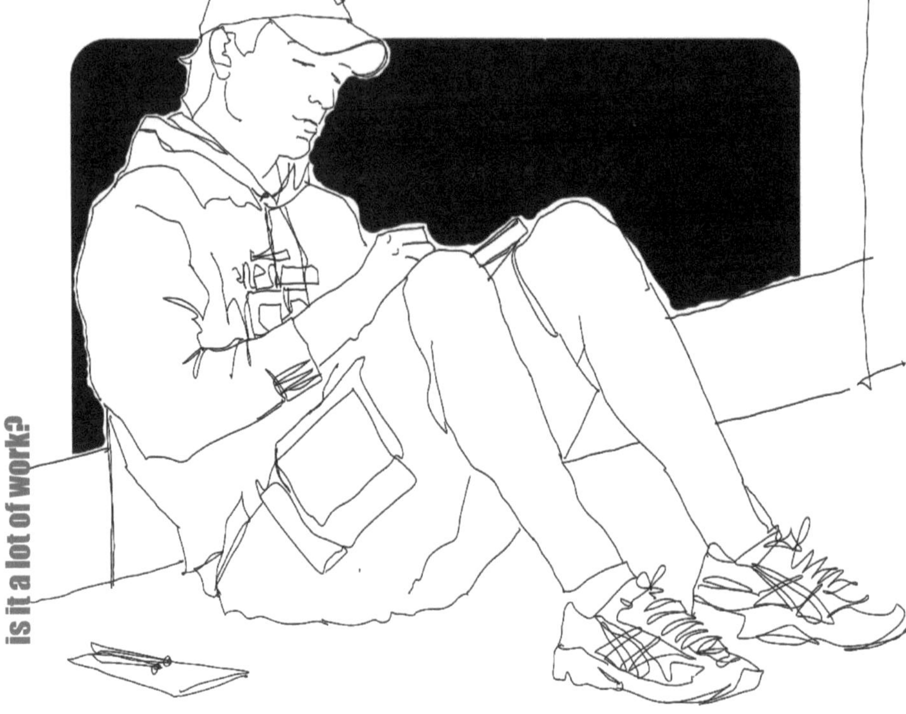

"A daily record of events or occurrences kept for private or official use. ... A record of events or matters of personal interest kept by any one for his own use, in which entries are made day by day, or as the events occur. Now usually implying something more elaborate than a diary."

The Oxford English Dictionary

Conceptually speaking, graphic journaling is a term used to describe a graphically oriented reflective process, an effective methodology whose ultimate purpose is to attain a better understanding of the world around us. Keeping a graphic journal, or **"journaling"** is a creative human task usually associated with enlightened individuals regardless of their respective field of expertise or profession. It functions as a gatherer of thoughts and images into a collective singularity for the sole purpose of developing a better understanding of an issue, place, or event. It allows us to challenge and question the norm while being engaged in the process of being. Many great thinkers and artists throughout time have kept a journal of sorts and used it as an indispensable tool to sift through their thoughts and ideas.

The word itself, journal, is from the Latin word "Diurnal" meaning daily, and while the meaning implies recording the daily activities of a person, journaling is a long-term endeavor that involves dedication, patience, discipline, and a commitment to personal growth. The value of keeping a graphic journal is not in its content but in its inherit process of recording the information, carefully editing the content, reflecting upon and analyzing the information, and ultimately recognizing the emergence of the resultant understanding.

keeping a journal

Before discussing the topic of journaling in greater detail, it should be mentioned that the graphic journal that is the subject of this book is not the type of "Dear Diary" that the lovelorn teenager might keep. While it is true that the graphic journal can lead to a greater personal understanding of a myriad of issues, it's purpose as discussed in these pages is for personal growth in the area of the creative process.

The journal that is the focus of this book is usually a bound notepad, lined or unlined, and is typically carried by architects, artists, scientists, musicians, and writers to supplement and reinforce their process of thinking. It is a scratchpad for the brain... a two-dimensional planar environment that allows a creative individual to better understand the world. It tends to be personal, but not to the point that you might consider suicide if someone else reviewed it! I constantly share my journal with my students and clients when discussing ideas and projects.

As human beings, we tend to incline toward the written word, due to our conditioning since early childhood. We interact daily within a culture that values the word and only the word. I vividly remember my mother asking me to stop doodling and to learn to draw something meaningful such as a flower or a horse! Luckily, I never listened! Several of my architecture students also recall their parents asking them to read versus to draw in their college prep years, which is ironic since their success in the field of architecture hinges upon developing their drawing, exploratory, and analytical skills.

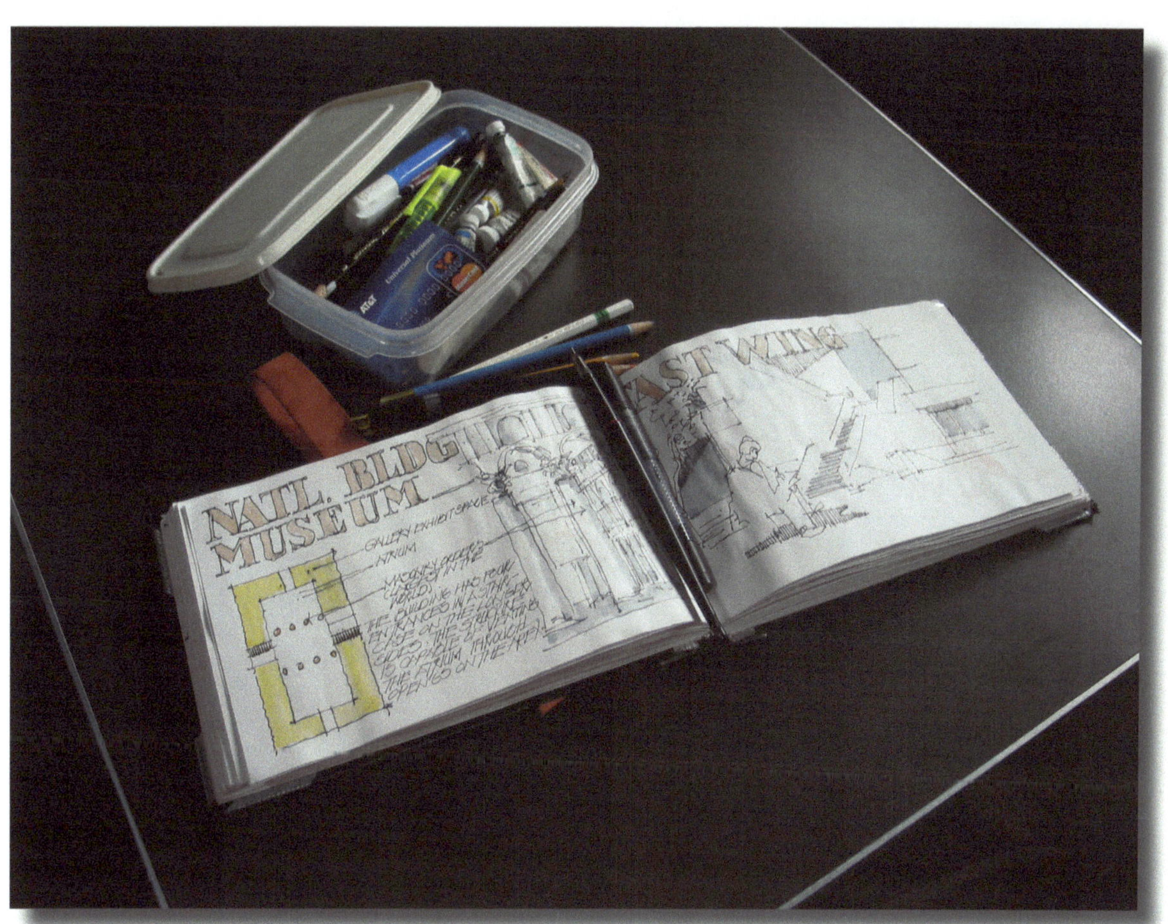

Fig. 01-1 A graphic journal and a plastic box of journaling tools, Moh'd Bilbeisi.

Fig. 01-2 Corporate and international symbols are easily recognized and transcend the language barrier.

The father of modern sociology, **Ibn Khaldoun** (1332-1406) declared that it is innate in our nature as humans to live together and to communicate. According to his book, *Al Mukadimah* (also known as *The Introduction*), he asserts that humans will evolve in their quest for stability and safety and this evolution should in theory propel language and art (as in graphic communication) to new realities, thus avoiding conflict and achieving prosperity. I find this disheartening since our educational system marginalizes the importance of drawing as a component of the process of thinking.

As much as we rely on our cognitive skills to understand, evaluate, and make decisions, our ability to process the information is limited by our inherent optical/graphic weaknesses. We communicate verbally by speaking and we supplement this communicative skill by writing; this is rather limiting since it is documenting our acoustical communication in a graphic fashion. We invented this faux pas once our alphabet and our lingual modus started to shift from the realm of the pictograph to the phonetic realm. Almost immediately, communication among humans became accurate and efficient, however sterile and overly non-creative. I would like to emphasize the term non-creative due to my belief that creativity is fundamentally based upon establishing connections between the symbolic and the literal. For example, as much as the word CAT designates a feline, a drawing of a cat will actually communicate the cat's physicality in terms of hue, value, size, character, activity, and context far better than the word itself.

Graphic/visual communication is everywhere around us. The media empires recognize its force and influence and use it to their advantage. Human beings are seduced and easily manipulated by the image. Almost everyone recognizes the corporate symbols of UPS, Chase Manhattan Bank, Apple Inc., etc. What made MTV famous was its ability to graphically transcend the limitation of the audio quality of the singer alone.

Journaling at the very fundamental level involves three proactive issues: **seeing, thinking, and sketching**. To do these well, active personal ignition is required.

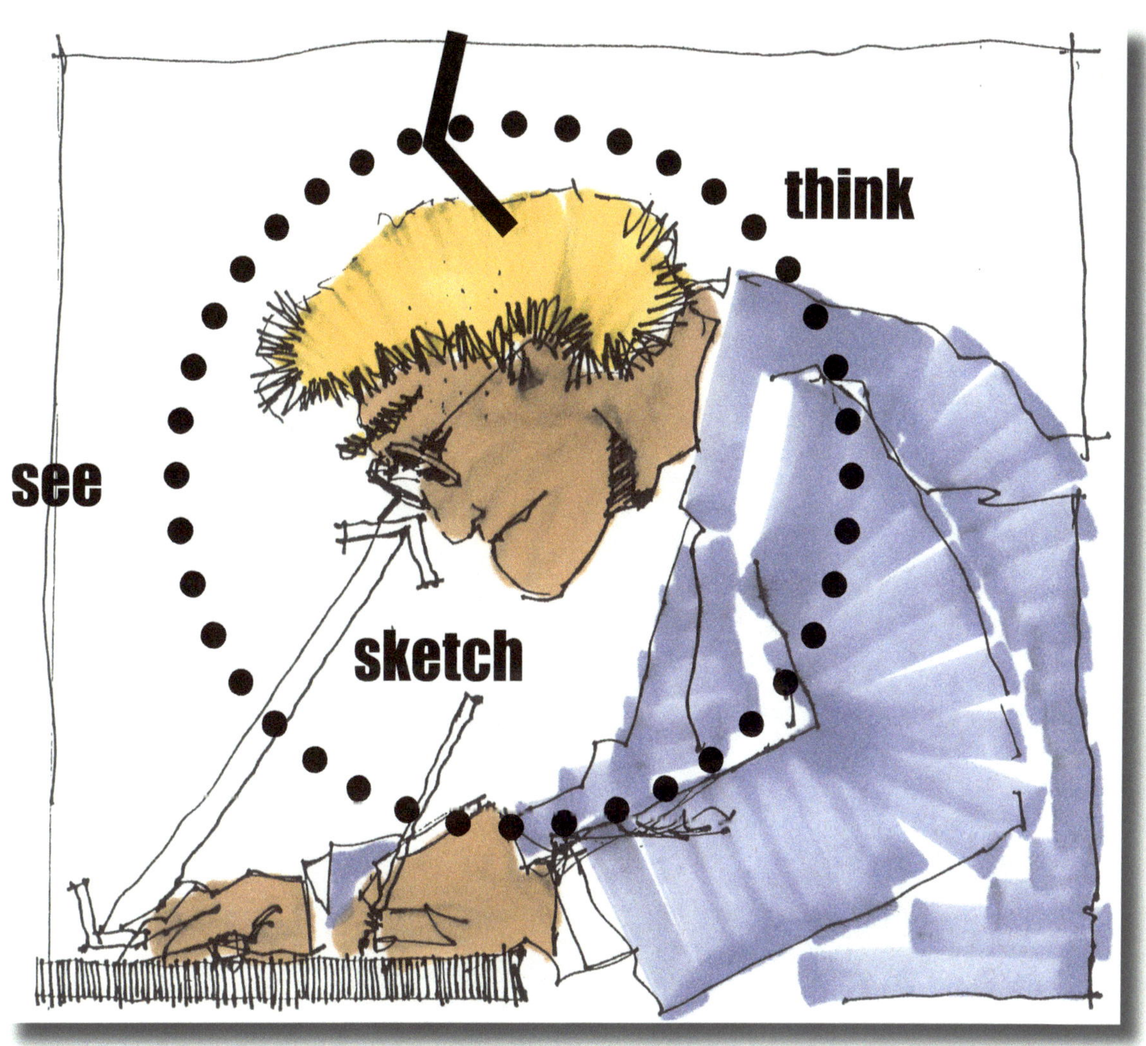

Fig. 01-3 The cyclical nature of the act of graphic journaling involves the eyes, the hands, and the brain.

SEEING

Seeing is fundamental to the act of journaling. The eye is the vehicle that transmits the information to and from the brain. Unfortunately, although it is a highly developed sensual organ, it is also highly susceptible to abuse and neglect. The aesthetic thinker Rudolf Arnheim wrote, "every child entering grade school in this country embarks on a twelve to twenty year apprenticeship in aesthetic alienation. Eyes they still have, but see they do no more."

THINKING

Thinking is the main reason behind keeping a graphic journal. There are a few important steps that ensure a sound thinking process when journaling:

keeping a journal

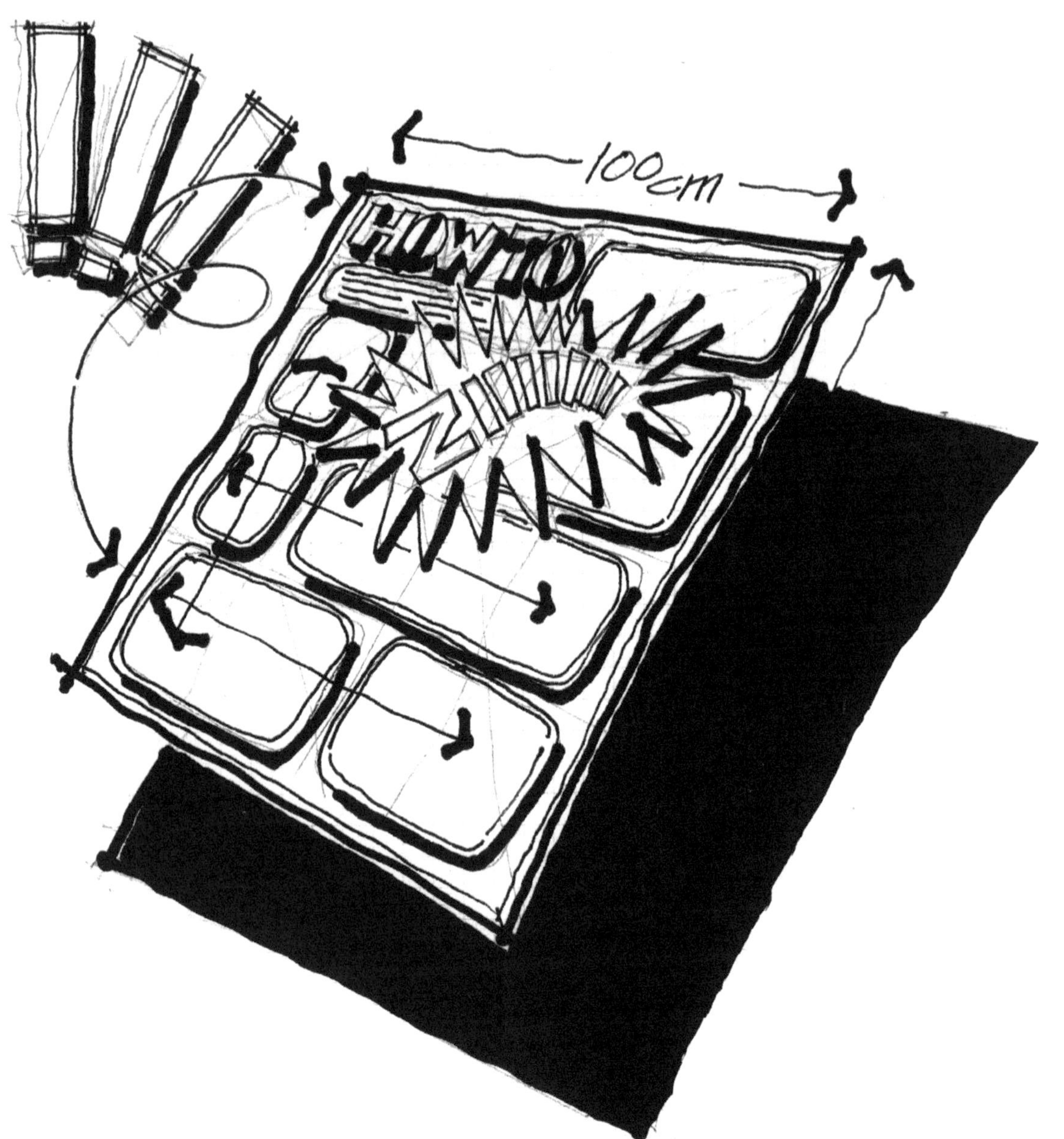

Observation: being interested, having the ability to pay attention to the details and to take good notes. This step requires patience and practice.

Discrimination: identifying the similarities, differences, and peculiarities of the issue, place, or event. This is purely a function of being accurate. Many refer to the color of the sky as blue and that is not necessarily correct. White buildings are never actually white. Be accurate.

Analysis: investigating the subject at hand ontologically to establish value. The subject of study is always veiled in layers of obscurity that hide its essence. Good analytical skills are crucial for honing the ability to isolate the essence for further study. Again, this skill is hard to master, yet attainable by repeated practice and diligent thought.

Synthesis: developing an outcome resulting from the analysis. It is a logical inference as the action from the cause, or as in the Kantian realm, describing the action of unifying the data into a comprehensive coherent whole. It is very possible to incorrectly synthesize one's analysis. Actually, the process of synthesis is inherently prone to errors due to its dependence on the analytical process which might be correct or faulty.

The journal helps us make better decisions since it facilitates note taking and offers a superior investigative platform.

SKETCHING

Sketching is a skill that must be acquired. It is elementary for the process of graphic journaling. Many students abandon journaling due to initially poor sketching skills, without going through the process long enough to actually improve! This book presents a wide gamut of sketching ability; though from different skill levels, each example shares the same goal: to communicate better and to explore.

The use of photography is in my opinion counter productive to the notion of graphic journaling. It is conducive to subject/object alienation and distancing. The proliferation of inexpensive digital cameras exacerbated the problem, pictures now have even less value since they can cost nothing to develop. When a person sketches, she is spending ample time studying the subject matter, including the physicality and the non-physicality of the context. A few seconds in front of the object with a camera is not enough to develop an understanding of the topic! A sketch can capture the nuances of light, color, human activity, and even the smell of a subject.

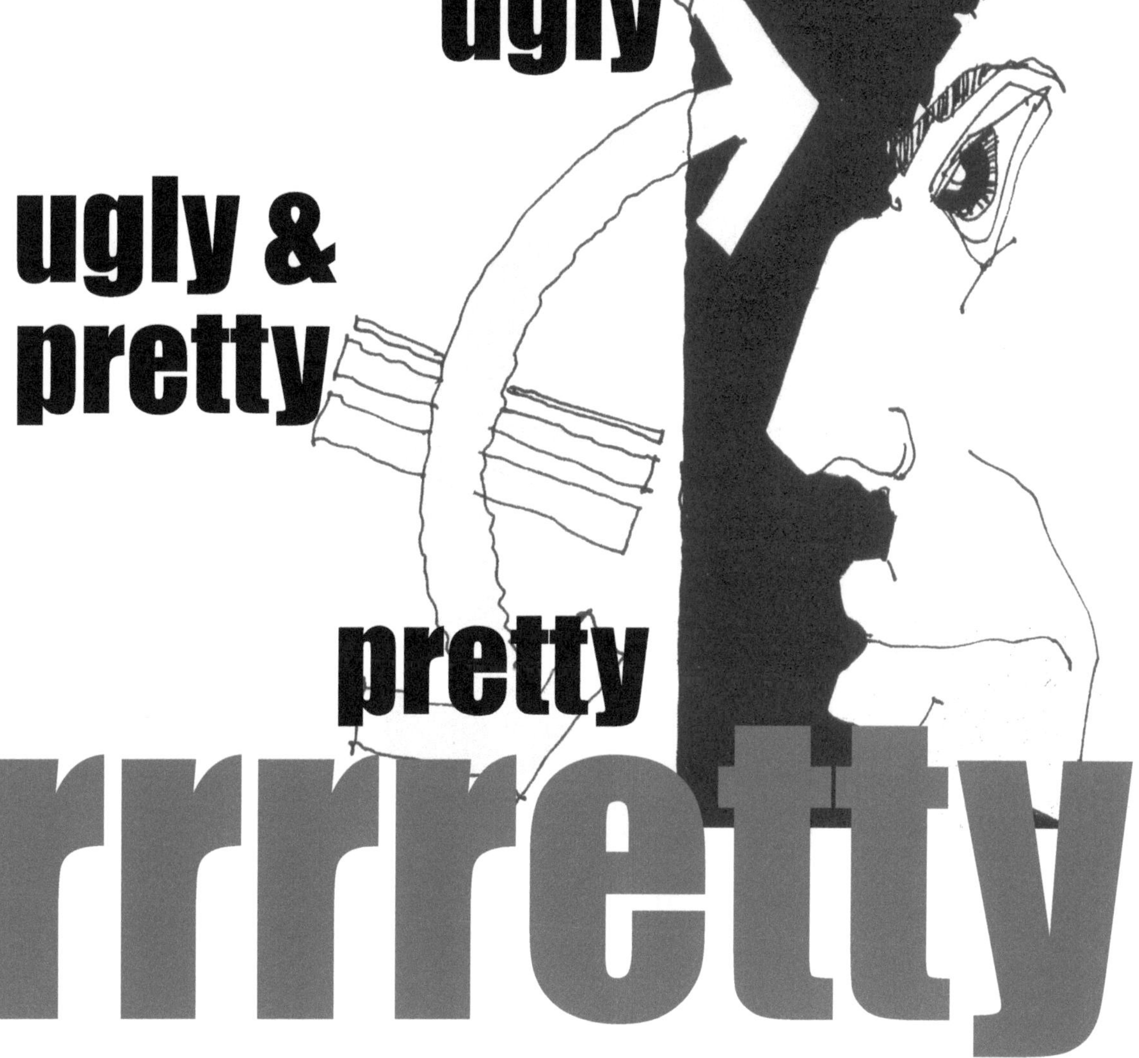

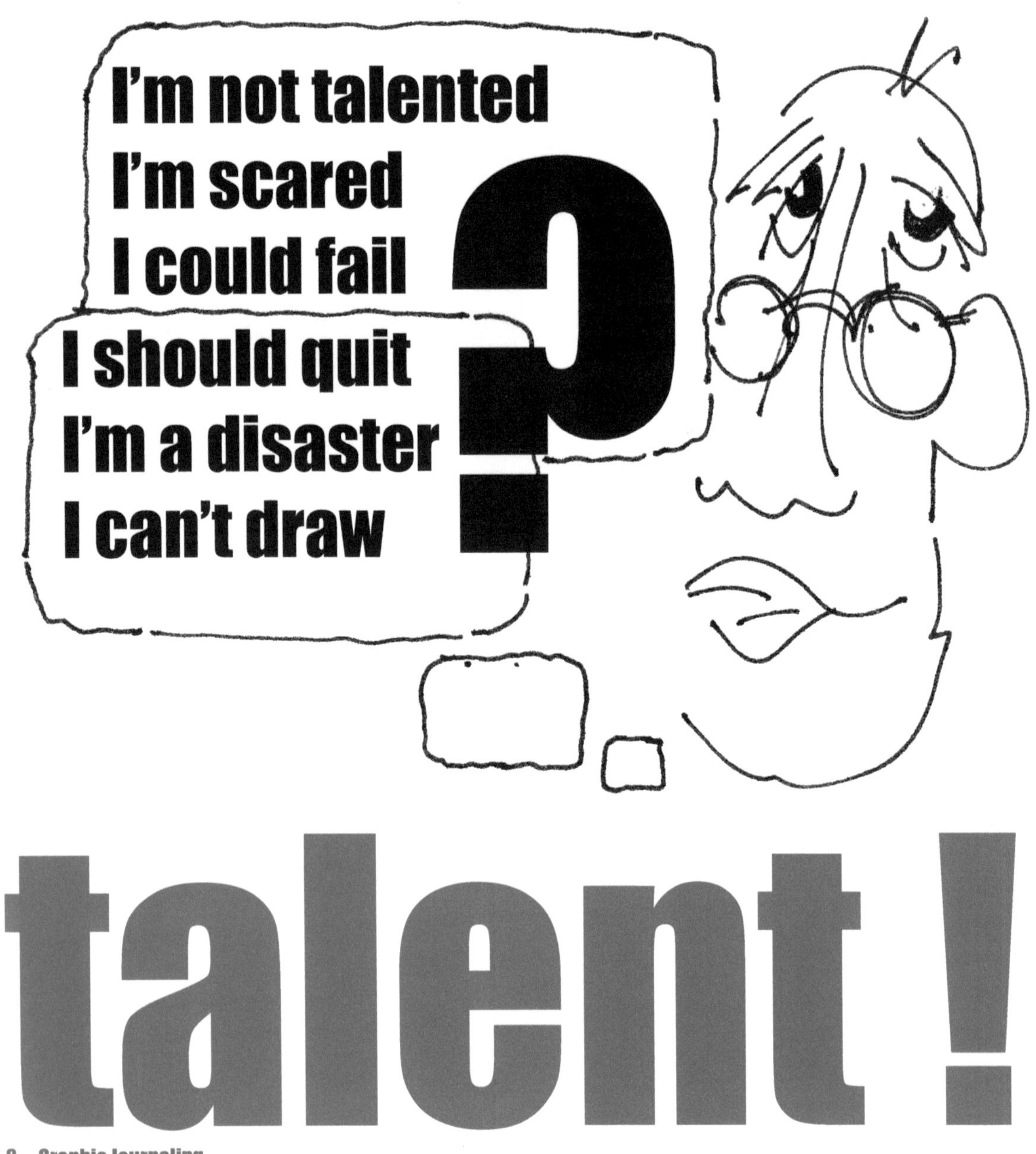

talent !

Talent is a mirage, stop chasing it because it does not exist. The concept of talent, the divine gift that is bestowed upon certain individuals and not on others, has crippled our advancement.

Throughout my years of experience as an architect, artist, and an educator, I have developed a distaste for the concept of talent: the theory of divine emanation that is received by certain individuals over others, thus catapulting them into the upper echelons of their respective fields. Schools of art and architecture have lost many promising individuals due to this universal misconception that has no academic merit.

If talent does not exist, then how do we explain the existence of a natural disposition among certain individuals to excel in certain fields? Is it environmental conditioning or superior parental upbringing? Is it luck; being at the right location at the right time? While no one is certain about this phenomenon, there exists a pattern that alludes to consistencies among the variables.

The so-called talented people work hard, perhaps harder than others. They tend to be self motivated, driven, and learn from their mistakes. Are they naturally talented? The answer is... no!

No one is talented by birth. Talent is reared and success is learned. Experts and child prodigies are made and not born. Studies conducted by many psychologists in the field of creativity emphasize motivation as the primary force behind talent.

Individuals who nourish, motivate, and support their offspring are the secret behind their children's ability, and ultimately, their success. They realize early on that success builds on success and each accomplishment will add a sound footing atop which their children will build.

If our parents did not provide the "talent food" when we were young, does this mean that we should give up? The answer again is... no! It only means that we should work and try harder. Some people get an early start, that about it. Giving up is a defeatist attitude and should have no place in our minds and hearts. Graphic journaling is about courage and expression. Learn to journal - then sketch, write, and journal away.

As humans, we are enamored with the notion of pretty. We seek pretty in our lives, and discard the non-pretty as being valueless, disturbing and irrelevant. This is a very dangerous notion. The danger lies within a thin path that differentiates these three qualities and suggests the following question: do artists draw, paint, or sculpt with pretty in mind?

The answer is ...**no**! The artistic and design heritage of the entire world is filled with the pretty and the not so pretty. Again, the society dictates and eventually shapes us by its popular standards - correct or incorrect. I recall my mother repeatedly asking me to stop wasting paper and to draw something pretty. I resisted, I drew whatever came to mind at the time.

Please be aware that the doodles/ drawings included on the pages of any successful graphic journal are not intended to be pretty. They are meaningful lines. They are personal. They are exploratory, impressionistic, and developmental. Striving toward substance and clarity is by far better than striving towards the pretty. If the sketches and page compositions become attractive as a result, well that is because skills are developing... an added bonus!

Is coloring within the lines better than outside the lines?

Success in graphic journaling is a function of an elaborate intentional exposure that will eventually lead to a command in the field of visual acuity. Journaling is an act of discovery and reflection. The answer to the question posed above is that it is besides the point. Coloring inside or outside the shape is inconsequential at best. Communication is what matters.

02 - TYPES OF JOURNALS

which journal type are you?

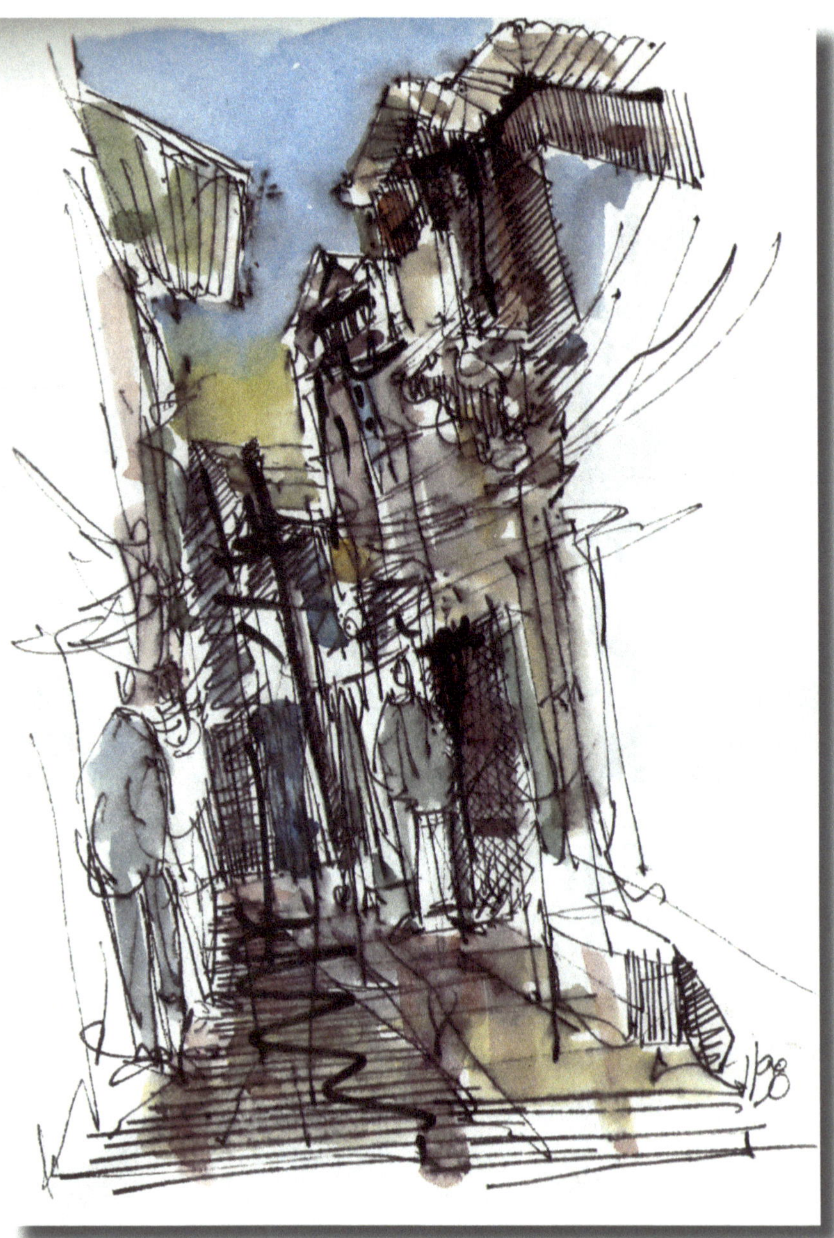

Deciding what type of journal to keep is not an easy task, especially if it is the first time undertaking this endeavor. Some individuals prefer to write and others prefer to draw. Some do both. Others prefer to include photographs or souvenir items such as ticket stubs and newspaper clippings. A good place to start this quest is to determine the purpose behind the journal, and then evaluate one's own personal abilities - graphic, artistic, and linguistic. Finally, one must consider the goal for personal growth behind the journaling process. Once these truths are addressed then the choices are narrowed and decision making will be easier.

There are three common journal types:

The text journal.
The photographic journal.
The graphic/drawing journal.

Fig. 02-1 Travel journal, Moh'd Bilbeisi. Pencil and watercolors on paper.

TEXT JOURNALS

Text journals are very popular and provide a wonderful venue for recording one's thoughts and experiences via the written word. It is also very common for these journals to include souvenir items to supplement the text. In this case, the journal simply acts as a recorder of events and impressions, but also allows for the opportunity to reflect on the thoughts and experiences in a healthy and hopefully beneficial way. As much as text journals are an effective method for recalling observations, they tend to be single faceted and one-dimensional. They fall short in the area of developing a keen sense of spatial observation and the visual awareness of the experience itself that are necessary for the journal to be used as a design tool.

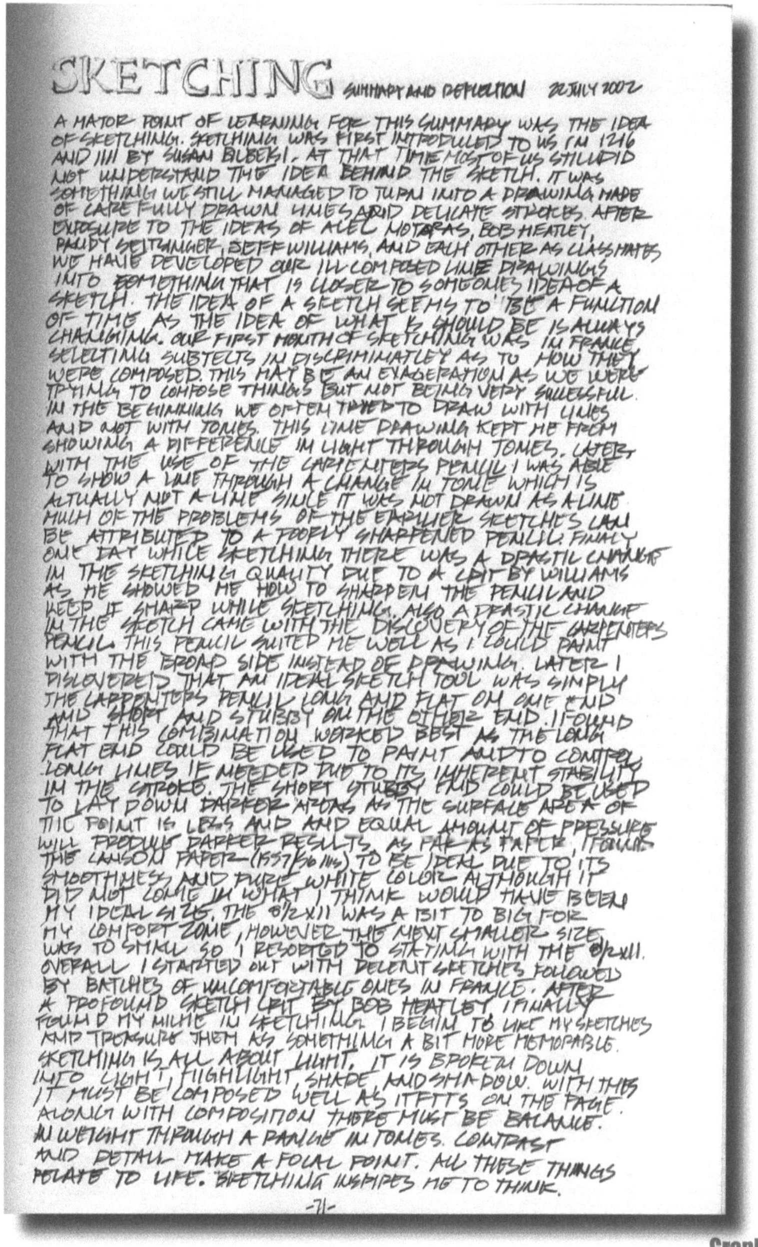

Fig. 02-2 The entire human experience is captured and recorded by the written word, Kyle Zerbey. Pencil on paper.

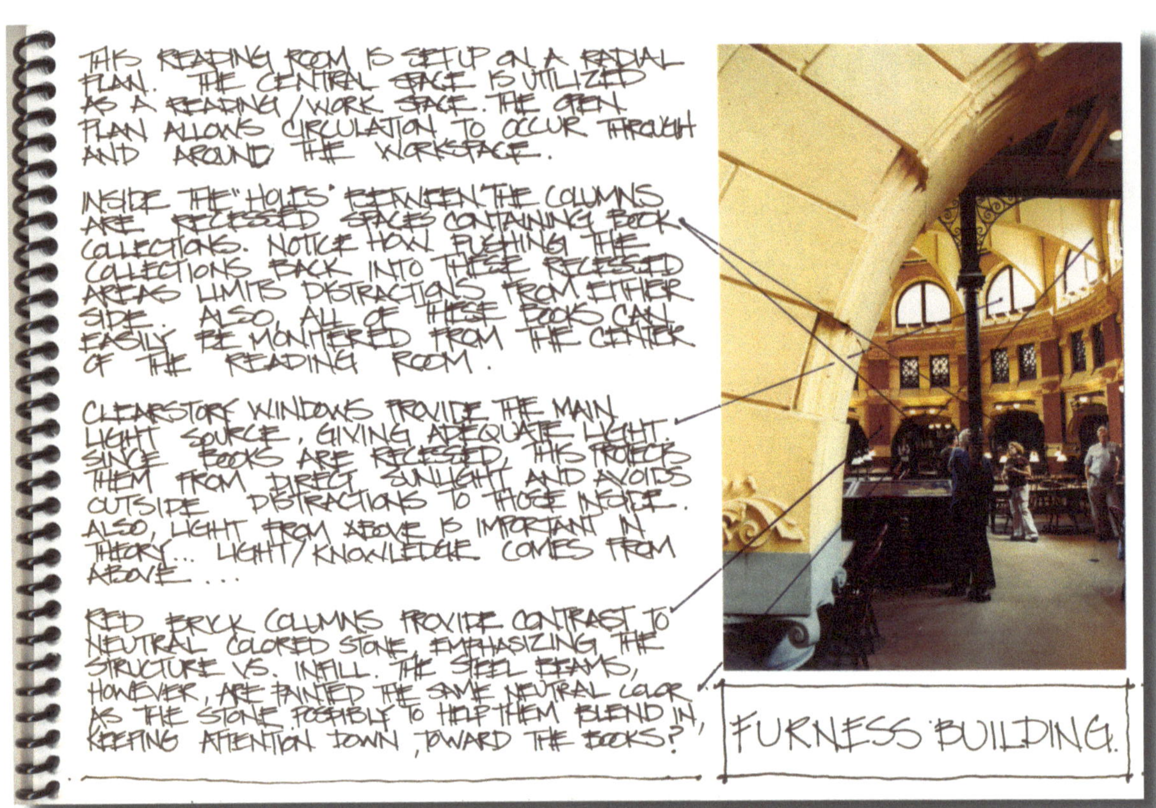

Fig. 02-3 The architectural experience is captured as commentaries that are supporting a photograph, Flynn Thomas. Ink and photographs on paper.

IMAGE JOURNALS

Some individuals prefer to use the camera to assist in the documentation of their experiences. They spend hours stalking the subject and composing the view; they understand the subject matter and their purpose for recording it before taking any photograph. Beware of clicking away at any object regardless of the subject matter! A simple truth is that machines tend to separate us from the experience, and to filter the humanity of the experience. Use a camera to supplement your journal and as an instrument to further study the subject matter. Great photographers do not take shots, they collect and capture events. In other words, use sparingly.

GRAPHIC JOURNALS

Graphic journals are the focus of this book. While the other types of journals - the textual and the photographic - are popular and relatively simple to start and maintain, the graphic journal requires a trained eye for acute visual comprehension, processing, and translation. This type of journal is more difficult to start and to maintain since it requires some degree of graphic skill that might not be available to all individuals... initially. The rewards of developing graphic skills and keeping this type of journal are many; whether it be as a design tool for an architect or a research tool for a botanist. The primary message of this endeavor is that you must begin the journey to reap the rewards!

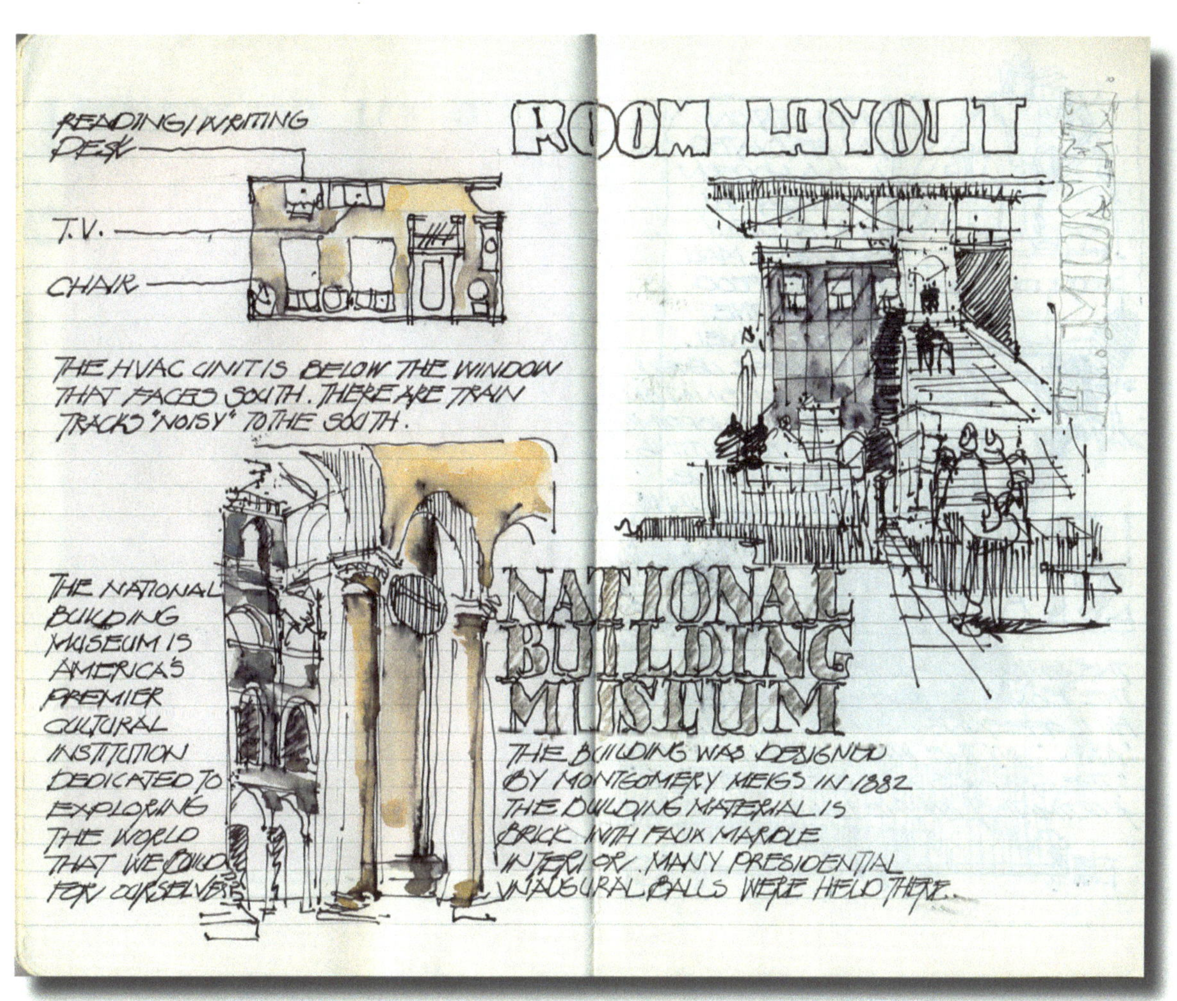

Fig. 02-4 A visit to Washington, DC., Moh'd Bilbeisi. Ink and watercolors on paper.

03 - RELAXATION

natural exercises to perform

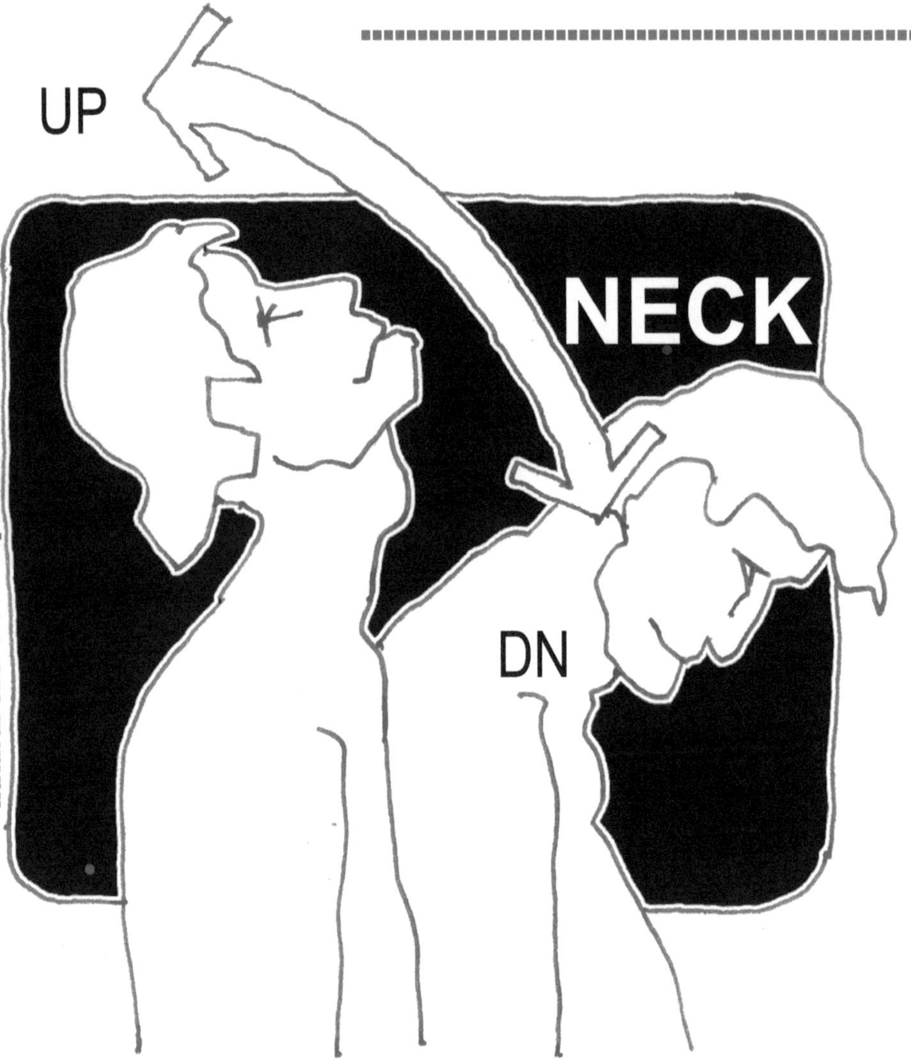

UP

NECK

DN

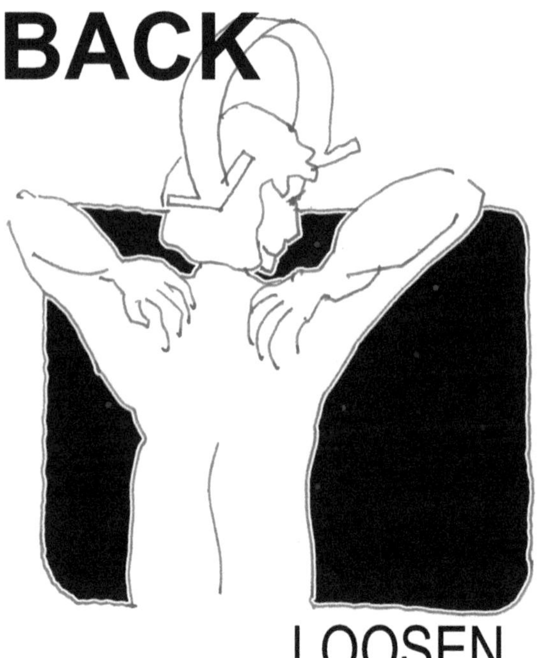

SIDE

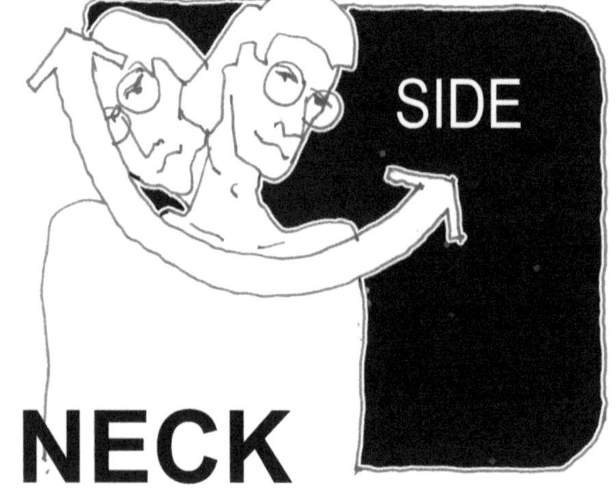

Human physiology plays an important role in the creative process. In general, a tense body produces tense drawings; a relaxed body produces relaxed drawings. If you feel a knot between your shoulder blades, this is an indication that you are tense. Clear your mind and focus your creative energy. These suggested physical exercises are a few that might loosen the muscles and calm the mind. **Do not be nervous, relax**.

UP

SHOULDERS

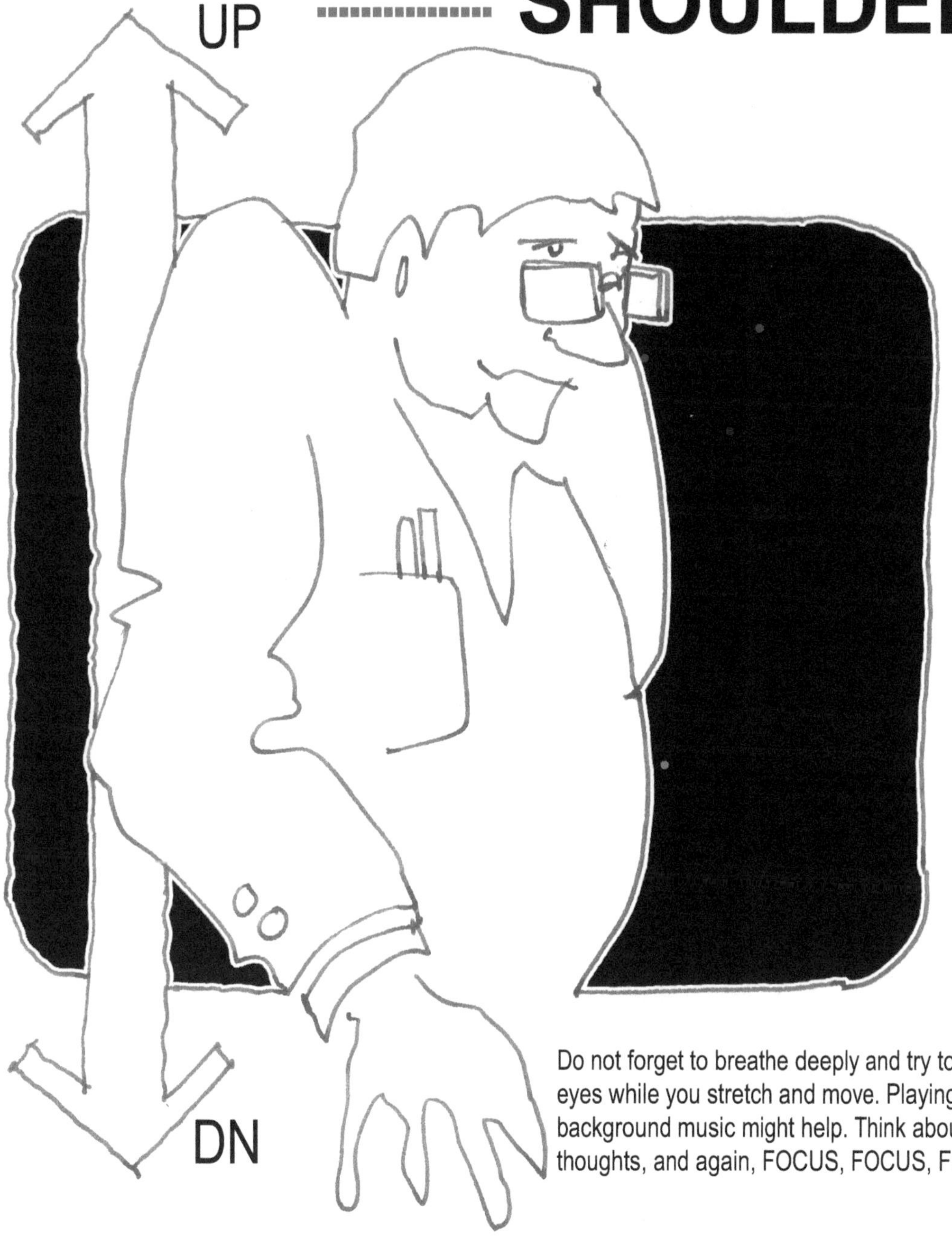

DN

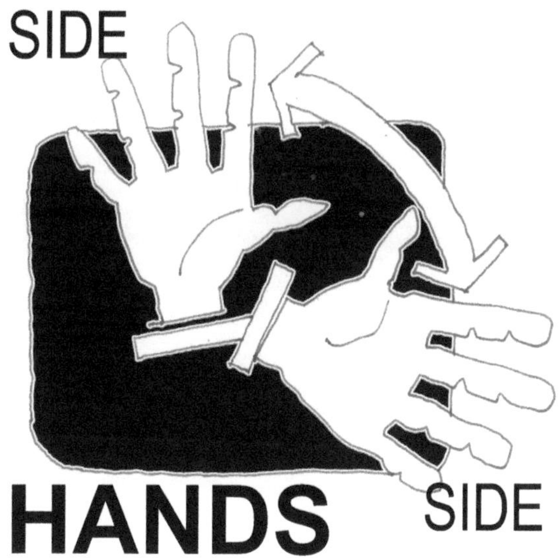

HANDS

FEET

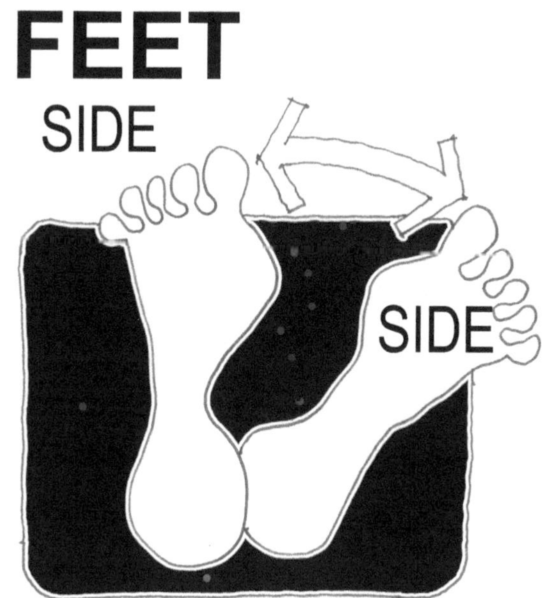

Do not forget to breathe deeply and try to close your eyes while you stretch and move. Playing ambient background music might help. Think about happy thoughts, and again, FOCUS, FOCUS, FOCUS.

04 - ERGONOMICS

the need to be comfortable

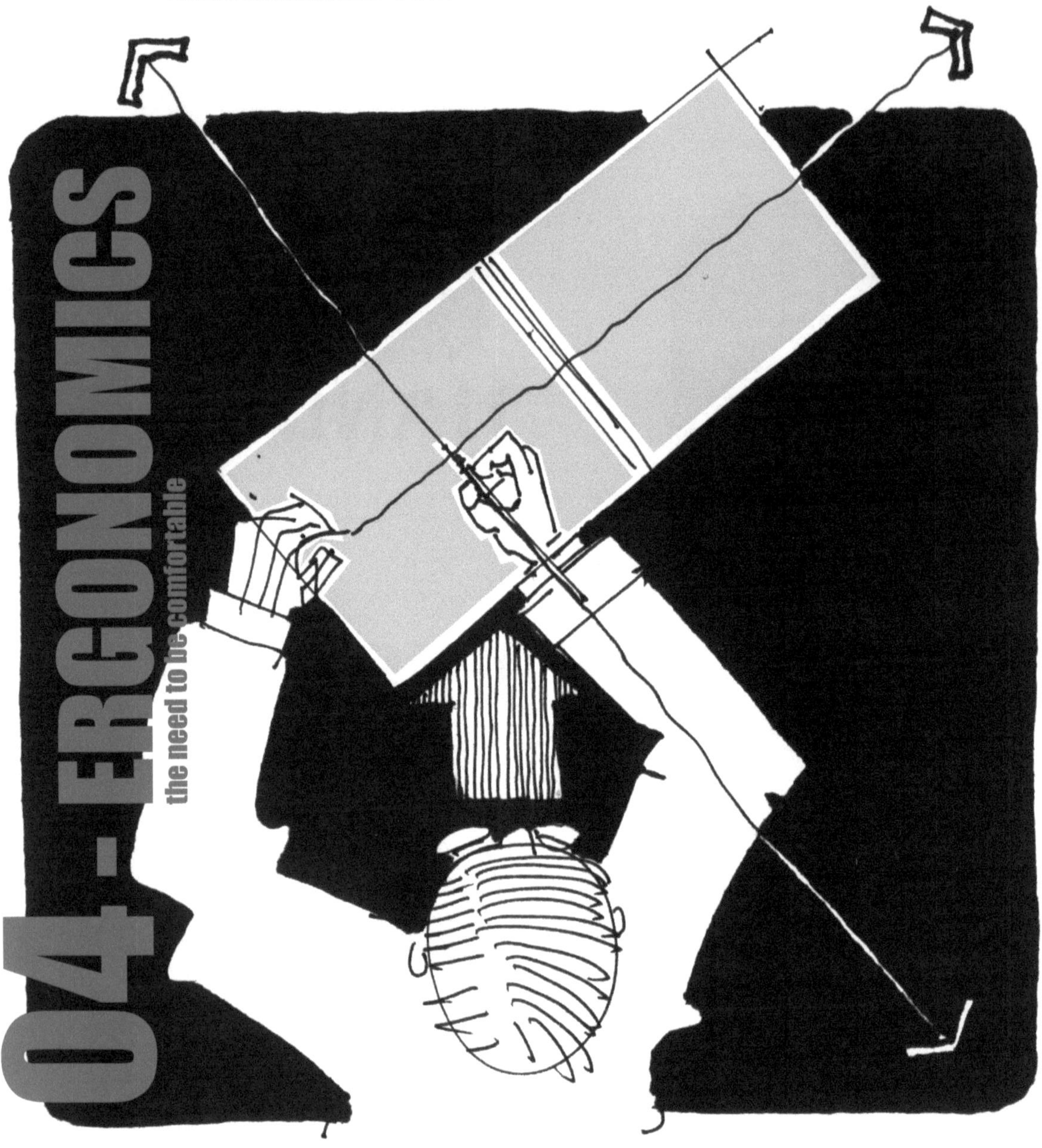

Correct and healthy ergonomics are crucial for the act of journaling. A comfortable and efficient sitting position will make the experience more enjoyable and contribute immensely to the quality of the journal entries. If you are not completely comfortable while journaling, your hand will lack support and the journal (sketchbook) itself will not be stable enough to provide a dependable writing/ drawing surface.

SEATING

Many individuals prefer to sit at a table when journaling, although such a luxury might not be available when journaling in the field unless you are sitting at a sidewalk cafe in Paris! If a table and a chair are not available, seek support by either sitting down on the ground or using a wall or a bench as a support surface. If you are journaling in a public place, *ask first* before sitting. Some museums do not permit visitors to sit on the floor.

LIGHTING

When drawing, lighting is crucial for two reasons: to provide adequate and correct illumination on the work surface, and to lessen the eye fatigue associated with poor, colored, or incorrect lighting. Be aware that over lighting has the same effect as under lighting and will lead to the same poor conditions. There is no general formula that predicts correct lighting levels, so trust your eyes... they do not lie!

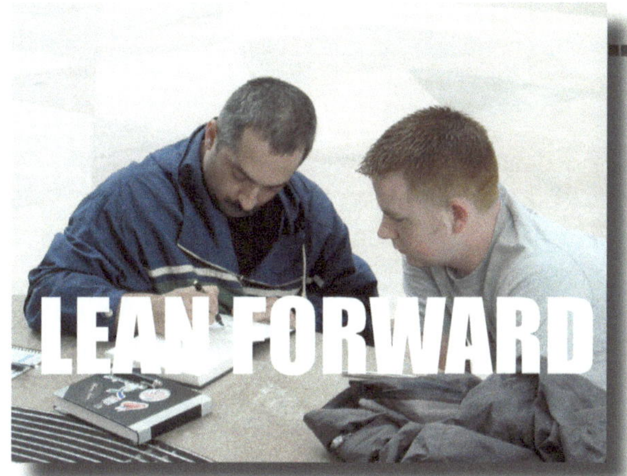

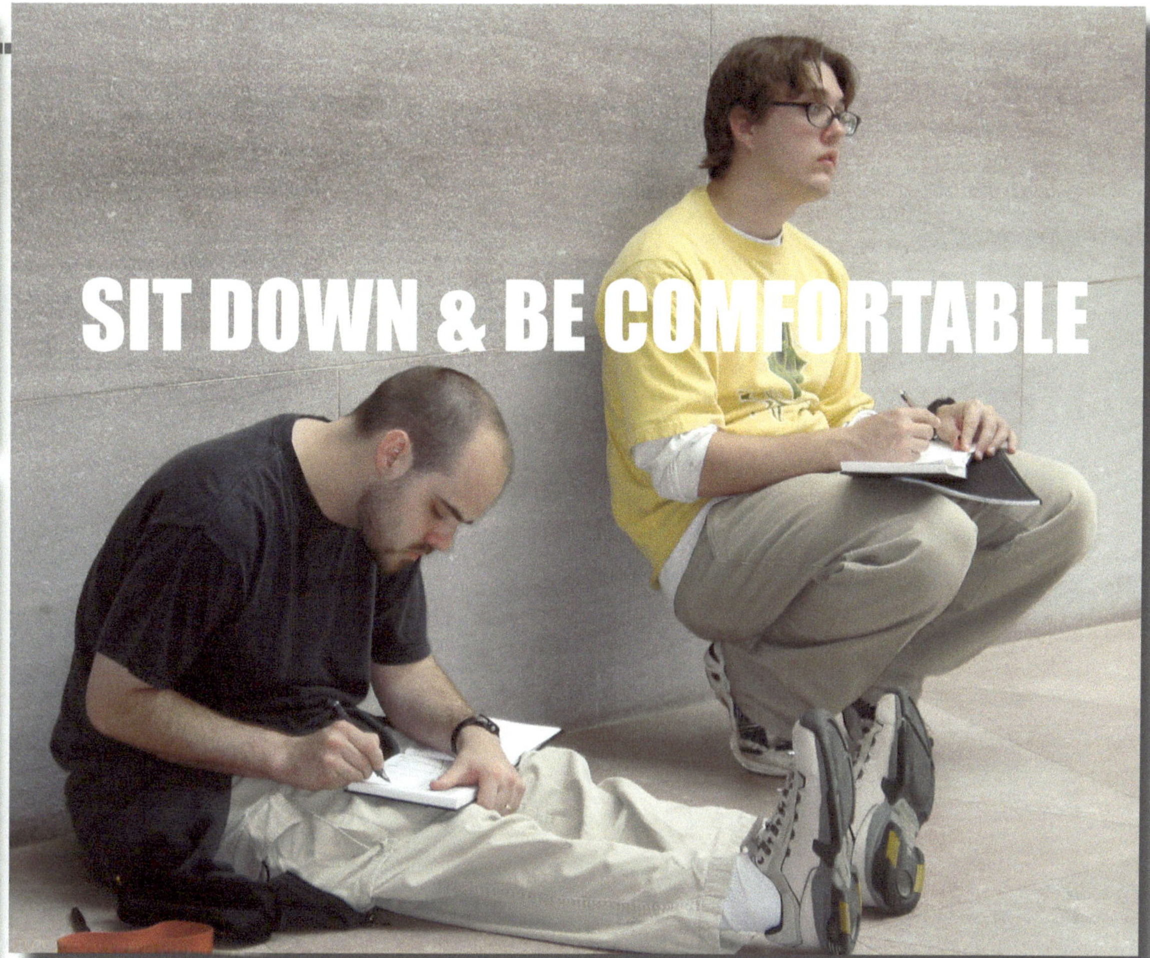

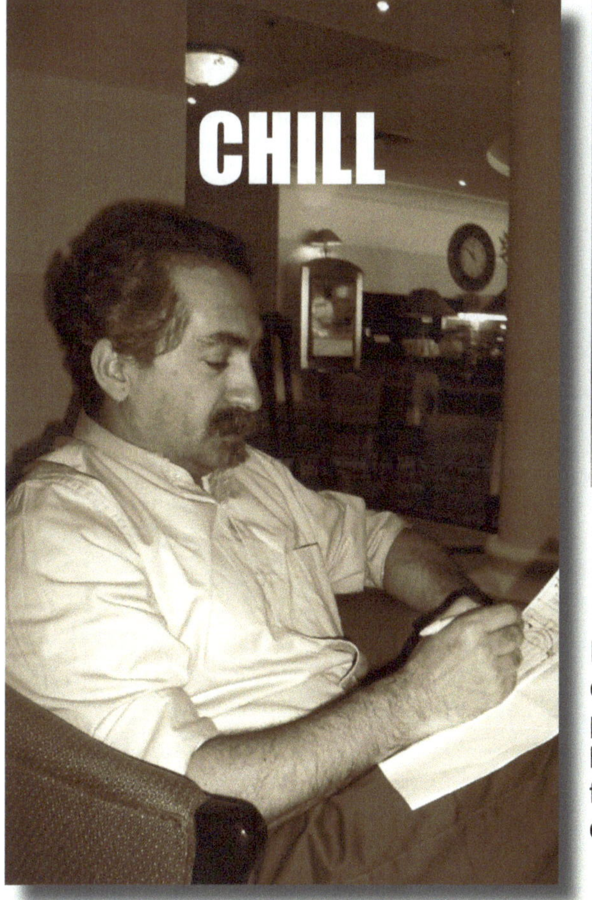

SIT DOWN & BE COMFORTABLE

POSITION

In addition to adequate lighting and reasonable climatic protection, rotate the journal so that the pages are perpendicular to the axis of the forearm/hand which is carrying the drawing instrument. Your free hand should be stabilizing the journal itself by exerting some vertical pressure on the pages.

HAND/FOREARM

The hand and the forearm that are holding the writing/drawing instrument should be resting comfortably on the drawing surface to provide support. An unsupported hand and forearm will not be able to make controlled lines and, ultimately, will lead to poor performance.

05 - JOURNALING TOOLS

graphic journaling necessities

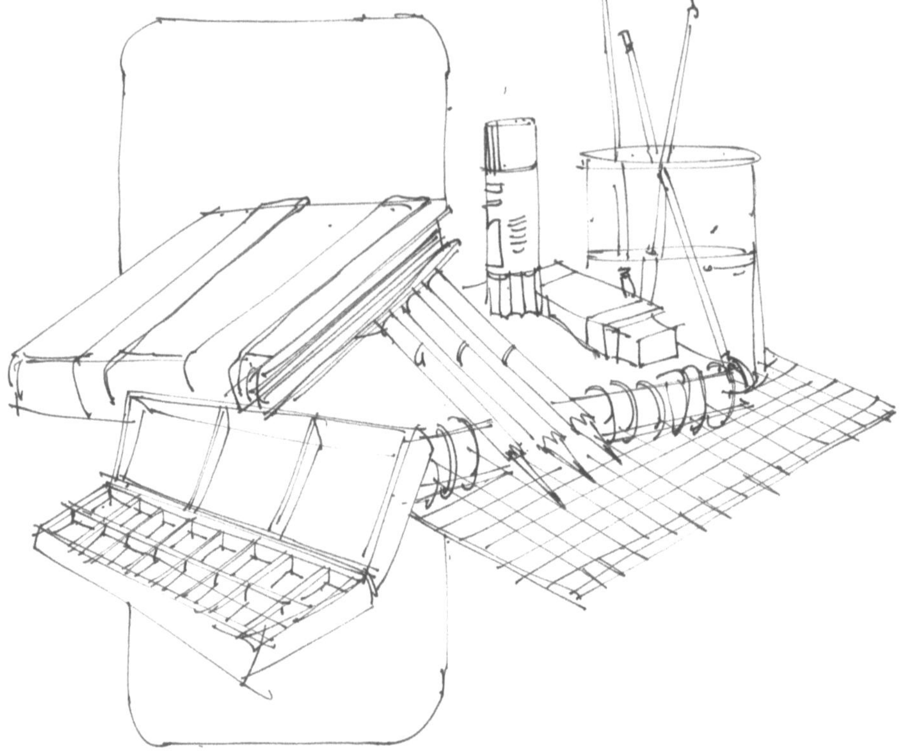

This description of the tools that are necessary to journaling is intended as a suggested guide. Experiment with several tools and determine which work best for you. Depend on your personal experience and act accordingly. For example, I was taught that the pencil is the best drawing instrument but now I prefer a fountain pen. I still use the pencil for some sketching and definitely for complex layouts for watercolors; however, we all have our personal preferences. Journaling is a personal act.

There are so many choices in terms of media, tools, and technique when it comes to journals and journaling. Having said that, there is unfortunately a proliferation of art supplies that are either inferior in quality (catering to fans of low initial cost) or superior in price (catering to fans of high initial cost thinking that it will produce a better result). My advice is to listen to knowledgeable individuals who are offering you their opinion free of charge and for no reason other than to help. Always be on the look-out for new products and please, please make it a habit to visit your local art store to try their new products. Once you find a product that you are comfortable with, stick with it and use it… use it regularly until you are convinced about its performance.

A person is incapable of graphic journaling without a sketchbook. Simply stated, a sketchbook is a tablet of blank or ruled paper sheets that are bound together. There are many of these to choose from!

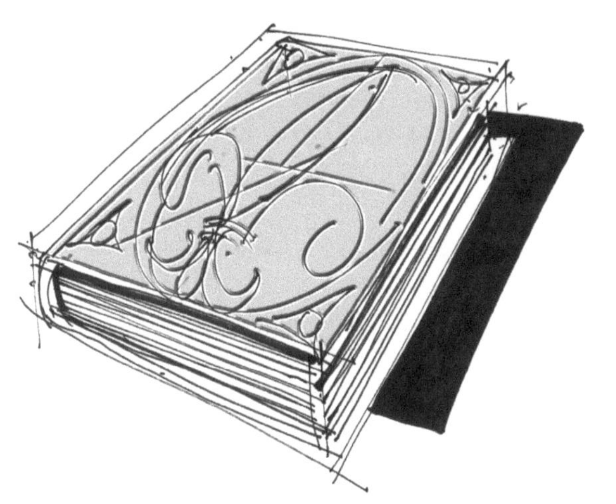

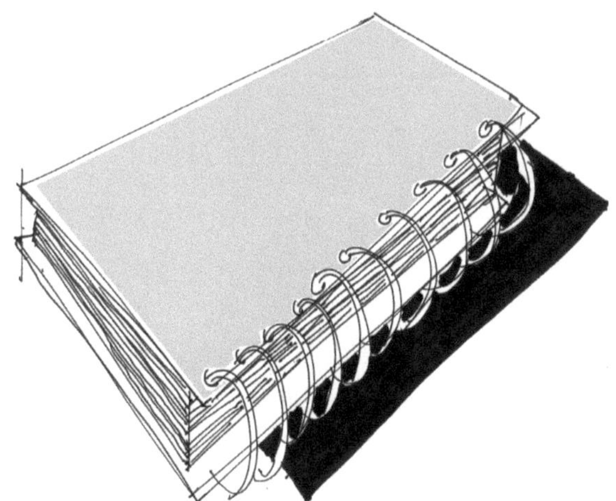

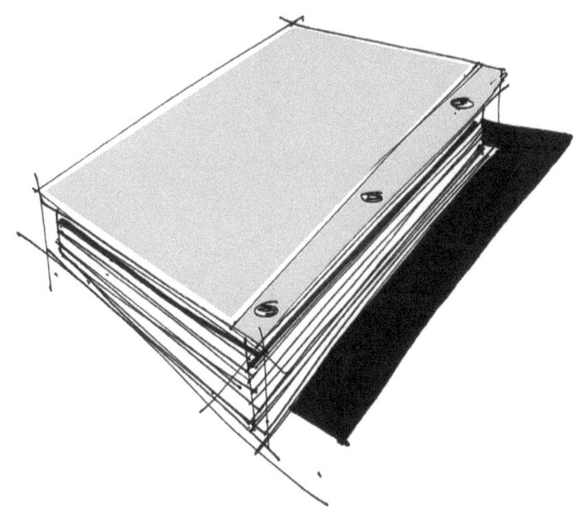

DECORATIVE

Decorative or decorated journals tend to draw attention to themselves through indulgence of the cover design, or designs on the pages themselves. The paper is generally of poor quality. They also tend to be heavy and cumbersome. They are better suited for writing than drawing, as the paper usually works best with ballpoint pens. They hinder the graphic journaling process because they are incapable of being completely opened so that they can be used as a two-page layout.

SPIRAL BOUND

Spiral bound journals are available in art stores throughout the United States. They are not popular in Europe or the Middle East. Some are of questionable paper quality, but they can be opened completely flat to enable the user to draw comfortably without the book trying to close itself. It is difficult to use as a two-page layout, however, because of the spiral. The cover is not as durable as the hard-back journals which shortens its lifespan significantly.

PRONG BOUND

Prong bound journals are economical and popular among the do-it-yourselfers. They enable the insertion of any type and color of paper. Mixtures of paper types can be compiled by inserting sheets of watercolor paper, for example, to diversify its use. The proper choice of cover is crucial or the durability of the journal will be compromised. This type of sketchbook is almost impossible to use as a two-page layout.

journaling tools

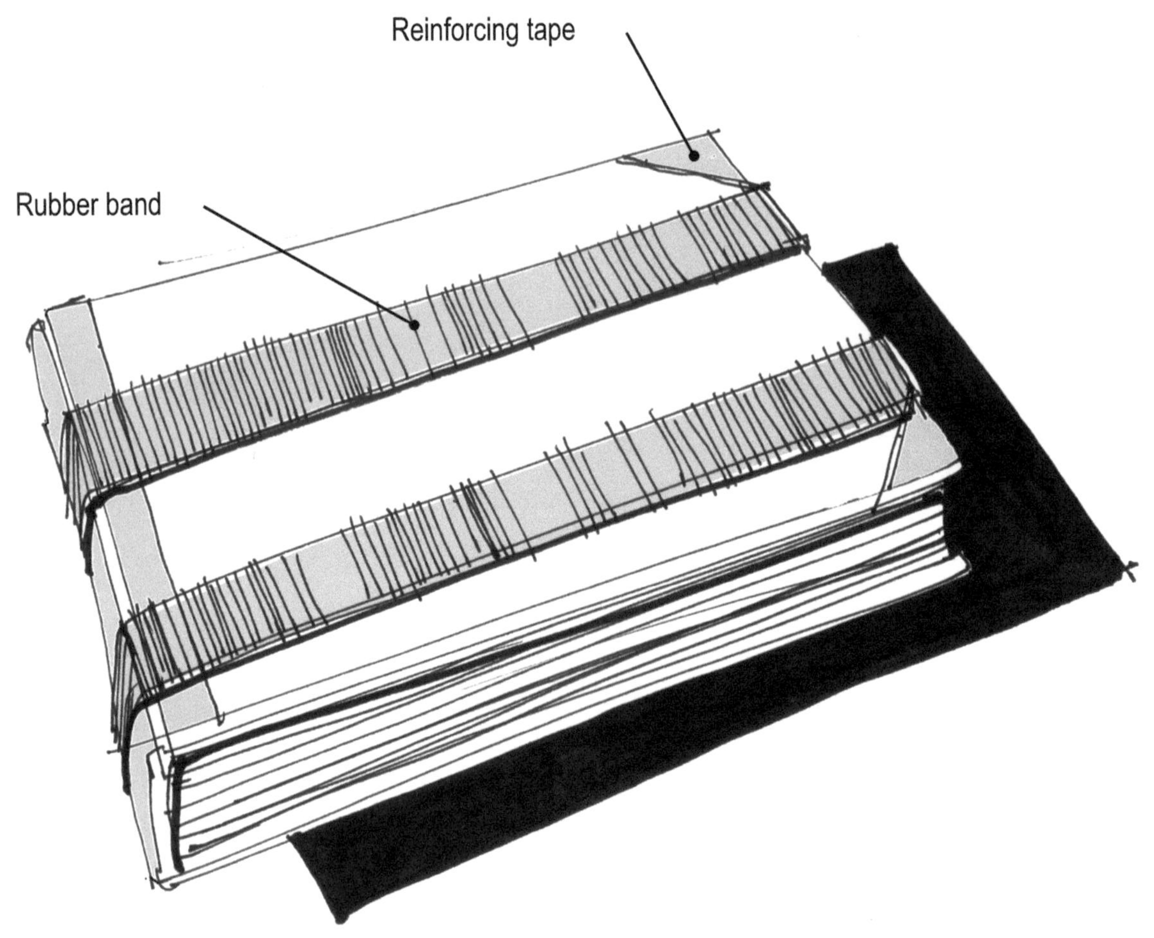

Fig. 05-1 It is a good idea to reinforce the corners of the sketchbook and to keep it tightly closed to avoid damage.

Twenty plus years of graphic journaling have taught me a few things about sketchbooks. First, the **ultimate sketchbook does not exist**. My journey began with a few years of experimentation with sketchbook types; I subsequently determined what my criteria for a sketchbook are. A good sketchbook must conform to the following:

<u>It must have a hard cover</u>. This increases its durability and lifespan. It can also be used as a projectile in times of distress. The spine and the corners of the sketchbook cover should be reinforced. If they are not done so by the manufacturer, I usually reinforce them with fabric or fiberglass tape.

<u>It should be kept firmly closed when not in use</u>. This reduces the susceptibility of the sketchbook pages to tear due to torquing and accidental impact. I use two 1 inch mega rubber bands to restrain the pages when transported or not in use. Some individuals use extra large monkey clips to keep the sketchbook closed; however, they tend to scratch the cover and annoy anything else that comes in contact with them.

<u>The format of the sketchbook, whether portrait or landscape, is a personal issue</u>. The landscape format is wonderful for panoramic compositions; however, they tend to have a shorter lifespan than the portrait format because of the spine length to page length ratio. The portrait format opens in a more compact manner, which makes it a bit easier to deal with when doing journaling in the field. I have used both, and I enjoy both.

The sketchbook should be capable of being used effectively as a two-page layout. Some sketchbooks are impossible to open and lay flat and that is very irritating and counter productive.

High quality paper inside the sketchbook is very important. The weight is the first consideration - to perform aqueous washes or use a fountain pen or felt tip pen, a heavier paper is required. The second consideration is the color, which affects your ability to use it without straining your eyes in bright light or outside under direct sunlight. Generally, off-white paper is more gentle on the eyes yet devastating when performing watercolor washes. Sometimes sheet color is a compromise.

Ruled, non-ruled, or grid paper is a personal choice. Some prefer the proverbial blank page to begin their work. If you are incapable of drawing a level line on the page, then you might entertain a sketchbook with ruled paper. Grid paper is useful for those individuals who prefer more accuracy. Ruled and grid paper assist in controlling lettering. They are all useful and should be selected to cater to your needs and the way you use the journal.

Bonus features. Some sketchbooks have a small pocket to keep a map or a receipt. Some sketchbooks have a sturdy string or a ribbon to mark your place or a particular page. These features are very useful and proven in the field.

These are *my* sketchbook requirements! Consider these points and find your own ultimate sketchbook.

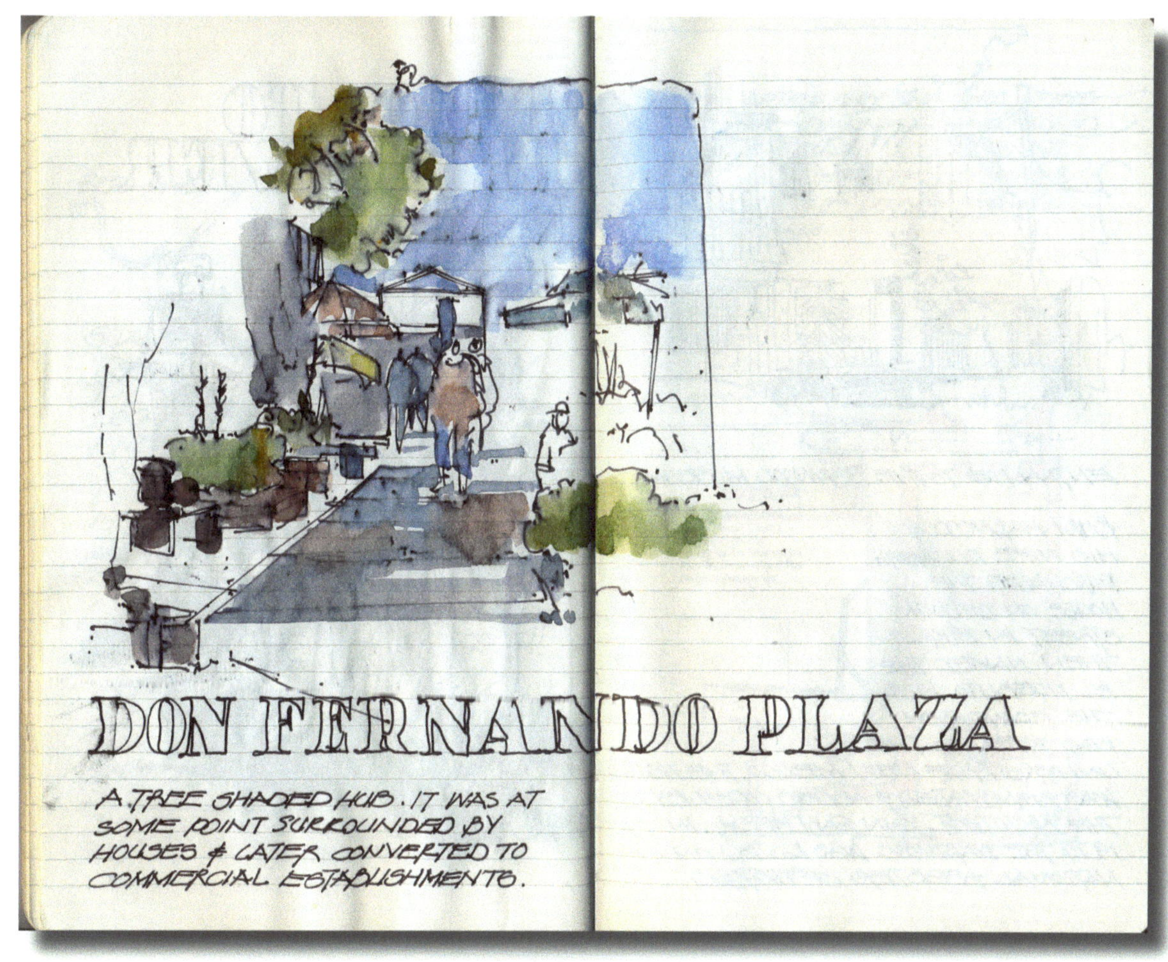

Fig. 05-2 A street scene in Santa Fe, New Mexico, Moh'd Bilbeisi. Ink and watercolors on paper.

journaling tools

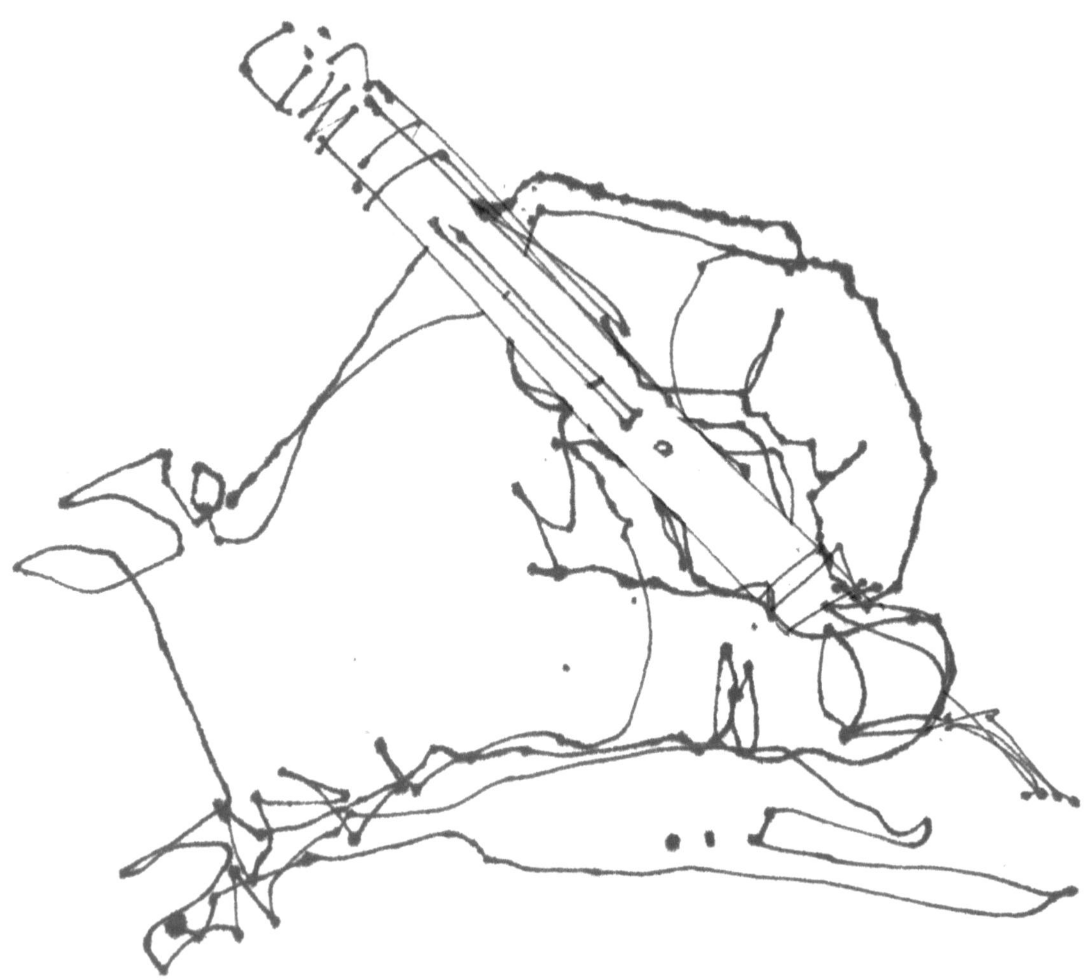

Graphic journaling is impossible without certain tools. Again, there are so many choices in terms of media and technique, but one always has to be wary of price and value. Make it a habit to visit your local art store to try their new products. Once you find a product that you are comfortable with, stick by it and use it… use it regularly until you are convinced about the performance of the product.

SUPPLIES

Your supplies should be small enough to take with you into a museum, each individually and within some sort of carrying device (small backpack, zippered pouch, or pencil box). Because you never know what circumstance you might encounter, be prepared! The following is a suggested list of journaling supplies:

- **5 1/4 inch x 8 1/4 inch blank, lined, or gridded hardback quality sketchbook.**
- **A good fountain pen.**
- **A few pencils - 2H , HB, and 6B.**
- **A small ruler, 6" or so.**
- **A few colored pencils.**
- **A small eraser.**
- **A sharpener.**
- **A glue stick.**
- **A quality compact watercolor paint set.**
- **A quality # 10 watercolor brush.**
- **A tightly sealed water container for watercolors.**
- **A small piece of absorbent fabric.**

PENS

Pens are drawing instruments that use ink as a vehicle to mark a paper. They have the advantage of being versatile, durable, and produce a relatively permanent (lightfast) line. A quality fountain pen is an excellent choice unless cost or availability is a prohibitive issue. Rollerball and felt-tip pens are other viable options. Ballpoint pens are inexpensive and available everywhere. They tend to produce a relatively dry line whose quality is inferior to other ink pens, since the instrument requires the user to press the pen downwards on the paper as one slides the pen, which compromises both the line and the lateral movement of the hand.

ROLLERBALL & FELT-TIP PENS

Rollerball and fine felt-tip pens are far superior to ballpoint pens because their line quality is so much better. The ink tends to be a bit more wet than that of the ballpoint, however, which makes it prone to smearing and bleeding through the page. Page weight and quality will affect the performance of the rollerball or felt-tip. Try before you buy!

Unfortunately, art/color markers usually bleed through the paper, depending again on the quality and thickness of the paper, so use them sparingly if you *really* have to. They can work well, but be careful!

FOUNTAIN PENS

It makes perfect sense to respect the medium that translates your important thoughts onto paper. Using a quality fountain pen can improve your penmanship and the graphic quality of your lines.

A good quality fountain pen with a medium semi-flexible nib is very effective as a drawing and a writing instrument. This pen uses fountain pen ink, which is an aqueous solution with a suspended pigment. The ink is usually water soluble and comes in different grades and hues. The nib on a fountain pen is flexible, semi-flexible, or rigid depending on the nib material and form. Gold is usually selected as the premier material for the nib since it is more flexible and resistant to ink corrosion than steel. Older (vintage) pens are also more flexible than today's productions; however, the feed mechanism of today's fountain pens are far superior to the vintage pens.

If you decide to purchase a fountain pen, consult a reputable vender and get the best fountain pen for your budget. Avoid chain and office supply stores - they have no idea about what they are selling. Art supply stores and of course fountain pen stores will offer you the best selection and advice. Once you purchase a fountain pen, use it and use it often. Do not allow others to use it because the nib actually gets shaped by the specific way you hold and use the pen. Flush the pen regularly with cold water to ensure its longevity and line quality.

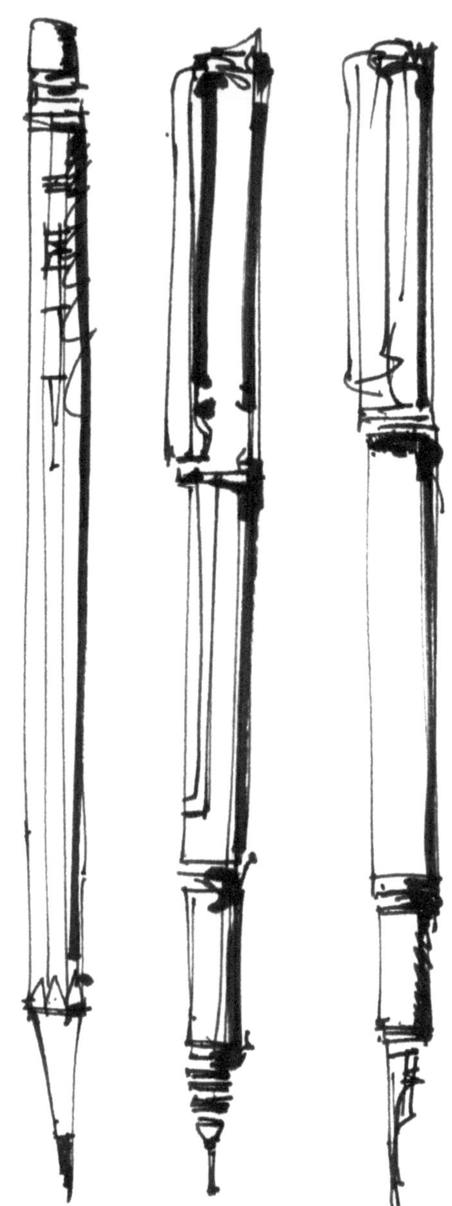

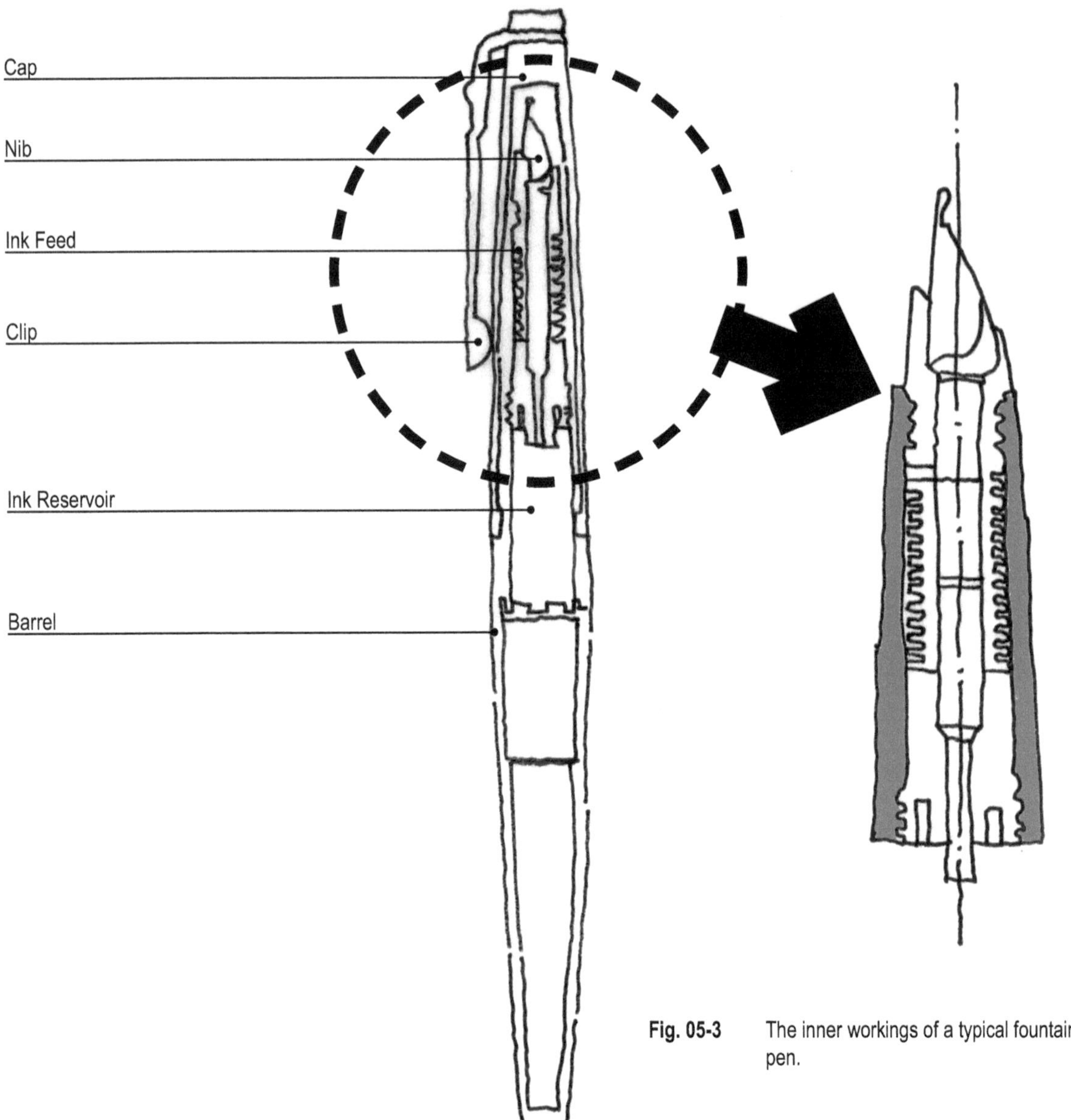

Fig. 05-3 The inner workings of a typical fountain pen.

Selecting a fountain pen is very important. Over the last 100 years, pen manufacturers have introduced and marketed a vast number of models. Technology and market forces have dictated the materials used, the design, and filling mechanism. The principle employed for an efficient fountain pen is the same whatever the model - a uniform transfer of ink from the reservoir to the nib and thereafter to the writing surface. The efficiency of the fountain pen can be improved through a basic knowledge of its working principles, a fault-finding procedure, and good maintenance. Most modern fountain pens are precision instruments and very reliable.

COMPONENTS

Case: this normally consists of a barrel, shell (gripping section), and a cap with an attached clip.

Reservoir: this could be permanent or a replaceable filling type (converter) or a throw-away cartridge.

Feed system: this basically transfers ink from the reservoir to the nib via small channels.

Nib: this is the point of the fountain pen that makes the actual marks and lines. Nibs are usually made of gold, steel, or gold plated steel. Gold nibs are very flexible yet not very durable. A harder material such as iridium is usually applied to the tip of the nib for longevity. The design of the nib reflects the writing characteristics of a particular pen.

Tines: these are the two equal sides of the nib separated by the slit which channels the ink from the reservoir to the paper. A medium nib is the best nib for drawing and sketching. Many individuals also like to experiment with calligraphy nibs; there are three types of calligraphy nibs: **oblique, reverse oblique,** and **italic**. An oblique nib is one in which the tines have been cut at a downward angle from right to left; this provides a thick line on the downward stroke and a thin line on the horizontal stroke. Oblique nibs are good for left-handed people who "push" their pens. Reverse oblique nibs are cut at an angle which slopes downward from left to right. An italic nib, also known as a stub nib, has a sharp, straight cut across the tip. It is generally used for calligraphy writing. With italic nibs, the writing is slower and strokes are more deliberate.

Ink: which is drawn away from the nib during the course of drawing is replenished from the feed channels that take ink from the reservoir to the nib. Unless the ink taken from the reservoir is replaced by air, the pen will stop working. On a well-designed pen this control is so regulated that the flow of ink from the nib to the paper appears constant. In a situation where the pen is subjected to a sudden increase in temperature or decrease of external pressure, the air in the back of the reservoir expands forcing the ink through the feed channels. This ink is removed from the feed by the use of an overflow system, consisting of a series of slots that fill with ink.

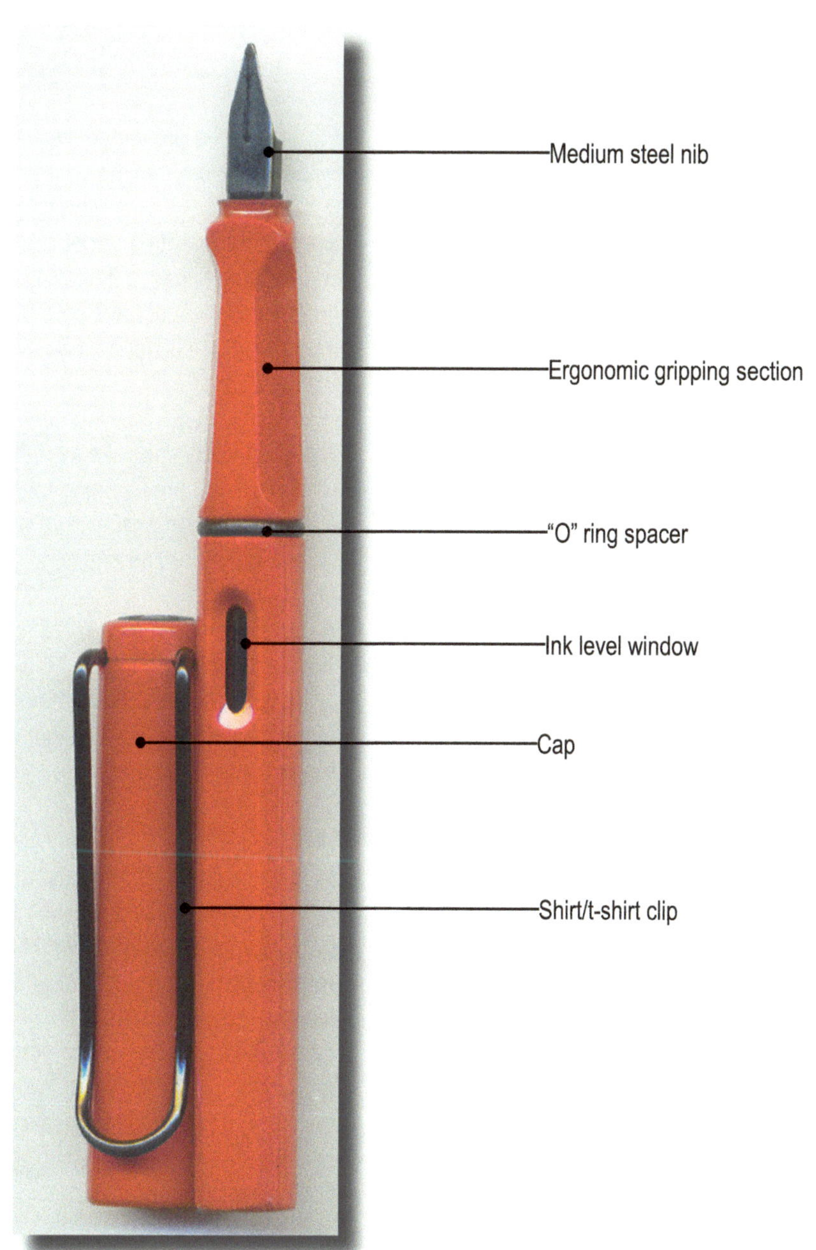

Fig. 05-4 The Lamy Safari fountain pen, ergonomic, reliable, and very attractive.

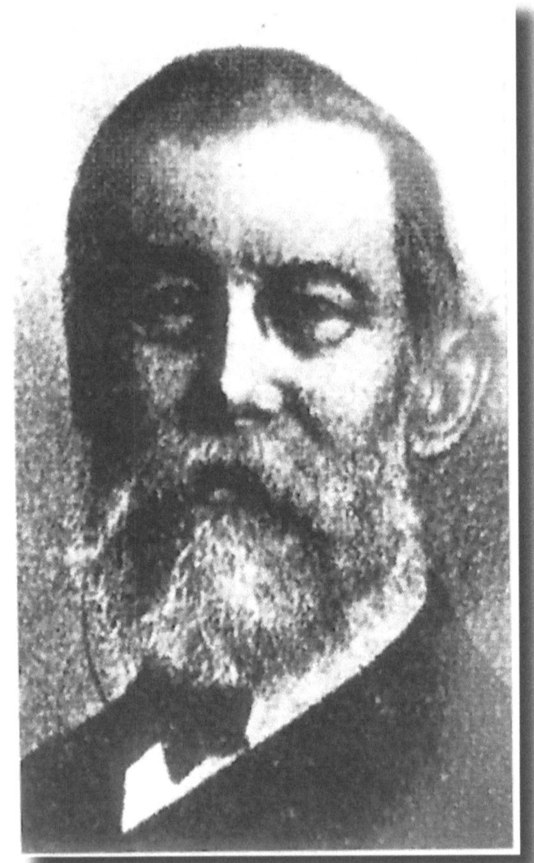

Fig. 05-5 Lewis Edson Waterman, the inventor of the modern fountain pen.

CHOOSING A PEN

Fountain pens are very personal. Consider the following before making your purchase:

Size: a barrel with a larger diameter is usually more comfortable because it alleviates pressure on the fingers (you do not have to grip the barrel as tightly). If you have small hands, however, a wide barrel may feel awkward.

Weight: many of us like the initial feel of heavy pen, but if you are planning to draw or write for a prolonged period of time, that weight will cause fatigue on your hand and wrist.

Balance: the pen should rest easily within your grip. Try placing the cap on the other end of the pen while using it. Pens with thicker barrels will generally feel better capped, whereas longer pens may feel top heavy and off balance.

Nib: these come in different widths, ranging from extra-fine to extra broad depending on the manufacturer. Individuals with smaller or lighter handwriting will do better with finer points. Nib widths vary from brand to brand. A Parker medium, for example, runs wider than a Lamy medium. Fine nibs release less ink, thus finer pens sometimes feel scratchy on the paper. Nib material impacts the flexibility; if you tend to press firmly when writing, try using a stiffer nib such as a steel nib. Gold or iridium tipped nibs are more flexible.

Ink Capacity: pens which fill via a built-in piston hold more ink than those that use a disposable cartridge or a removable converter. The piston allows you to draw ink directly into the pen from the ink bottle, but it cannot be re-filled unless you have a bottle of ink handy. Disposable cartridges are great when traveling, but are prone to flow problems - the pen will sometimes skip or not always "start" when the pen touches the paper. Removable converters are reliable and very popular.

Price: determine your price range and compare the available pens in that range. Two pens of the same price may differ greatly in quality and performance. Furthermore, a pen does not have to be expensive to write well!

CARING FOR THE PEN

Do not press hard when writing. This will damage the nib. A good fountain pen should glide effortlessly across the paper.

Use fresh ink. Do not use bottled ink that is more than a year old. If you do use old ink you should first examine it for any mold that may be growing on the surface. Then stir the old ink to make sure that there are no lumps or sediment on the bottom - a sign that the ink is solidifying. Thinner inks, like Waterman, Sheaffer, or Pelikan, are less likely to solidify than thicker inks. If the ink has not been used for several weeks, shake the bottle before filling the pen, as the ink particles may have settled a bit.

Store your ink bottles away from direct sunlight. This practice will help keep the ink from fading.

Wash your pen. Your pen should be washed every few weeks and when changing ink colors. Use only cool water when washing the pen. Distilled water will work best; tap water sometimes contains particles which may clog the feed. Never use hot water or alcohol as this will damage the feed or other parts of the pen. With a piston filled pen, wash the pen by filling and emptying it with water - repeat this until the water is clear. If the pen uses a cartridge or converter, soak the nib section in water overnight. If the pen is very dirty, add a small amount of Formula 409 or household ammonia to the water.

Clean it before storing it. If you do not plan on using your pen for a prolonged period of time, wash and empty it of ink before storing it away.

Choose your papers carefully. Avoid using chemically treated paper, which usually has a slick feel. It does not absorb ink well. Ink will collect in the nib and will ultimately clog the feed. If your pen skips after using treated paper, wipe the nib with a lint-free cloth. If this does not work, wash the pen with water.

Avoid leaks. When traveling by plane, either fill the pen completely or leave it empty in order to avoid leakage. Under normal daily circumstances, keep the lid on when the pen is not in use.

Do not loan your pen to anyone. Amazingly, the nib adjusts to your writing style - pressure and angle.

Remove the cap carefully. Pen caps are removed by a threaded screw action or a pressure pull-out cap. If your pen has a pull-out cap, do not use both hands when removing the cap. Instead, hold the pen in one hand, grip the cap between your index finger and thumb, and then gently push the cap up.

Avoid clogging. When not using the pen, keep it stored vertically with the nib pointing up to prevent ink from settling in and clogging the feed.

Lubricate if necessary. If the piston mechanism is tight or squeaky, do NOT use petroleum-based products such as Vaseline or WD40 to lubricate it. The most effective lubricant is Superlube, also known as Teflon.

use me

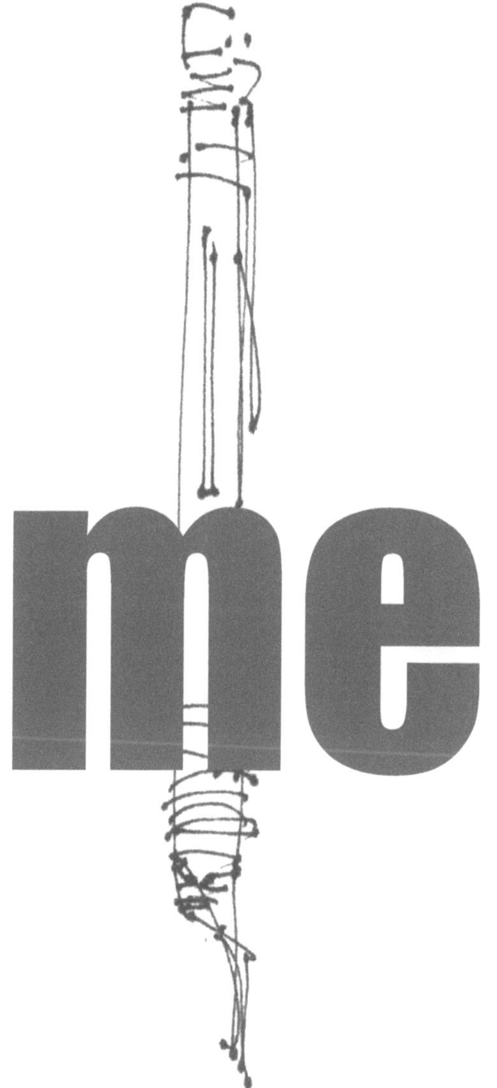

If your pen does not "start" right away, ink has probably dried and clogged the nib and/or the feed. To start the ink flowing again, resist the urge to press down hard on the pen. Instead, wet the point of the nib with water or ink of the same brand and color. If that does not work, place the nib under running cold water or wash the pen thoroughly.

pencils

Wood pencils are as diverse as the species of wood that they are named after. They come in different shapes and sizes, and vary in quality, performance, and price.

The modern "lead" pencil is devoid of any traces of lead for health reasons. The "lead" nomenclature is vestigial from when lead was used to mark parchment. The dark marking core within any wood pencil manufactured today is actually made from a hardened paste of graphite, clay, and plasticizers such as wax. The wood surrounding the core is either a soft wood or an inexpensive plastic resin that provides less rigidity and weight.

Graphite pencils are made in a variety of hardnesses which affect the tonal value and feel when marking upon a drawing surface. This hardness is usually expressed as an H (hard) or a B (black), with sequential gradations. A 4H pencil is harder than an H, and a 6B is softer than a B. Unfortunately, there is no international standard that controls these two variables. Within a certain brand of pencils, however, such categorization tends to be accurate and reliable.

Try several brands of wood pencils and compare their feel and tonal value. A 4B wood pencil is a great tool to sketch with and to do the layout. Be aware that a pencil sketch will smudge and smear, and has to be "fixed" by using an artist's fixative or hair spray.

The degree of vertical pressure that a person exerts on the tip controls the tonal value. Push hard if you want to make a darker line and lighten your pressure when you need to draw a lighter line. The tip of the pencil dispenses the line weight. Sharpening a wood pencil with a small folding pocket knife is very healthy for the pencil and ensures a customized tip - pointed, chiseled, etc. If you lack the control or time necessary for using an open blade, a regular pencil sharpener will suffice. Use a piece of sandpaper to chisel the tip to the desired profile.

Mechanical pencils are generally better suited for drafting rather than sketching. Lead holders or clutch pencils have improved in quality recently and many manufacturers are producing engineered products that can accommodate the thick dark lead suitable for sketching and layout.

Colored pencils are similar to graphite pencils except that the core contains a somewhat hard paste of colored chemical pigment and either a clay or wax hardener. This explains the waxy/chalky feel of different colored pencils. Avoid buying the so-called Color systems (boxes that contain tens or hundreds of different colors); buy and use a few colors such as black, sepia, white, red, green, blue, and yellow.

Charcoal pencils and sticks tend to smudge and flake off as the page in the journal is opened and closed. As mentioned earlier, a can of artist's fixative or hair spray will remedy the situation; however, your journal will start to smell like a chemical laboratory and might set off the bomb detectors at international airports.

Experience taught me to abandon graphite and charcoal pencils due to their inability to produce a true and permanent black line. When not using my fountain pen, I use a black colored pencil to sketch and a regular HB pencil to do the layout.

A good quality white eraser is nice to have - for use sparingly, in addition to a good pencil sharpener and a small ruler. The ruler can help with title layout and with the basic lines of a drawing layout, but do not use it to hardline your sketches!

A good glue stick is a must when journaling. Avoid the cheap brands. Always put the cap on the glue stick when you are finished using it to keep it fresh.

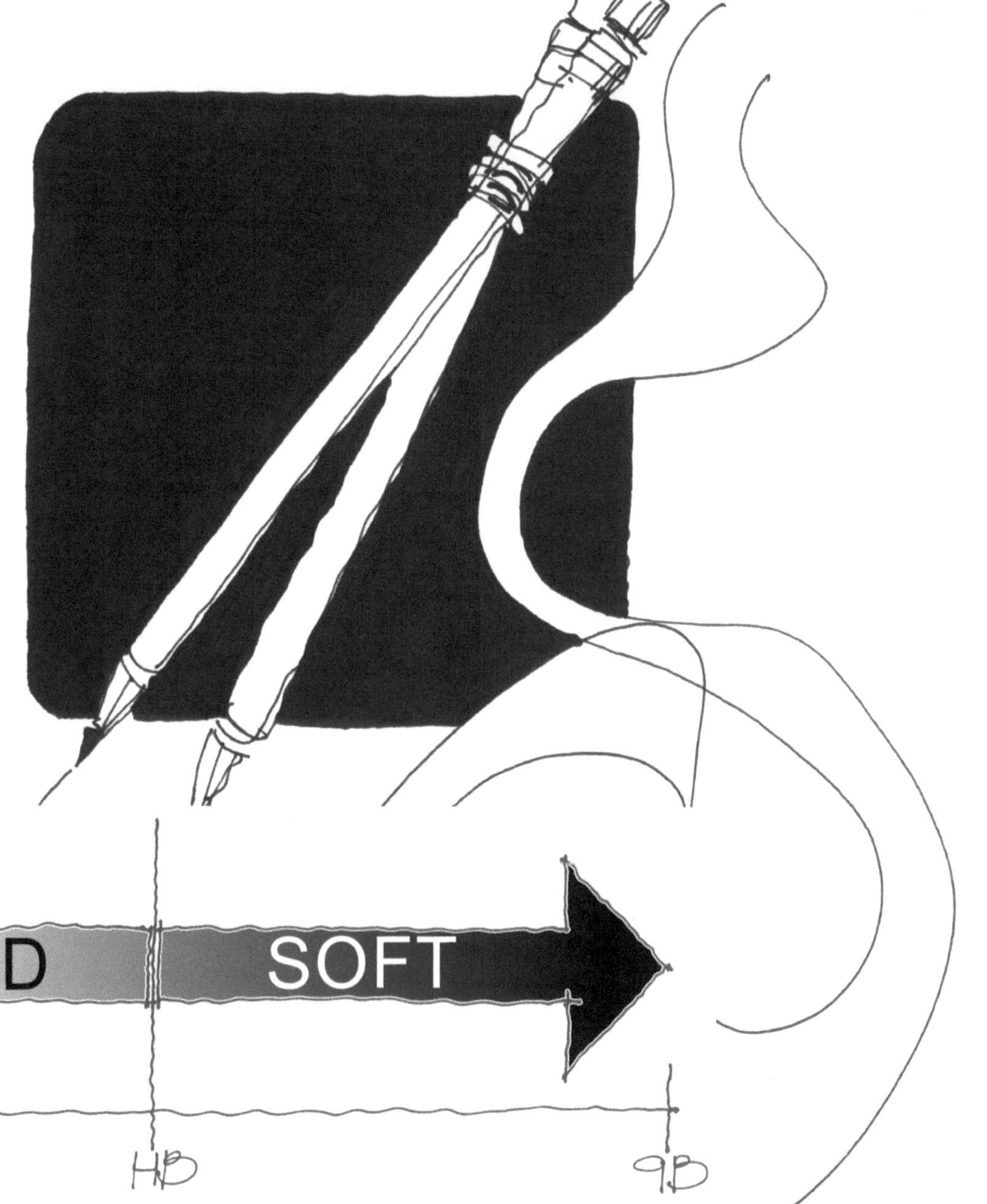

06 - SKETCHING

technique and composition

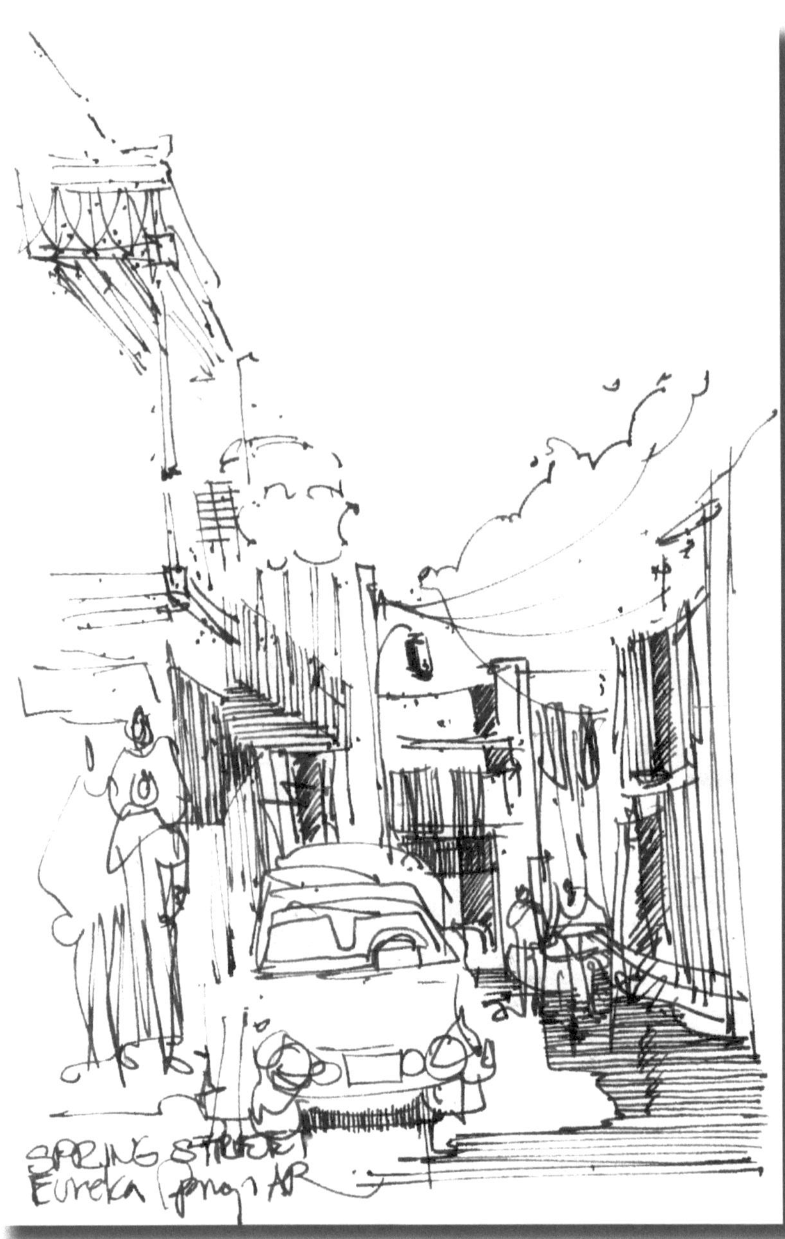

INTRODUCTION

One of the most important aspects of graphic journaling is sketching. While some advocate sketching as an independent activity and an end in itself, sketching in this book is advocated as a complement to analysis and the written text. The two activities combined are what constitute graphic journaling... the act of gathering visual data that is outside the realms of writing and sketching alone.

Sketching requires thought which, in turn, builds understanding. Sketching cannot be detached from seeing and thinking about the fundamental nature of the subject matter being represented. The knowledge and understanding gained through drawing from life directly enhances our ability to draw from the imagination.

While sketching is dependent upon our ability to see, it can never emulate reality. It heightens our senses and sharpens our perception of the subject matter. Sketching has the unique ability to help us focus on the essence of the experience engaging us. Graphic representation is how we record our thoughts as we interact with the subject matter and ultimately the essence of the experience. The ability to convey an experience or idea, whether real or imagined, with a sketch is a fundamental skill that every person should strive to possess.

Fig. 06-1 Journal page, Moh'd Bilbeisi. Ink on paper.

Sketching is a word that describes an act of drawing that involves seeing and feeling at the same time. Simply put, sketching involves the following five acts to various degrees of intensity:

- **Ability to acquire and develop drawing skills.**
- **Ability to see clearly.**
- **Ability to sense accurately.**
- **Ability to focus.**
- **Ability to think abstractly.**
- **Ability to isolate and integrate simultaneously.**

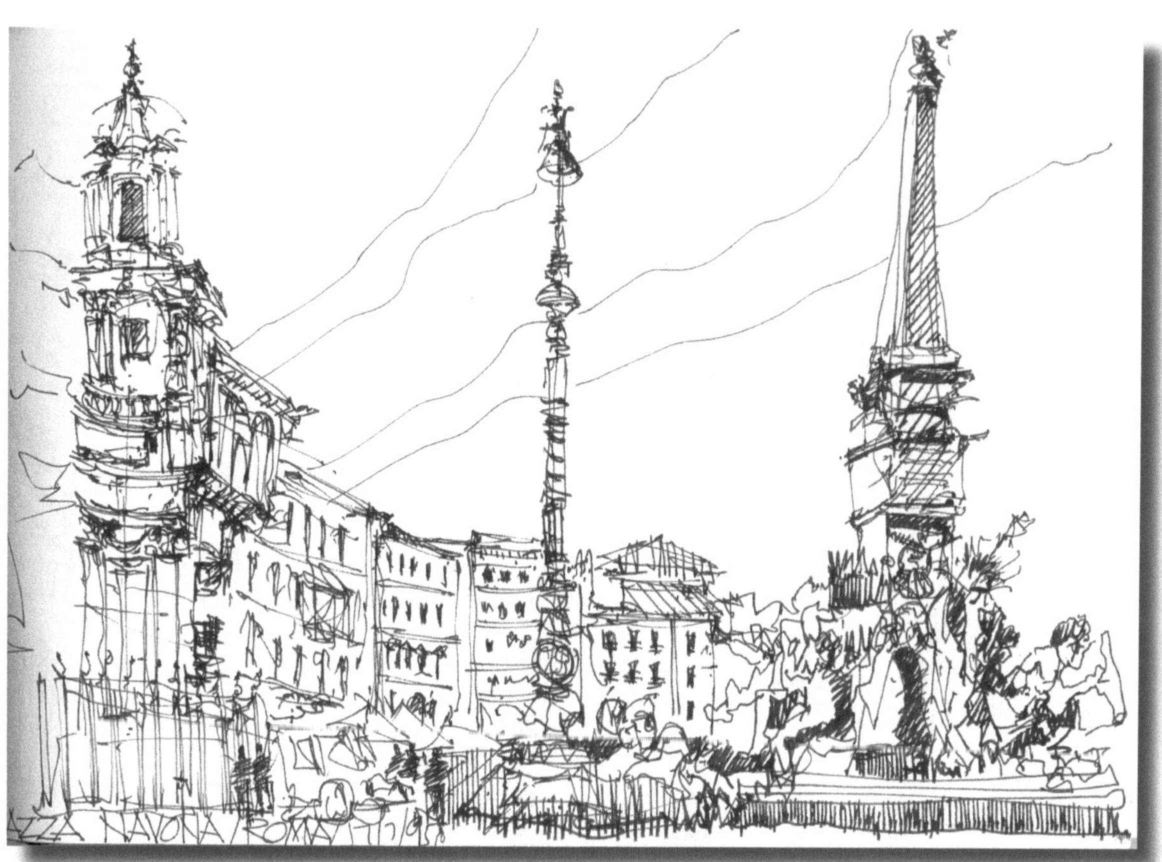

Fig. 06-2 Journal page, Moh'd Bilbeisi. Ink on paper.

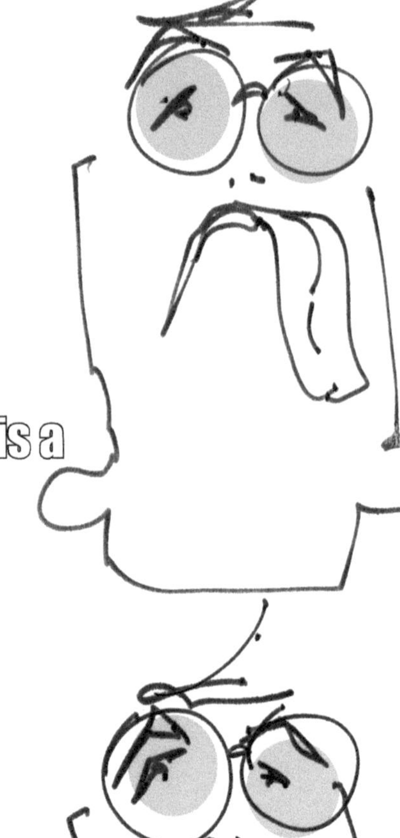

Do not stick-out your tongue. It is a bad sketching habit.

Do not clench your teeth. It is also another bad sketching habit.

TECHNICAL SKILLS

Technical proficiency as it relates to sketching is an acquired skill. No one is born naturally talented in drawing. Developing this skill is like learning a new language; it involves exposure and immersion in the act itself. This means that in order to become a good sketch artist, one needs to practice, practice, and practice. Again, similar to learning a new language, if the skill is not practiced daily, then it is lost.

The very first technical skill to master is to control your breathing while sketching. Puckering, holding one's breath, and protruding the tongue are not good for sketching and will add a degree of stress that will eventually hinder the quality of the sketch.

A sketch artist needs to be familiar with the abilities and limitations of the drawing and coloring instruments. Ideally speaking, the drawing instrument should be relatively light in terms of weight and dependable in terms of performance. Soft pencils, roller ball, felt tip, and fountain pens easily fit this definition. These drawing instruments produce variable line qualities with varying degrees of permanence. Experiment with all of them and you will eventually develop a preference. Keep your drawing and coloring instruments inside a protective bag, especially the pencils since they tend to shed graphite. Refer to Chapter Five for detailed information regarding drawing and coloring instruments.

SEEING, SENSING, & FOCUS

Seeing is different from looking. Humans have eyes and they look; however, the majority of us do not see. By seeing, I mean developing the ability to look and study the object/objects and the event at the same time. It also includes looking and gathering the necessary details to enable us to develop a clear understanding.

Practice this skill by looking at objects for a certain amount of time and asking yourself questions about the colors and the other details associated with the object. Another good exercise is to look, study the object, and later write a narrative describing it in terms of form and color. Challenge yourself and do the previous exercises while looking at an object, a building, or even a street. Keep in mind that the secret is being able to look with interest and being able to focus and sense the surrounding environment holistically.

It is not easy; however practice makes perfect.

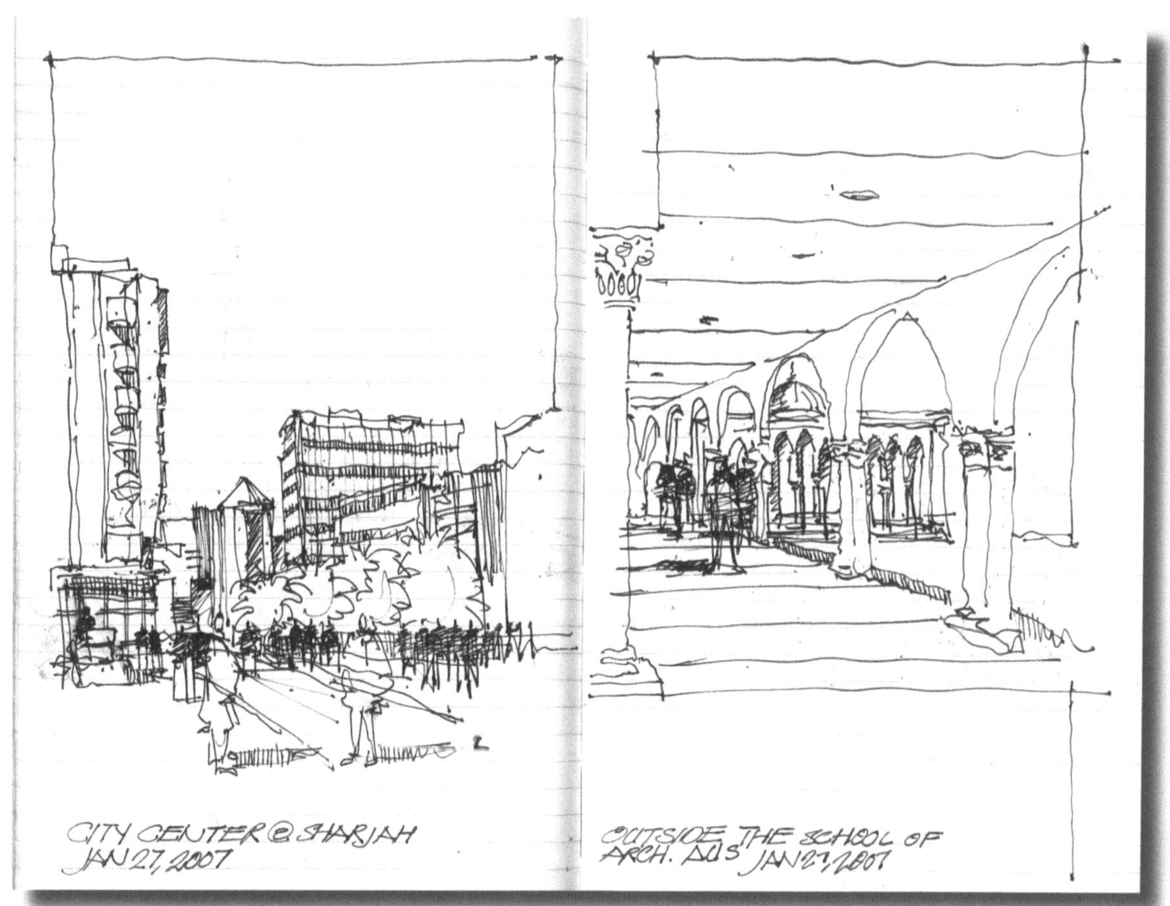

Fig. 06-3 Journal page, Moh'd Bilbeisi. Ink on paper.

PRACTICE MAKES

PERFECTPERFECT

PERFECTPERFECT

ABSTRACTION, ISOLATION, & INTEGRATION

Abstraction is considered by many experts as the highest form of thinking. Abstraction, as a word, is associated with the verb, to extract, meaning to remove. All interpretive references allude to a complex thinking modality that involves reductionism to extract the ideal. This particular skill is acquired through rigorous training at schools of architecture and design. Abstraction is important to graphic journaling and sketching since it allows the individual to focus and extract the essence of the subject matter instead of concentrating on embellishment and self indulgence.

A good sketch artist is a person who is able to look at the subject matter and isolate its essence. This information must then be integrated on the pages of the journal in a meaningful way.

The issue of **isolation** and **integration** in sketching is a complex act that involves the sketch itself, the text, and the diagram. While there exists a hierarchical relationship among these three elements, the graphic journalist is in charge of composing the layout so that it purposefully communicates the idea and the feeling. The logic of graphic progression in sketching such as progressive rendering or detailing might be intentionally manipulated by the sketch artist in order to manipulate the focus and character of the sketch.

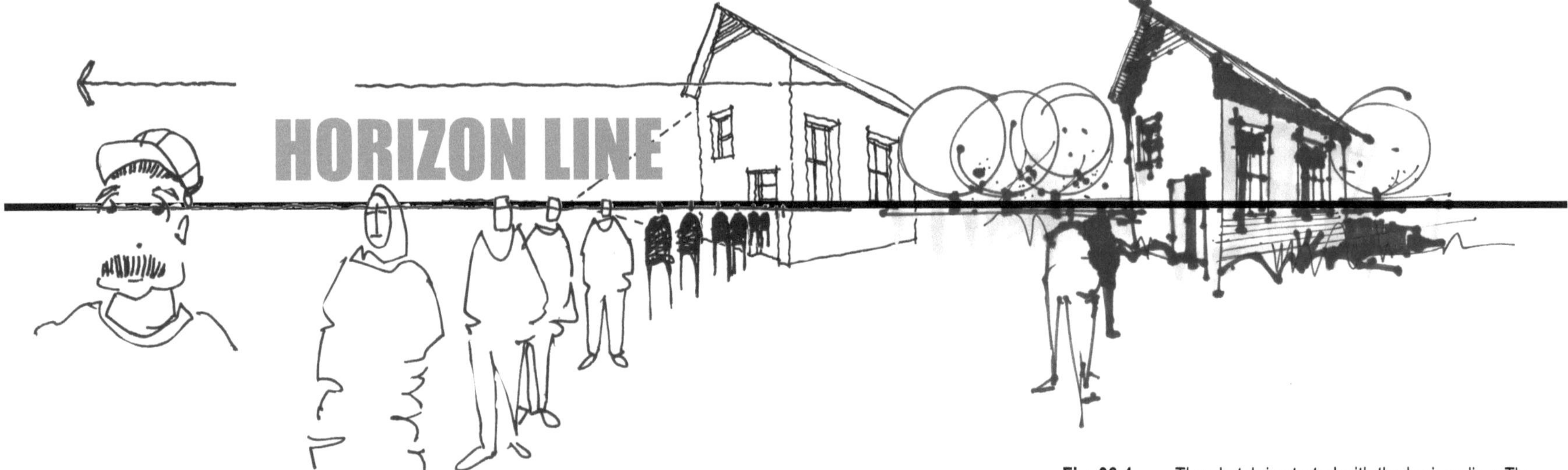

Fig. 06-4 The sketch is started with the horizon line. The people, the house, and the foliage were isolated and integrated into the sketch. Note that the degree of abstraction is increased as objects recede toward the background, yet the degree of abstraction for the house was decreased to achieve focus. Shade and shadows were added to complete the sketch.

The following five topics are arguably the most important issues when sketching:

1- View selection
2- Page composition
3- Proportioning
4- Line quality
5- Texture

VIEW SELECTION

Identify something interesting to sketch! Do this by walking around, looking, sensing, and studying the object and the setting... essentially "hunting your prey". Once you identify a target, move around until you have a focus and the best, most interesting frame to highlight that focus.

PAGE COMPOSITION

To put it on the paper, determine if the sketch should be a horizontal or vertical orientation, and consider how it will fit on the page itself. Generally speaking, most people fail to leave any white space, or if they do, it is an accidental edge which does not contribute to the overall effect of the finished sketch. So draw smaller, and think about where the "breathing room" should be on the page.

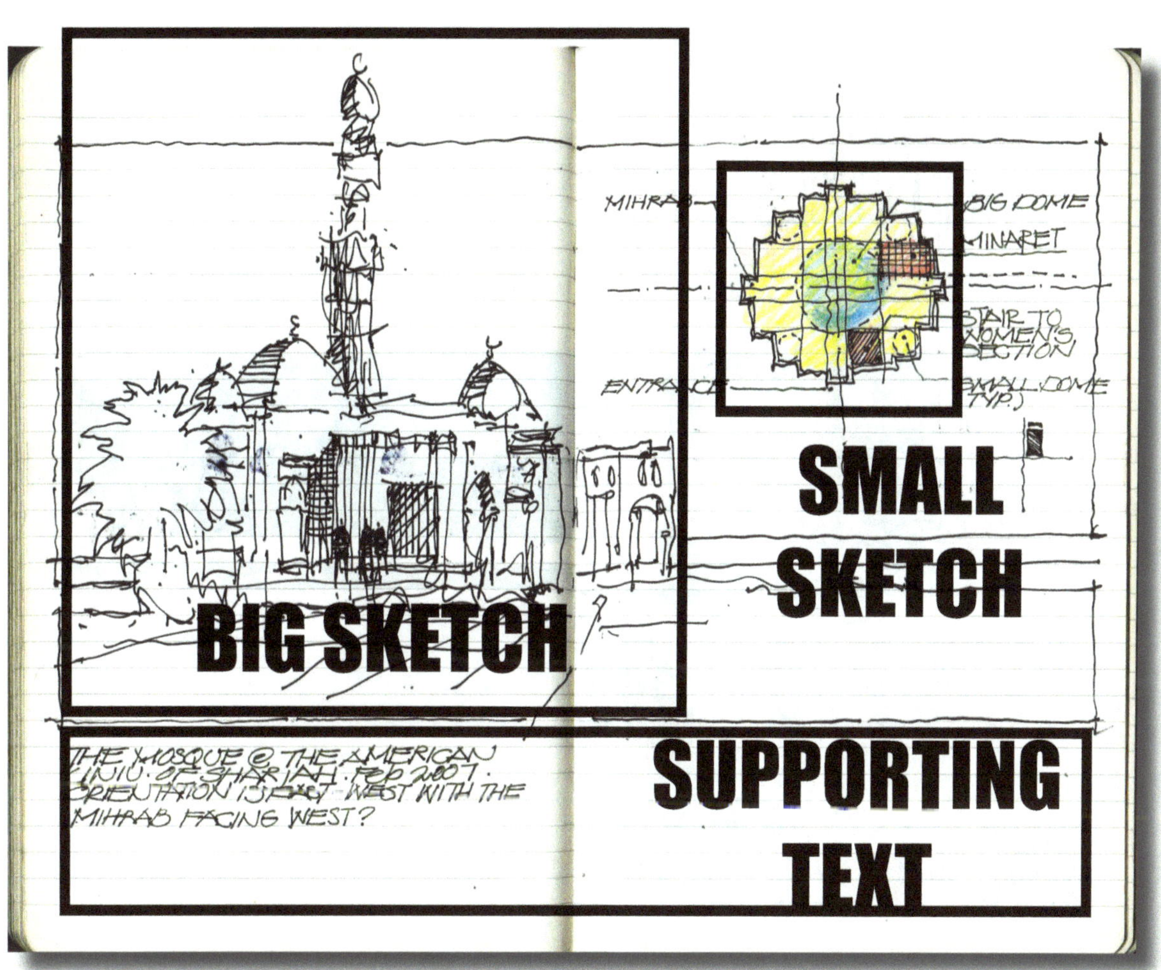

Fig. 06-5 The two pages of the journal are acting as a single composition. It has a sketch of the overall view, a sketch of the plan, and supporting text. Three elements acting as one, Moh'd Bilbeisi. Ink and colored pencils on paper.

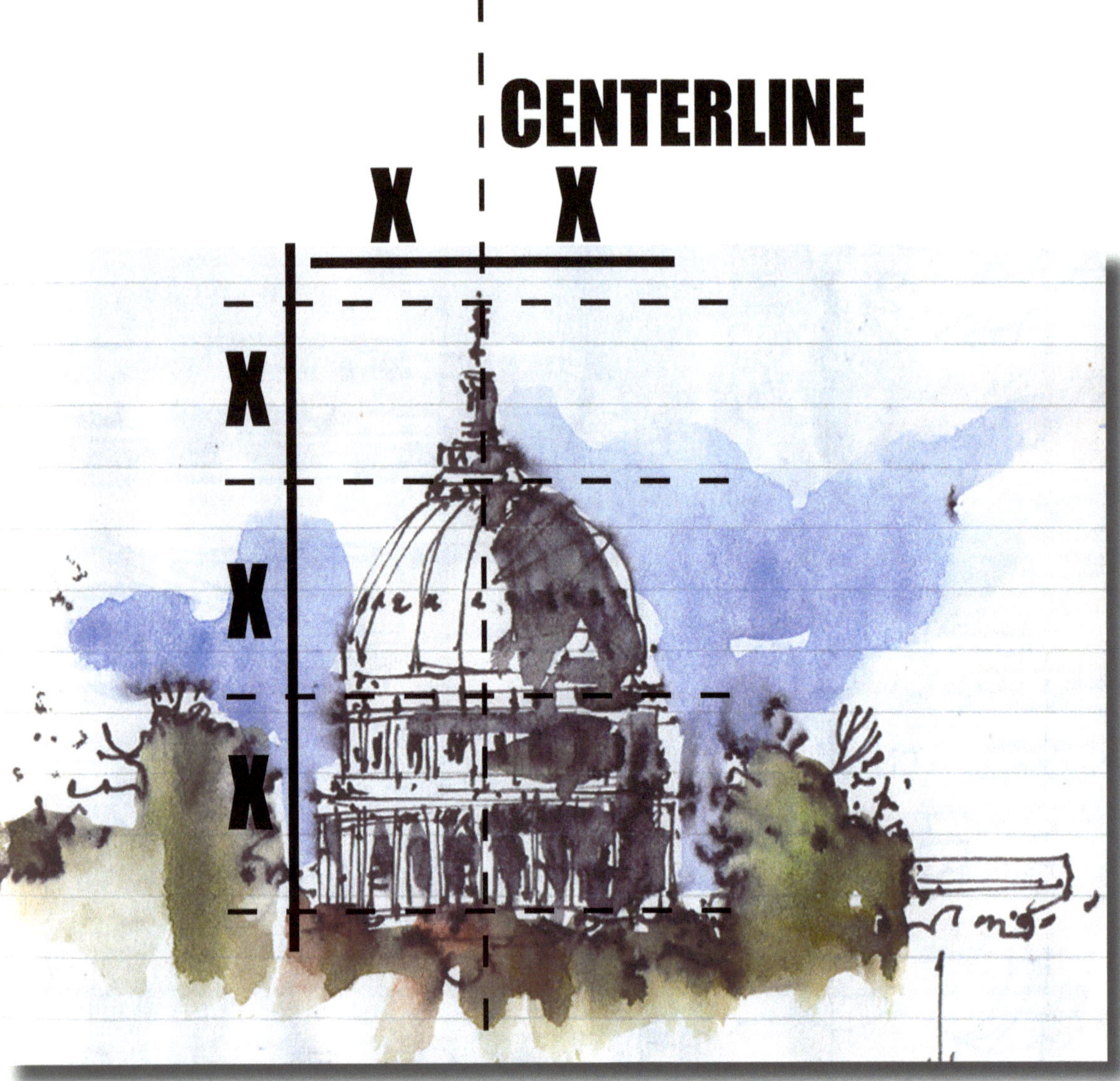

Fig. 06-6 Journal page, Moh'd Bilbeisi. Ink and watercolors on paper.

PROPORTIONING

This is a term that describes how big or small the objects are in comparison to each other. Some sketch artists use their pencil or a view finder as a benchmark to measure distances and angles, and then transfer these onto the paper. In other words, the sketch has a scale; however, it is not in inches or centimeters, it is in the relationship of objects in the view to one another.

As a rule, draw and fit comfortably the tallest or widest object - the master element - on the paper first. This will ensure the correct size and placement of the sketch on the page and sets the tone for the logical progression of the journal entry. Failure to do so will produce ill-fitting and disproportionate sketches. An experienced sketch artist will eventually master this skill without depending on any tools other than a good eye and a good brain.

In this example, the height, width, and divisions of the dome are sketched as repetitive ratios based on a predetermined length of a line. The other dimensions are determined as a ratio that is based on this master line. Again, this strategy requires practice and, once mastered, it will become a valuable tool in sketching and journaling.

LINE QUALITY

Experiment with line quality. Use different pens and pencils, chisel the pencil point and change the angle of the point to the paper. The eye is naturally attracted to points and intersections. Start your line with a serendipitous point and end it with a point. This is referred to as the **"Hit-Go-Hit"** method. A variation on this technique is to rub your pen or pencil on the paper several short strokes prior to stroking the line proper. Move your arm as you extend the line on the paper. Failing to do so will result in an unintentional curved line.

A **perfectly straight line (PSL)**, vertical, diagonal, or horizontal, is an impossibility. A slight intentional graphic wiggle (movement) will remedy the futile attempts to produce the PSL and add character to the line. Questions about how much wiggle are also impossible to answer. Some individuals prefer a slight wiggle and some prefer a really wiggly line.

A wiggle is good, but **AVOID HAIRY LINES**. Hairy lines give the false impression that one of the lines might be the right one. Teach yourself to scribe the most correct line with the fewest iterations possible. This produces a clear line and ultimately a powerful sketch.

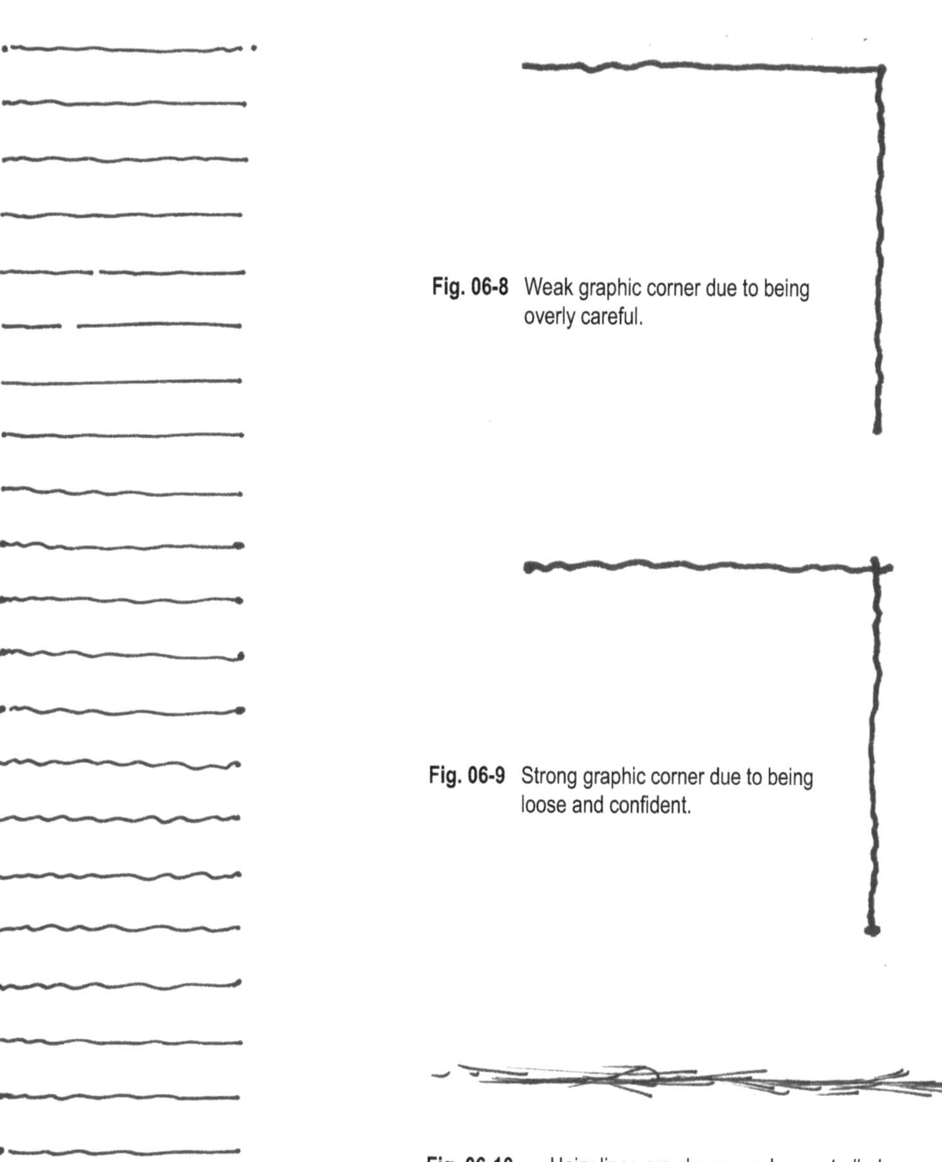

Fig. 06-8 Weak graphic corner due to being overly careful.

Fig. 06-9 Strong graphic corner due to being loose and confident.

Fig. 06-10 Hairy lines are shaggy and uncontrolled lines. These must be avoided.

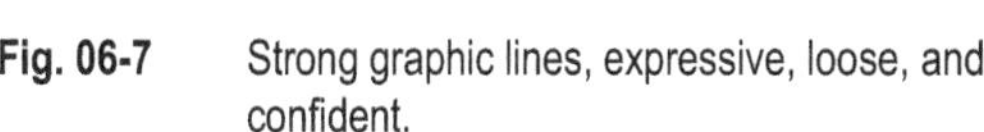

Fig. 06-7 Strong graphic lines, expressive, loose, and confident.

SHADE/ SHADOW/ TEXTURE

Again, more experimentation. Shade, shadow, and texture are fundamentally about graphically depicting the object's interaction with artificial or natural light. If the object is facing away from the light source then it is in shade and if it is blocking the light then it is casting a shadow. Some designers tend to simplify the graphic issues of shade and shadow by depicting the two as a homogeneous area of value. While this might be effective to add life to the sketch, note that within the areas of shade or shadow, there exists a value modulation that ranges from light to dark. Also, not all shade or shadow is gray in terms of color. Objects casting shadows tend to reflect the adjacent hues and reflect them back on the shadows.

Texture is a more complex issue when it is discussed in sketching and graphics. Texture, as an optical phenomenon, is recognized when viewed at a short distance from the textured object. As the distance increases, the texture starts to fade and transform into hue. This is a good point to emphasize since sketching is a reductionist process that involves depiction at a distance. Note that this is not a law nor a rule; however, it explains why the texture of brick vanishes when viewed from a distance and is replaced with a hue.

Sketching in pen limits the number of methods to depict graphic value that indicates texture, shade, or shadow. The pencil on the other hand is very capable of indicating texture and graphic value due to the versatility of its drawing medium, graphite, and the practicality of the tip since it can be shaped by using a pocket knife or sandpaper file.

HATCHING

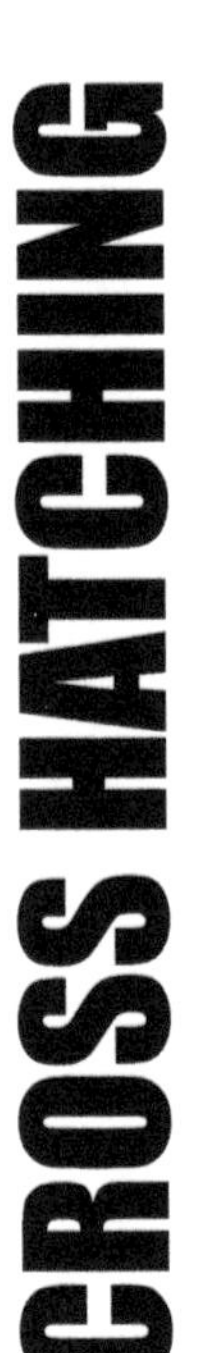

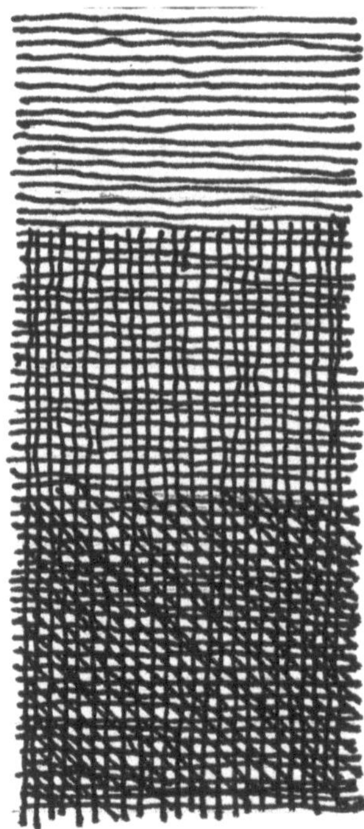

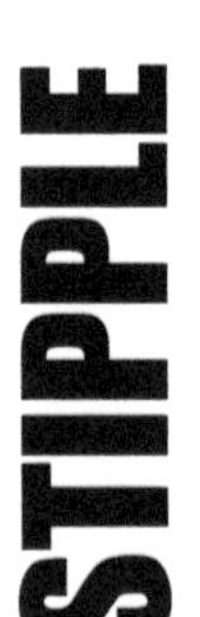

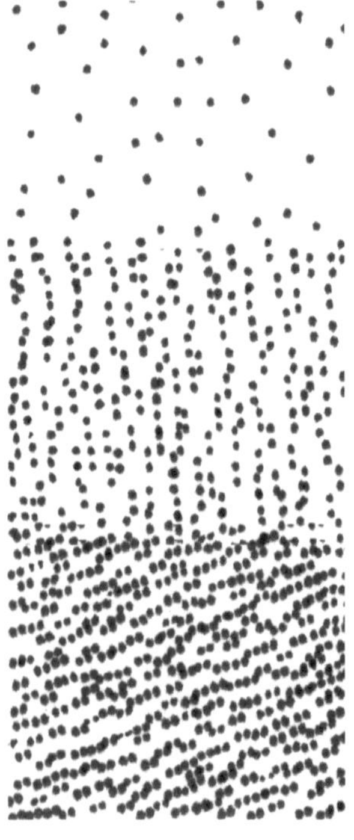

CONTOUR DRAWING AND GESTURE DRAWING

The act of drawing is divided into two distinct methods. The first is known as **contour drawing**, which is an ingenious strategy of defining form, not by value or hue, but by abstracting the hue/value difference between two adjacent areas to a line... a contour line. The second method of drawing is referred to as **gesture drawing**, which is more about depicting value and hue as the object is interacting with natural or artificial light.

Sketching, as a drawing endeavor, could be accomplished via either method... a contour drawing or a gesture drawing. Combining both is rather problematic; however, it is commonly exercised by many designers and artists at varying degrees of success.

Since sketching involves speed and quickness, contour drawing tends to be favored by many as the drawing method to exercise. It requires discipline, concentration, relaxation, and confidence.

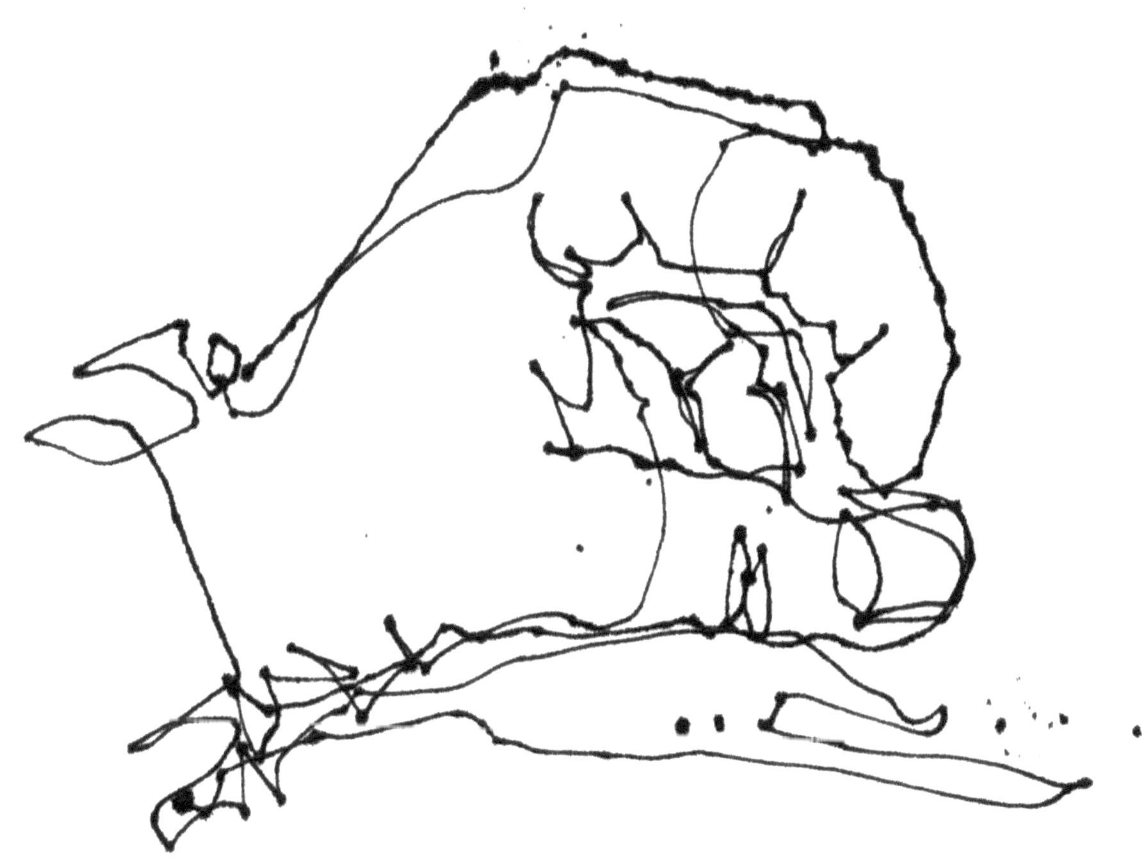

Fig. 06-11 A ten second contour drawing of a hand on a table, Moh'd Bilbeisi. Ink on paper.

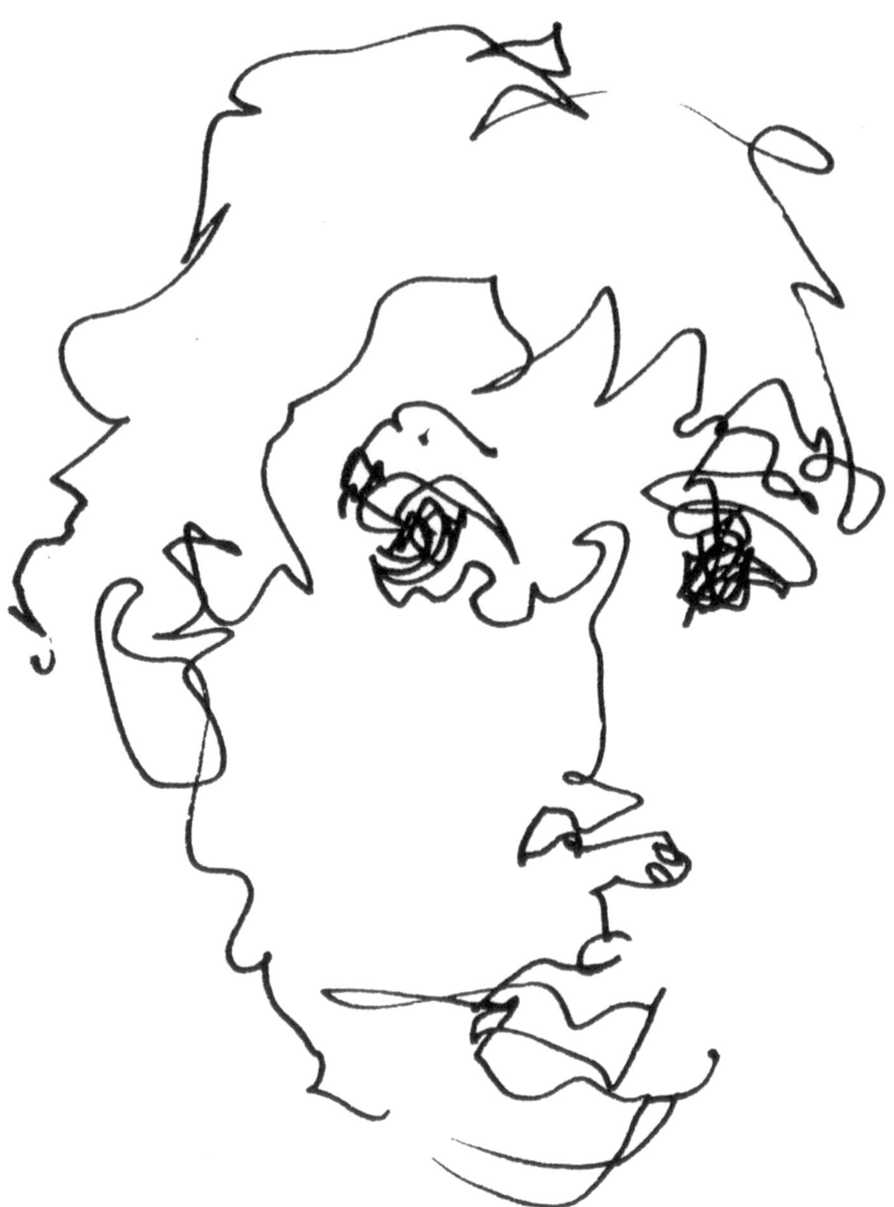

HOW TO CONTOUR DRAW

The following is a step by step guide to achieve an effective contour drawing:

1. Concentrate. Contour drawing is an intellectual act. One needs to focus so as to correctly depict the value difference between adjacent surfaces.
2. Keep your pen on the paper at all times. Modulate the pressure on the tip/ nib and move your hand quickly across the drawing.
3. Draw slowly in small, bordered areas and draw faster when you get to larger and simpler shapes.
4. When overlapping shapes, allow the pen to leave the shape and start on the new, adjoining shape.
5. Consider each completed shape as a measuring tool for the next shape. Learn to judge dimensions comparatively.
6. Connect each shape to an adjacent one. If there is not a shape to follow, invent one (it sounds confusing, but it is possible).
7. Transfer yourself to the subject matter, think of your pen or pencil as an extension of your arm. Scribe away.

GRAPHIC COMPOSITION

Simply stated, Graphic composition is the **spatial relationship** between the parts and the whole and vice versa within a defined boundary. In this case, the defined boundary is the journal page. This dialogue between the different parts within this predetermined boundary is what transmits the information. This requires an efficient and effective communication between the transmitter and the receiver. Effective graphic composition is what distinguishes the work of the professionals from that of the amateurs.

The concept of graphic composition is often referred to, yet hardly explained within graphics books or even live workshops. This is partially due to its non-scientific nature and also due to its cultural bias. For example, the Western world perceives graphics as starting from the left and ending with the right. The Eastern world does the opposite. Unlike science, the topic of graphic composition is not factual. It is rather philosophical, interpretive, and requires ample training to be understood and practiced effectively. The following concepts should shed some light on this interesting topic.

Graphic composition, as a defined graphic discipline, was first studied scientifically by the Gestalt theorists and the work of environmental psychologists at the end of the eighteenth century. Their work in visual perception led to some fundamental beliefs that perception is active rather than passive, and that the human eye is constantly seeking a wholistic pattern. This holistic pattern is beyond the sum of its parts. The observer is in a constant search for a patterning bond that holds the image/ drawing together. According to the Gestaltists, humans favor simplification, and study complexity by recognizing or inducing patterns. They also explain that the human eye favors points and intersections over lines.

While the work of the environmental psychologists is by no means complete or beyond debate, it does explain several graphic tendencies, specifically our obsession with the dot and pattern making. Their studies made considerable contributions to the topic of graphic composition and communication.

FIGURE/ FIGURE-GROUND

SUMMATION OF PARTS

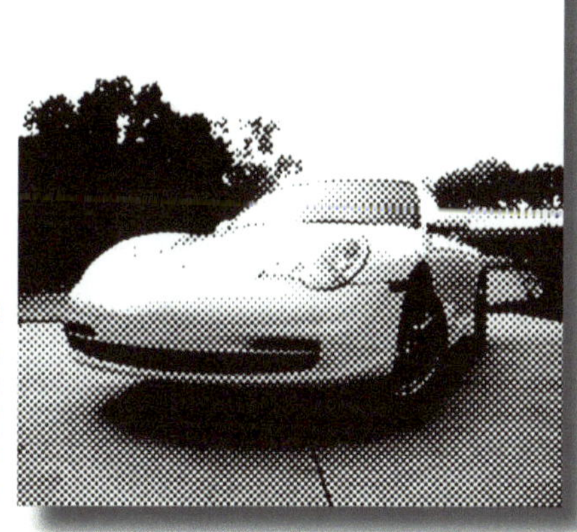

PATTERN

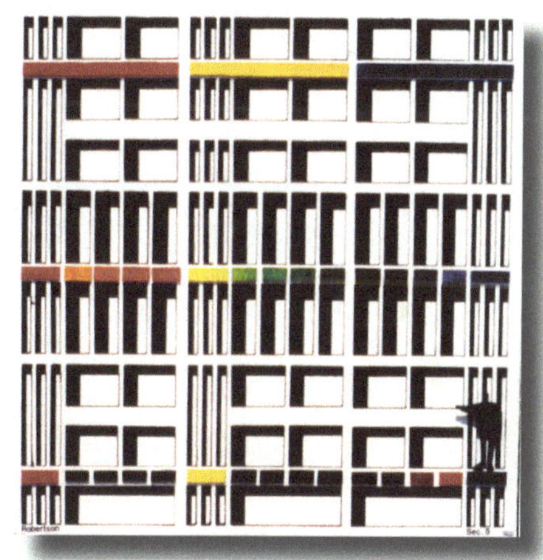

Fig. 06-12 Is it a chalice or the facial profiles of two individuals? Moh'd Bilbeisi.

Fig. 06-13 The overall image is composed of dots of different sizes, Moh'd Bilbeisi.

Fig. 06-14 Different rectangles composing a single facade, Adam Lanman.

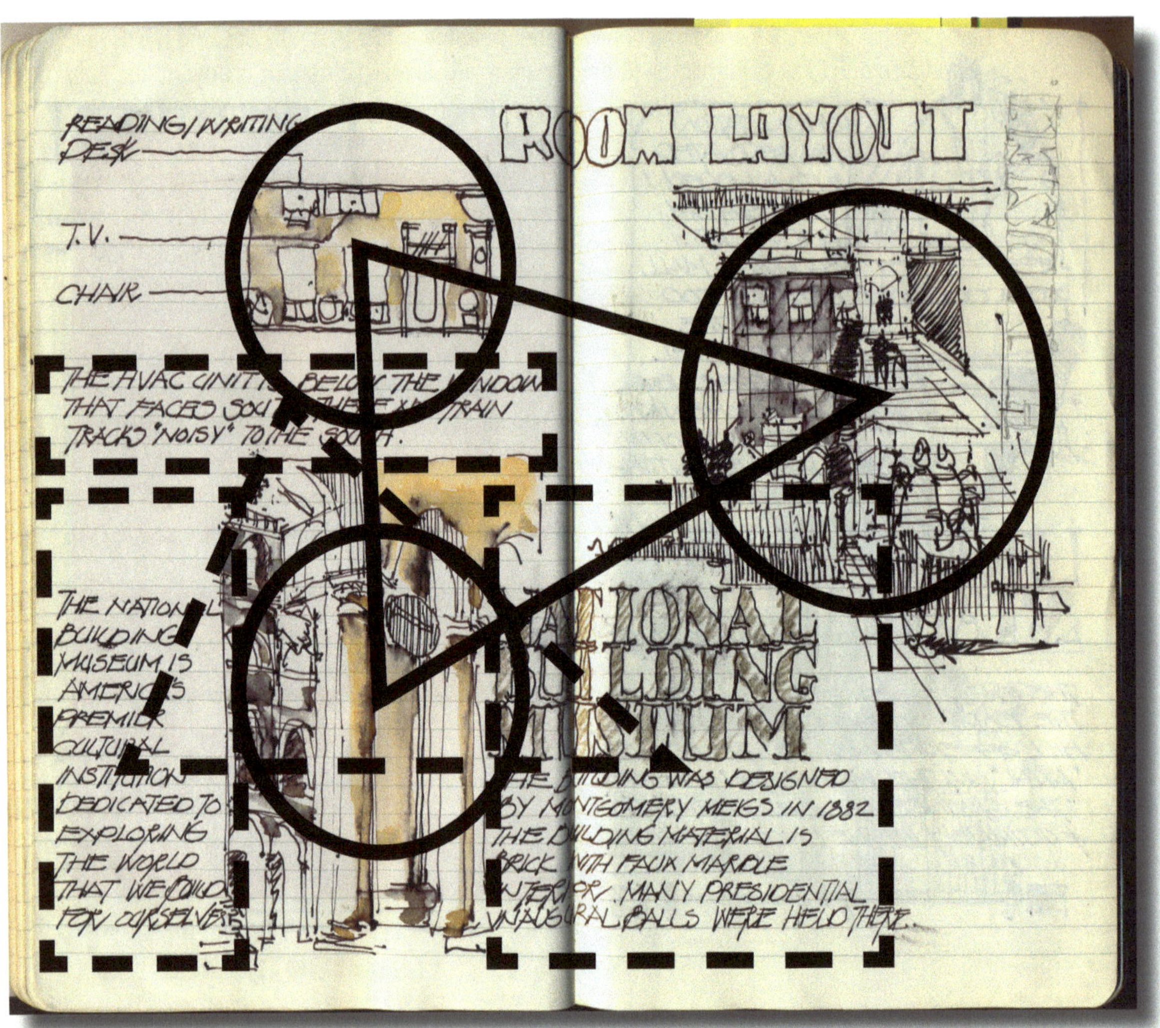

Fig. 06-15 Relationships between similar and dissimilar elements. Note the geometrical superimposition created by the text and the sketch, Moh'd Bilbeisi. Ink and watercolors on paper.

The following compositional tips, "C-Tips," are the most common graphic composition strategies utilized to facilitate communication and produce an attractive layout.

C-TIP 1

RELATIONSHIPS

Geometrical: the designed arrangement of the text, the image, and/ or both in relationship to each other.

Images and text occupy different areas on the page, but relate to one another in a geometrical fashion. This allows communication between them. This geometrical arrangement can be built upon a grid, or in a radial, circular, or triangular pattern.

C-TIP 2

SEQUENTIAL PERCEPTION

Directional: the placement of the graphic parts to influence compositional direction... up, down, across, and toward. This perceptual trait is based upon the progressive placement of the graphic parts to foster effective overall communication.

A good example of this type of communication is sequential art or comic art. Comic strips are generally read from left to right in a stacked series of straight lines, occasionally punctuated by a larger image. In some instances, they are read diagonally or down and then horizontally thus moving the eye constantly and adding to the dynamic nature of the composition.

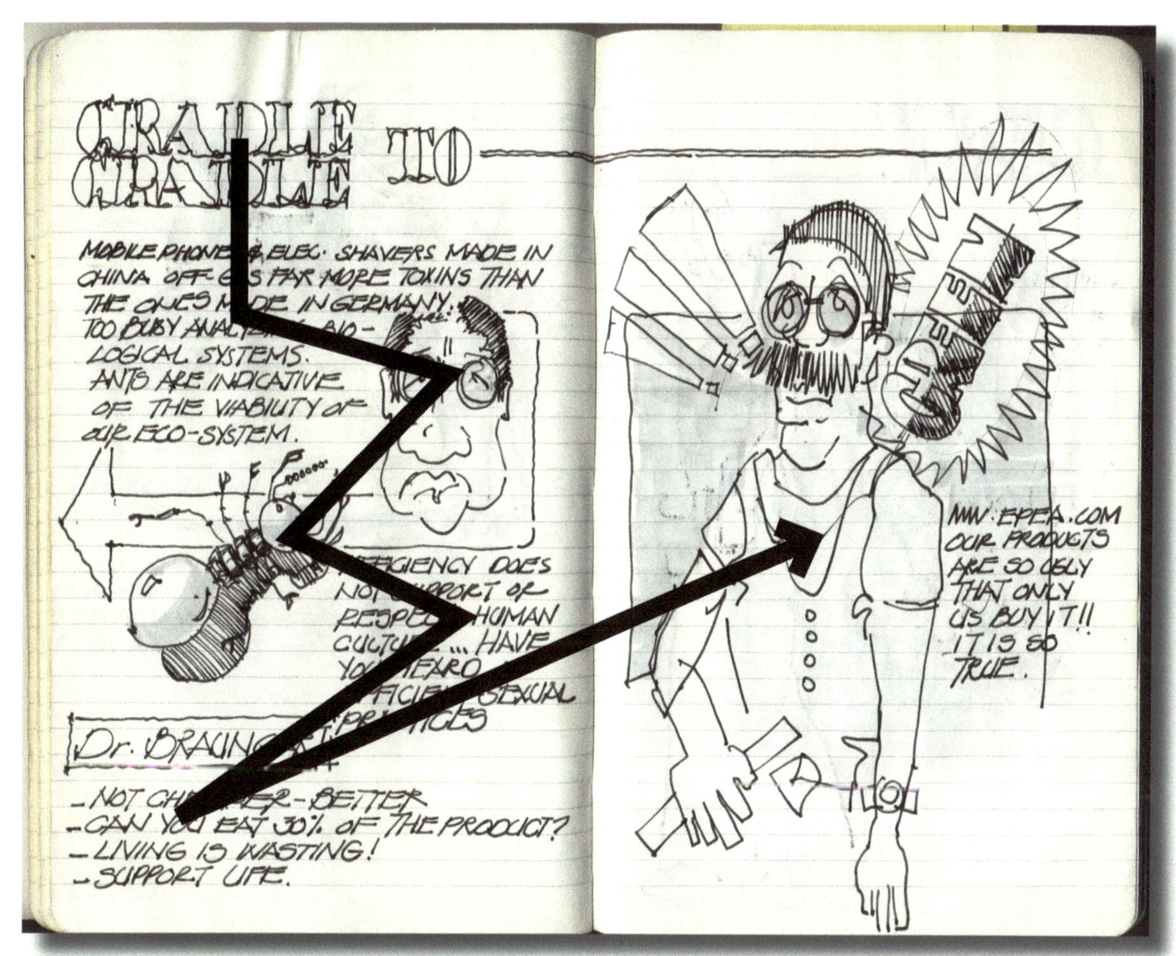

Fig. 06-16 Sequential perception created and enhanced by the placement of text and sketches, Moh'd Bilbeisi. Ink and watercolor on paper.

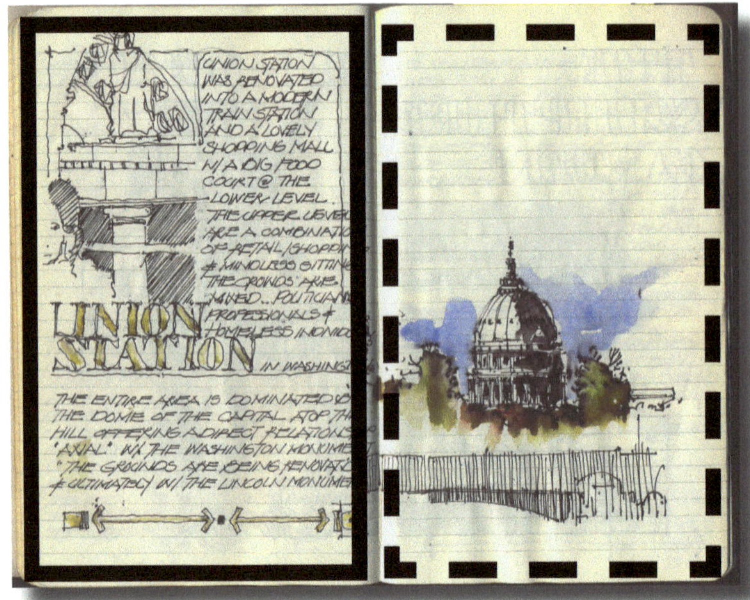

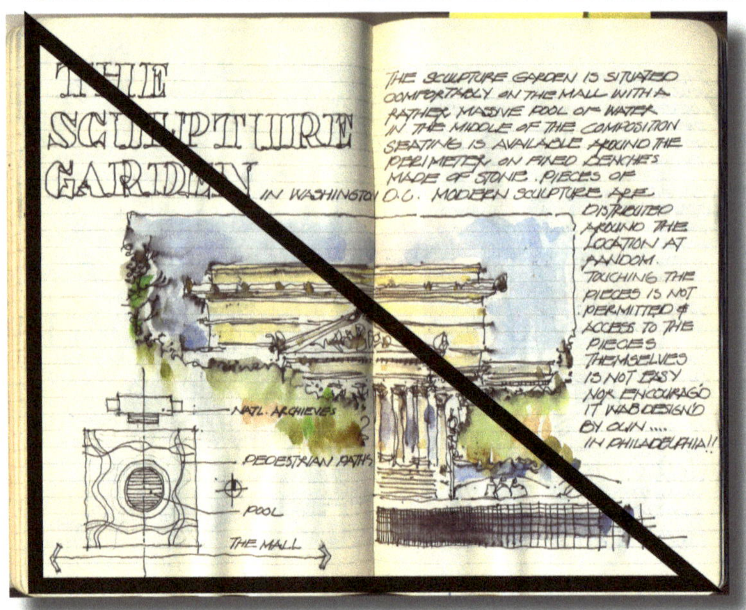

C-TIP 3

BALANCE

Graphic value: the optical value of an image, a drawing, or text. Squinting is a good way to determine the graphic value of an element on the page. Balance between different graphic elements in a composition is crucial since the human eye favors darker values over lighter ones.

Topical: the meaning or subject matter of a graphic element. Grouping similar topics ensures an efficient communication. Intentional misallocation and fragmentation might be desirable to add more interest to the subject matter and exude a youthful flair. Be careful with this one!

Fig. 06-17 The layout is divided equally between the sketch and the supporting text, Moh'd Bilbeisi. Ink and watercolors on paper.

Fig. 06-18 The layout is divided diagonally between the sketch and the supporting text, Moh'd Bilbeisi. Ink and watercolors on paper.

C-TIP 4

CRESCENDO

Gradual and immediate: the rhythm of the graphic composition. Communicating the subject matter on the page is more efficient when organized from general to specific or from low to high value. Immediate or sudden variations in this process can create a dramatic effect that might work to the advantage of the composition.

The upper left-hand side of the page is very important since it designates the starting point for reading the text or the sketch. The lower right-hand side is equally important since it designates the end. Manipulate these two positions according to the importance of the elements to be communicated.

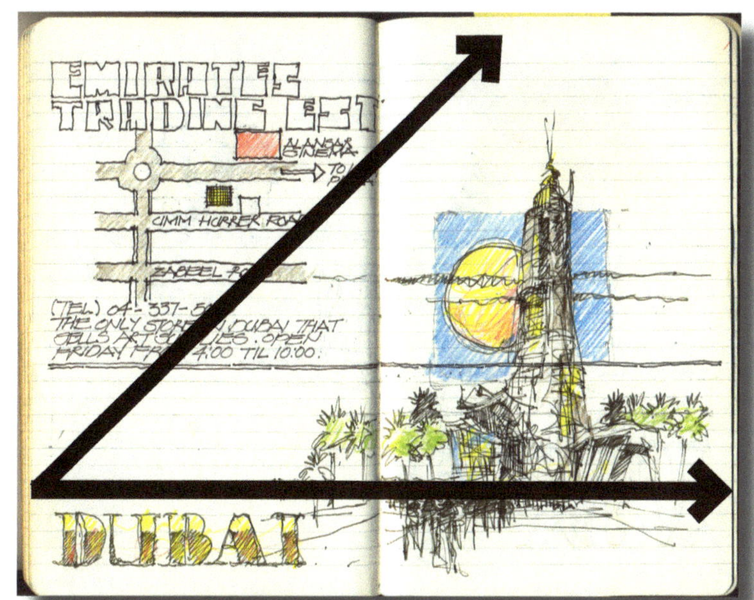

Fig. 06-19 The sketch is gradually increasing in height and importance toward the lower right-hand side of the page. The rest of the info is purely supportive, Moh'd Bilbeisi. Ink and colored pencils on paper.

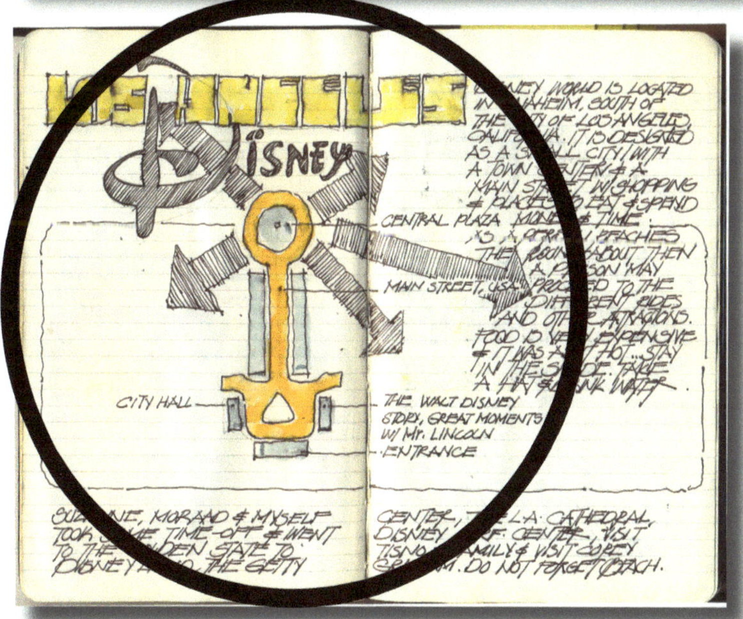

Fig. 06-20 The sketch is immediately situated towards the upper left-hand side of the page with the supporting text occupying the perimeter, Moh'd Bilbeisi. Ink and watercolors on paper.

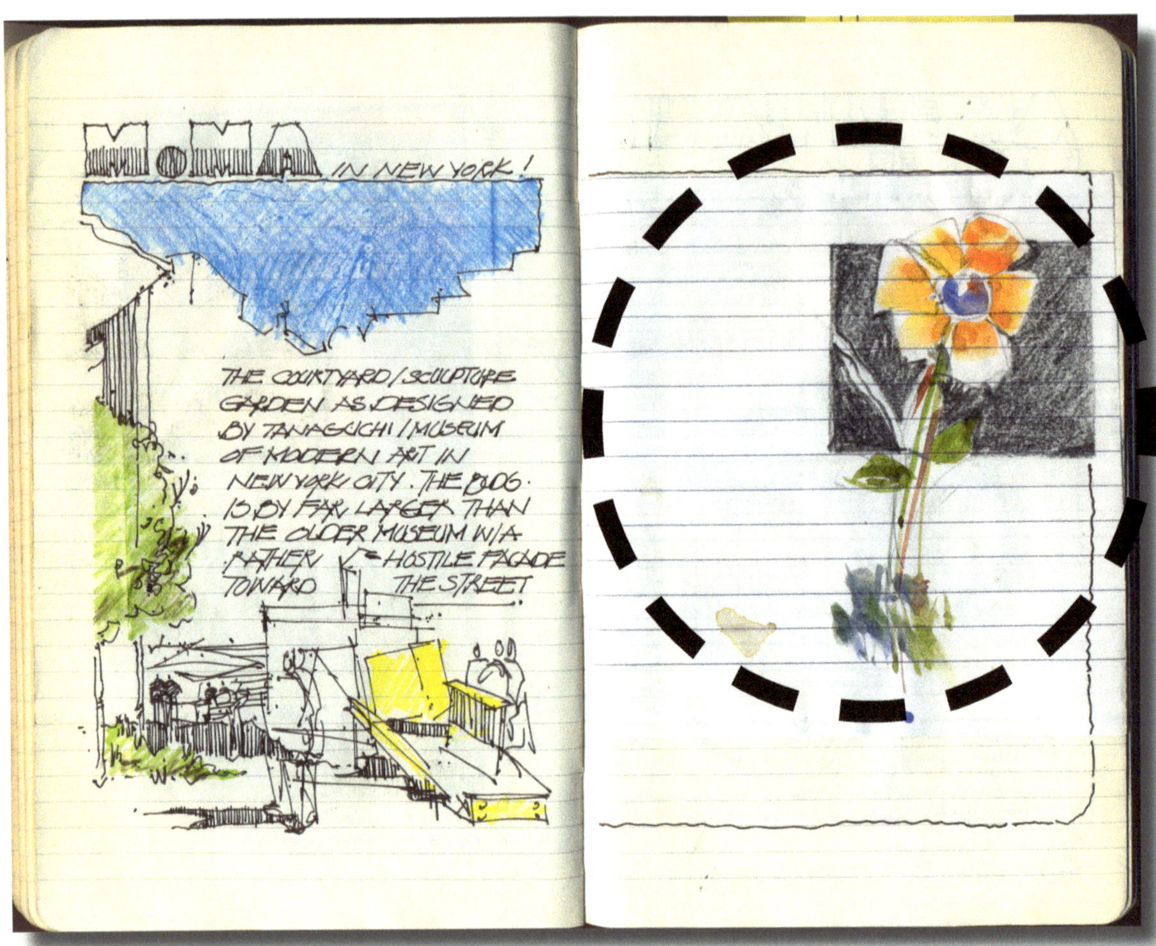

C-TIP 5

CHARACTER

Gender and emotion: the intrinsic message of the medium as well as the choice of subject matter. Certain fonts, images, and sketches are attractive to different genders and age groups. Some images or fonts evoke strong emotions - which can be positive or negative, thus heightening an emotional response.

Fig. 06-21 Certain images appeal to certain individuals. Addressing this human quality can be very effective in graphic composition, Moh'd Bilbeisi. Ink and watercolors on paper.

C-TIP 6

DRAMA

The notion of shock: the inclusion of something which is out of the ordinary. Drama is achieved by writing and/ or including images to attract attention by shocking the viewer via subject matter, scale or the color of the graphic elements. The eye almost immediately goes to this location on the page prior to viewing anything else on the page.

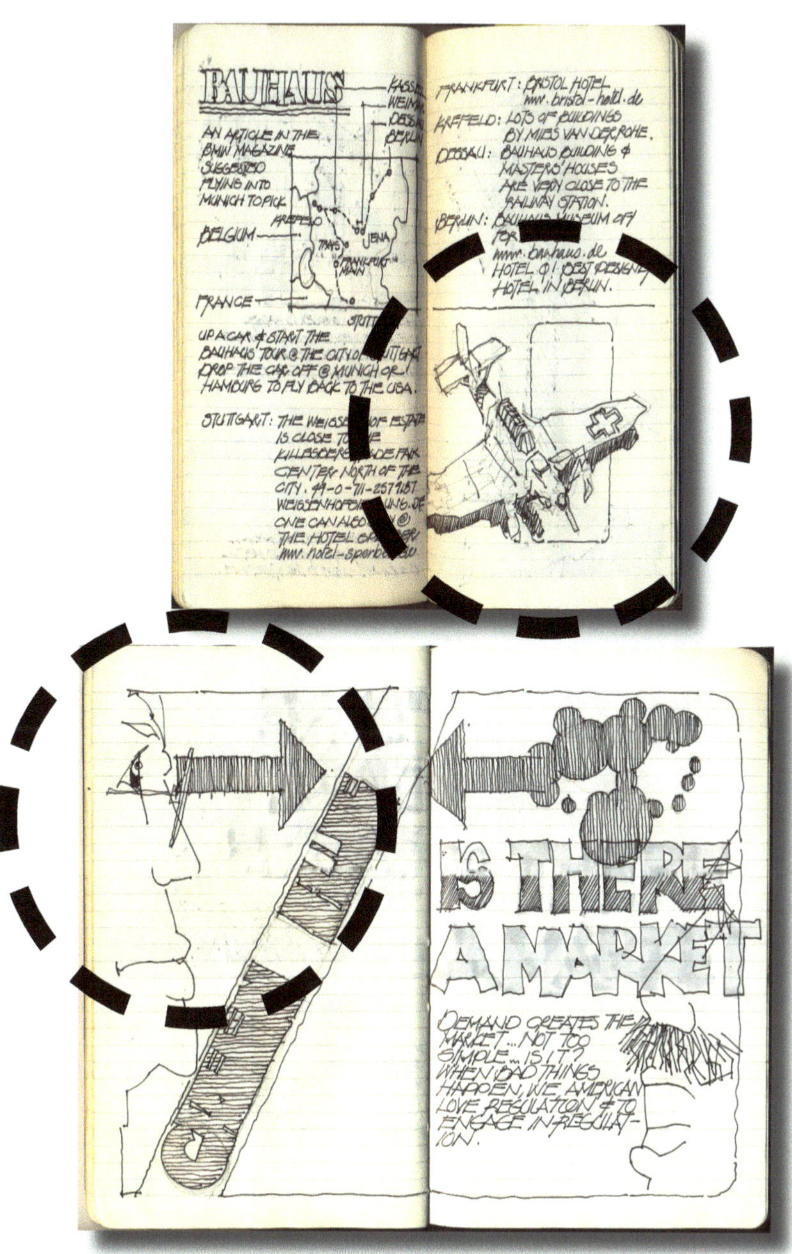

Fig. 06-22 The sketch of a German Stuka bomber in a journal entry about the Bauhaus, Moh'd Bilbeisi. Ink on paper.

Fig. 06-23 An exaggerated and stylized sketch intentionally placed to attract attention to the subject matter, Moh'd Bilbeisi. Ink and watercolors on paper.

C-TIP 7

FOCUS

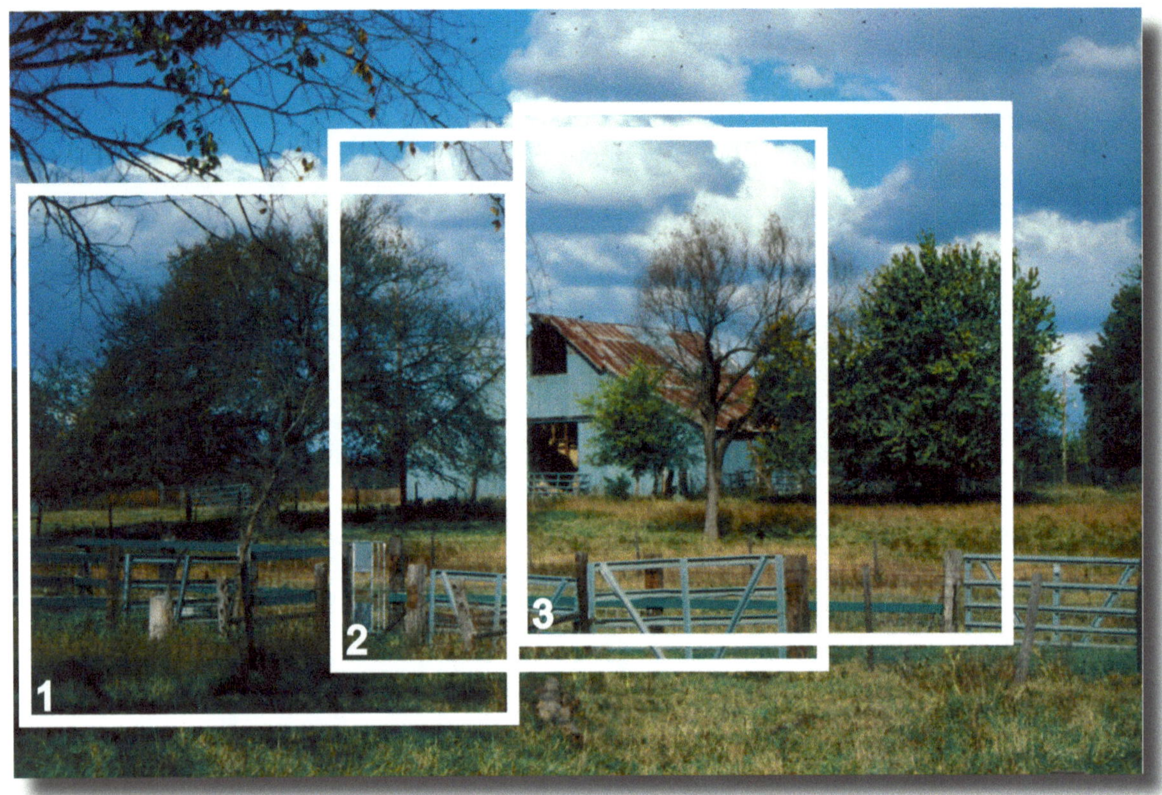

Fig. 06-24 A single view can be sectioned into many different views, each with a separate and distinct point of interest... or focus.

View selection: a view needs a focus. Views without a focus are somewhat pointless. Remember, you are communicating! Carefully select a view that communicates the desired atmosphere or message. To begin, study the view as a series of frames, each with its own focal point. Until you become efficient at view selection, feel free to use a cardboard frame or picture mat, or an empty photo slide frame to assist your effort. Once practiced, you will have the imagination to simply identify the proper view using only your brain.

The composition should relate to the message of the journal entry. For example, compositions 1 and 3 invoke a pastoral character, while composition 2 emphasizes a more rural/ farm image investigation. The view should correlate to the message, it is that simple.

Composition one: The focus is the tree in the foreground with shading to the right of the foliage indicating the sun located at the top left of the view. This divides the composition into two halves, the first is light and the second is dark. The tree is situated at the center of the viewing frame and the bottom is anchored by the fence and some low vegetation. The horizon is acknowledged by a band of vertical hatching with an intentional lift toward the right-side to add a degree of dynamism to the sketch. The entire composition is maintained within the boundaries of an imaginary square to contain the sketch.

1

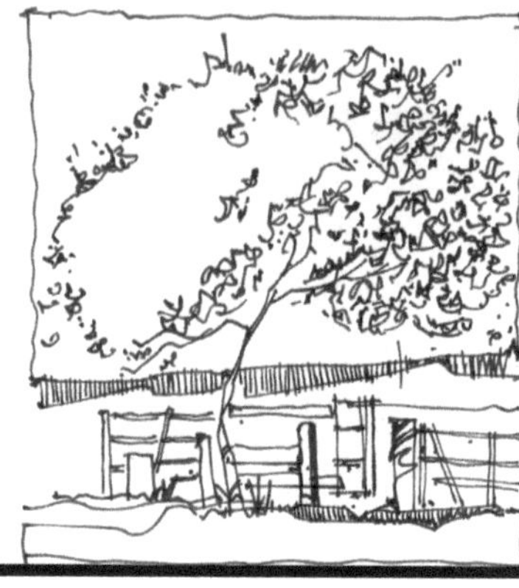

Composition two: The focus is the barn in the background. It is situated at the center of the viewing frame with shade and shadows indicated on the barn structure only. Two adjacent trees are flanking the subject and situated in the middle ground. The bottom is anchored by the fence and the low vegetation. The horizon is acknowledged by a band of vertical hatching with a fade effect towards the right-side. The entire composition is maintained within the boundaries of an imaginary square to contain the sketch. This is achieved through lines that seem to belong to the trees which suddenly form a frame.

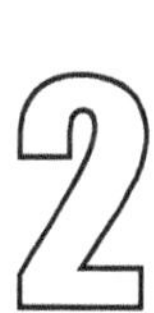

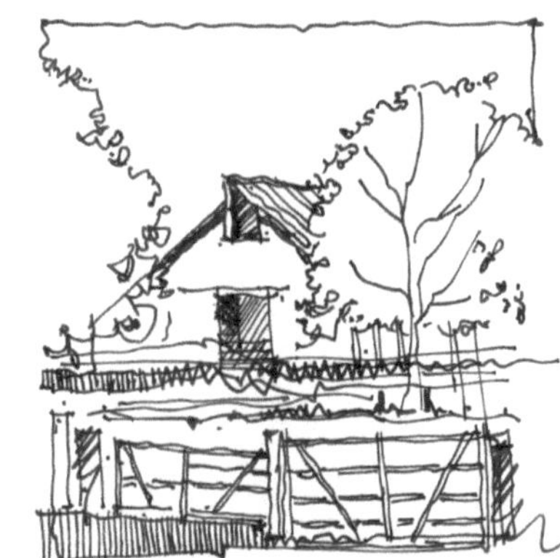

Composition three: The focus is the tree in the middle ground. It is situated at the center of the viewing frame with shading to the right of the foliage indicating the sun located at the top left of the view. The bottom of the tree is delineated with a low value and the fence located at the foreground has very little detail to maintain focus on the tree. The barn structure is located in the background with very little detail. The horizon is acknowledged by a band of vertical hatching with a fade effect towards the right-side. The entire composition is maintained within the boundaries of an imaginary square by using lines that connect to existing elements within the sketch.

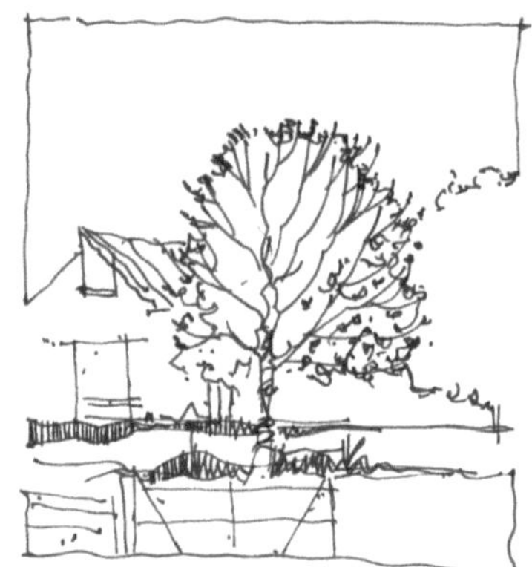

07 - watercolors

enhancing the journal entries

Transparent watercolors are arguably the most important medium in the graphic journalist's tool box. They are capable of adding so much dynamism, character, and hierarchy to the pages of the journal! Due to their aqueous nature they need very little preparation time and will not seep through the journal's pages or add odor as do colored markers.

Watercolor paint is a finely ground pigment - a natural substance such as iron oxide (rust) or a chemical compound- that is held together by a water soluble medium such as gum arabic or other chemicals. Once it is subjected to water, the ground pigment will run across the fibers of the paper and produce the beautiful watercolor effect. Once the paper is dry, the pigment is held together again by the medium. Unlike oils and modern acrylics, watercolors are very susceptible to damage and bleaching by sunlight. This is partially why watercolor has not achieved the classical stature of other painting mediums.

While the detailed, step by step application of this medium is beyond the scope of this book, the general information necessary for the graphic journalist is provided. The medium is complex, requiring a skill level that is acquired only through constant and consistent effort and practice. The quality of the watercolors, the water, the paper, the brush, and the application technique play a crucial role in the process of watercoloring. The following recommendations and suggestions are subjective in nature, based upon personal experience. There is no substitute for experimentation to develop personal preferences!

WATERCOLOR PAPER

Watercolor paper is crucial to the process of watercolor painting. It is an interactive medium, designed and manufactured specifically to produce the luminous character that distinguishes watercolor painting from other painting media. As a general rule, high-quality paper will produce the best results, while low-quality paper will produce dull washes and uneven pigment absorption. *Be aware that most sketchbooks are not watercolor-friendly!*

Watercolor paper is available as individual sheets, bound sheets in a journal, or in watercolor blocks. Blocks are stacks of watercolor sheets that are glued on four sides to control the paper deformation (cockle) due to the process of water application. Watercolor paper is also categorized by weight, thickness, texture, and color. Some watercolor paper manufacturers add or delete certain chemicals to control the archival quality of the sheets.

In the past, the weight of the watercolor paper was measured by pounds per ream (500 22" x 30" sheets), but currently it is measured more accurately in grams per square meter (gsm) or (g/m^2). The thickness of the paper used to be a function of its weight; modern high-tech presses now produce heavy paper in thin sheets. This means that the thickness or thinness of the watercolor paper is not necessarily a function of its weight. Thick paper does tend to be more rigid than thin paper. A minimum watercolor paper weight is 200 g/m^2.

The texture is a function of the manufacturing process and typically falls in the following categories:

Heavily textured
Cold press- Moderately textured.
Hot press- Lightly textured.

Some paper manufacturers manipulate the color of the paper by modulating the degree of bleaching in the manufacturing process - the process of turning the color of the paper from dull gray to white. The whiteness of watercolor paper is not necessarily consistent, and certain watercolor techniques will work better if executed on a less bright paper. The amount of sizing, a water resistant coating that holds the fibers of the paper together, also affects the way watercolors interact with the paper. Experiment and be selective.

My favorite brands of watercolor paper are **Fabriano** and **Arches**. They both come in various sizes and textures, and are available worldwide.

Watercolor sketchbooks or wire-bound pads are usually quite thick and are not readily available. While they are totally capable of accepting the watercolor washes, the paper is much too rough to use with pens. Quality sketchbooks indicate the weight of the paper on the cover, which is a good guide to judging whether the paper is capable of accepting watercolor washes. The curling and seeping associated with the use of watercolors on thin paper can be controlled by limiting the amount of water applied to the paper.

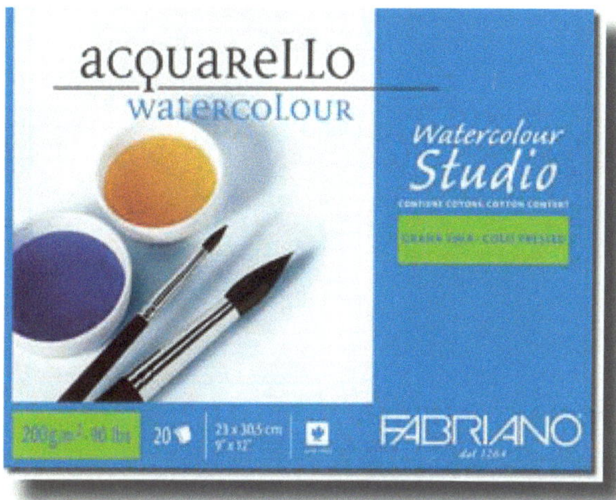

Fig. 07-1 Watercolor block tablet of 200 g/m^2 paper weight, by the Italian manufacturer, Fabriano.

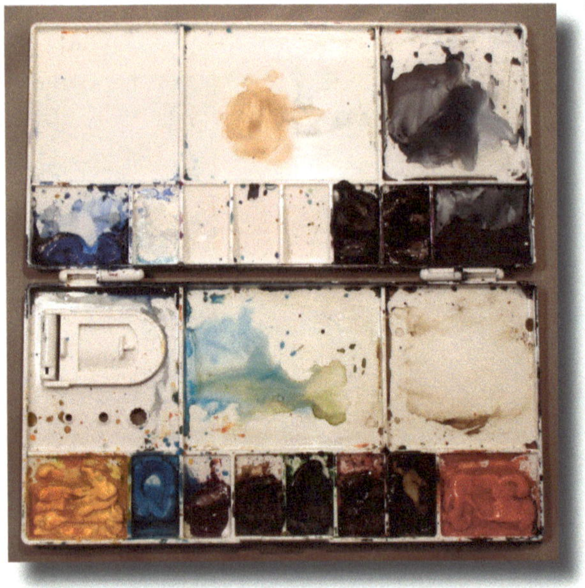

WATERCOLOR PAINT

As previously mentioned, watercolor paint consists of a finely ground pigment (natural and/or artificial) that is bound by natural gum arabic or a chemical binding agent. Generally speaking, watercolor paints are water soluble and are either transparent or opaque. If they are opaque, they are referred to as **Gouache** or **Poster** paint and if they are transparent, they are referred to as transparent watercolors.

Transparent watercolors, the common watercolor paints, come in many quality grades and price ranges. Some are formulated to be used by professional painters (artists' grade) and these are usually expensive. Some are formulated to be used by amateurs and aspiring watercolorists (student grade) and can be either inexpensive or really cheap. Avoid the cheap!

Transparent watercolor paints come in dry cakes/ pans or tubes. Cakes are economical and versatile, though they can dry out quickly. The tubes can also be wasteful because they dry out if not emptied completely from the tube and used in a short period of time. The easiest way to make a travel palette is to acquire a plastic folding watercolor tray and fill its wells with your favorite watercolor paints from tubes.

Be aware that watercolor paints are very susceptible to UV light. The lightfastness of the paint is usually indicated on the packaging or on the tube itself. Note that there is no universal standard to evaluate lighfastness between the different brands of watercolor paints. Consult the manufacturer's paint charts for comparative permanency ratings. Also be aware that the best method for keeping watercolor paintings from fading is to avoid exposure to sunlight, and if needed, place behind glass with a UV protection coating.

Fig. 07-2 A plastic watercolor palette box, filled from watercolor tubes.

The following is a list of the minimum watercolor paints necessary for the graphic journalist to own:

Cadmium Red
Cadmium Yellow
Raw Sienna
Burnt Sienna
Payne's Gray
Cobalt Blue
Hooker's Green

WATERCOLOR PAINTBRUSHES

When considering what watercolor paint brushes to purchase, there are three factors that must guide your decision-making process:

Quality: Simply stated, good watercolor brushes are expensive. A good watercolor brush has to perform two important functions; the first is to be able to hold and retain water and the second is to be able to produce "bounce" a resistance to deformation. Brush bounce is an important factor when buying a watercolor brush, the brush should have a bit of spring when you push on it. Kolinsky sable brushes are a joy to use; however, they tend to be pricey. Brown sable brushes that combine natural and synthetic hairs are wonderful to use and are moderately priced. The Da Vinci brush company manufactures a wonderful synthetic watercolor brush that is collapsible and very usable

Shape: The shape of the watercolor brush is also important. The tip of the brush must be pointed, not angular. The length of the barrel of the brush is an issue since it influences the balance in the hand.

Size: Brush manufacturers use different numbering systems to designate brush sizes. A round brown sable watercolor brush with 1 1/4" bristles (#10 or #12) will serve one well during travel.

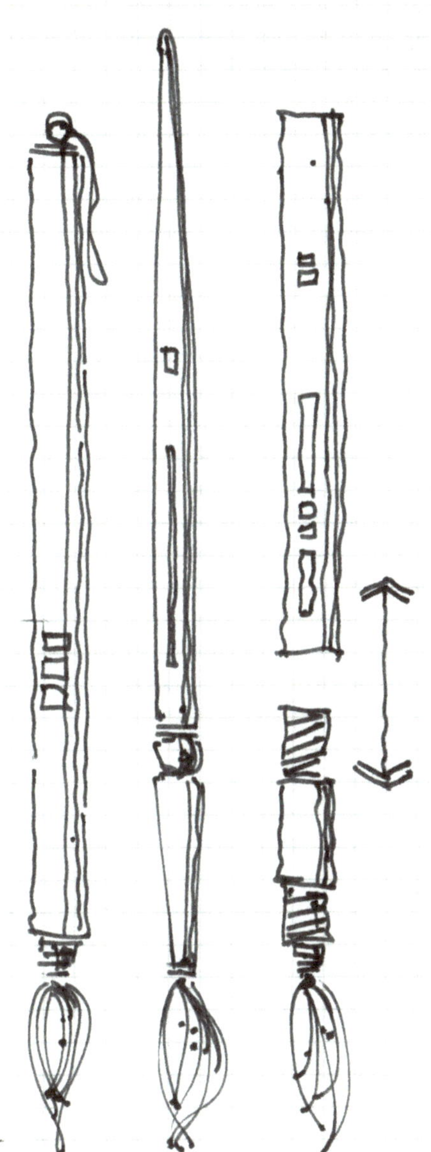

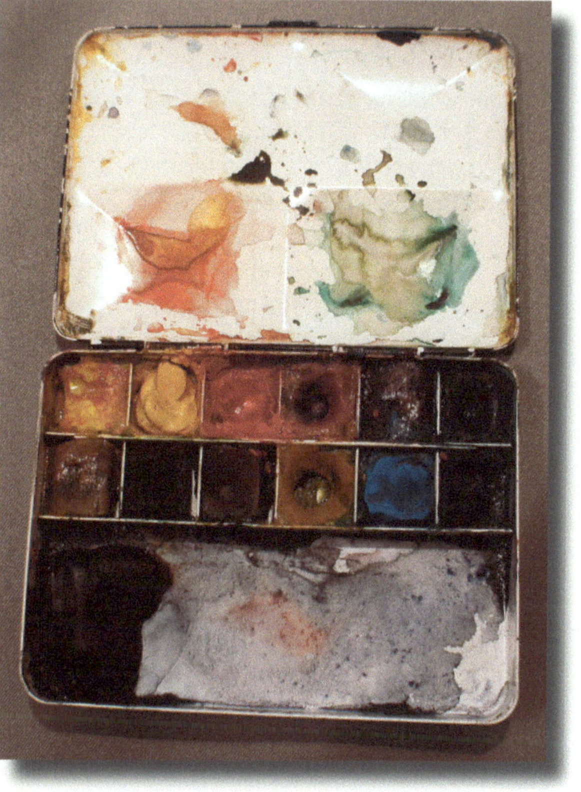

Fig. 07-3 Travel watercolor set in a metal box by the British manufacturer Winsor & Newton.

Fig. 07-4 From left to right, Chinese bamboo brush, a typical watercolor brush, and a collapsible travel watercolor brush.

COLOR THEORY

In a graphic journal, watercolors can be used to highlight a sketch or a part of a sketch, or to achieve a level of contrast with the background. Selecting the right color to use is an important decision when working with a journal entry. Understanding the theory of color is crucial to this process.

Color theory is also crucial to the process of mastering watercolors. The fundamentals that must be understood are the attributes of color, the ways in which colors relate to each other, and how humans perceive them.

Johannes Itten (1888-1967) of the Bauhaus is the color theorist who is most associated with our modern conception of color. He established a comprehensive system of color that depicts the three primary hues (yellow, red, and blue) as the anchors of this system, with the rest of the hues the result of systematic relationships between these three primary hues.

Itten is also credited with defining every color by its three distinct characteristics: hue, chroma, and value. **Hue** is the color itself - yellow, red, or blue. **Chroma** is the color saturation or intensity, and **value** is the lightness or darkness of the color. High value means light and low value means dark. These three factors interrelate to produce millions of colors!

Color perception differs from one person to the next. The attributes and categories of color, culturally speaking, also differ substantially. For example, Asian cultures group colors into two categories. The first is referred to as **cool** colors, which are greens, blues, and purples. The second category is **warm** colors, which are the reds, yellows, and oranges. Some cultures venerate certain colors due to their rarity in their respective environment, while others prefer a color because of its abundance in their immediate environment. Desert cultures venerate the color green, whereas the color blue is very popular among cultures that inhabit coastal areas.

The **primary colors** - yellow, red, and blue - are the hues that can not be produced by mixing other colors. The **secondary colors** are produced by mixing any two primary colors. For example, yellow and red produce orange, red and blue produce purple, and blue and yellow produce green. The **tertiary colors** are the ones produced by mixing a primary color and a secondary color to produce colors such as yellow green or red orange.

And finally, in strict color theory terms, white reflects all color and black absorbs all color. Gray is most successfully created by mixing a primary color with its companion secondary color - blue with orange, for example. With paints, this is not always true because of the chemicals that have been introduced into the paint formulas.

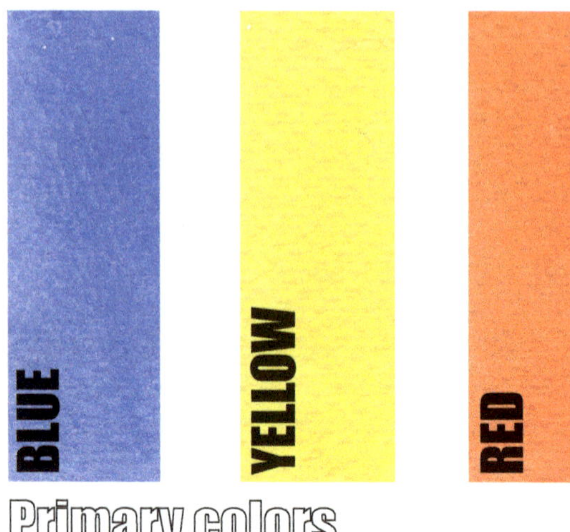

Primary colors

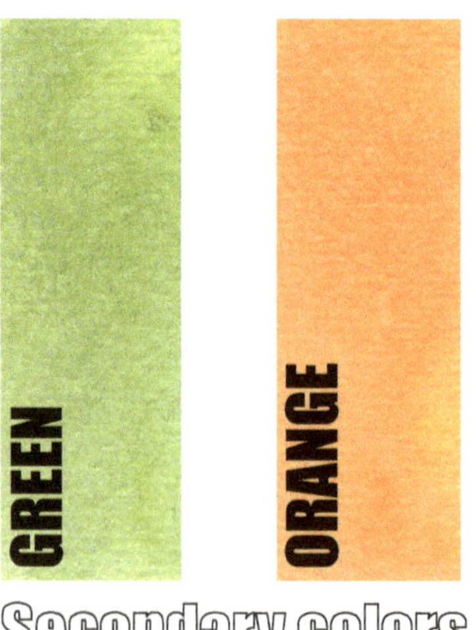

Secondary colors

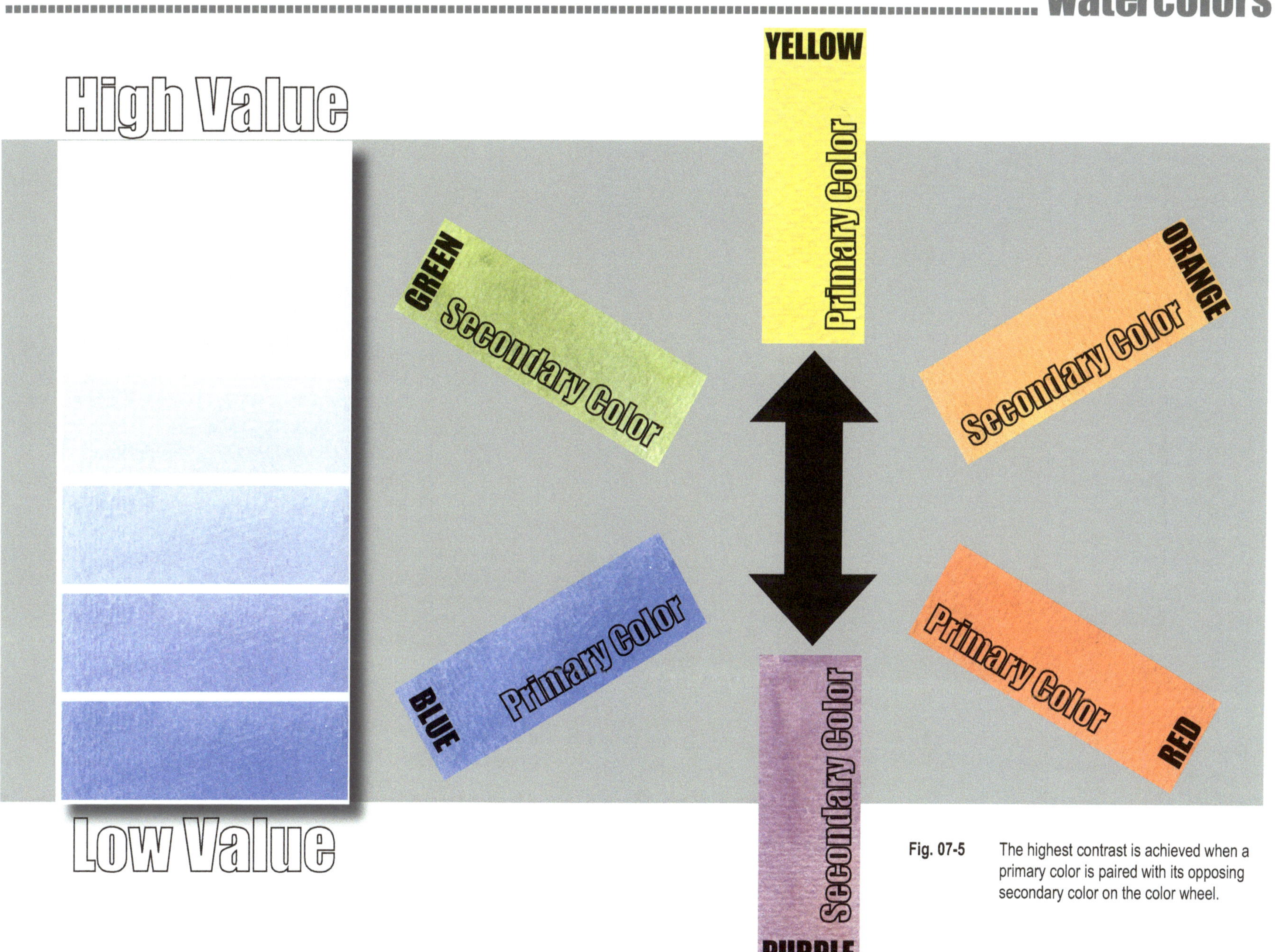

Fig. 07-5 The highest contrast is achieved when a primary color is paired with its opposing secondary color on the color wheel.

watercolors

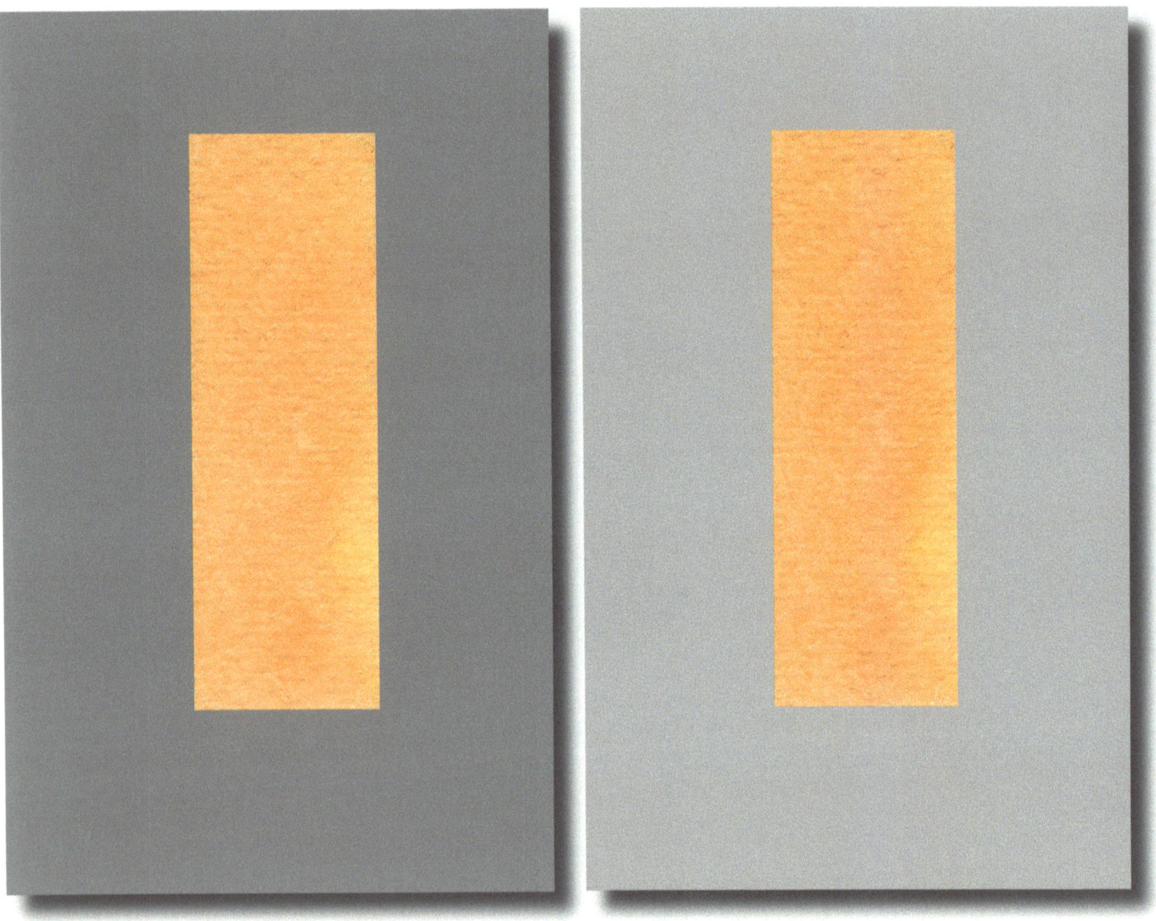

Fig. 07-6 The orange color appears brighter or darker depending upon the color adjacency.

A human's awareness of color is fundamentally relative. This means that the perception of color is dependent upon other factors, most notably color adjacency. For example, the color orange appears brighter if superimposed upon a lighter background versus a darker one. Other factors that affect the perception of color include the media itself, the paper, the angle of viewing, and even the cultural and physiological background of the viewer.

MIXING WATERCOLORS

Mixing watercolor paint is not as simple as mixing oil or acrylic paints. The process of mixing is dependent upon four distinct variables: the amount of water added to the watercolor paint; the type, color, and thickness of the paper; the size and quality of the brush; and the application or mixing technique.

Water - adding more water makes the paint lighter (high value) and increases its transparency. Learn to use watercolors, not water. Use water sparingly and avoid making puddles on the paper. Use a paper tissue if that happens.

Paper - study how watercolors react with the paper of your journal prior to its application. The colors will appear differently if the paper has some grayness or yellowness in it. On a heavily textured paper, watercolors **vein** (create small puddles) on the paper surface and produce a textured effect.

Brush - use a quality brush, test its ability to carry watercolors, and snap it after you dip it in water.

Technique - do not mix more than three hues. Over mixing will produce a disgusting gray or brown hue that will dull your sketch. This is why there is a vast amount of watercolor hues available for purchase at art supply stores. Learn to mix the watercolors on the paper as opposed to mixing on the plastic palette. The goal behind mixing watercolors is to gently entice the hues to work together!

Fig. 07-7 Watercolors are mixed toward the center of the slide. Note how certain colors are more prone to mixing and producing attractive hues than others. Veining is a function of how much water was used and the type of paper involved.

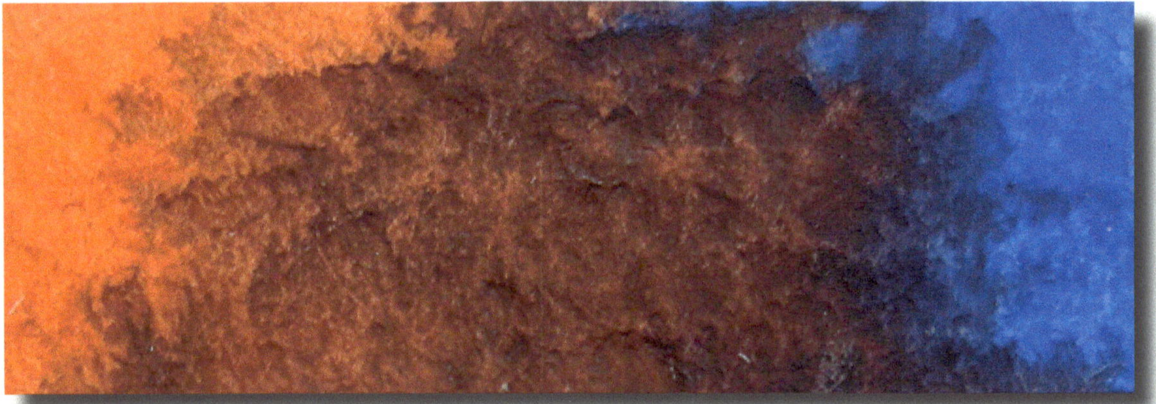

Fig. 07-8 The value of the top rectangle is manipulated by lifting the watercolor paint off the paper. The bottom rectangle is manipulated through adding a different hue while keeping the same value.

WATERCOLOR LIFT

Watercolor lift is another aspect of the techniques of watercolor application. Lift means the ability to change the graphic value of a hue from low to high or vice versa. This can be achieved by adding more water to the watercolor hue that is already on the page, or through the removal of the watercolor hue from the page by dabbing the area with a damp brush or a tissue. Lift is especially important when dealing with light, shade, and shadows.

Manipulating the hue (color) while maintaining the value is an important watercolor technique. It allows for a shift in interest without too much disturbance to the overall color scheme. Learn to use hue as a graphic value generator in itself, for example, cadmium yellow is a high value hue and cobalt blue is a low value hue.

WATERCOLOR WASHES

Watercolor, in its simplest form, is an aqueous solution of colored pigment. Watercolor washes generally fall into three distinct categories:

The Flat Wash - a thoroughly mixed paint solution that is applied consistently to avoid any hot spots. This is the easiest to apply and produce consistent results.

The Graduated Wash - a paint solution that is applied to the paper and then continued with clean and clear water until it achieves a gradual change in value. This wash is a bit tricky since it involves some lift to absorb the pigment, and a steady hand to avoid brush marks.

The Variegated Wash - a wash in which two different hues are gradually routed towards an acceptable mixed hue. This wash is arguably the hardest to achieve.

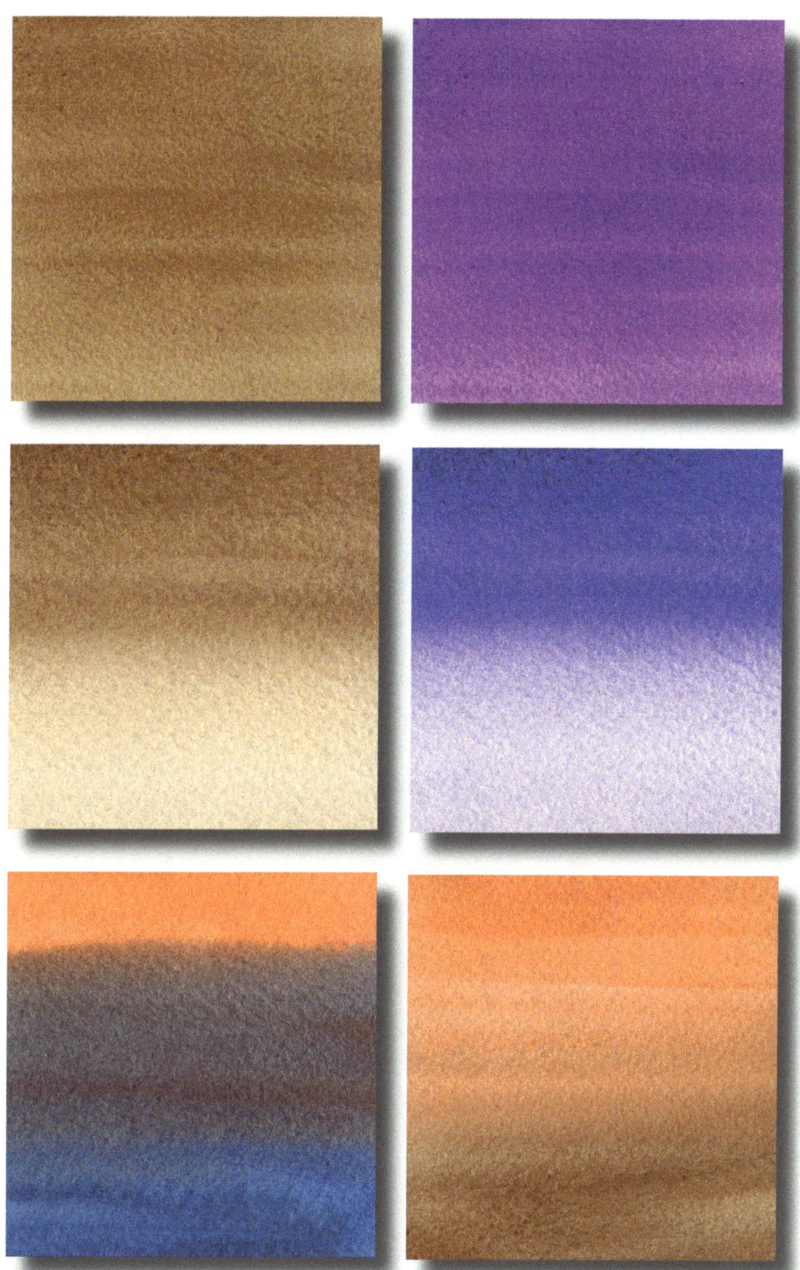

FOUNTAIN PEN INK WASH

Fountain pen ink is a relatively water soluble solution, even after it dries. Cold, clean water will activate the dry ink on the paper and cause it to run. Surprisingly, many different hues will become apparent due to the ink's solvency, usually purples, reds, and blues. Different colored inks from different manufacturers will produce different hues and wash characteristics. This feature can be used effectively on a sketch within a journal if drawn by using a fountain pen. It adds emphasis and graphic value within a journal entry. Learning to control the brush and the amount of water is crucial when utilizing this rather casual graphic technique.

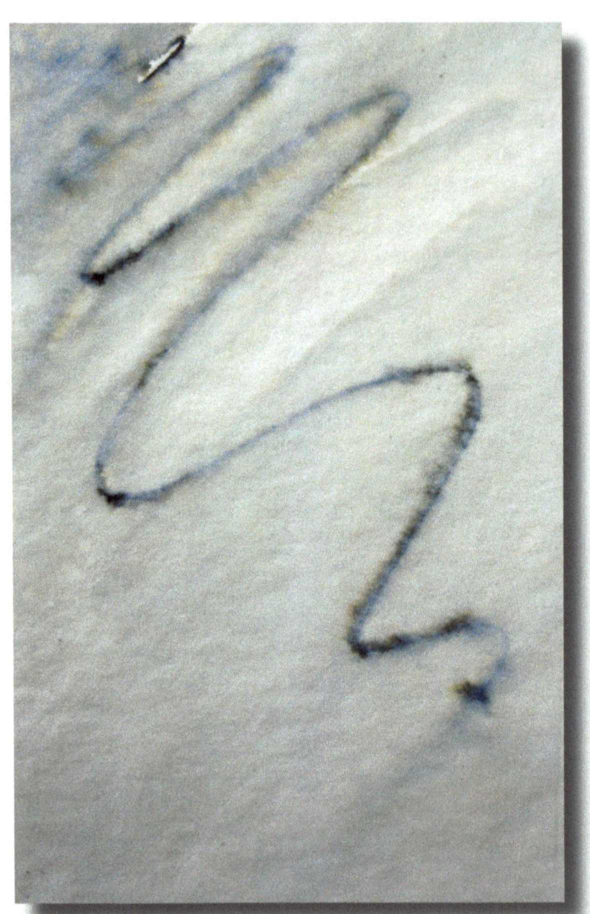

Fig. 07-9 The ink line was scribed first and then a cool water wash was applied to the paper. Note the different colors produced by the wash.

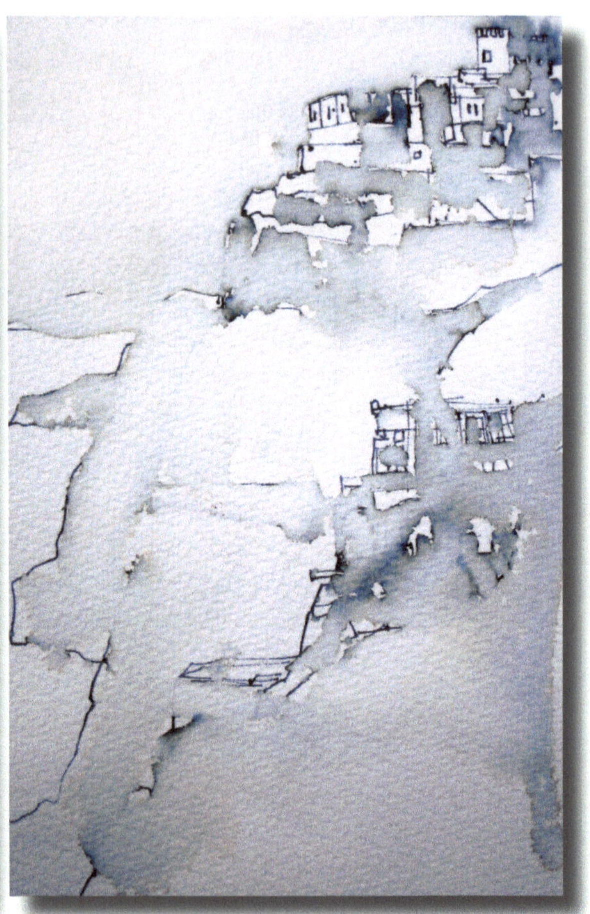

Fig. 7-10 Santorini, Greece, Moh'd Bilbeisi. Fountain pen ink and water on watercolor paper.

INDIA INK WASH

India ink is a permanent waterproof ink that was invented in China and later attributed to India by the British. It can be diluted from an ink stick on a grinding stone or a bottle with different amounts of clean cold water to produce different gray values which can be directly applied as graphic washes or as a brush strokes.

The quality of the ink and type will affect the end result. Certain India inks are formulated to work more effectively on synthetic surfaces such as vellum and Mylar and certain types and brands work best on paper with natural fibers. Read the label on the bottle of ink carefully before buying and using the product. Note that India ink is sedimentary. It behaves more like a suspension than a solution when mixed with clean water. Always stir before the application.

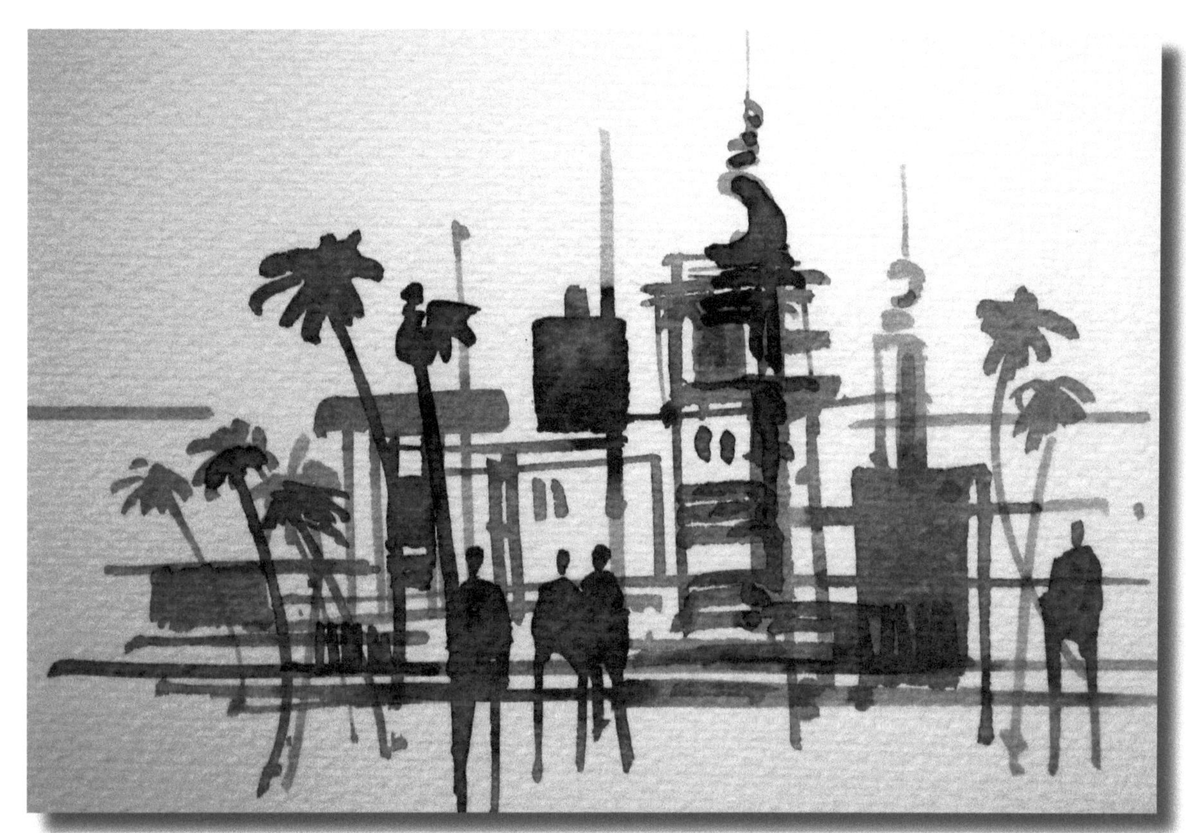

Fig. 07-11 Old Sharjah, Moh'd Bilbeisi. Ink wash on watercolor paper.

08 - LETTERING

communicate, communicate, communicate

THE PROCESS OF GRAPHIC JOURNALING INVOLVES BOTH THE IMAGE AND THE WRITTEN WORD... THE TEXT. THE PROCESS OF UNDERSTANDING THE JOURNAL ENTRY ... GETTING IT, INVOLVES A HIGH LEVEL OF ABILITY TO JUMP AND PROCESS THE INFORMATION BACK AND FORTH BETWEEN THE TEXT AND THE IMAGE. THIS ENSURES A GOOD UNDERSTANDING OF THE SUBJECT AND THE TRANSFORMATION OF THE TWO TYPES OF INFORMATION INTO A SINGLE WHOLE ... COMPLETE.

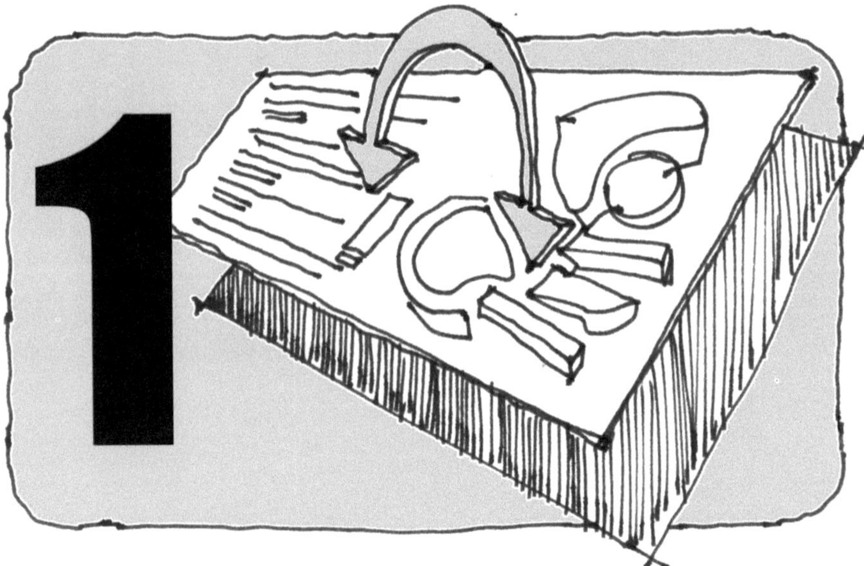

Graphic journal entries are never complete without notation to supplement the sketch or the diagram. Successful journal entries are usually titled properly and annotated with adequate supporting text. Designers, artists, architects, and graphic journalists prefer the look and feel of a hand-lettered text over the type generated by computers; however, we can learn many things from digitally created fonts that will enhance the overall appearance of the text. Good lettering will contribute immensely to the overall success of the journal entry.

The location of the journal entry's title or the supporting text is a matter of page composition and communication strategy. Locating the title towards the top left corner of the page is an invitation to read the title first before proceeding to the rest of the graphic or textual information on the page. On the other hand, locating the title towards the bottom right corner is an invitation to view the graphic or textual information on the page first and the title last. Note that this issue is cultural and based on the the behavior of individuals who read and write from the left to the right.

The location and quality (penmanship and style) of the supporting text that accompanies the drawings in graphic journaling are also questions of composition since they serve two functions; to communicate hierarchy on the page and to further explain the graphic content of the journal entry. Consistency is very important when it comes to lettering since it presents a uniform level of support that leads to better readability and character legibility.

There are several attributes that must be considered with regard to lettering:

SIZE

The first is the font size, this issue controls hierarchy within the composition. Large upper case fonts are read first. Technically speaking, 72pt font is 1" in height, 18pt is 1/4" in height. Use the appropriate size according to the importance of the text.

FONT

The second quality is the font itself. Serifs are easily read. Highly stylized fonts are very personal and if the readability of the text is not important then they are totally acceptable to use. To teach yourself new fonts, simply type out an alphabet on a computer and trace the letters until you feel comfortable with them.

FORMALITY

The third quality is the formality of the text. Some subject matters require a more rigid use of text, while others can be quite casual. Script fonts are rather romantic in nature and provide a much needed softness and serendipity, depending on the looseness or rigidity of the other text items. Rigid sketching and diagraming will need a script font to soften the composition. Loose sketching and diagraming will need a formal font to add formality to the journal entry. Use the appropriate level of formality for the subject at hand.

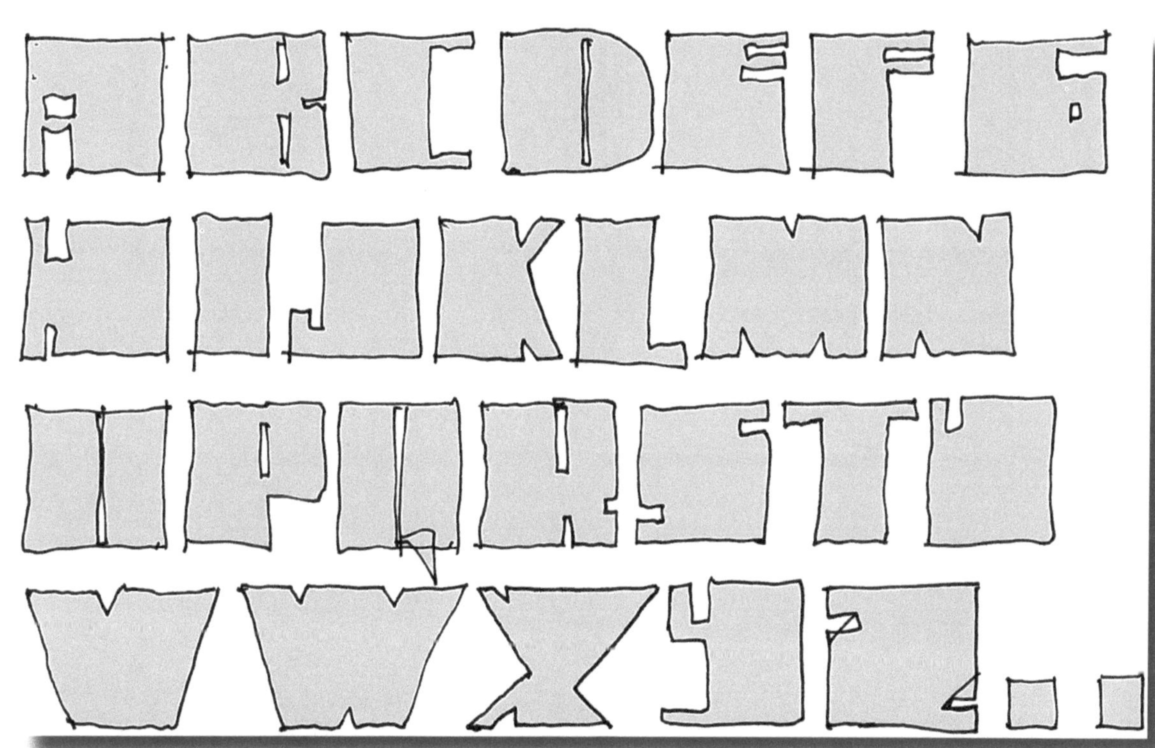

Fig. 08-1 Large and/or stylized fonts can be ideal for journal entry titles, Moh'd Bilbeisi. Ink on paper.

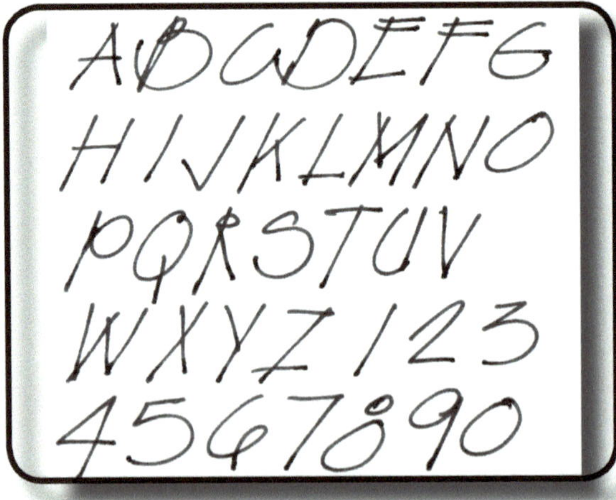

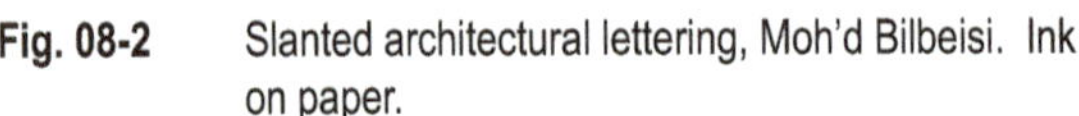

Fig. 08-2 Slanted architectural lettering, Moh'd Bilbeisi. Ink on paper.

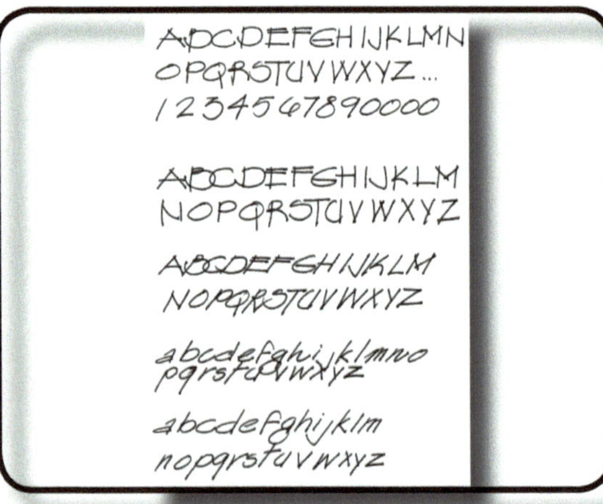

Fig. 08-3 Different styles of architectural lettering in upper and lower cases, Moh'd Bilbeisi. Ink on paper.

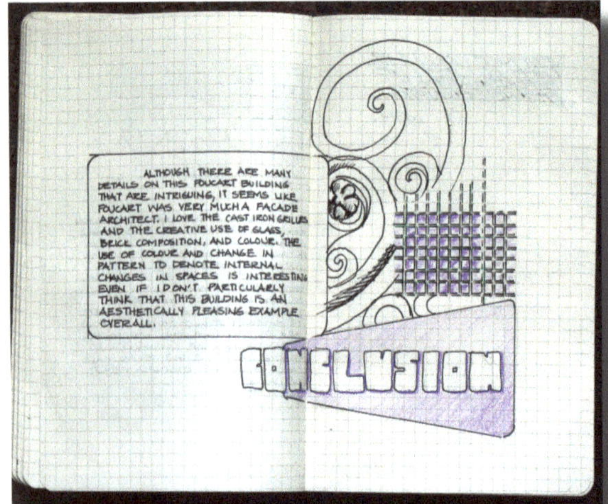

Fig. 08-4 Pronounced lettering presence, Lauren Cadieux. Ink and colored pencils on paper.

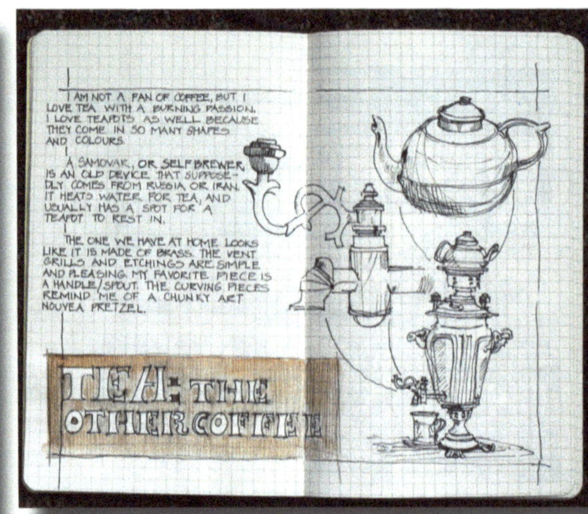

Fig. 08-5 Stylized font and layout prominence, Lauren Cadieux. Ink and colored pencils on paper.

LOCATION

The fourth issue is the location of the text itself: surrounding the image, below the image, atop the image, or to the side of the image. This is truly a compositional issue.

There are no rules concerning the addition of the text to the image in the journal. Here are a few pointers that should aid in the process of adding text to the journal entry.

PENMANSHIP

Good penmanship is critical. This requires practice and patience. And lots of hard work! Your hand written text should be legible and readable, yet casual and loose so as to be completed in a timely fashion.

CONSISTENCY

Consistency is important. Teach yourself to write and draw with the same amount of quality and care associated with the act itself. For example, all your letters should be upper case. All vertical strokes must be thin and all the horizontal strokes thick. If your hand is hurting or you have a headache, do not draw or write. Go home and take a nap. If you are tired or hungry, do not even dare to open your journal, it would be a hopeless case. Just do not do it. Make your work important to you, but also something you would be proud to show others.

GUIDELINES

Use guidelines - there is no way of getting around this for a beginner. Even experienced graphic journalists can slip - every once in awhile, my lettering starts to dip towards the bottom of the page for no obvious reason. I have to go back to the basics and use guidelines until I get it straightened out. Gridlines can be lightly drawn onto the journal pages, or a digitally created "cheat sheet" of guidelines can be slipped behind a journal page to aid in keeping the lettering aligned. An easier way is to use a journal with ruled paper.

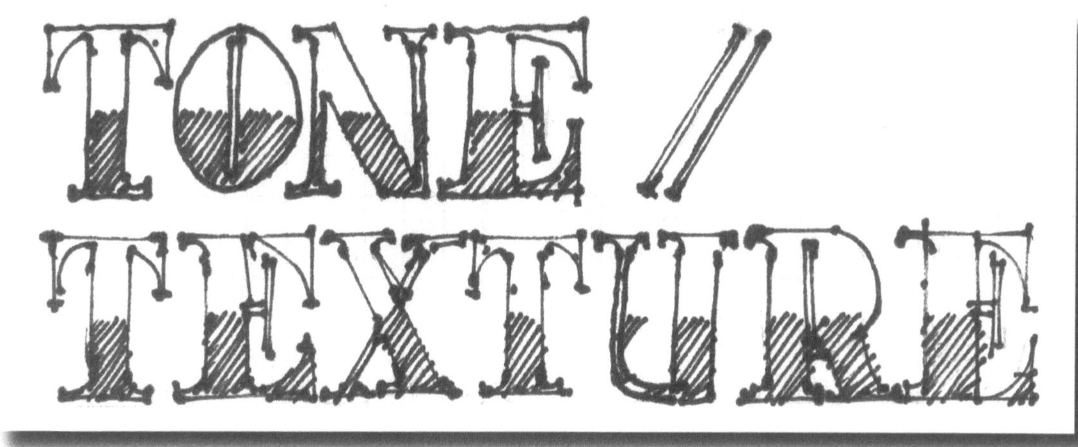

Fig. 08-6 The use of a juicy pen produced intense font corners that add to the looseness of the journal entry. The bottom half of the letters is diagonally hatched to add weight to the words, Moh'd Bilbeisi. Ink on paper.

TITLES

Do make titles for your journal entries. This aids in the overall effort to organize the material, and will help you find the entry at a later date! Also title and date your sketches, this is often overlooked but is an important aspect of the communication process. Do not be afraid to underline certain sentences or paragraphs to communicate emphasis.

PRACTICE

Practice, Practice, Practice. There is no other way to master the art of lettering. Experiment and have fun; eventually you will develop your own style of lettering which will become as unique as your fingerprint upon your journal.

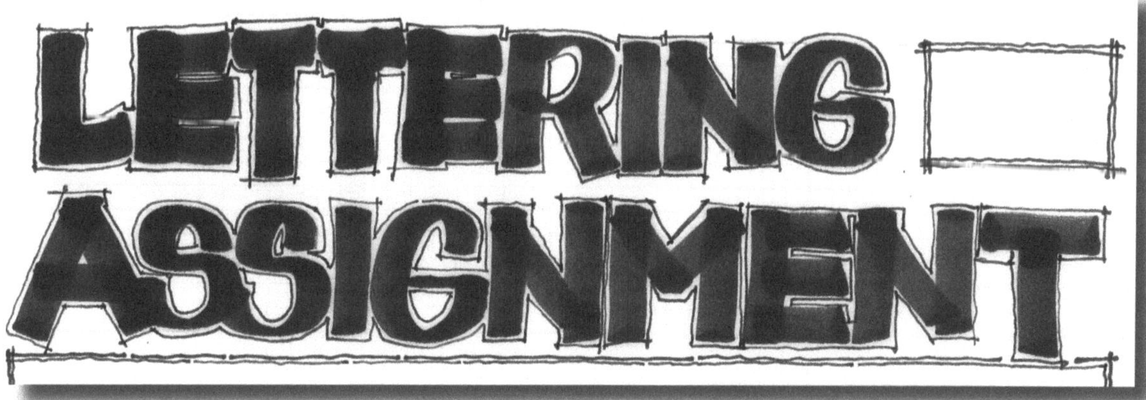

Fig. 08-7 Outlining the letters separates the text from the page adding a 3-D effect to the composition, Moh'd Bilbeisi. Ink and marker on paper.

lettering

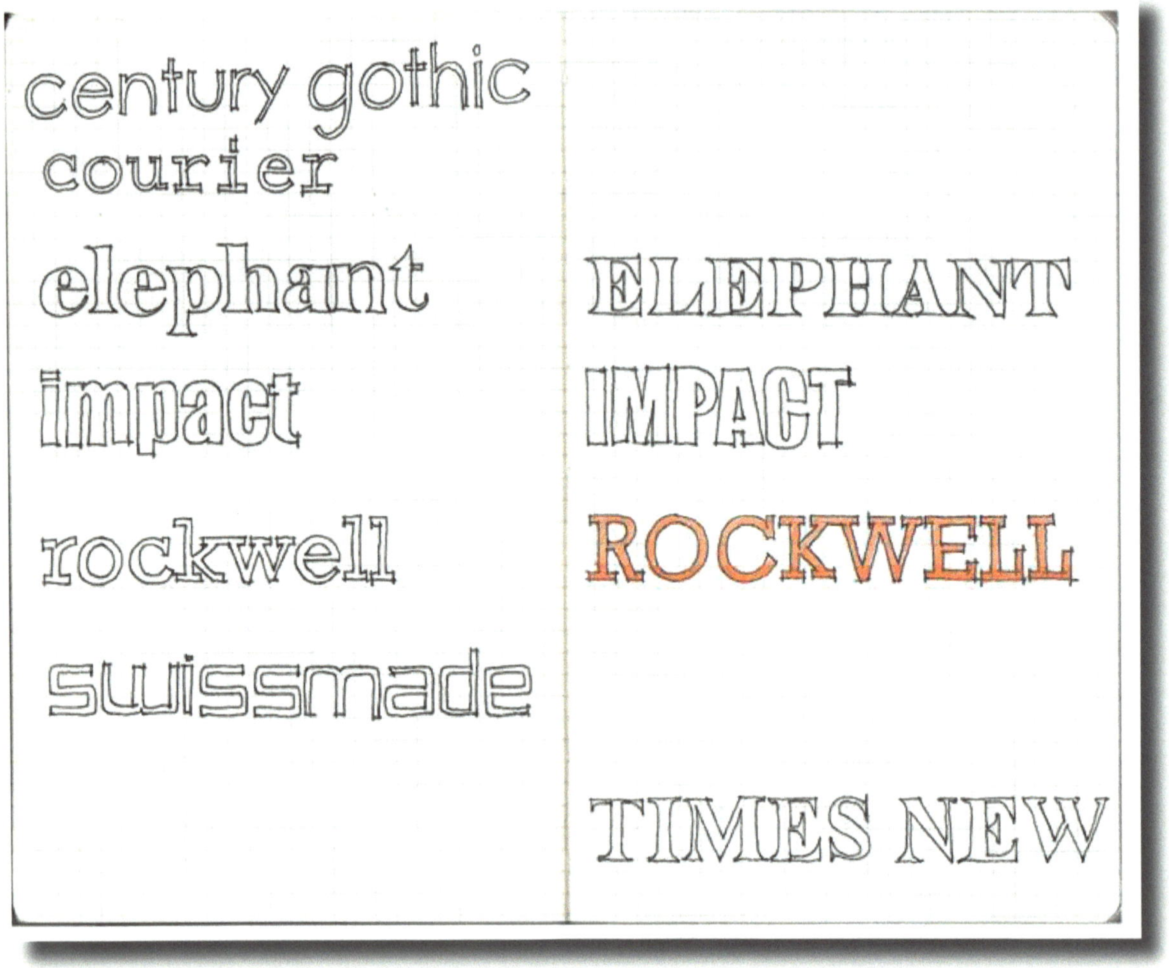

Fig. 08-8 The font - shape and size - affect the visual perception of the image, influence the composition, and ultimately affect the graphic communication. Adding a lower value toward the bottom anchors the text and adds weight to the letters, Josh Moratto. Ink and colored pencil on paper.

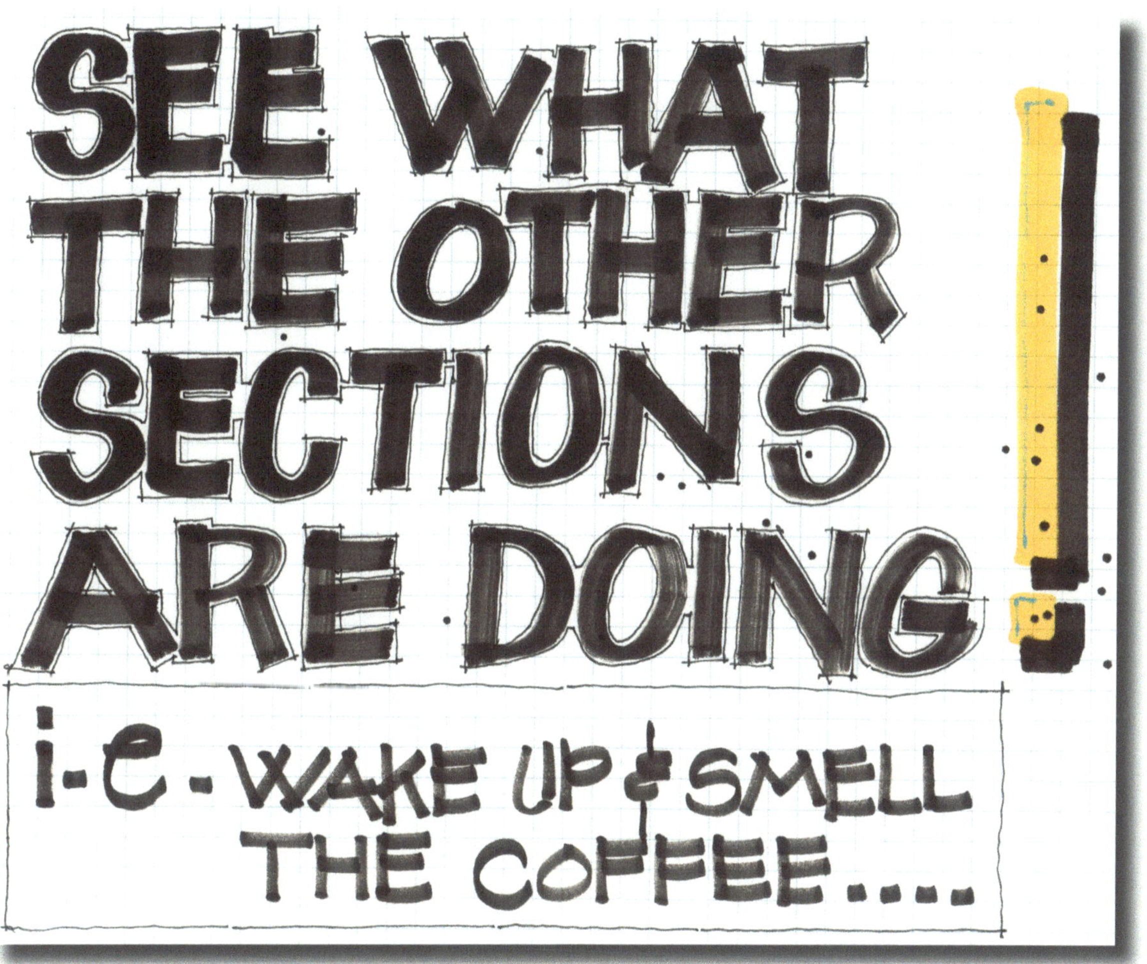

Fig. 08-9 The addition of an accent color accentuates the text. Random stipple (disease) animates the composition and adds to the looseness or informality of the composition. The horizontal and vertical strokes are clearly executed with thin and thick lines. The use of a grid is very helpful in making good lettering, Moh'd Bilbeisi. Ink and marker on paper.

09 - JOURNALING PARADIGMS

case studies

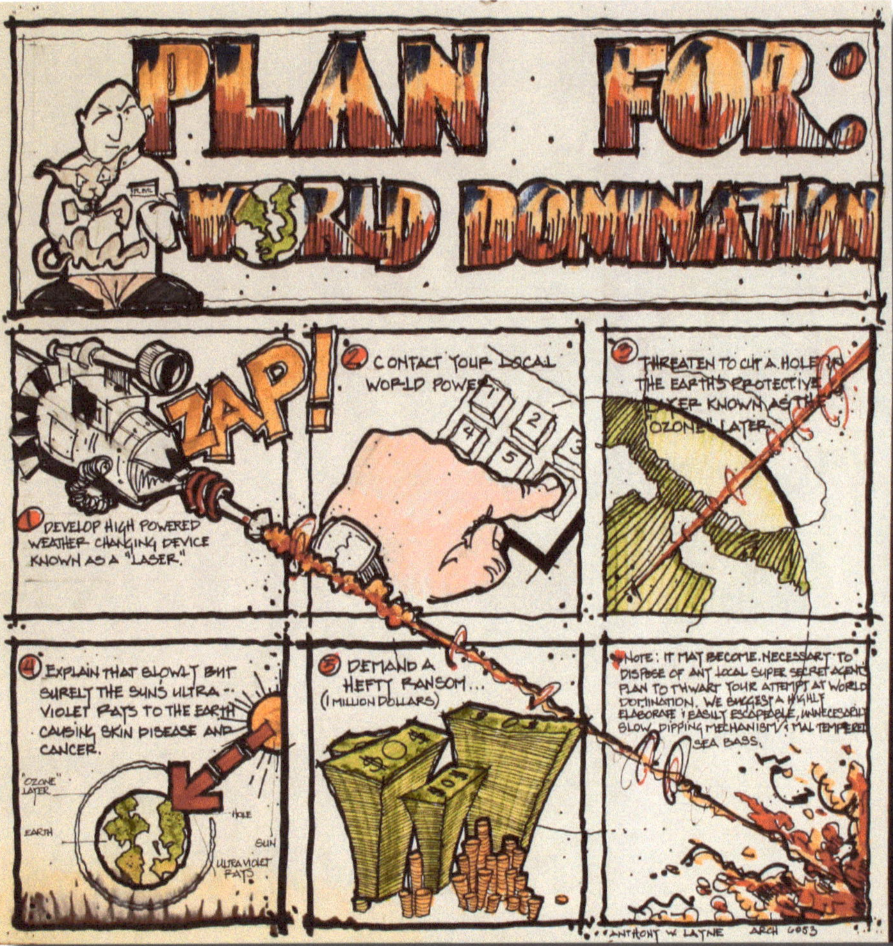

Fig. 09-1 Plan for world domination (sequential art), Tony Layne. Ink and marker on paper.

Graphic journaling is a very personal creative act. There are different ways a graphic journal may be used - to document, to imagine, to think, and to analyze. As the journal is really a tool of self-development, it also assists one to become. In this collection, the following examples of graphic journaling are organized into two general categories:

Experiential Graphic Journals:

These include, but are not limited to, journal entries that involve travel experiences, travel sketches, class notes, and field notes.

Imaginative Graphic Journals:

These include, but are not limited to, design sketches, design details, graphic thinking, and flights of fantasy.

The selection process of these individual example entries emphasized variety and breadth, spanning the available gamut in terms of content and technique. Since these are the products of architects and architecture students, there is naturally a focus on all things architectural and design related.

The following paradigms demonstrate a commitment to the act of graphic journaling. Some of the journal entries were created by novices and some were executed by seasoned individuals who have spent years honing their skills. A wide range of technique and skill is included in this collection, but all have one thing in common - the love of graphic journaling.

These graphic journaling paradigms were executed as reactions towards places, spaces, events, and thoughts. Some of the entries were done hastily and some were done with ample time to react, to record, to reflect, and to correct. Any spelling or factual errors are not intentional. The personal opinions, graphic or textual, are the sole property of the author of the specific journal entry.

The intention here is to present the following journaling paradigms in their purest form, unabridged and unedited.

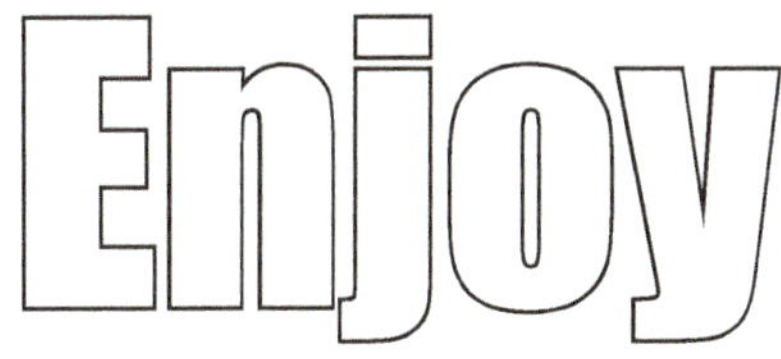

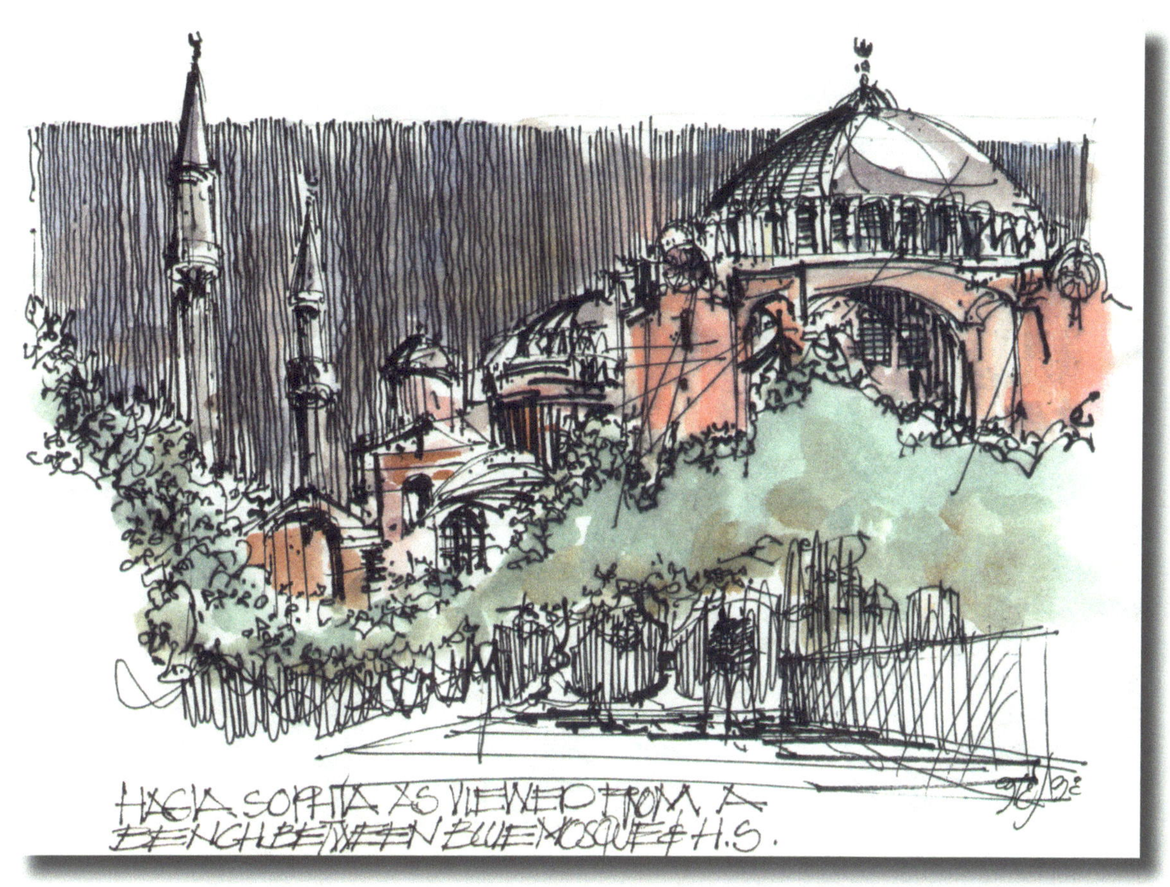

Fig. 09-2 One page journal entry, Moh'd Bilbeisi. Ink and watercolors on paper. Istanbul, Turkey.

credits

Experiential Graphic Journals [EGJ]

Bilbeisi, Moh'd	EGJ-1
Goh, Kah Leong	EGJ-2
Holstedt, Sarah	EGJ-3
Johnson, David	EGJ-4
Jump, Meredith	EGJ-5
Lanman, Adam	EGJ-6
McCool, James	EGJ-7
Moratto, Josh	EGJ-8
Moss, Marvin	EGJ-9
McQuillen, Lauren	EGJ-10
Parker, Geoff	EGJ-11
Ra, Sueng	EGJ-12
Richardson, Nathan	EGJ-13
Salmons, Jacque	EGJ-14
Smardo, Scott	EGJ-15
Splinter, Janelle	EGJ-16
Thomas, Flynn	EGJ-17
Vogt, Eric	EGJ-18
West, Shannon	EGJ-19
Williams, Ryan	EGJ-20
Womack, John	EGJ-21
Zerbey, Kyle	EGJ-22

Imaginative Graphic Journals [IGJ]

Badran, Rasem	IGJ-1
Bilbeisi, Inad	IGJ-2
Bilbeisi, Moh'd	IGJ-3
Condia, Bob	IGJ-4
Lanman, Adam	IGJ-5
Laseau, Paul	IGJ-6
Majkowski, Alex	IGJ-7
Pride, Mitch	IGJ-8
West, Shannon	IGJ-9

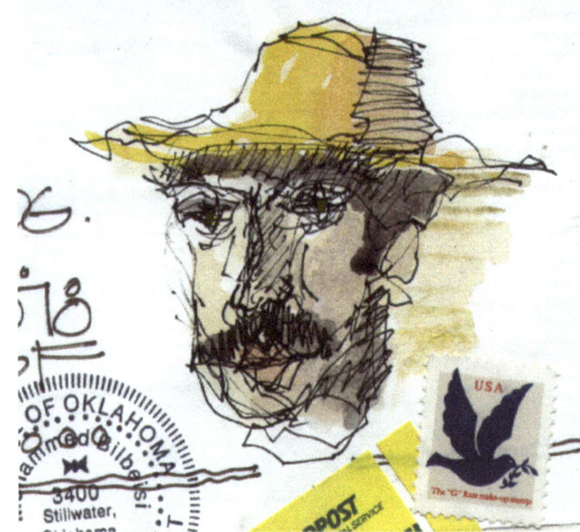

Badran, Rasem is an author, a lecturer, an artist, and a practicing architect in Amman, Jordan.

Bilbeisi, Inad is a practicing architect in Providence, Rhode Island.

Bilbeisi, Moh'd is an author, an artist, a professor, and a practicing architect in Stillwater, Oklahoma.

Cadieux, Lauren is a fourth-year student at Oklahoma State University School of Architecture in Stillwater, Oklahoma.

Condia, Bob is an author, an artist, a professor, and a practicing architect in Manhattan, Kansas.

Goh, Kah Leong is a practicing architect. He is based in St. Louis, Missouri.

Holstedt, Sarah is practicing architecture in Seattle, Washington.

Johnson, David is a practicing architect in Beijing, China.

Jump, Meredith is a practicing architect in Chicago, Illinois.

Lanman, Adam is an artist, a professor, and a practicing architect in Oklahoma City, Oklahoma.

Layne, Anthony is a practicing architect in Minneapolis, Minnesota.

Laseau, Paul is an author, a professor, an artist, and a practicing architect in Muncie, Indiana.

McCool, James is an artist and a practicing architect in Anchorage, Alaska.

Moratto, Josh is practicing architecture in Los Angeles, California.

Moss, Marvin is practicing architecture in Austin, Texas.

Majkowski, Alex is practicing architecture in New York, New York.

McQuillen, Lauren is a practicing architect in Seattle, Washington.

Parker, Geoff is a practicing architect in Oklahoma City, Oklahoma.

Pride, Mitch is practicing architecture in Ithaca, New York.

Ra, Sueng is a professor and a practicing architect in New York, New York.

Richardson, Nathan is a practicing architect in Boston, Massachusetts.

Salmons, Jacque is practicing architecture in Seattle, Washington.

Smardo, Scott is practicing architecture in San Francisco, California.

Splinter, Janelle is practicing architecture in Dallas, Texas.

Thomas, Flynn is an artist and a practicing architect in New York, New York.

Vogt, Eric is an artist and a practicing architect in Tulsa, Oklahoma.

West, Shannon is an artist, a musician, and a practicing architect in Tulsa, Oklahoma.

Williams, Ryan is a practicing architect in Dallas, Texas.

Womack, John is a professor, an artist, and a practicing architect in Stillwater, Oklahoma.

Zeiler, Dane is a fourth-year student at Oklahoma State University School of Architecture in Stillwater, Oklahoma.

Zerbey, Kyle is a practicing architect in Seattle, Washington.

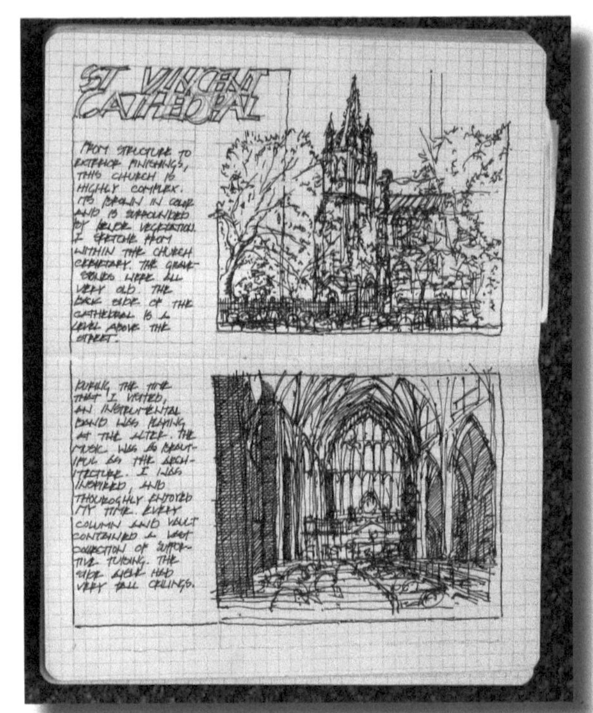

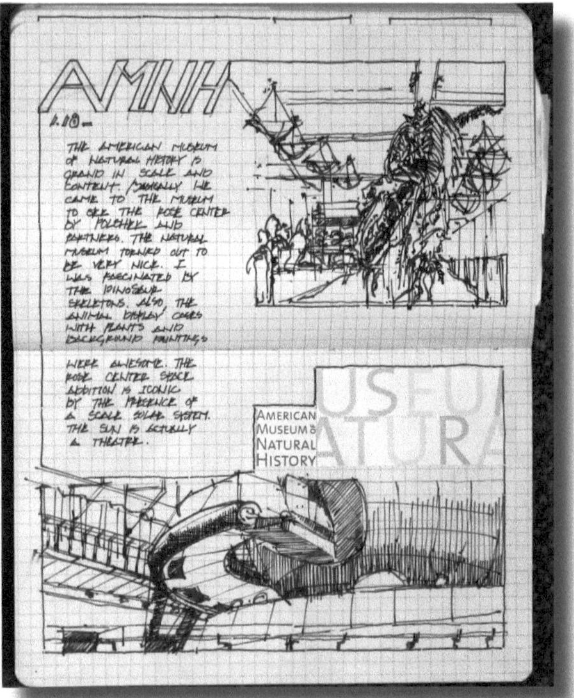

Fig. 09-3 Travel journal entries, Dane Zeiler. Ink on paper.

EGJ-1.1

MOH'D BILBEISI

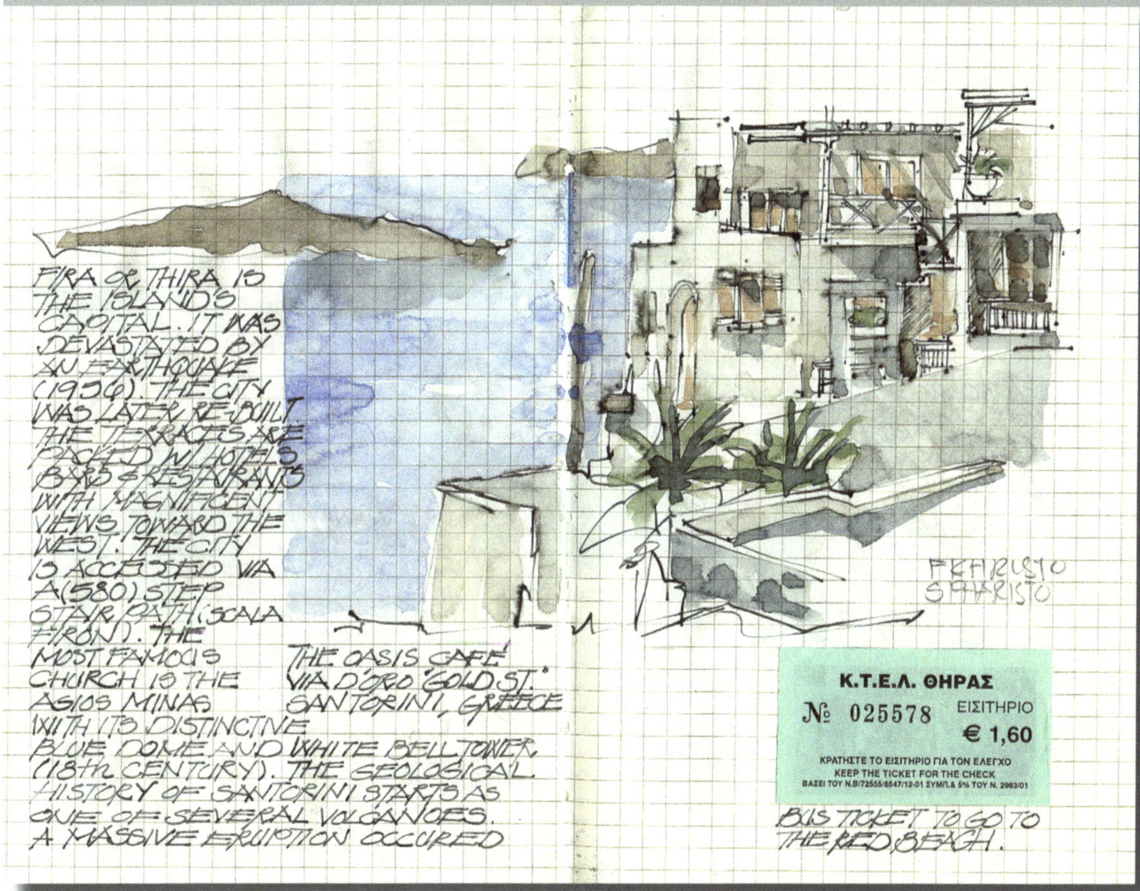

A two-page composition where the sketch and the supporting text are in a diagonal relationship. The text frames the composition on the left side, while the sketch holds the corner on the right. The sketch is highlighted with watercolors. A bus ticket anchors the journal entry and stops the circular flow of the composition. All the elements within the composition are placed to form a single rectangle on the pages.

Fig. 09-4 Two-page journal entry, Moh'd Bilbeisi. Ink and watercolors on paper. Santorini, Greece.

EGJ-1.2

MOH'D BILBEISI

The map of the islands is floating atop the blue watercolor wash representing the sea in the perspective sketch. The perspective sketch forms a bookend for the composition. The top line holds the vertical edge of the composition and the supporting text creates the same effect at the bottom. The watercolor wash is kept away from the ink lines to avoid producing an ink wash. All the elements within the composition are placed to form a single rectangle on the pages.

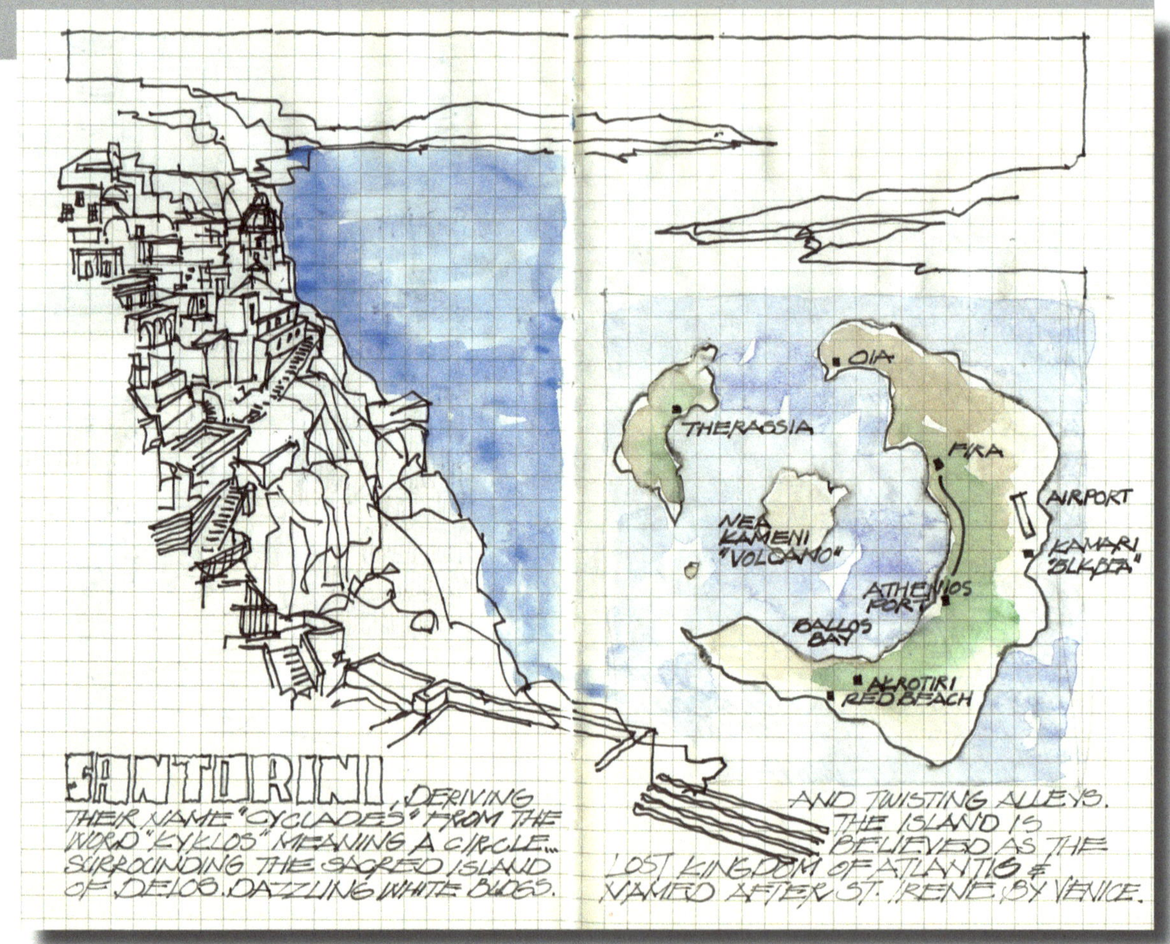

Fig. 09-5 Two-page journal entry, Moh'd Bilbeisi. Ink and watercolors on paper. Santorini, Greece.

EGJ-1.3

MOH'D BILBEISI

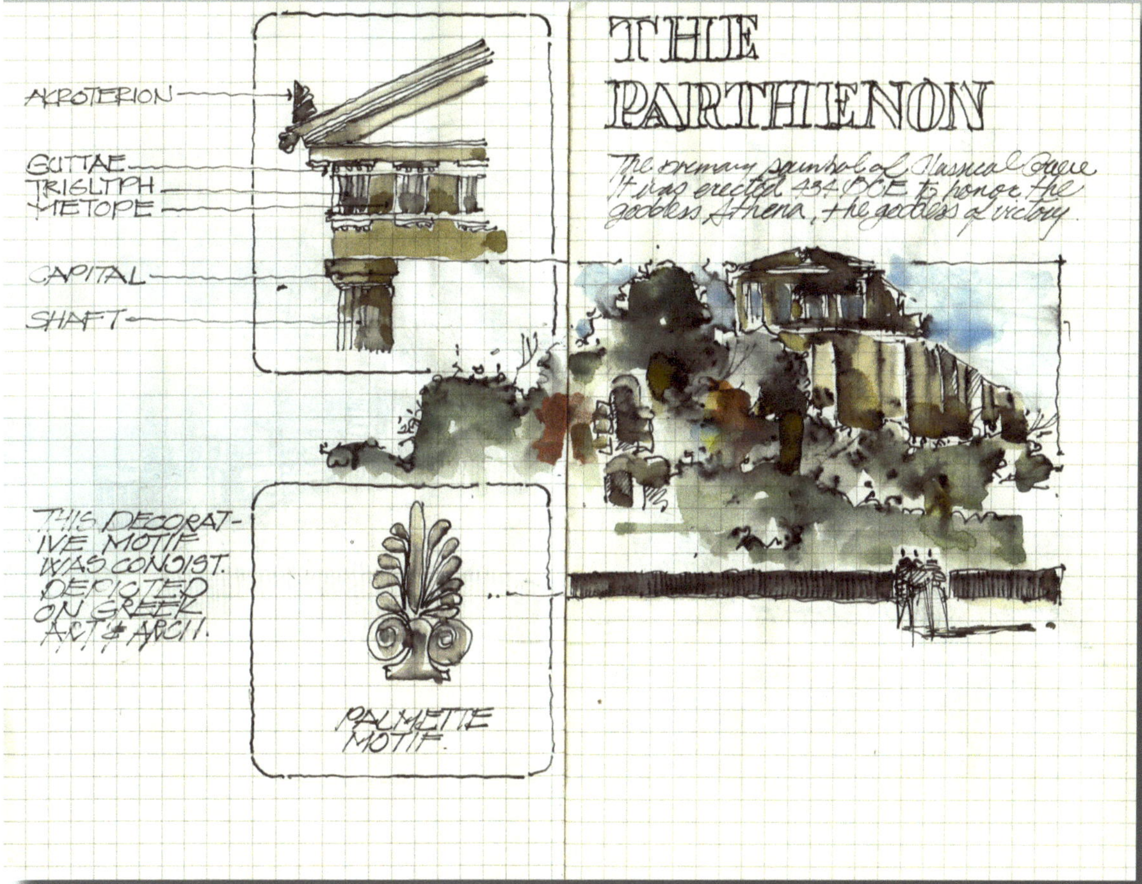

The layout consists of three rectangles of various sizes that form a triangular relationship across the two pages. The main sketch to the right is dominant due to its size and low graphic value. The two cameo sketches at the left are a bit more technical and treated as support sketches to establish hierarchy. Watercolors are applied loosely to produce an additional fountain pen ink wash. The font for the entry title is intentionally chosen to emphasize the classical nature of the subject matter.

Fig. 09-6 Two-page journal entry, Moh'd Bilbeisi. Ink and watercolors on paper. Athens, Greece.

EGJ-1.4

MOH'D BILBEISI

This composition is treated as two separate pages with an implied topical connection. The sketches are occupying the bulk of the space and the text is framing the left side of the layout. Lower graphic value is achieved through vertical hatching and the sketches are highlighted with color. The vignettes are strategically aligned with the supporting text.

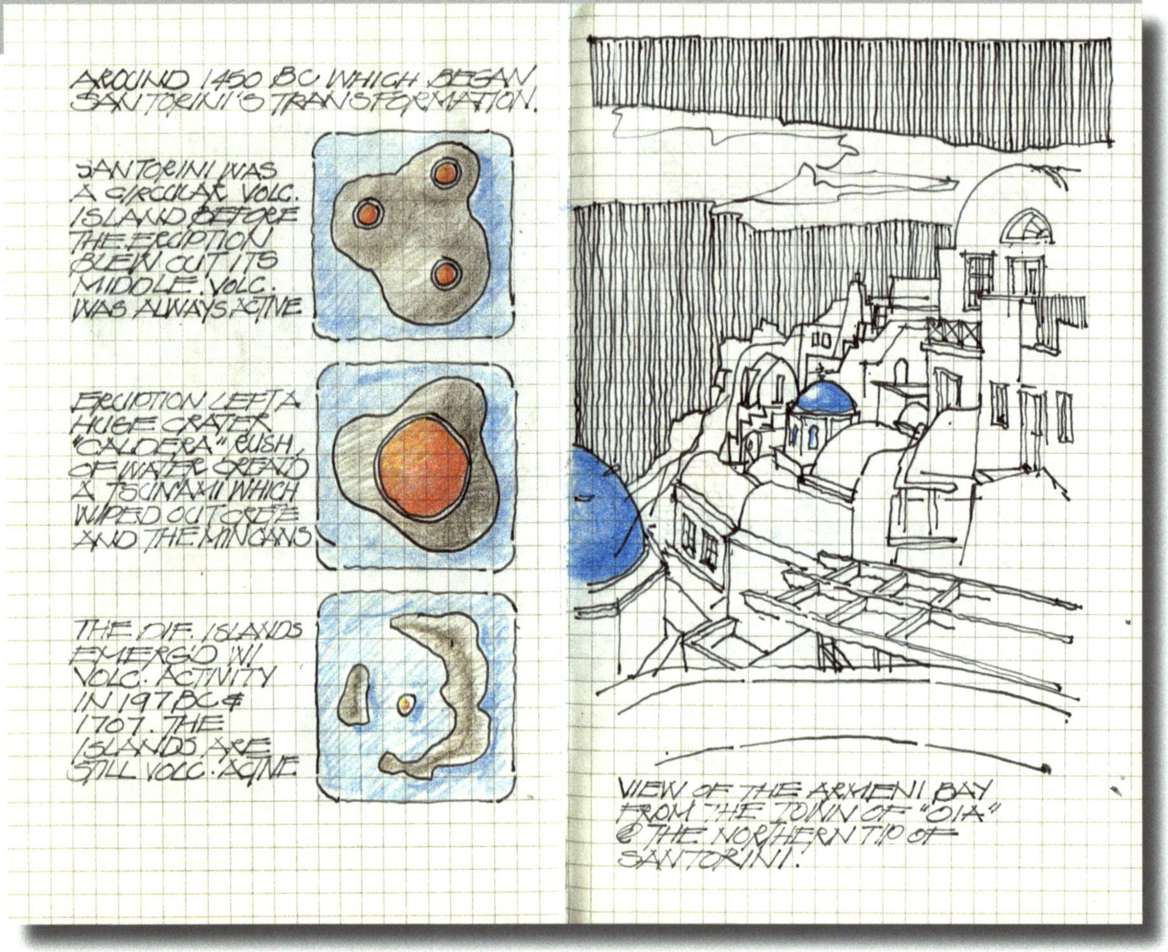

Fig. 09-7 Two-page journal entry, Moh'd Bilbeisi. Ink, and colored pencils on paper. Santorini, Greece.

EGJ-1.5

MOH'D BILBEISI

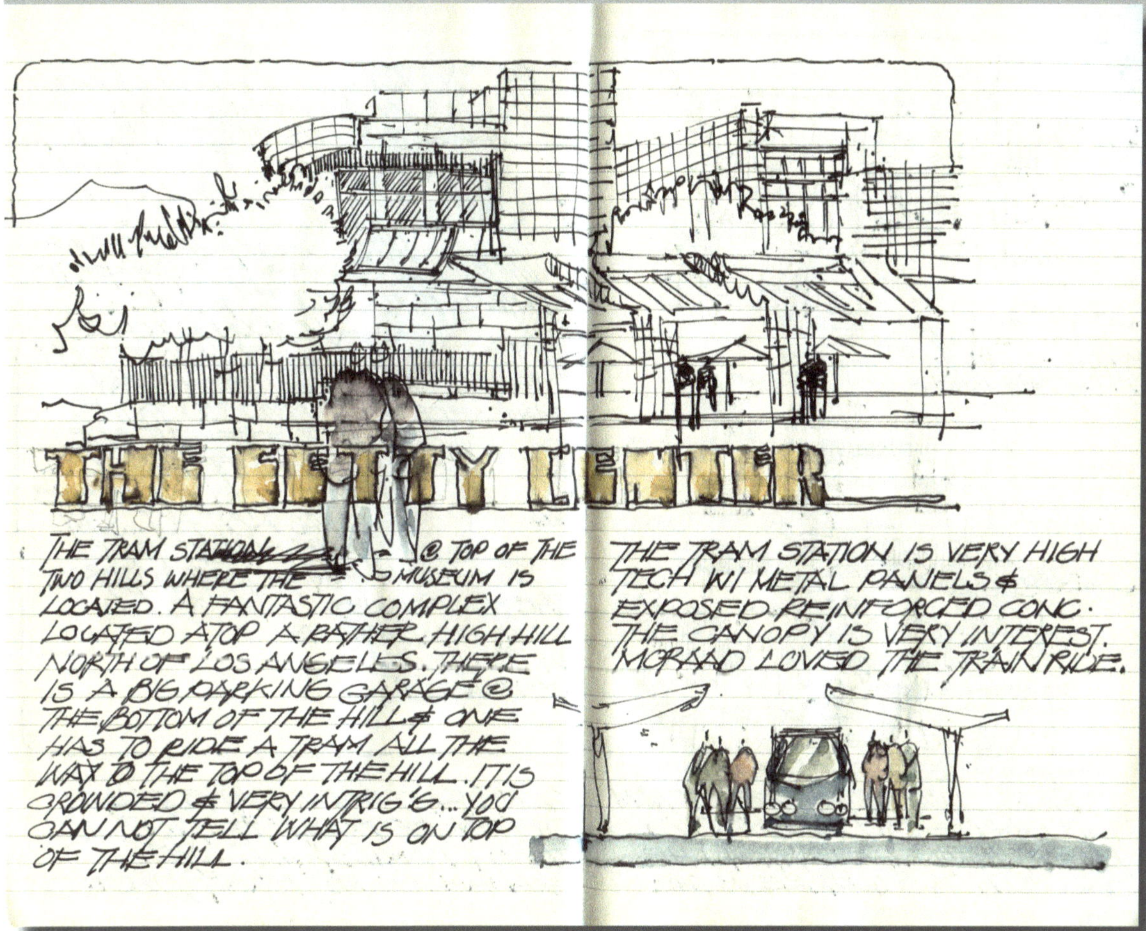

The journal entry is divided horizontally into equal halves that are separated by an implied graphic line, the entry title. The supporting text at the bottom has the lowest graphic value and acts as an anchor for the sketch at the bottom. A small detail sketch is added to the layout to further explain and communicate the subject matter. Watercolors are applied selectively to highlight the entry title and the small sketch.

Fig. 09-8 Two-page journal entry, Moh'd Bilbeisi. Ink and watercolors on paper. Los Angeles, California.

EGJ-1.6

MOH'D BILBEISI

The composition is divided diagonally into two equal triangles; the left upper triangle containing the sketches and the right lower triangle containing the supporting text. The entire entry is terminated towards the top with a compositional line. Graphic value is achieved through hatching.

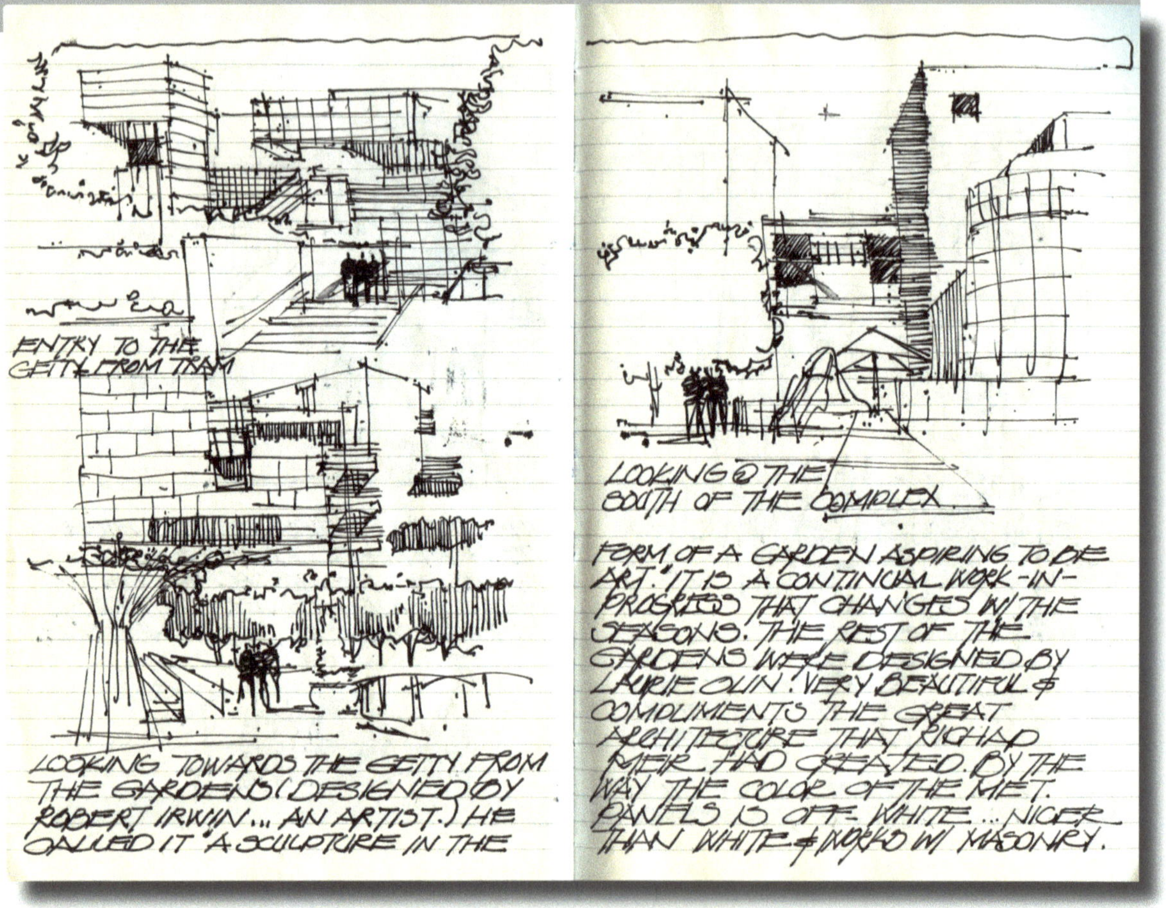

Fig. 09-9 Two-page journal entry, Moh'd Bilbeisi. Ink on paper. Los Angeles, California.

EGJ-1.7

MOH'D BILBEISI

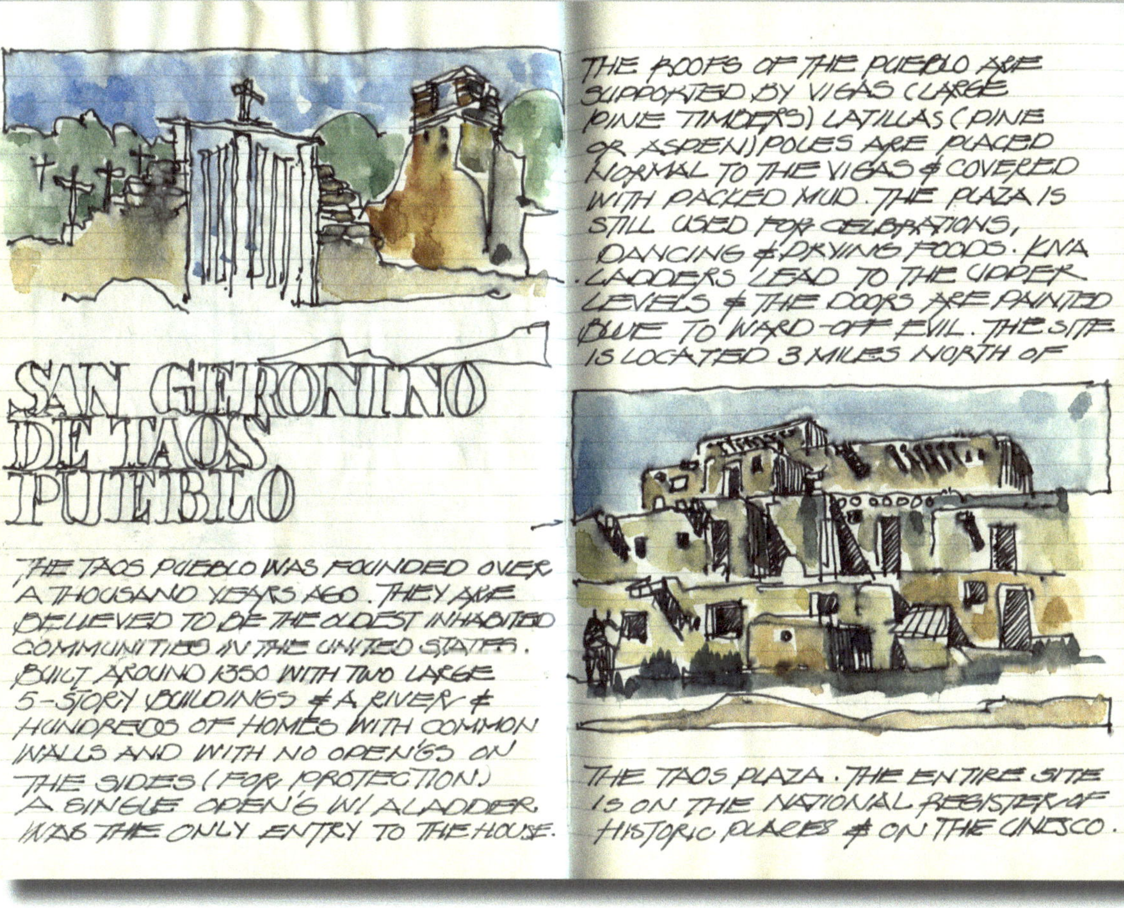

Fig. 09-10 Two-page journal entry, Moh'd Bilbeisi. Ink and watercolors on paper. Taos, New Mexico.

The journal entry is divided into four rectangles with alternating positions, sketch/text, text/sketch. The entry title is situated almost dead-center on the first page to anchor to the entire layout. Watercolors were added to highlight the sketches, and with control produce interesting fountain pen ink washes.

EGJ-1.8

MOH'D BILBEISI

The layout is divided equally between the sketch and the supporting text on two adjacent pages, A vignette is situated within the text and its distractive effect is nullified by making it a line drawing devoid of color. An entry title is added to align the text page with the sketch page. The bottom of the right hand page is compositionally unresolved.

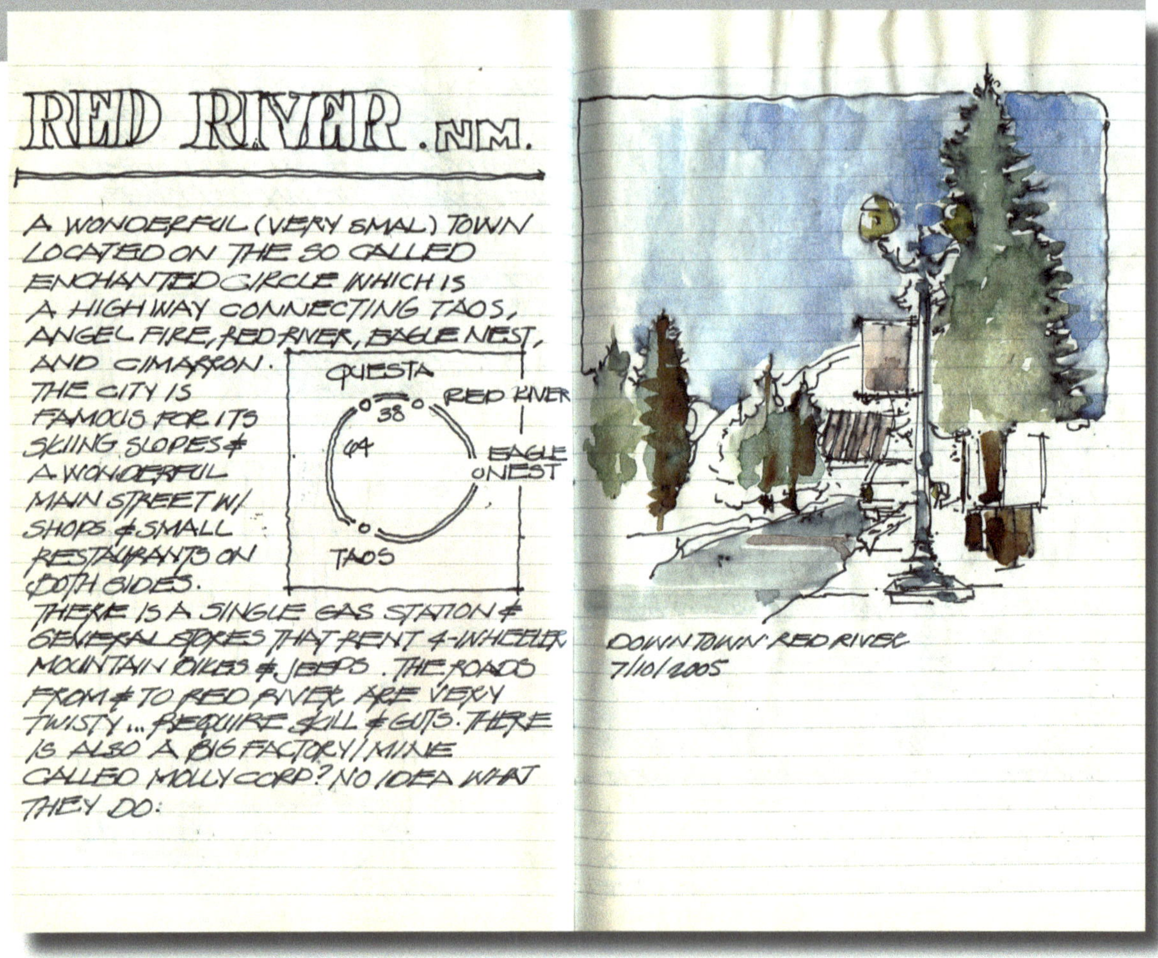

Fig. 09-11 Two-page journal entry, Moh'd Bilbeisi. Ink and watercolors on paper. Red River, New Mexico.

EGJ-1.9

MOH'D BILBEISI

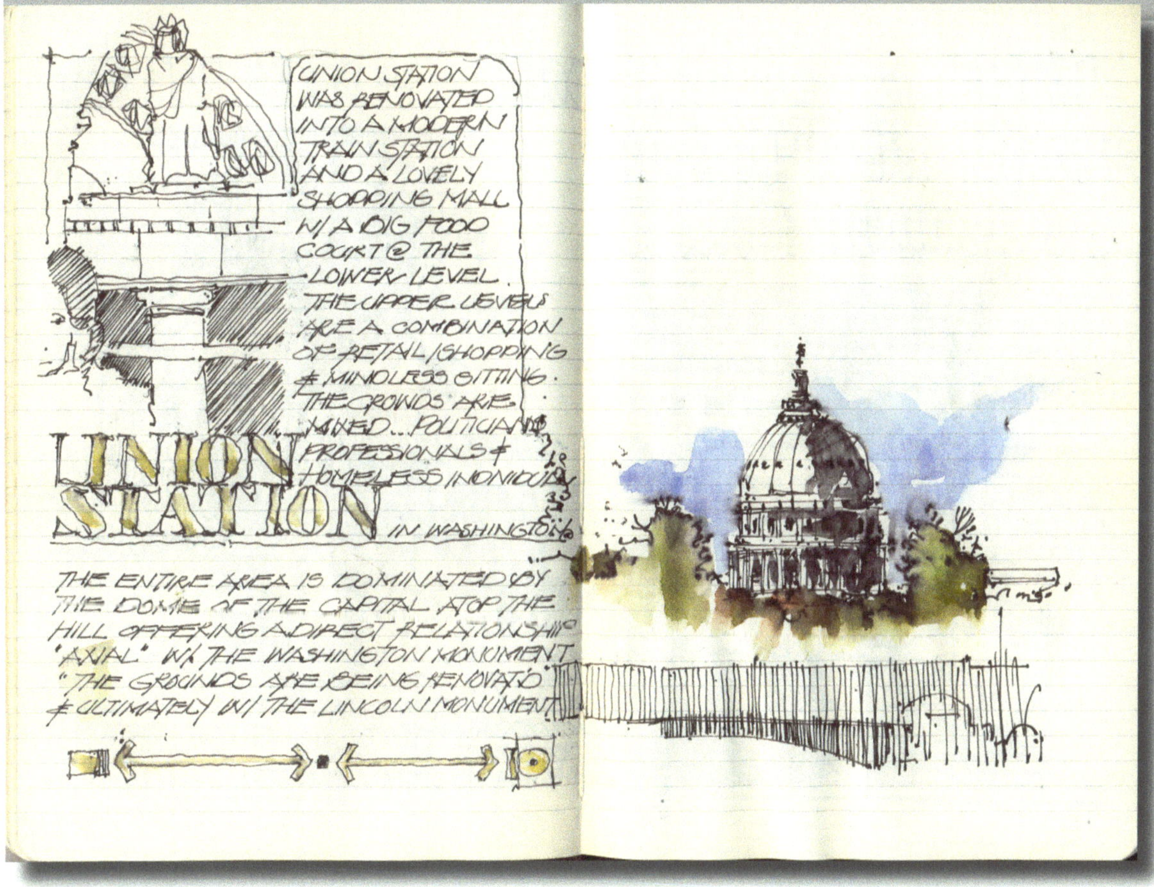

An imbalanced two-page journal entry; the important sketch is emphasized by its surrounding white space, allowing it to occupy the full right hand page. The sketch on the left page is not as important, so it is almost totally consumed by the supporting text. Watercolors were added to highlight the sketch and the entry title. Note the simple diagram and the area of low graphic value at the bottom of the page to form a base for the composition.

Fig. 09-12 Two-page journal entry, Moh'd Bilbeisi. Ink and watercolors on paper. Washington, D.C.

EGJ-1.10

MOH'D BILBEISI

This complex composition consists of three different topics, each with a sketch and a corresponding supporting text. The sketches form a triangular relationship that is superimposed upon the text. There are two entry titles, the major is the one highlighted by a watercolor wash. Only two of the sketches have watercolor application, with the third sketch achieving the same graphic value through the use of fountain pen ink wash and hatching.

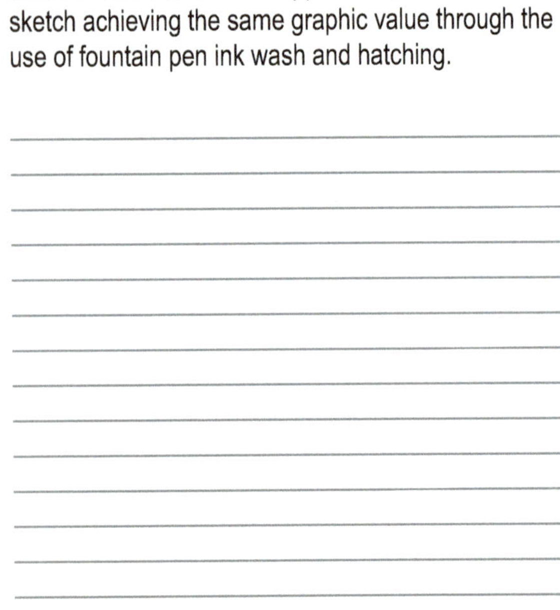

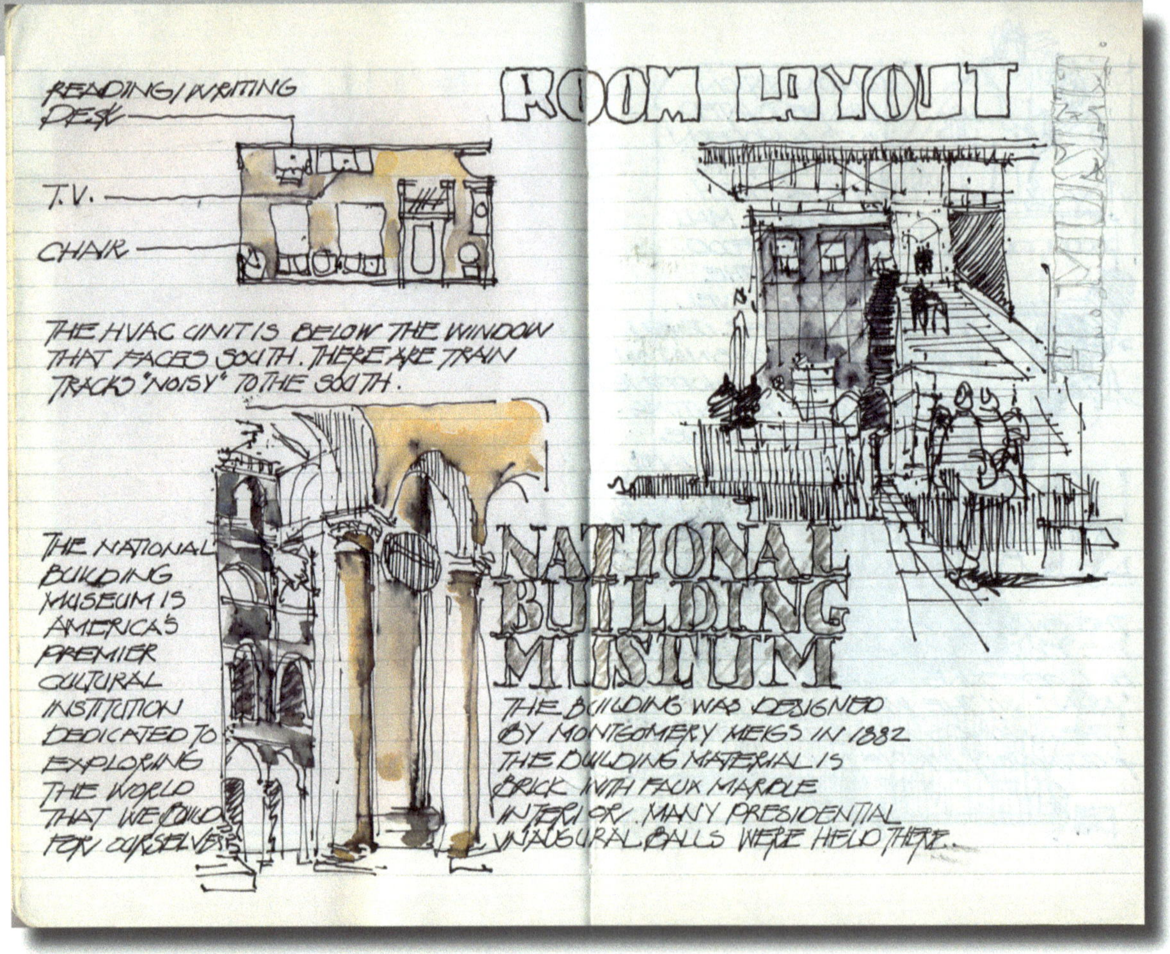

Fig. 09-13 Two-page journal entry, Moh'd Bilbeisi. Ink and watercolors on paper. Washington, D.C.

EGJ-1.11

MOH'D BILBEISI

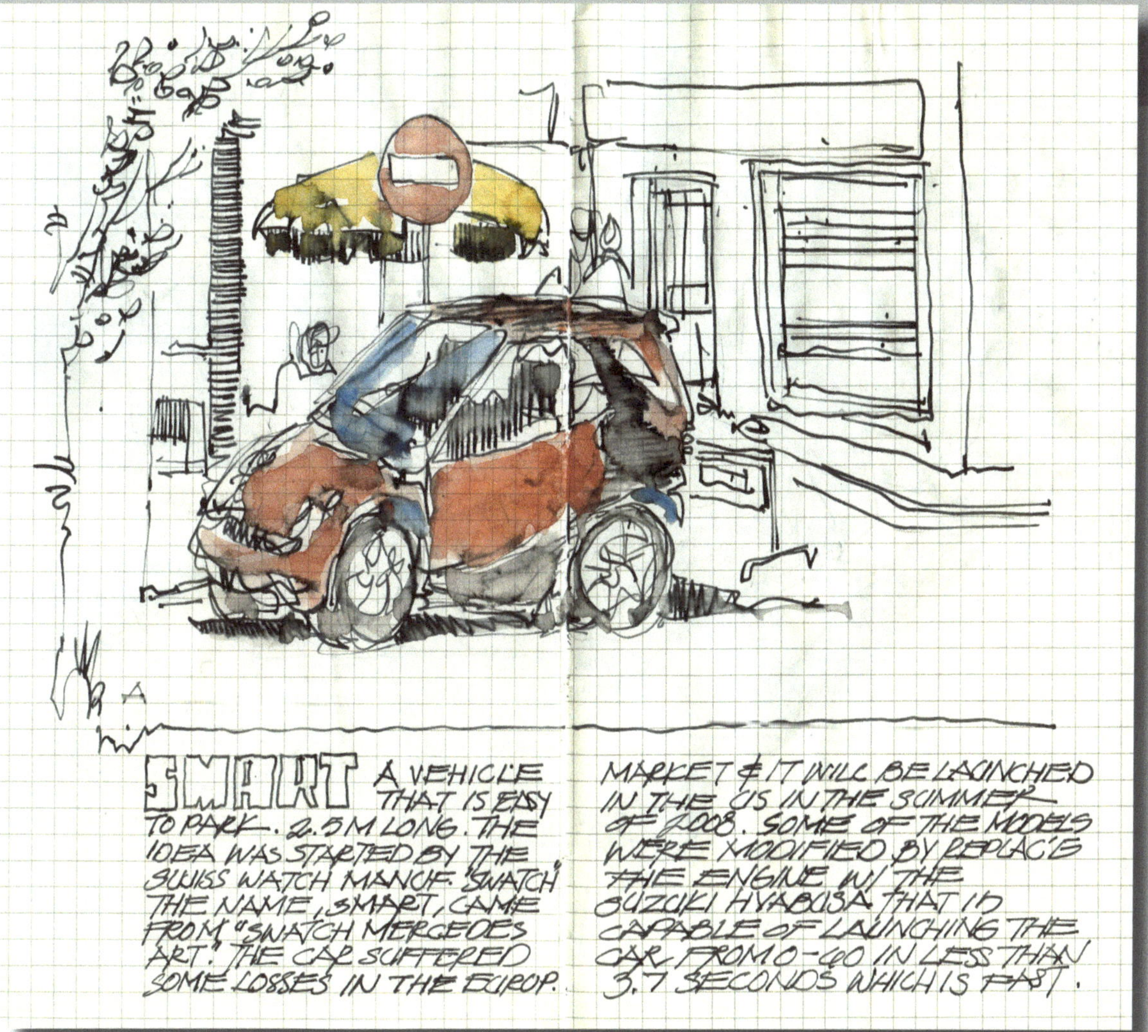

Fig. 09-14 Two-page journal entry, Moh'd Bilbeisi. Ink and watercolors on paper. Athens, Greece.

This composition is divided horizontally into thirds. The top two thirds are dedicated to the sketch and the bottom third to the supporting text. The tree in the sketch to the left is holding the left side of the layout, and joins a horizontal line that separates the text anchoring the bottom. Watercolors are used to highlight the main subject matter (the car) and to emphasize its colorful attribute.

EGJ-1.12

MOH'D BILBEISI

This journal entry is of a technical nature. The two-page layout is divided into sections ranging from a band of general information across the top half, to specific details below. Watercolors were added to the plan sketch on the left page to provide better contrast and increase its sense of hierarchy. The lower right detail sketch is superimposed upon a graphic frame with rounded corners to detach it from the page.

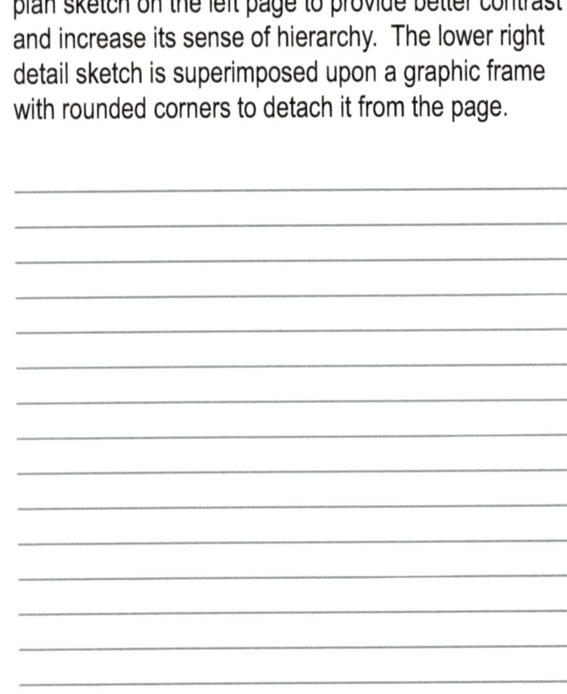

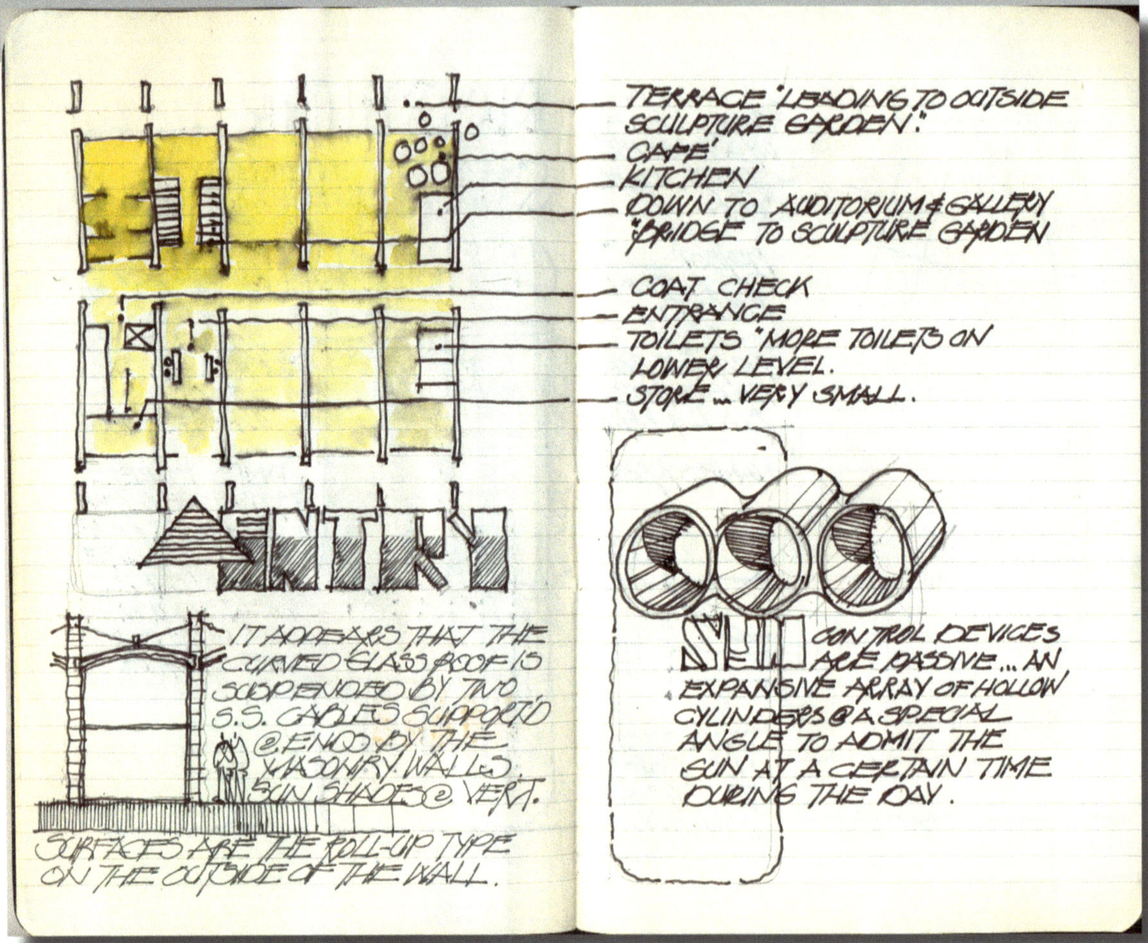

Fig. 09-15 Two-page journal entry, Moh'd Bilbeisi. Ink and watercolors on paper. Dallas, Texas.

EGJ-1.13

MOH'D BILBEISI

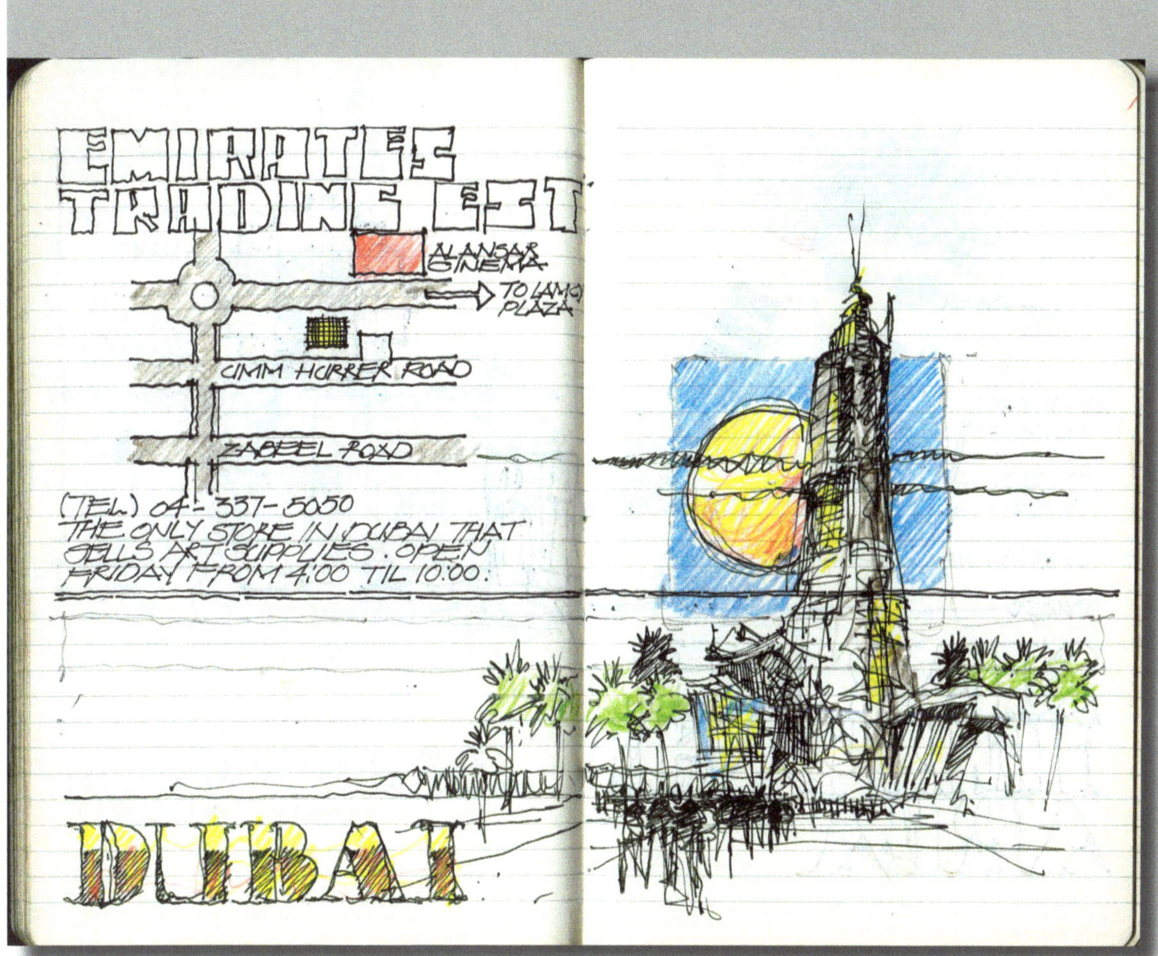

Fig. 09-16 Two-page journal entry, Moh'd Bilbeisi. Ink and colored pencils on paper. Dubai, UAE.

This journal entry is gradually increasing its intensity as it progresses toward the sketch to the right. A diagram is added to communicate location. The space between the two sketches ensures a much needed separation without compromising the integrity of the composition. The two titles are indicated with the major one highlighted through color and hatching. A graphic blue square is added behind the main sketch to separate it from the page.

EGJ-1.14

MOH'D BILBEISI

The ink line sketch is occupying the entire two-page spread. Trees anchor both sides of the sketch. Graphic edges are added to the top and the bottom to contain the sketch. Graphic value is achieved through hatching and the title is de-emphasized to place focus upon the sketch.

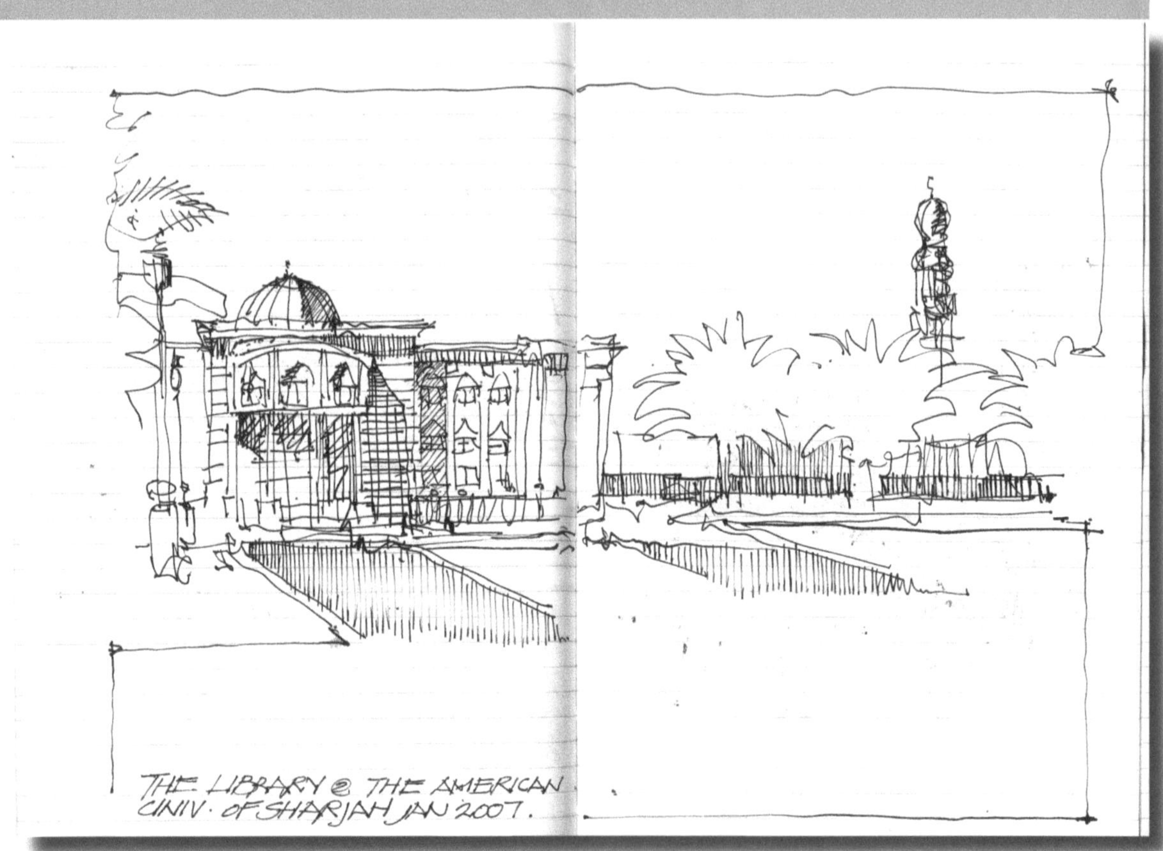

Fig. 09-17 Two-page journal entry, Moh'd Bilbeisi. Ink on paper. Sharjah, UAE.

EGJ-1.15

MOH'D BILBEISI

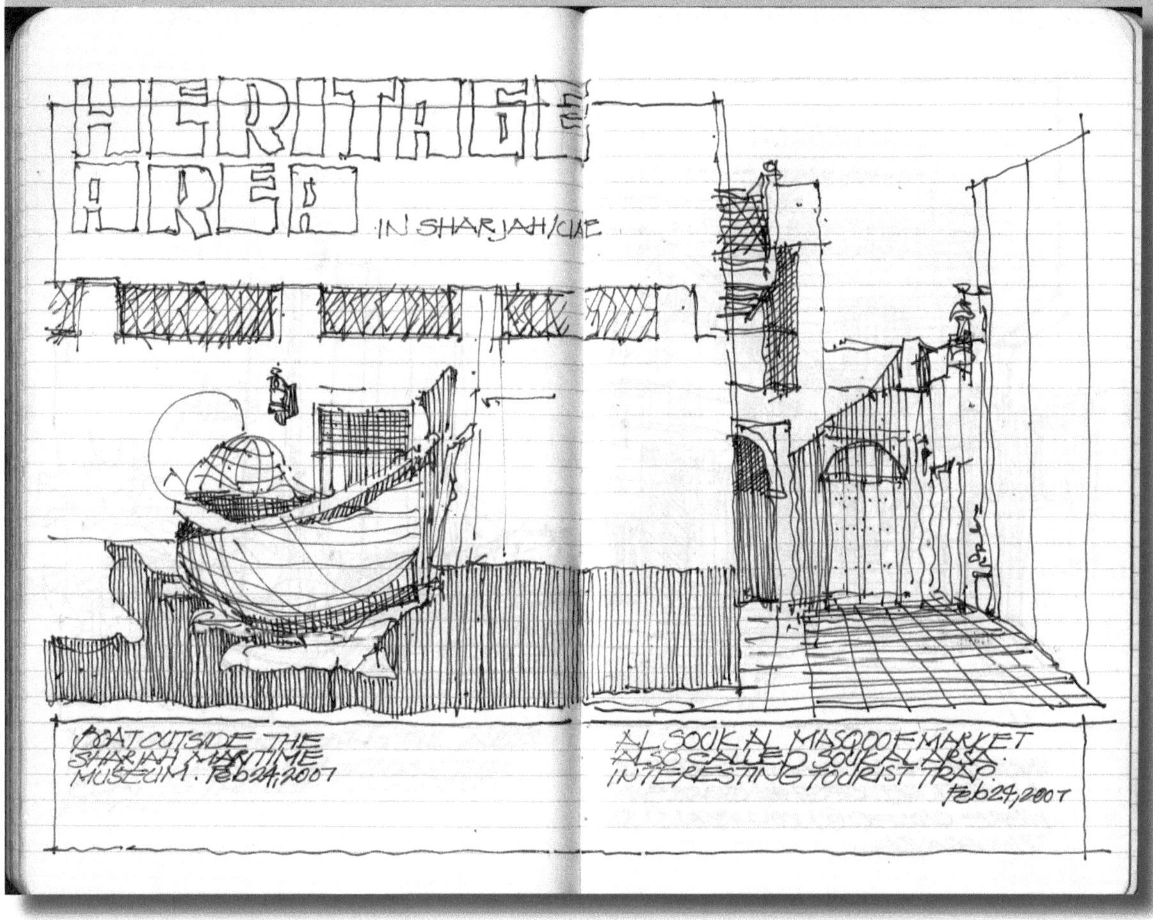

The layout is divided almost equally between the two sketches; however, the sketch to the left is partially superimposed upon the second sketch. The shadow of the boat is carried across to the second page to allow it to share the same graphic value. The frame for the supporting text spans the two-page spread in an attempt to unify the composition.

Fig. 09-18 Two-page journal entry, Moh'd Bilbeisi. Ink on paper. Sharjah, UAE.

EGJ-1.16

MOH'D BILBEISI

This composition uses the journal entry title and the supporting text as a method to anchor the left and the lower parts of the journal entry. The lower graphic values were kept to a minimum due to the intensity of the supporting text. The floor plan is floating towards the top right corner of the page as a supporting diagram to help communicate the subject matter. Graphic frames help define a rectilinear compositional shape.

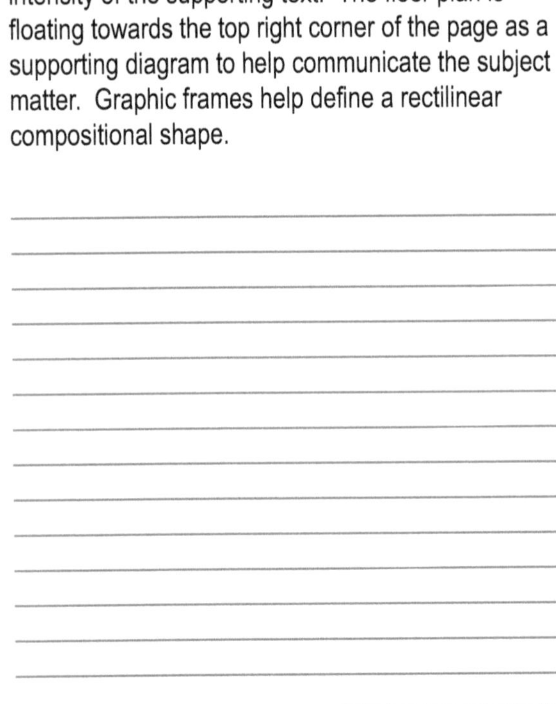

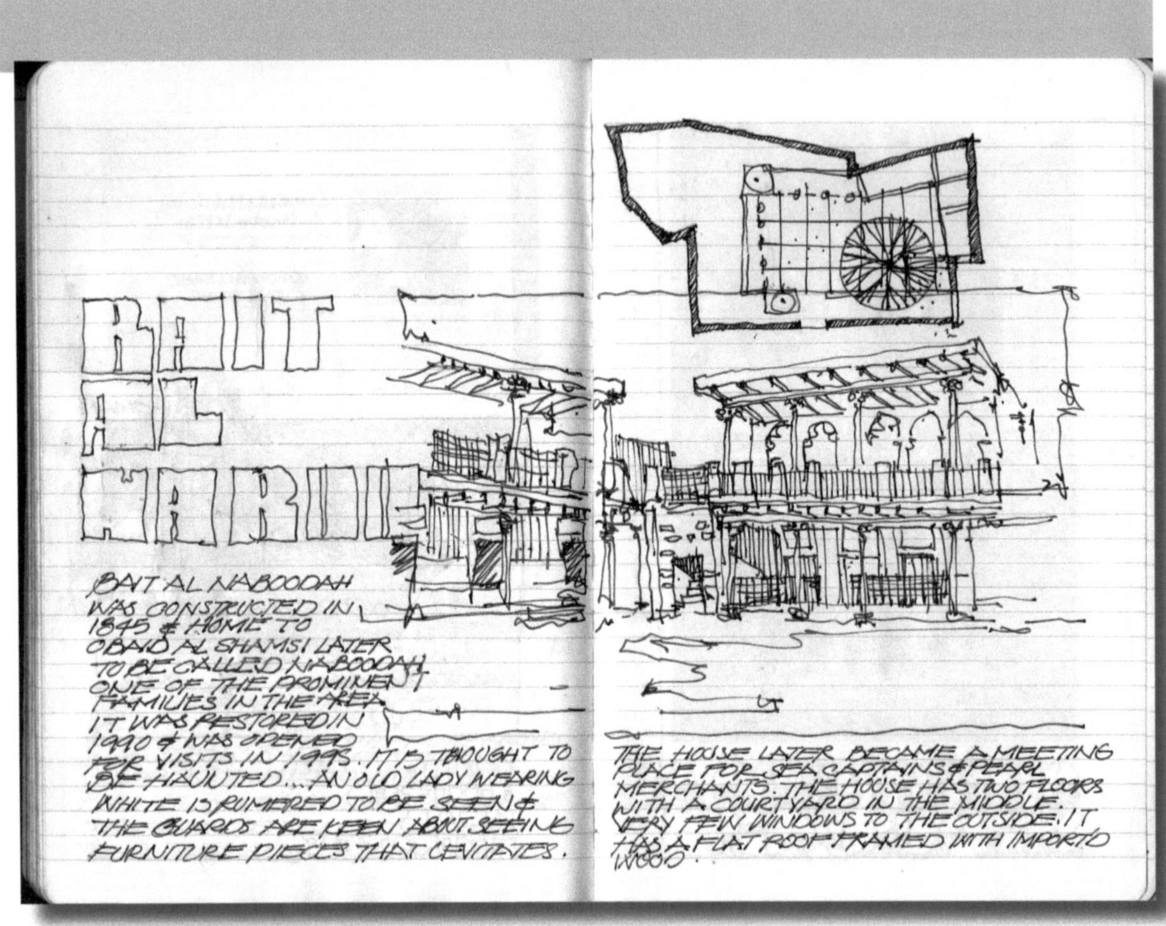

Fig. 09-19 Two-page journal entry, Moh'd Bilbeisi. Ink on paper. Sharjah, UAE.

EGJ-2.1

KAH LEONG GOH

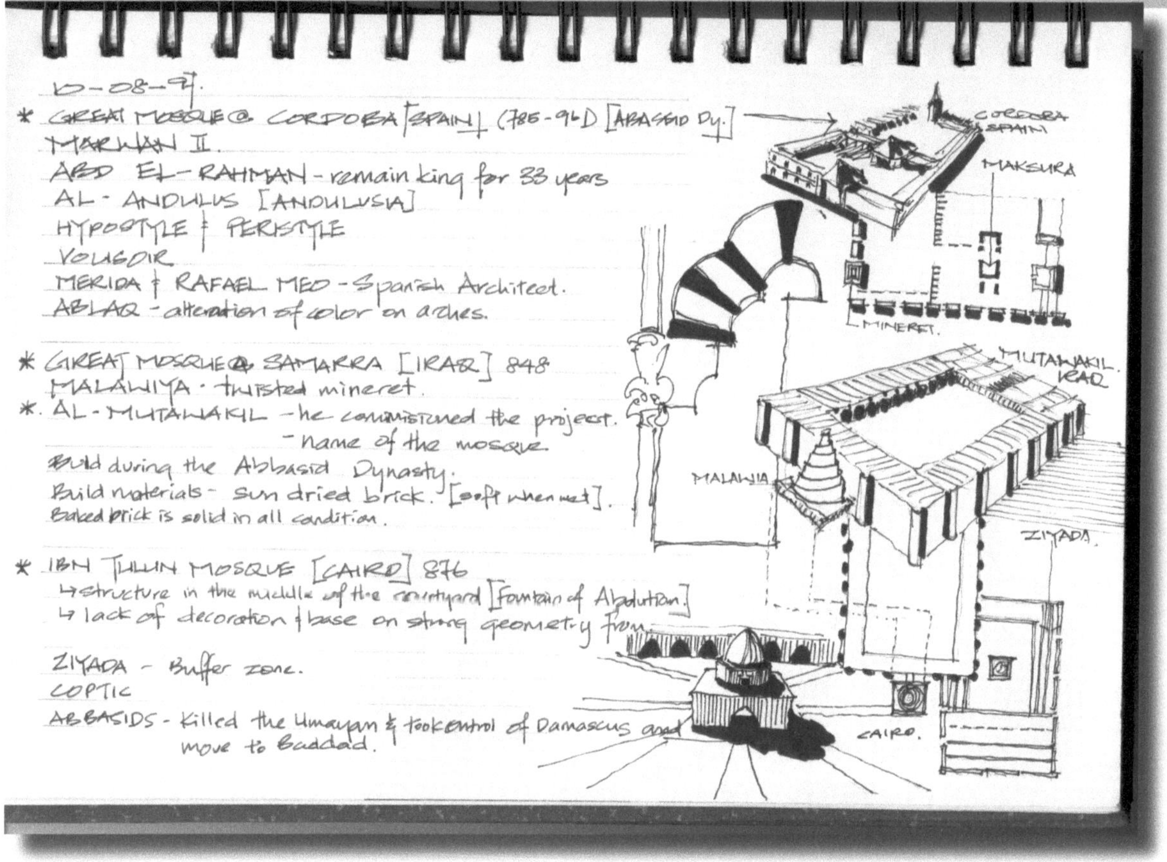

These class notes were composed on a page that was divided vertically into thirds. The left two thirds are dedicated to the supporting text and the right third is dedicated to the sketches, both orthographic and perspectival. The sketches are individually labeled. Each idea presented in the lecture has been documented in text and with a corresponding sketch for clarity.

Fig. 09-20 Single page class notes journal entry, Kah Leong Goh. Ink on paper.

EGJ-3.1

S. HOLSTEDT

The two-page spread is divided into four vertical strips with the main sketch occupying the first and third space. The sketches are graphically bracketed to give an illusion of detachment from the pages of the journal. The looseness of the sketches is complemented with an apparent informality in the supporting text. The title is integrated across the composition, and the overall graphic value is achieved through loose diagonal hatching in localized areas of high contrast in the sketches.

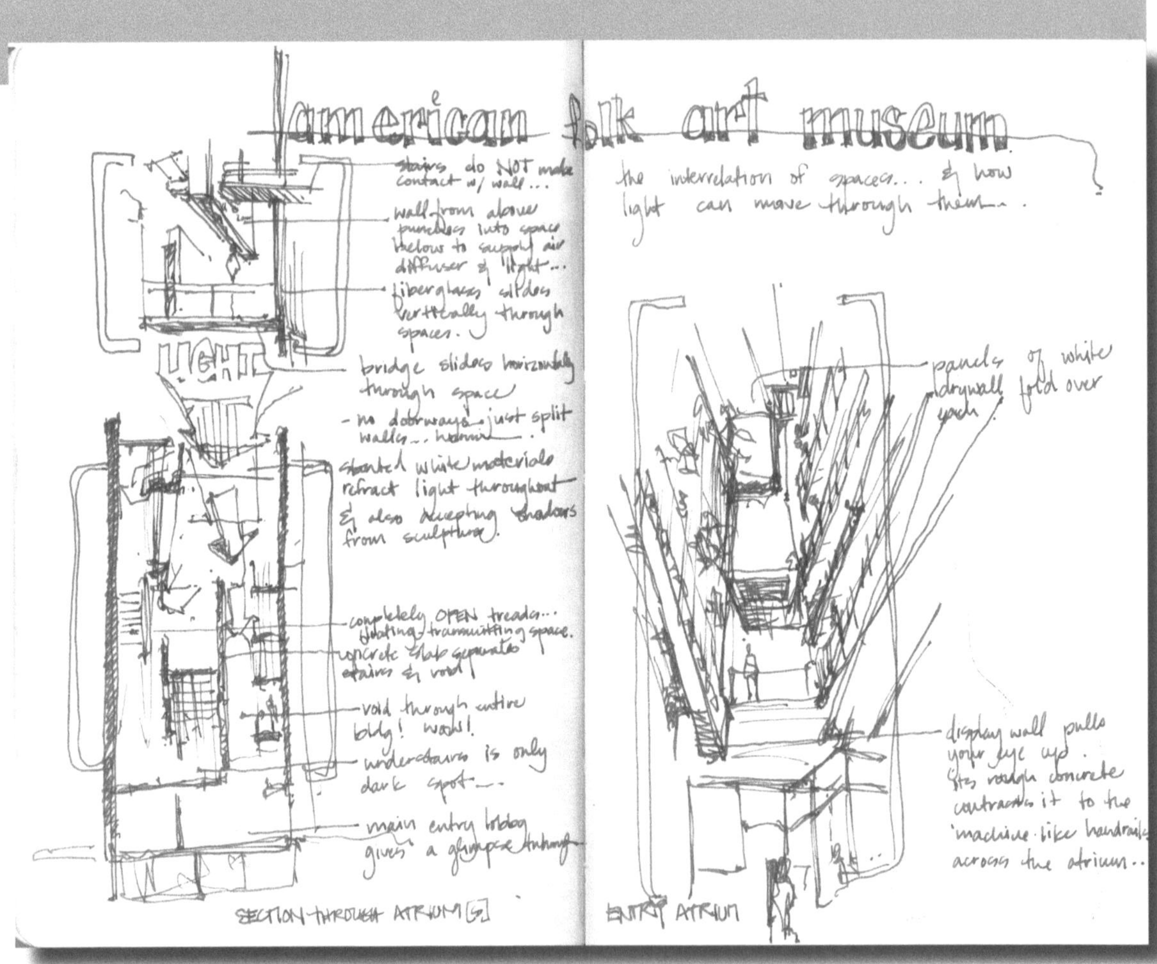

Fig. 09-21 Two-page journal entry, Sarah Holstedt. Ink on paper. New York, New York.

EGJ-4.1

DAVID JOHNSON

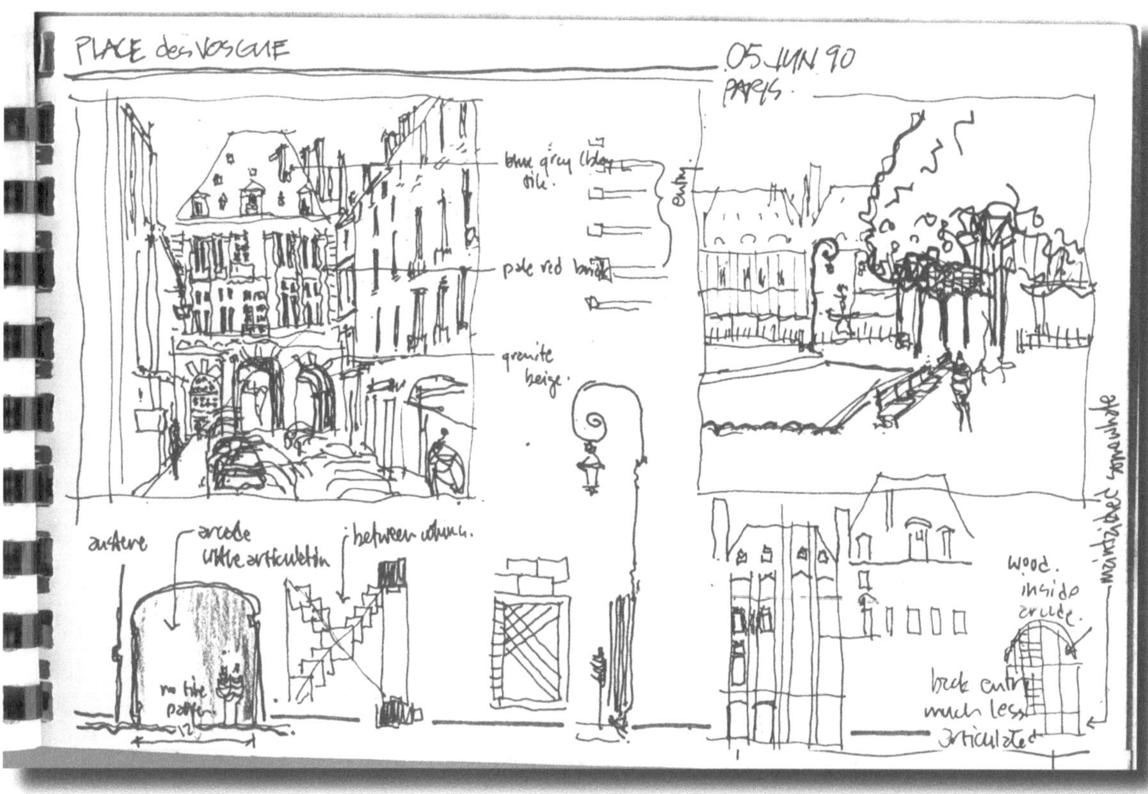

Fig. 09-22 Single page journal entry, David Johnson. Ink on paper. Paris, France.

This unique journal entry is divided vertically into halves and horizontally into thirds. The top two sketches are framed with the orthographic projections occupying the lower third. Graphic lines and brackets are used to contain the journal entry. There is some graphic value that was added to the sketches. The location and the date of the journal entry are noted.

EGJ-5.1

MEREDITH JUMP

The pages of this graphic journal were designed with a particular lecture course in mind. The pages are organized into vertical strips with the right strip being a repeated iconic logo. The rest of the page is divided equally between the sketch and the supporting text. The sketches are very diagrammatic and tend to be mostly orthographic projections to help illustrate the concepts. Clarity is very apparent in this class notes graphic journal entry.

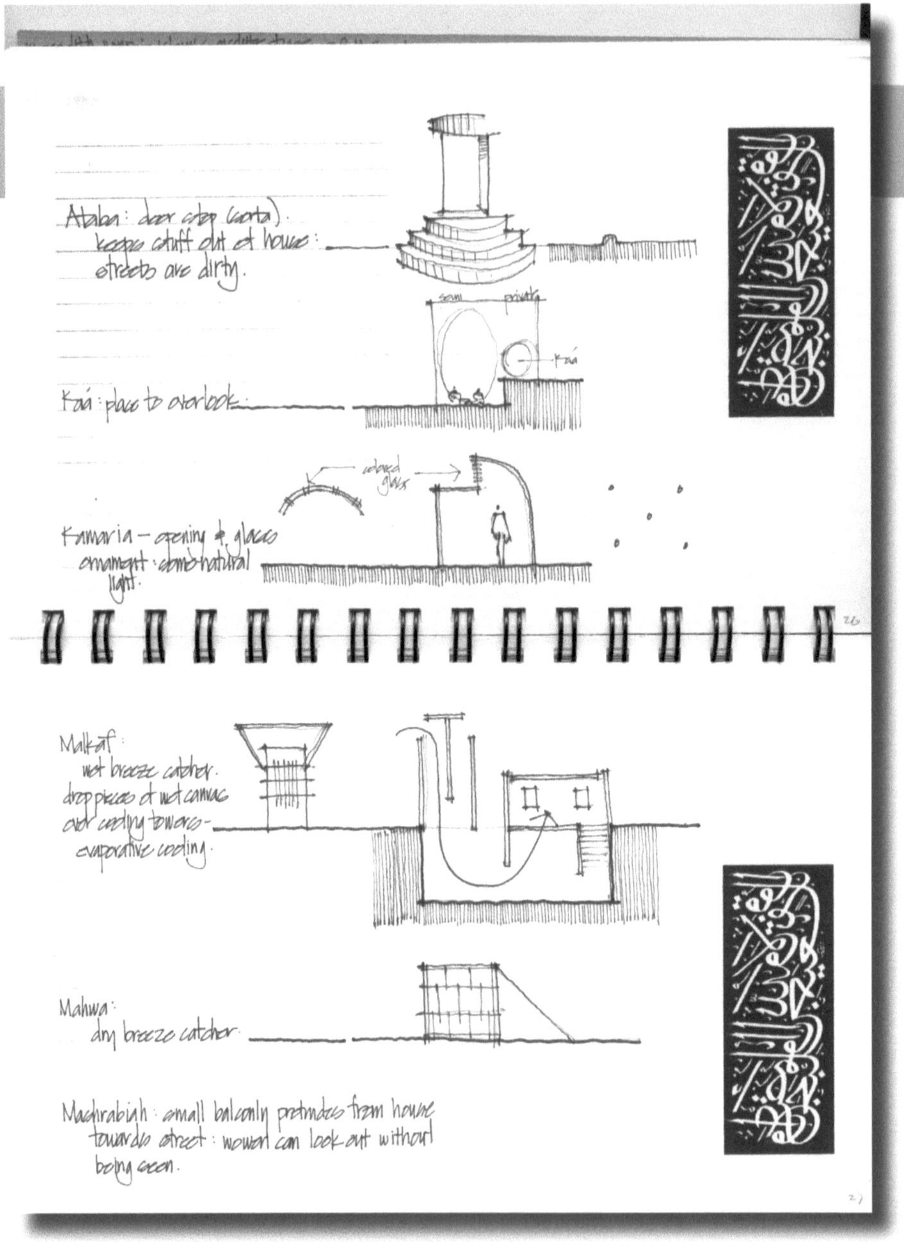

Fig. 09-23 Two-page class notes journal entry, Meredith Jump. Ink on paper.

EGJ-6.1

ADAM LANMAN

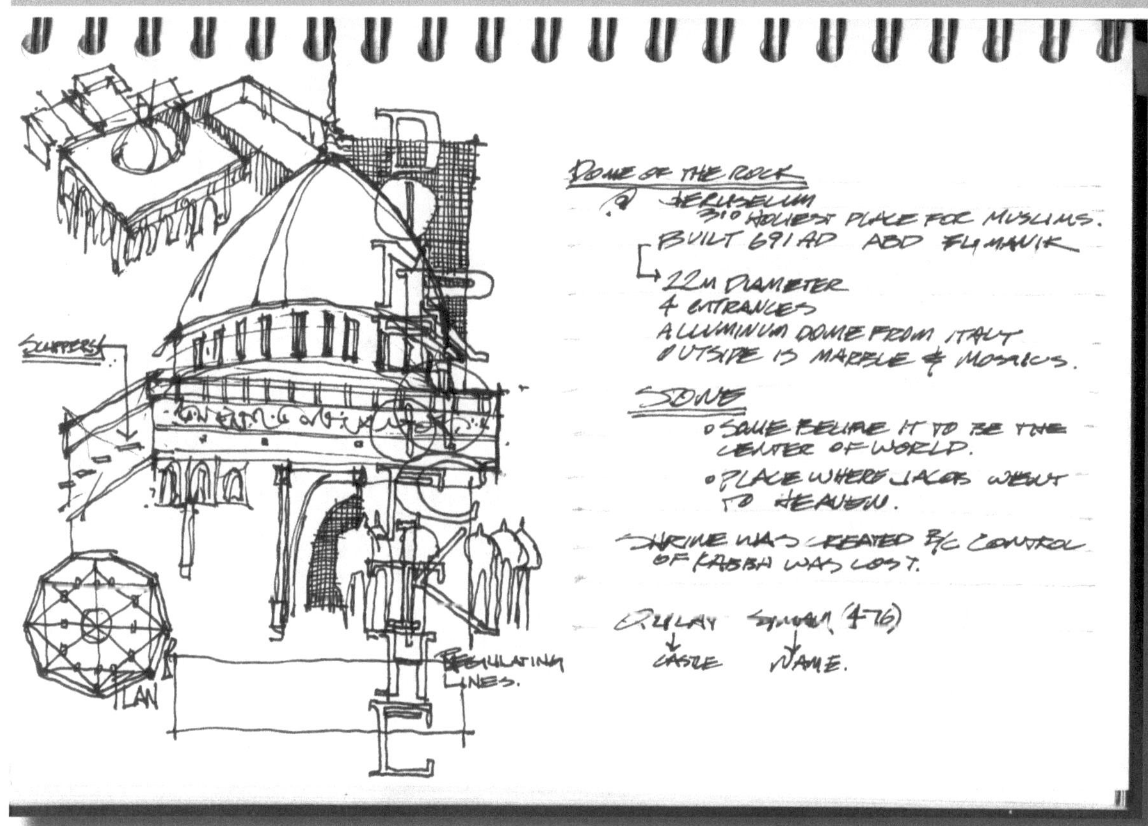

Fig. 09-24 Single page class journal entry, Adam Lanman. Ink on paper.

The page is divided vertically into halves. The left half is occupied by multiple diagrams and sketches while the right half provides the supporting text. This immediately establishes the supremacy of the sketch over the supporting text. The sketches are rather complex and superimposed upon one another. Sketches of people are added to indicate scale and character. A graphic low value frame is added behind the sketches to detach them from the page.

EGJ-6.2

ADAM LANMAN

The perspective sketch is the main topic for this travel journal entry. The highest part of the sketch is situated at the left side of the page with the sketch intensity fading towards the right edge. The outer edges of the sketch are outlined with a broad profile line to detach it from the page. The supporting text is located within the available margins without any relationship to the sketch. The inclusion of people to the extreme right side is intentional to indicate scale and add character to the sketch.

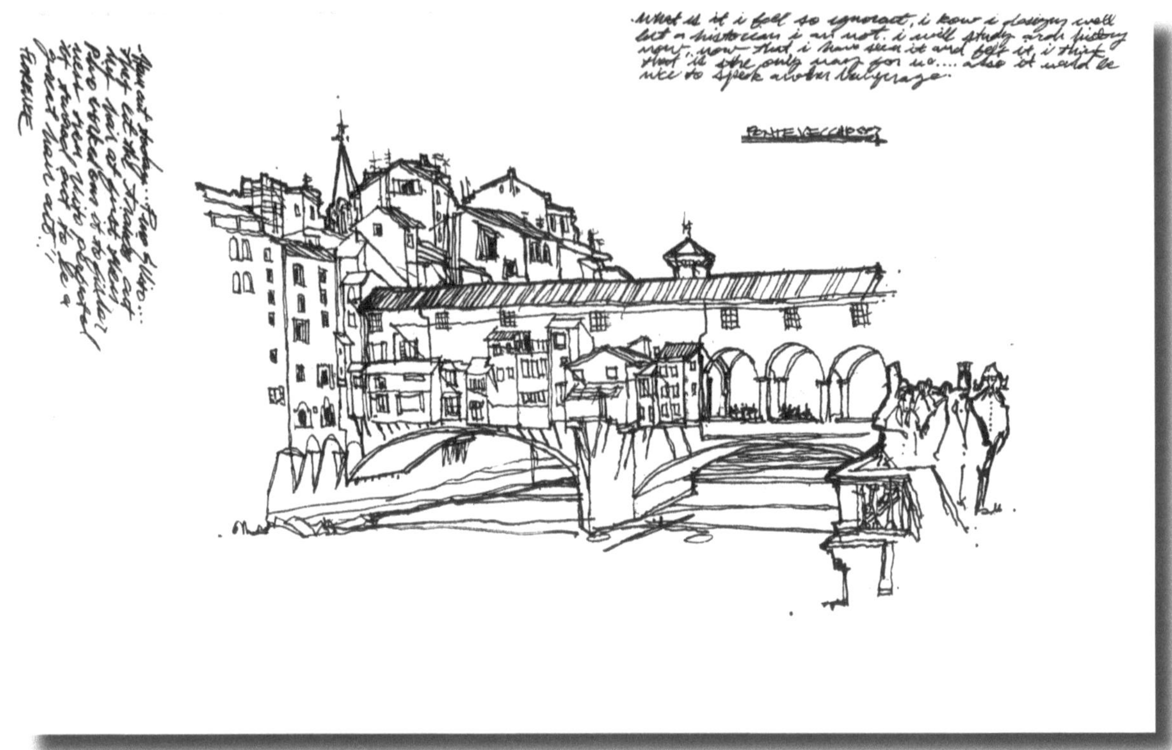

Fig. 09-25 Single page travel journal entry, Adam Lanman. Ink on paper. Florence, Italy.

EGJ-6.3

ADAM LANMAN

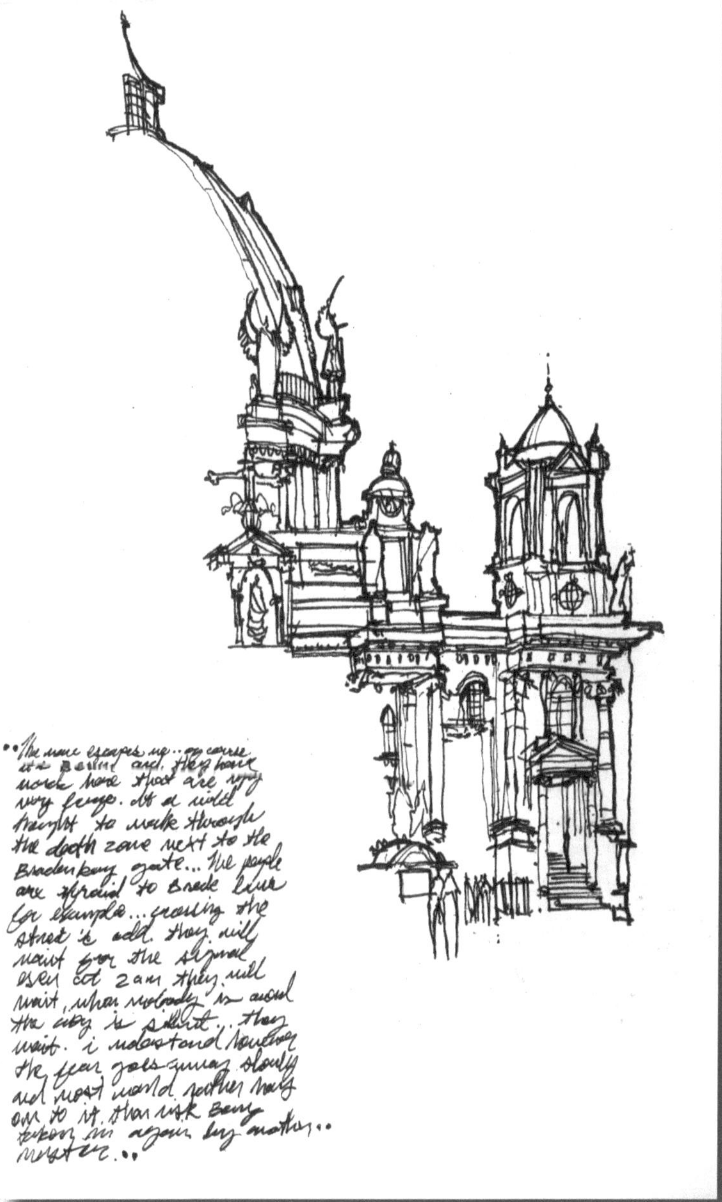

The page is divided diagonally into two triangles. The upper right triangle contains the sketch and the lower left triangle contains the supporting text. The sketch loses its detailed delineation as it moves towards the supporting text. This technique achieves focus without altering the graphic value. The inclusion of people at the base is a strong indicator of scale and character within the sketch. The supporting text is loose and complements the loose nature of the sketch itself. Its location mirrors the domed part of the sketch and illustrates a successful attempt to contain the composition.

Fig. 09-26 Single page travel journal entry, Adam Lanman. Ink on paper. Berlin, Germany.

EGJ-7.1

JAMES MCCOOL

The sketch is occupying the bulk of the journal entry without any supporting text except for the entry date. The sketch itself is highlighted through the use of colored pencils applied strategically to the view. Graphic value is indicated through the use of vertical hatching. The inclusion of people and street activity adds character and scale to the journal entry.

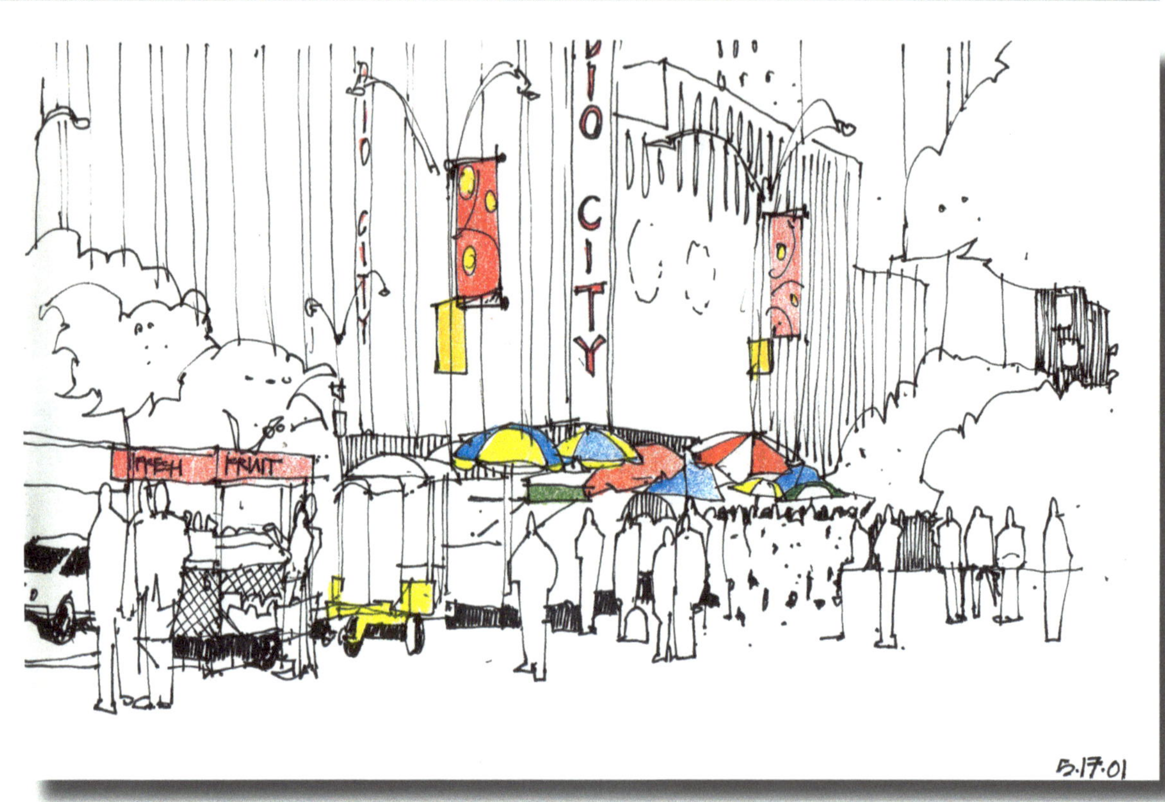

Fig. 09-27 Single page travel journal entry, James McCool. Ink and colored pencils on paper. New York, New York.

EGJ-7.2

JAMES MCCOOL

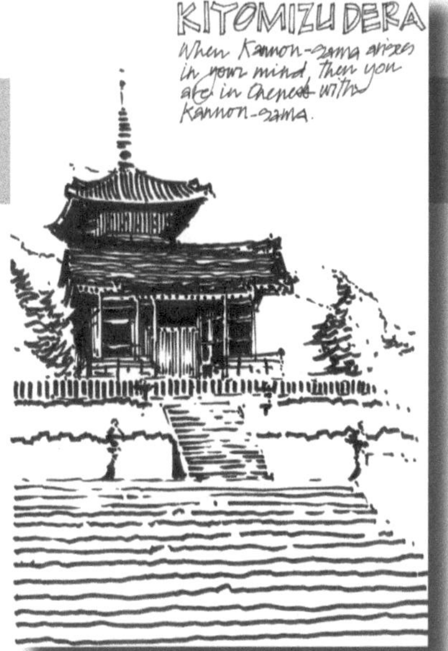

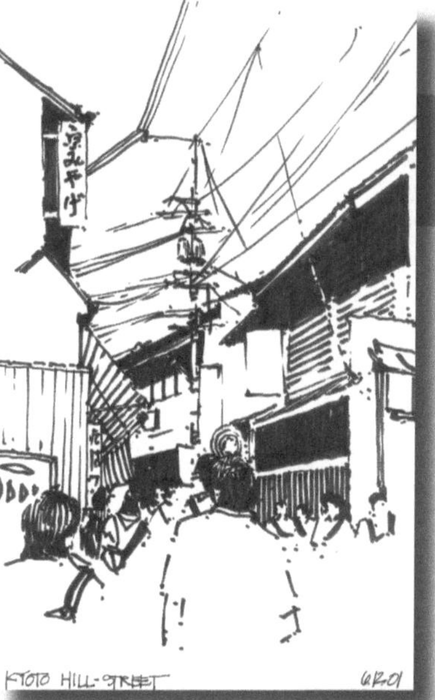

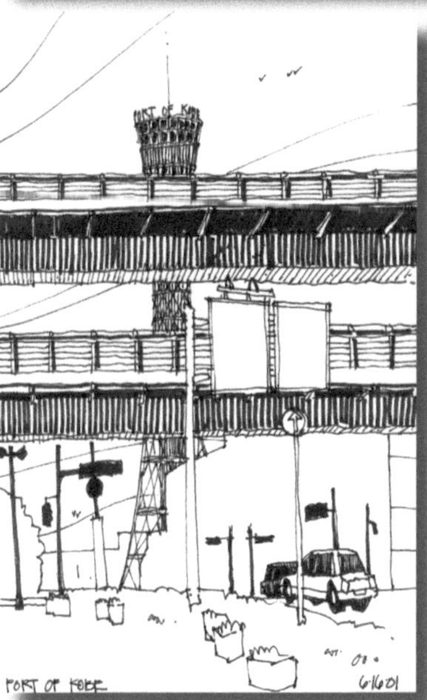

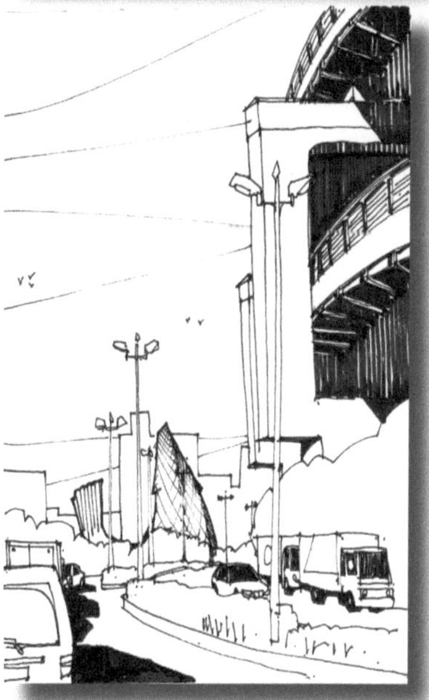

These four journal entries depend on high contrast to achieve prominence on the pages of the journal. The use of vertical and horizontal hatching with varying degrees of intensity is utilized to achieve graphic value within the sketches. There is very little text if any except for the dates of the entries. The inclusion of people and motor vehicles in the sketch successfully indicates scale and character. The vertical format of the journal entries offers a limited field of view and focus.

Fig. 09-28 Single page travel journal entries, James McCool. Ink on paper. Japan.

EGJ-7.3

JAMES MCCOOL

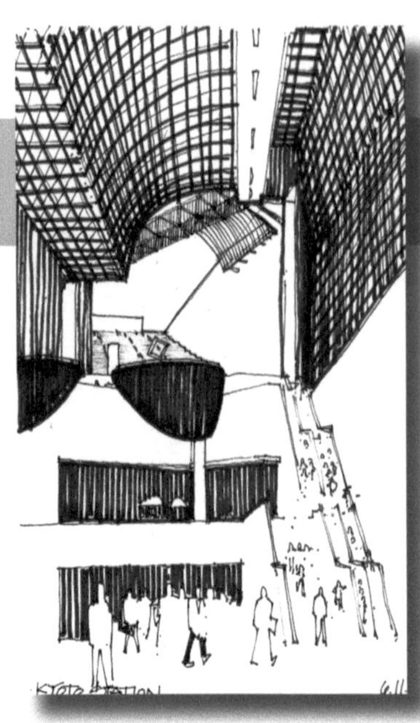

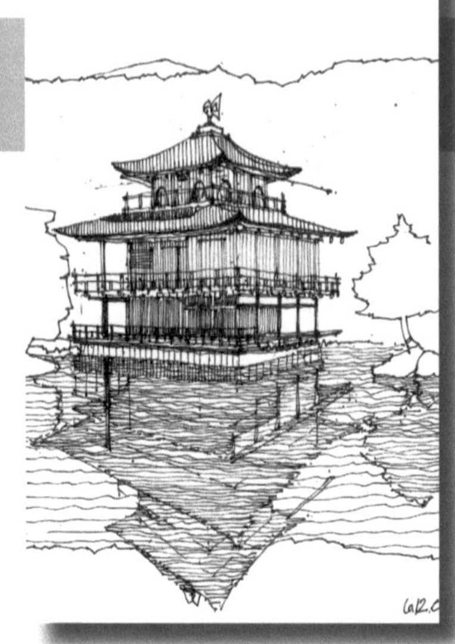

These three journal entries exhibit a mastery of sketching. They are sketched minimally, yet elaborately and loosely. The use of hatching indicates transparency, translucency, texture, and graphic value at the same time. There is hardly any supporting text except for the dates of the entries. The use of trees and people is effective in indicating scale and use.

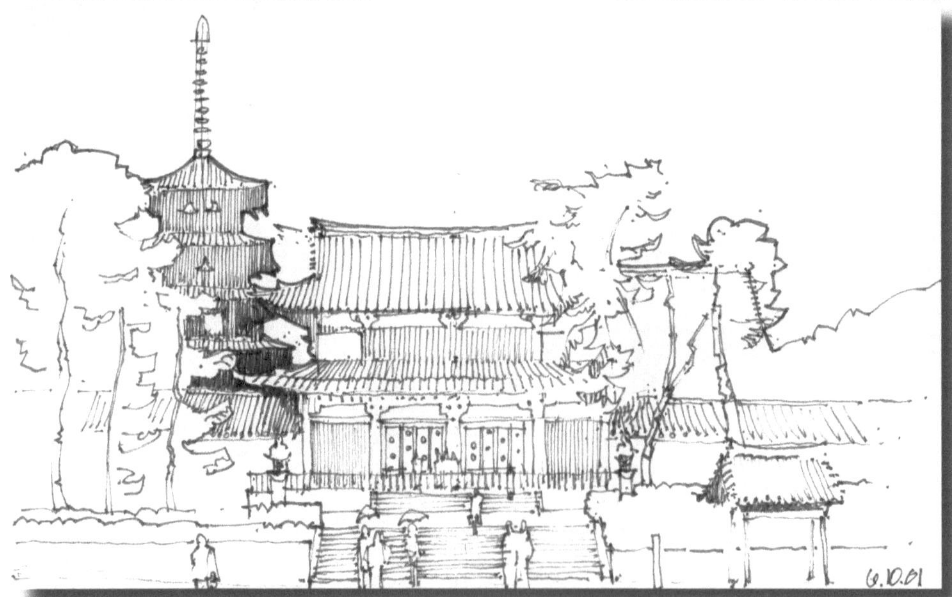

Fig. 09-29 Single page travel journal entries, James McCool. Ink on paper. Japan.

EGJ-7.4

JAMES MCCOOL

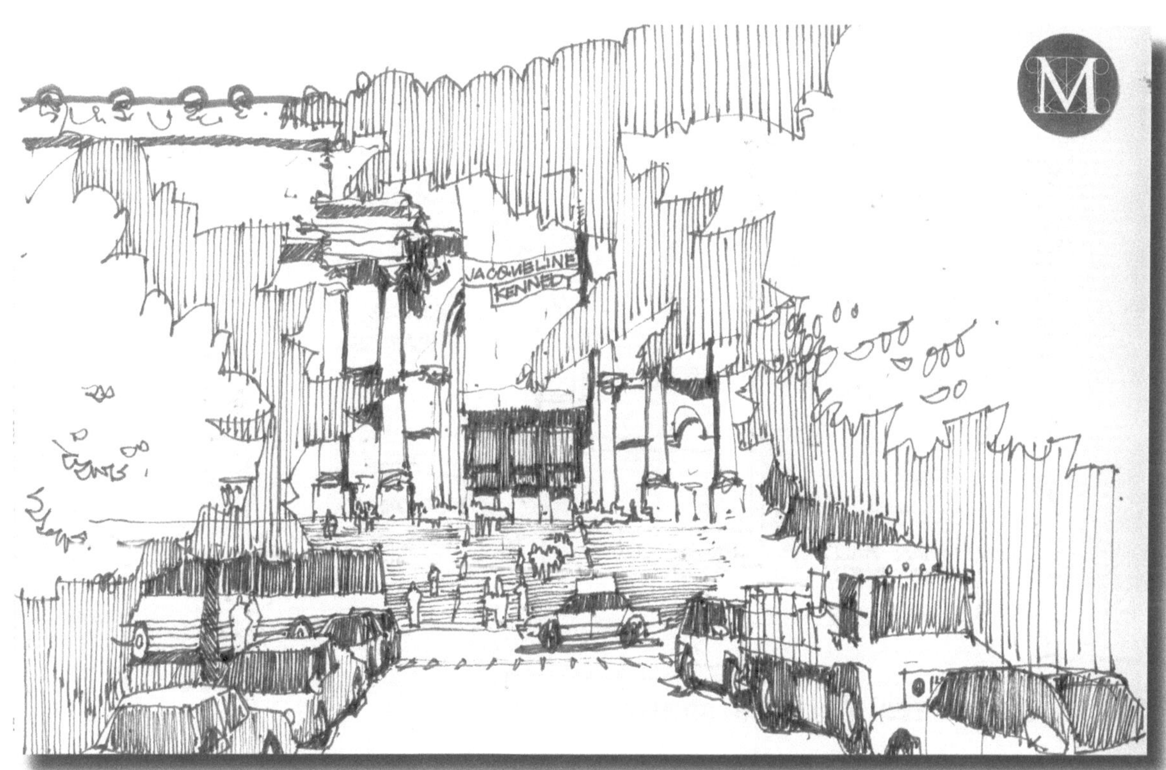

Fig. 09-30 Single page travel journal entry, James McCool. Ink on paper. New York, New York.

This single sketch journal entry indicates a strong perspectival tendency through the location of the automobiles at the bottom of the sketch. The subject matter is framed by the foliage indicated to the left, the right, and the top sides of the sketch. Graphic value is achieved through vertical hatching with variable degrees of intensity to show depth. The inclusion of automobiles and people add scale and character to the composition.

EGJ-7.5

JAMES MCCOOL

The directional nature of this composition is evident for two reasons. The first is the gradual decrease in terms of detail from the left to the right and the second is the increase in graphic value from the right to the left. Vertical hatching with varying degrees of intensities is successfully employed as a value generator. The absence of supporting text would render this journal entry meaningless except for the outline of the main subject matter which delivers the message in a quiet manner.

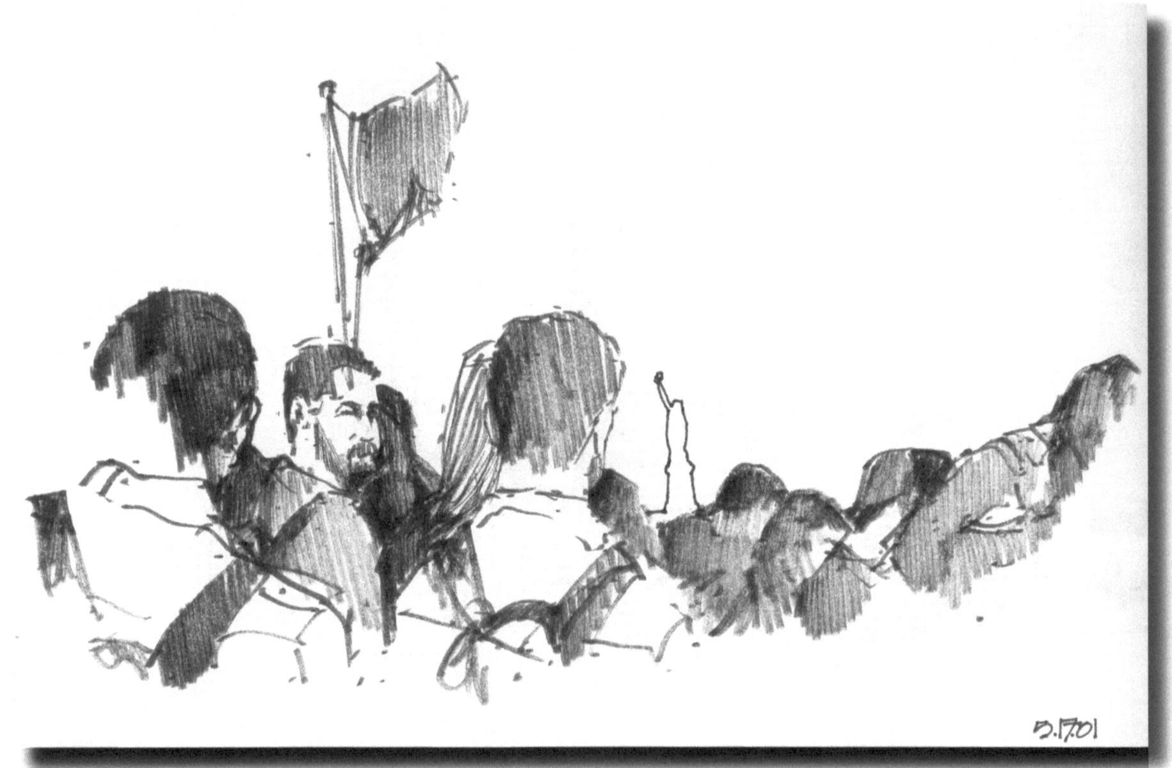

Fig. 09-31 Single page travel journal entry, James McCool. Ink on paper. New York, New York.

EGJ-8.1

JOSH MORATTO

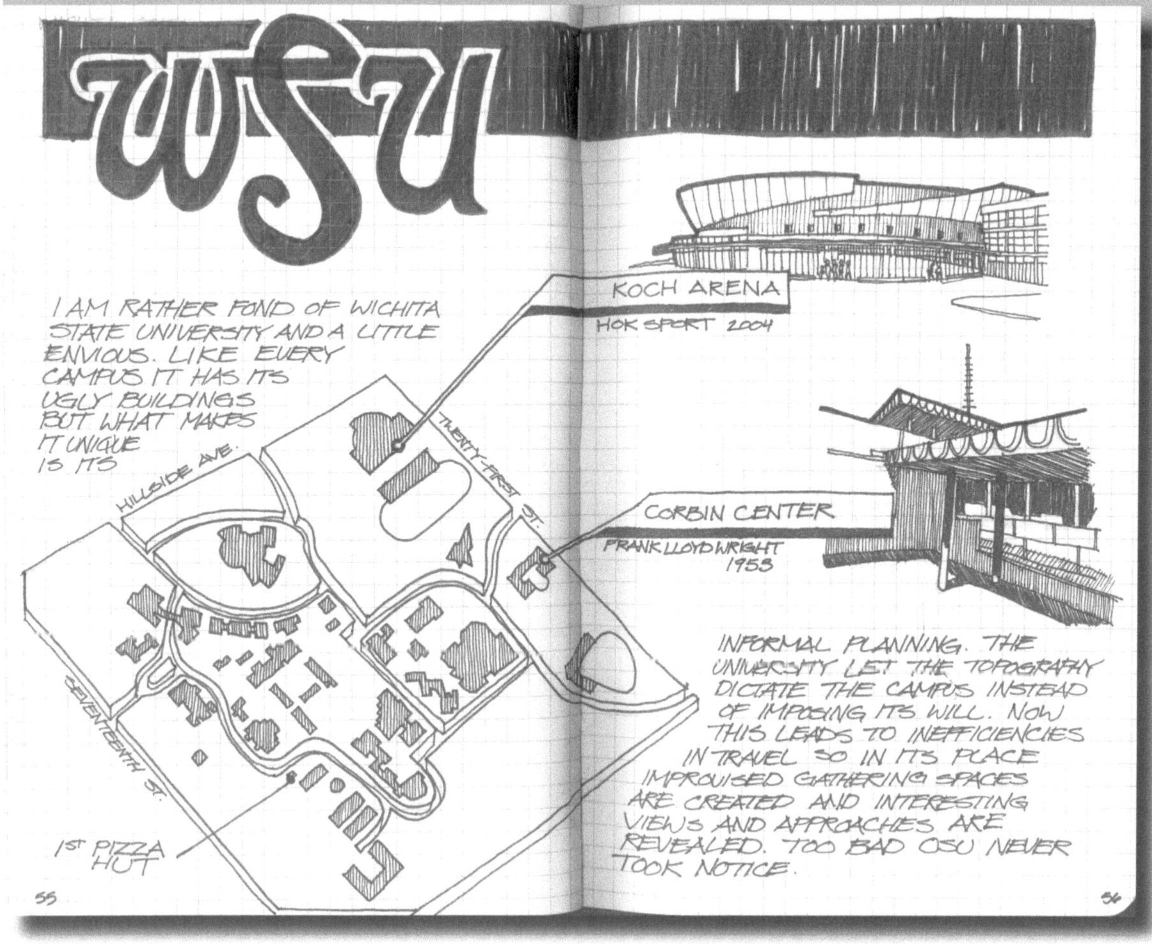

This journal entry is divided compositionally into four quadrants. Two of the opposing quadrants are occupied by sketches and the other two are occupied by the supporting text. The overall campus plan is related to the sketches of elements within the plan via a graphic connection marker that identifies the name and the date of the subject matter. Graphic value is achieved through hatching with a tendency towards high contrast. The composition is topped with an imposing hatched title that spans the two pages.

Fig. 09-32 Two-page journal entry, Josh Moratto. Ink on paper. Wichita, Kansas.

EGJ-8.2

JOSH MORATTO

This two-page layout is divided horizontally into thirds with the lower third occupied by the major sketch. Other diagrammatic sketches are included within the supporting text. The intensity of the vertical hatching creates a high contrast composition that is more technical than gestural in nature. The journal entry title is very prominent while unifying the top of the overall composition.

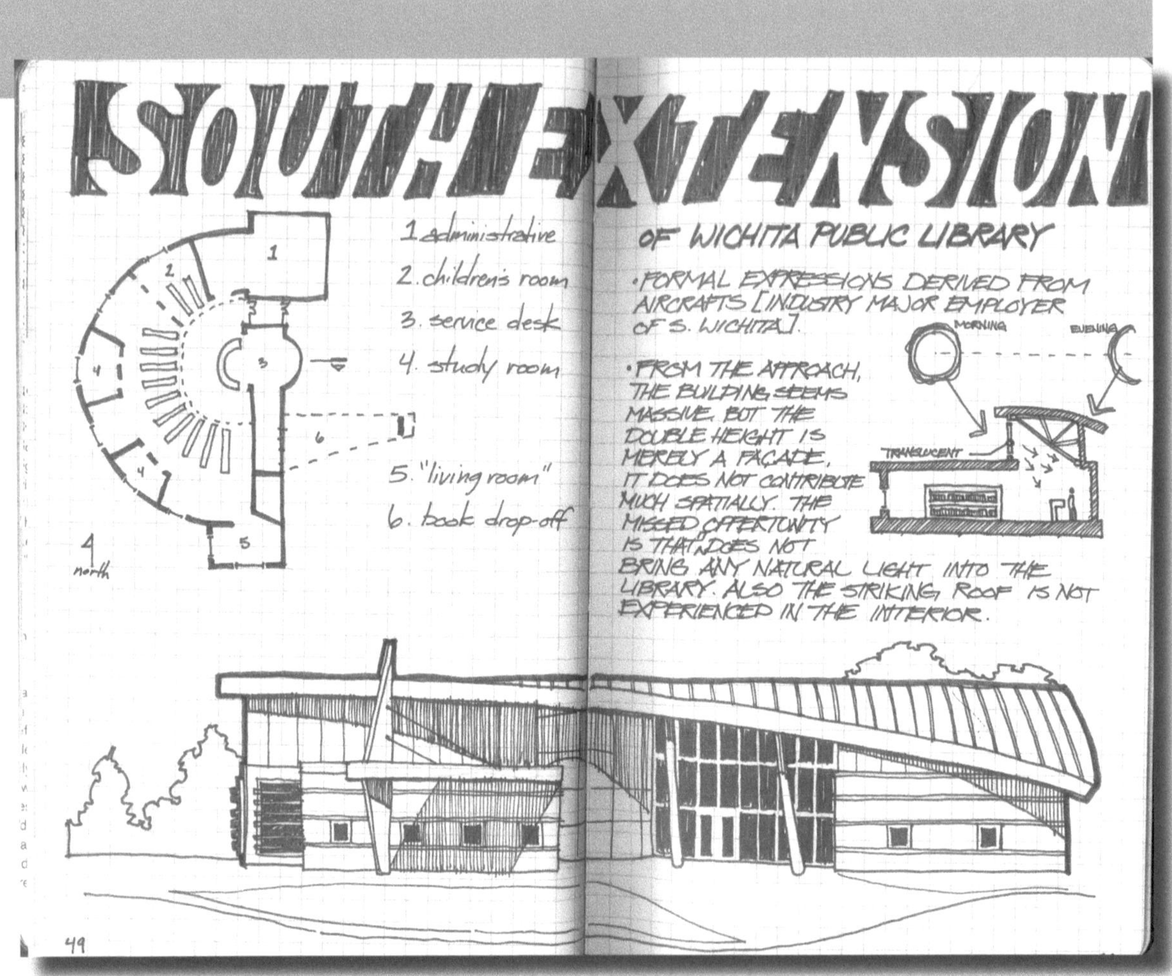

Fig. 09-33 Two-page journal entry, Josh Moratto. Ink on paper. Wichita, Kansas.

EGJ-9.1

MARVIN MOSS

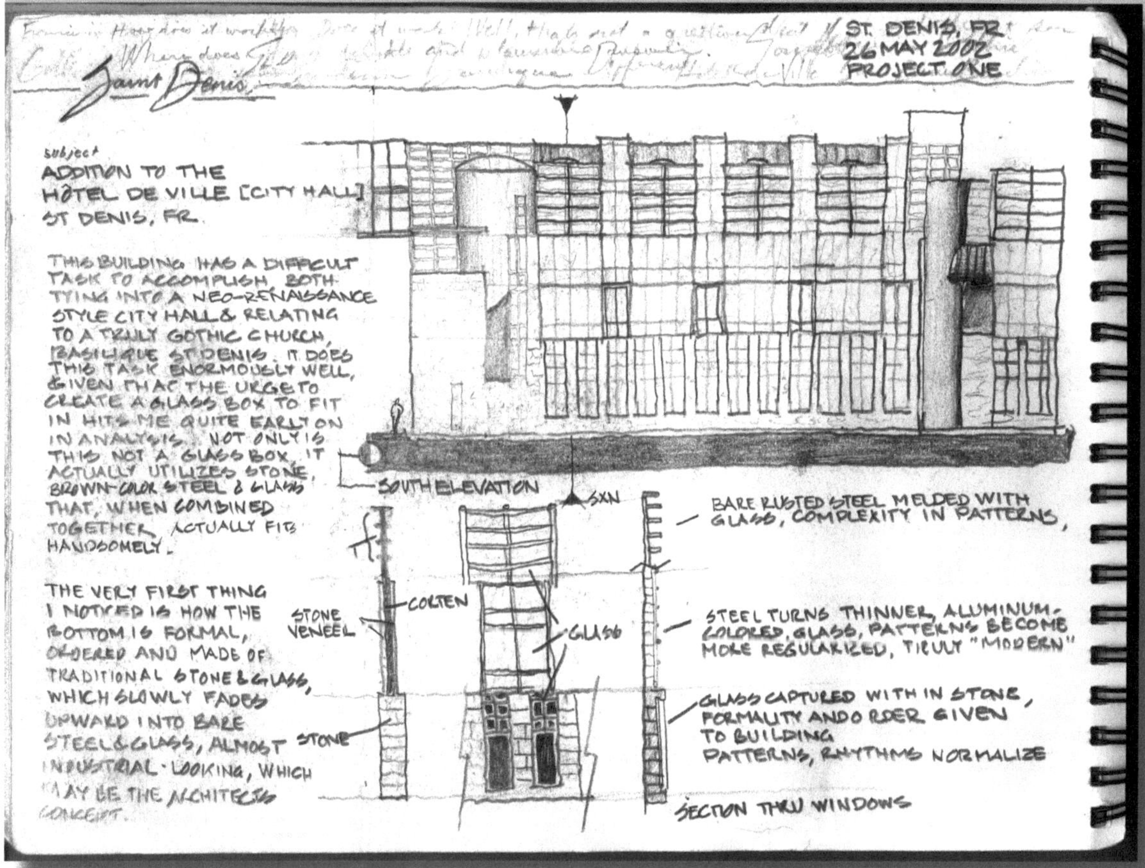

This journal entry composition is vertically divided into thirds and horizontally into halves. The sketch components are occupying the right two thirds with the left third dedicated to the supporting text. The sketches are orthographic in nature and indicate the pencil's ability to produces a wide variety of graphic value while exhibiting a weakness in producing high contrast. The journal entry is subtly titled and dated towards the top of the page.

Fig. 09-34 One page journal entry, Marvin Moss. Pencil on paper. St. Denis, France.

EGJ-9.2

MARVIN MOSS

This journal entry is divided vertically into two halves. Each half contains a sketch and supporting text. The two halves alternate content to accommodate the sketch. The use of a paraline sketch is very helpful in understanding a complex three-dimensional architectural condition. The page is titled and dated towards the top of the page.

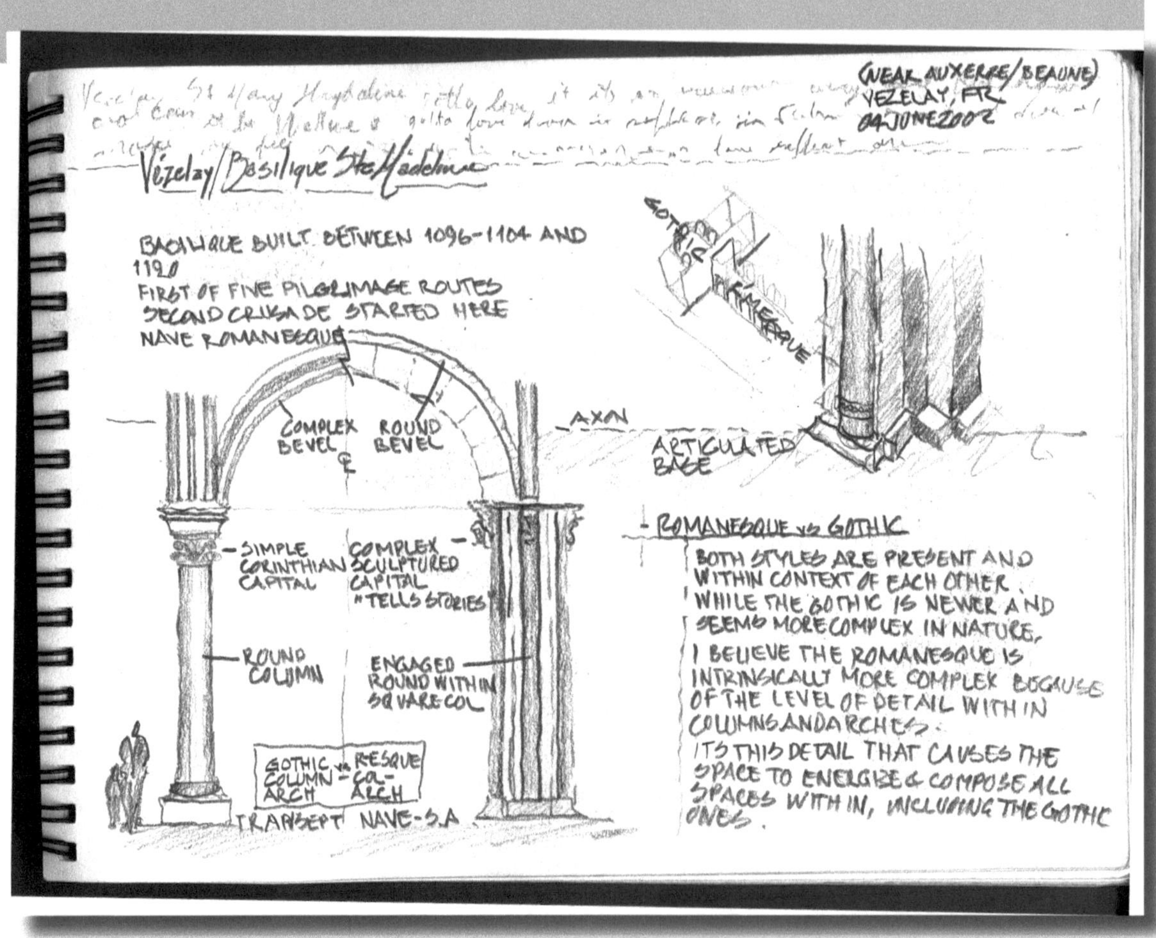

Fig. 09-35 One page journal entry, Marvin Moss. Pencil on paper. Vezelay, France.

EGJ-9.3

MARVIN MOSS

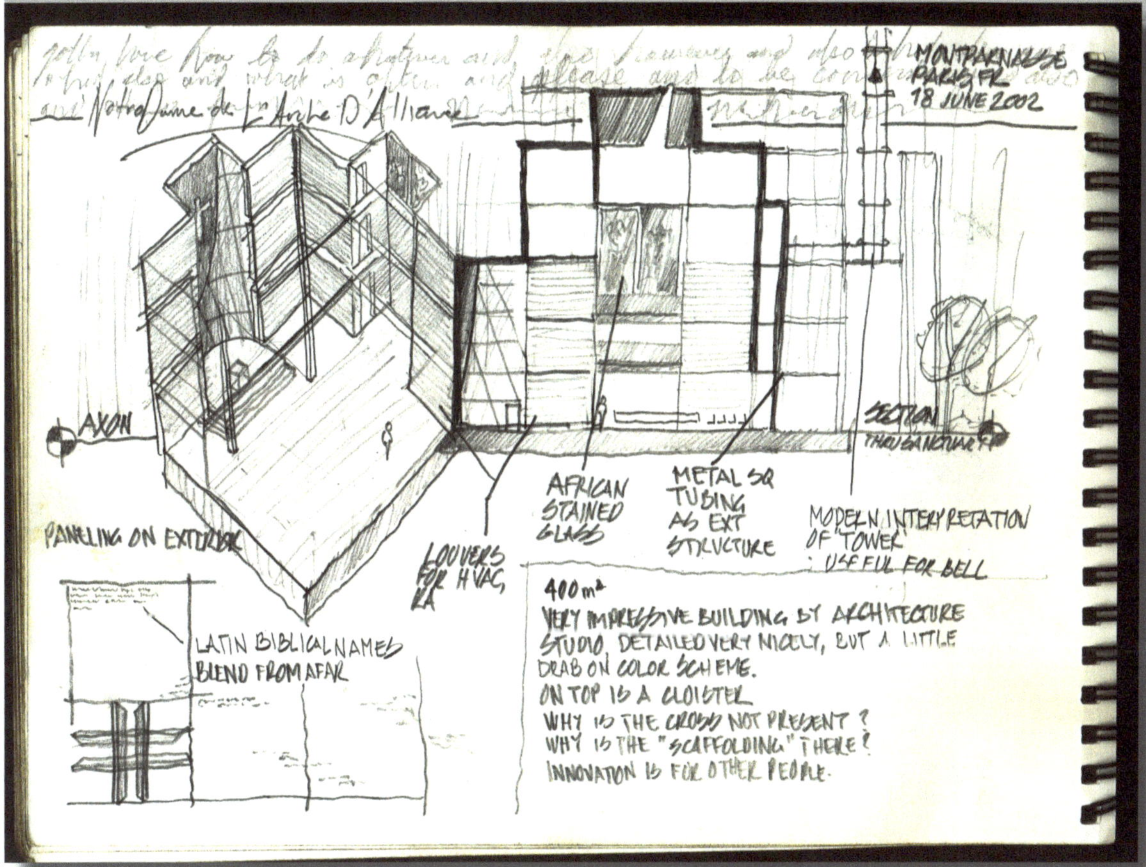

The graphic information presented here is unusual in that the major sketch is situated in the top right area, with the supporting sketches flowing from it in a counter-clockwise cycloidal movement. The major supporting text ends this movement at the bottom right side. Note the secondary text towards the top, superimposed on the title bar.

Fig. 09-36 One page journal entry, Marvin Moss. Pencil on paper. Paris, France.

EGJ-10.1

L. MCQUILLEN

This layout is simple yet effective. The page is divided vertically into two halves. Each half is again divided vertically into thirds - man, woman, text. The sketches are taking advantage of the drawing media's ability to produce value. Parts of the sketches appear to leave the dark background to add dynamism and drama.

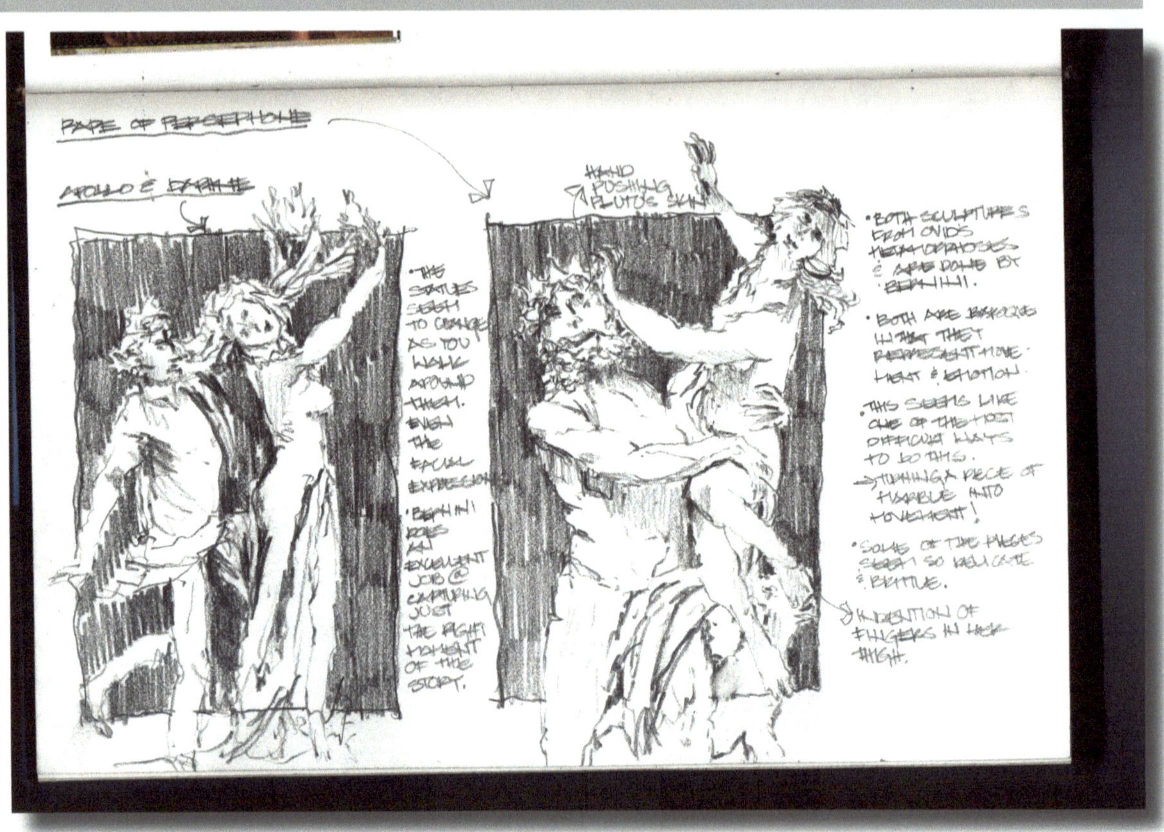

Fig. 09-37 One page journal entry, Lauren McQuillen. Pencil on paper. Italy.

EGJ-11.1

GEOFF PARKER

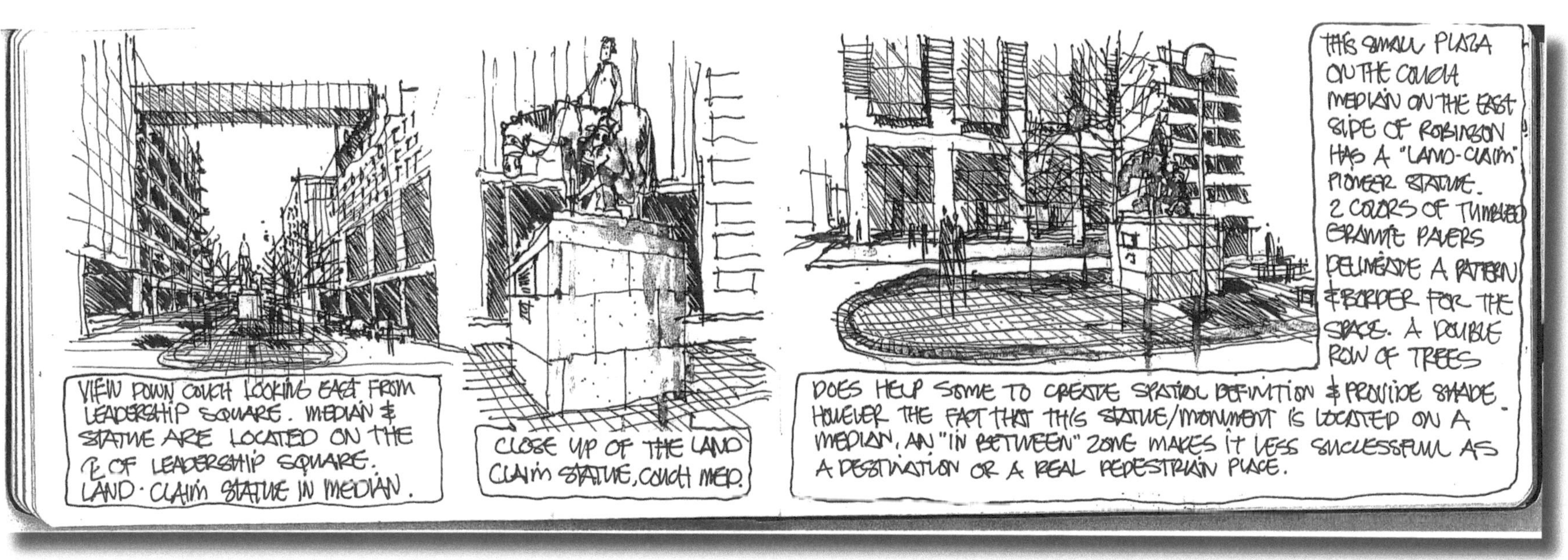

Fig. 09-38 Two-page journal entry, Geoff Parker. Pen on paper. Oklahoma City, Oklahoma.

This page is divided vertically into three sections of unequal dimensions. Each eye-level sketch is paired with an area of supporting text bound by a graphic frame. Graphic value is achieved through hatching and cross hatching and human figures are used to communicate scale and character.

EGJ-11.2

GEOFF PARKER

This two-page composition is oriented vertically and the layout is divided into four horizontal strips. Each strip contains a sketch with the supporting text located immediately below the sketch. The bottom strip uses photographs to communicate the subject matter. Graphic value is achieved through modulated hatching.

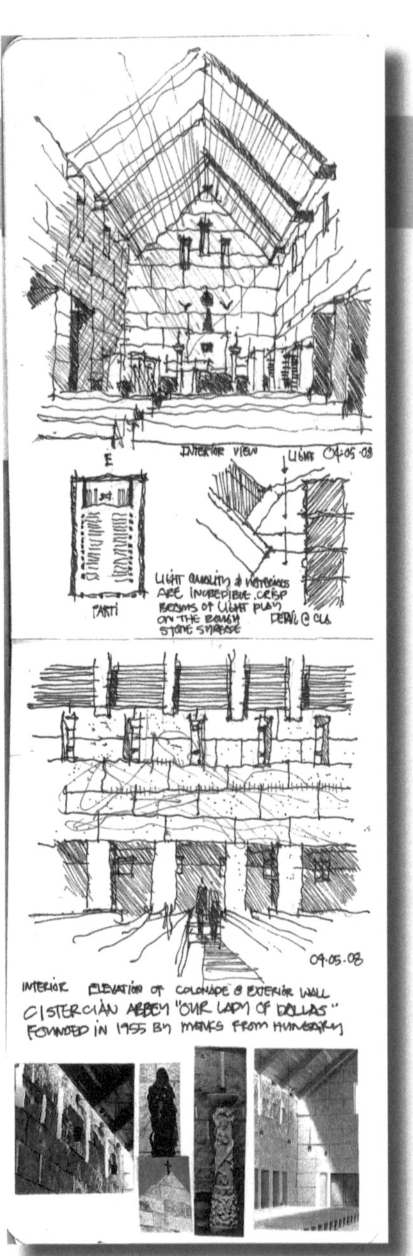

Fig. 09-39 Two-page journal entry, Geoff Parker. Pen and photography on paper. Dallas, Texas.

EGJ-12.1

SUENG RA

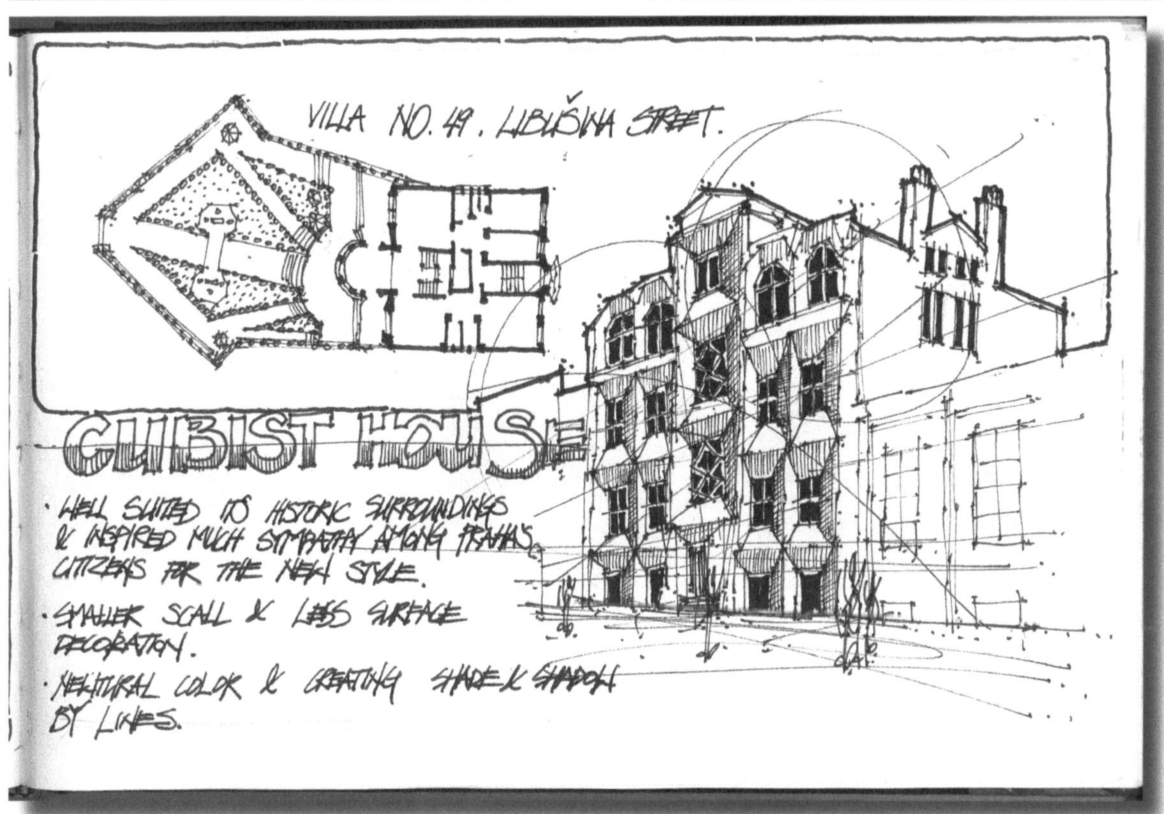

Fig. 09-40 One page journal entry, Sueng Ra. Ink on paper. Prague, Czech Republic.

The page is divided vertically into halves. The right half contains the major sketch and the left half is divided horizontally into two parts. The top part is dedicated to the secondary sketch and the lower part contains the supporting text. Hatching is used to achieve graphic value with the page title integrated within the overall composition.

EGJ-12.2

SUENG RA

This journal entry, graphic and textual, is presented as a horizontal strip of information superimposed on a blue background. This overlay technique detaches the graphic information from the page and adds a unique three-dimensional feel to the journal entry. Watercolors are used effectively to add graphic value and to communicate the character of the place.

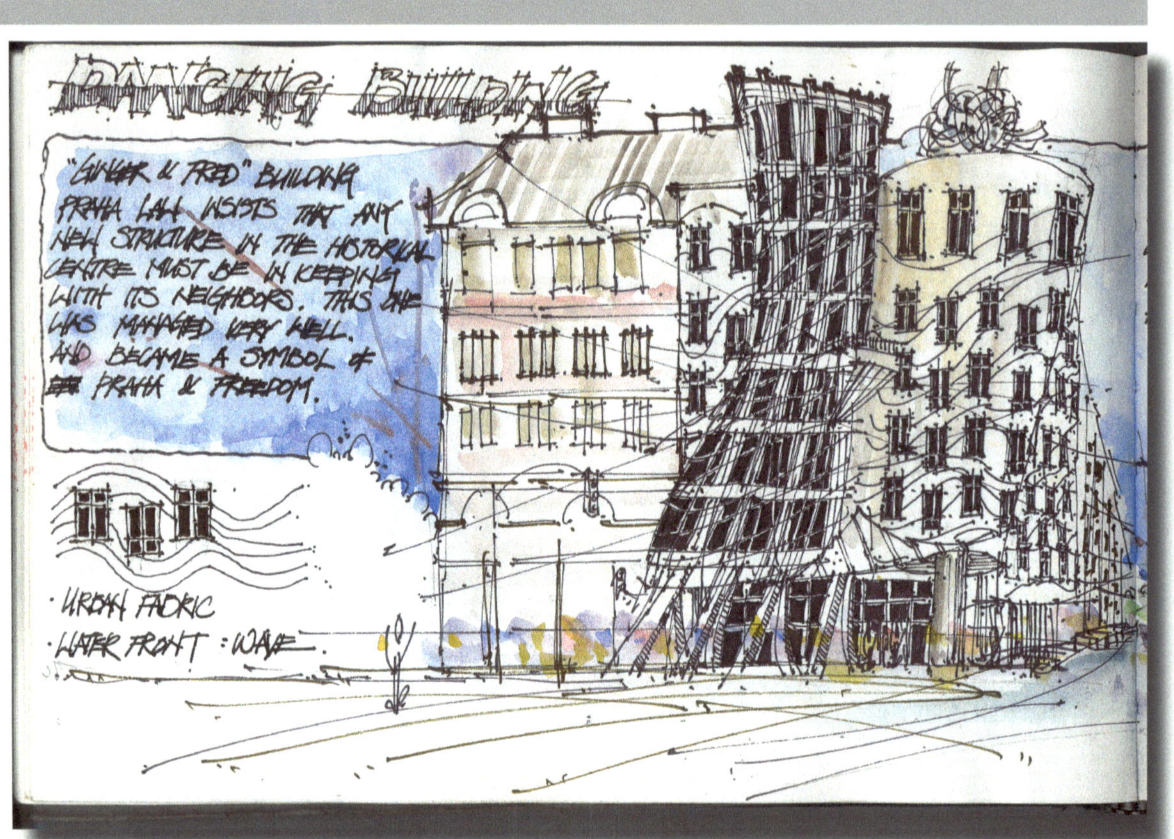

Fig. 09-41 One page journal entry, Sueng Ra. Ink and watercolors on paper. Prague, Czech Republic.

EGJ-12.3

SUENG RA

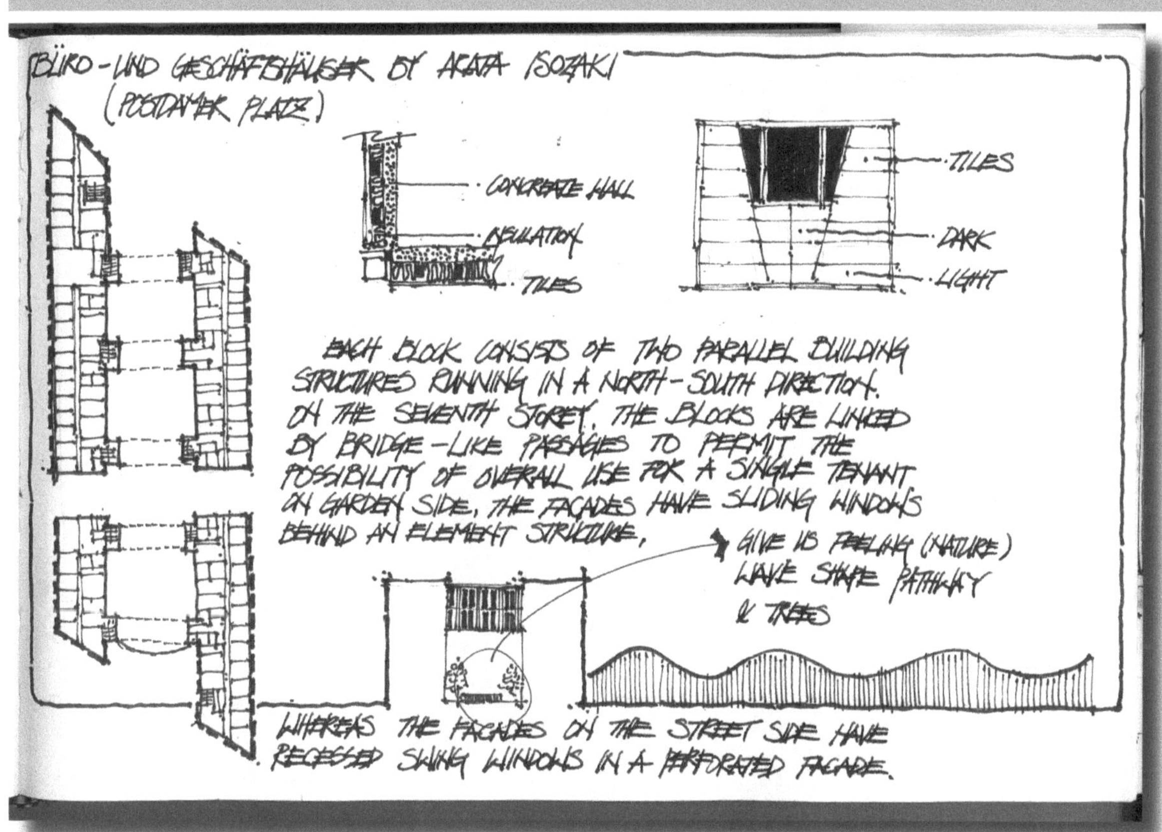

Fig. 09-42 One page journal entry, Sueng Ra. Ink on paper. Germany.

This journal entry layout is compositionally cycloidal, about the text in the center of the page. The title is connected to a frame that binds the collection of orthographic contour drawings together, even becoming the ground line of the section drawing at the bottom of the page.

EGJ-12.4

SUENG RA

This journal entry is divided into two horizontal strips of information. The bottom strip is dominated by the sketches, while the top strip became the domain for the supporting text and other diagrams. The sketches are orthogonal projections in line drawing form. Black is used to achieve high contrast in parts of the sketches; vertical hatching is used to anchor the bottom of the journal entry.

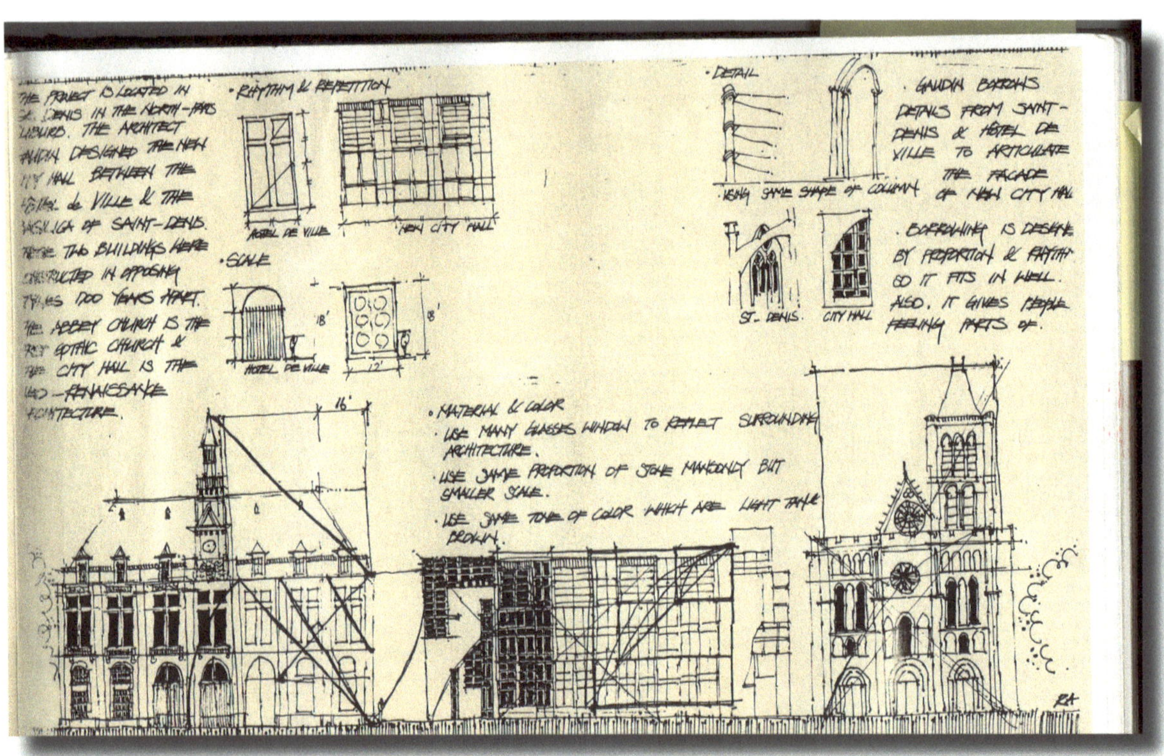

Fig. 09-43 One page journal entry, Sueng Ra. Ink on paper. St. Denis, France.

EGJ-12.5

SUENG RA

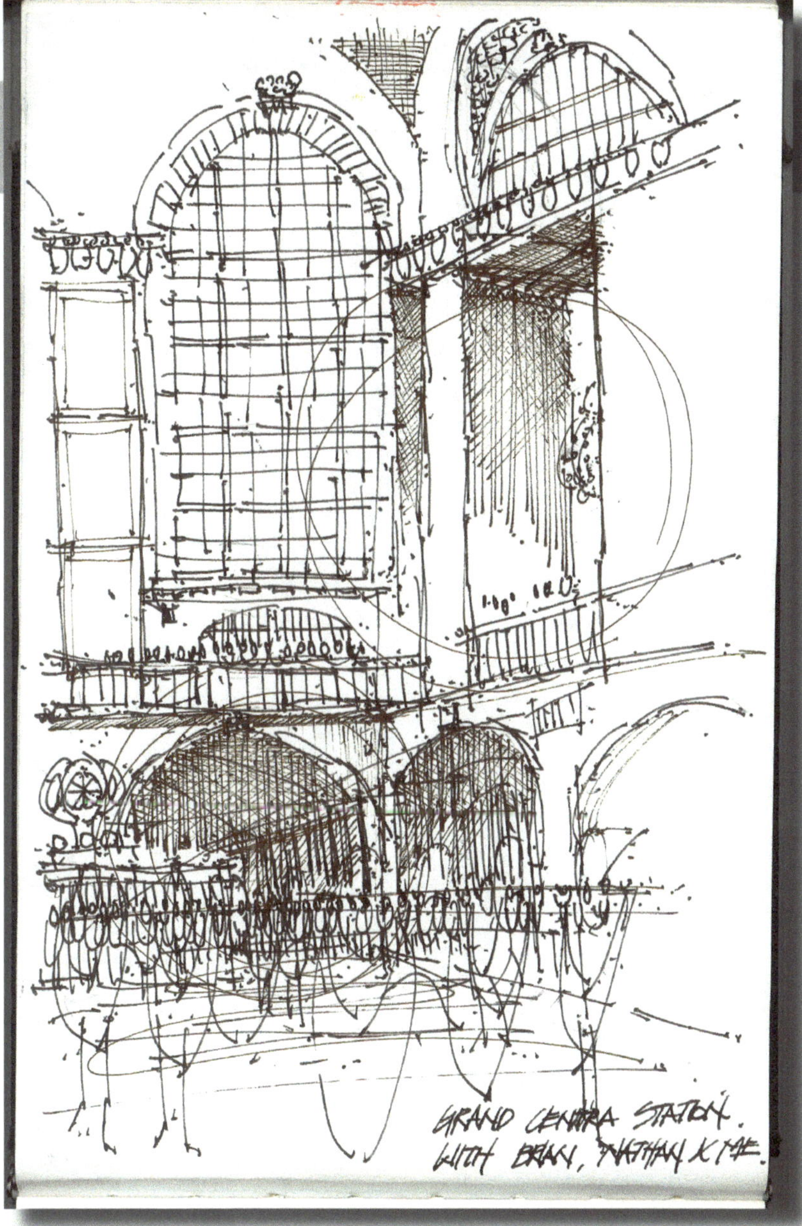

This journal page is dominated by a very intense interior view perspective sketch with no supporting text. Graphic value is achieved by hatching and cross hatching. Human figures are added and treated as transparent entities so as to not obstruct the view but to add a sense of character and scale to the space. Stipple/ graphic disease adds to the tactility of the sketch. A simple title is included towards the bottom right side of the page.

Fig. 09-44 One page journal entry, Sueng Ra. Ink on paper. New York, New York.

EGJ-12.6

SUENG RA

This is a very directional travel sketch, highlighted by the careful placement of watercolor strokes. The application of water to the sketch also interacted with the ink and gave it a wet, rainy feel. The vanishing point is intentionally shifted to the right side so as to greater reveal the left side. The addition of human figures and low graphic value towards the bottom added intensity to the already intense subject matter. The entry is contained by a graphic frame at the top, and the title and a few lines of text at the bottom.

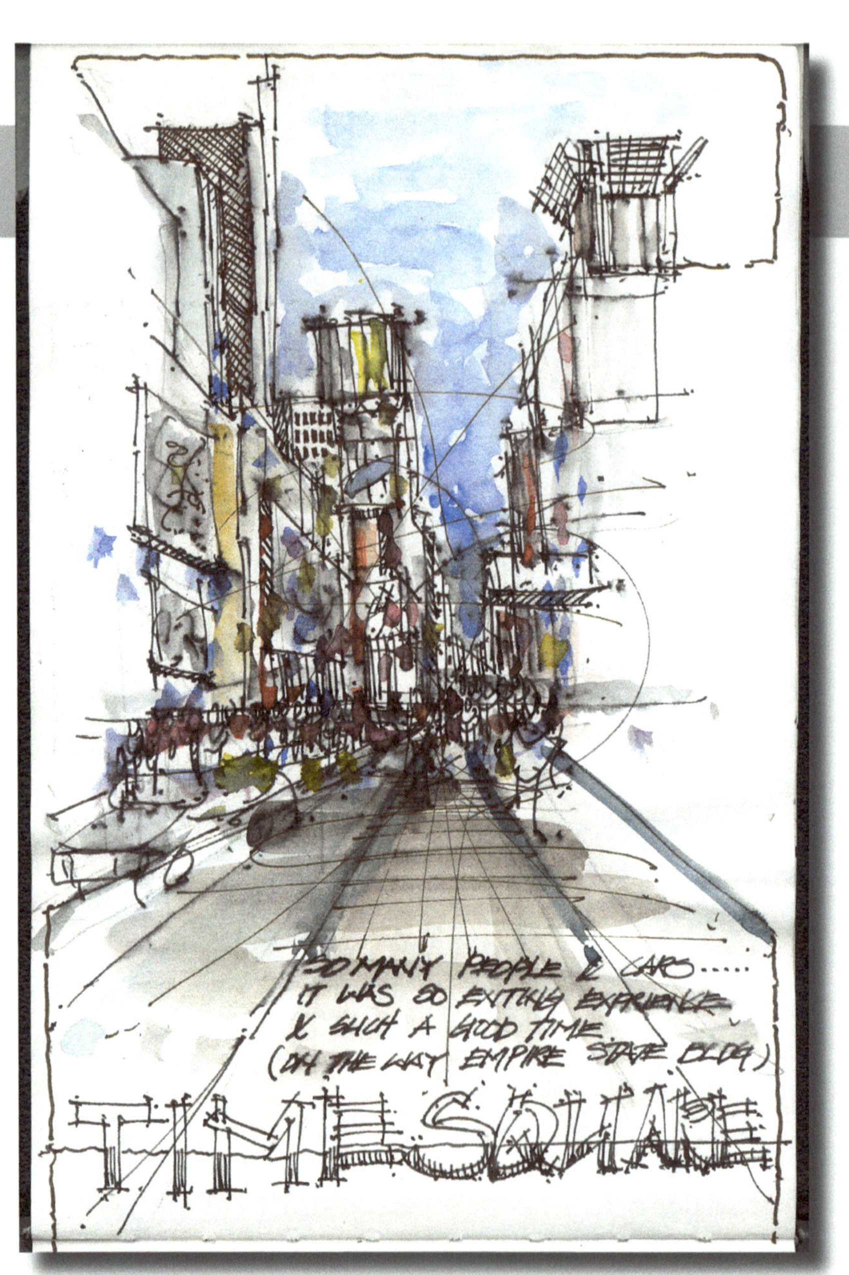

Fig. 09-45 One page journal entry, Sueng Ra. Ink and watercolors on paper. New York, New York.

EGJ-13.1

N. RICHARDSON

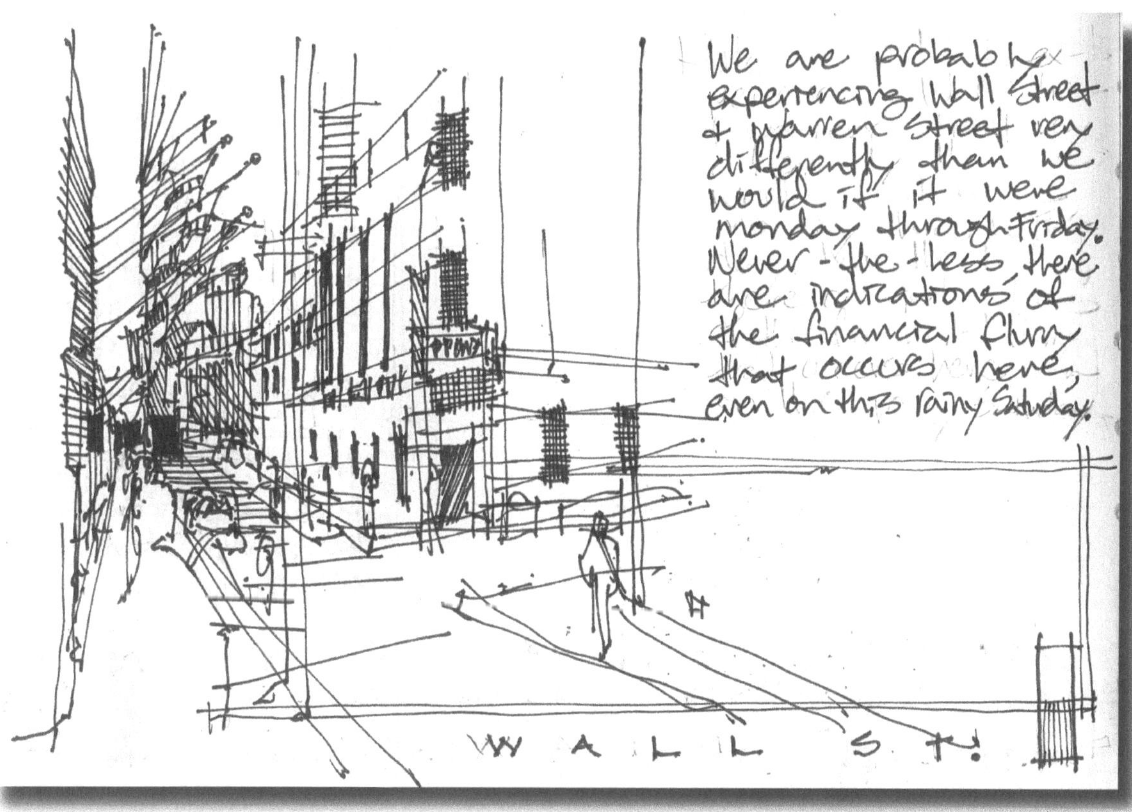

Fig. 09-46 One page journal entry, Nathan Richardson. Ink on paper. New York, New York.

This is a classic one third/two thirds vertical page layout. The street scene conveys an intense sense of perspective and the drawing technique and shading communicate the character of the subject matter. Graphic frames are skillfully integrated with the title and the supporting text is located in an empty area thus balancing the composition.

EGJ-13.2

N. RICHARDSON

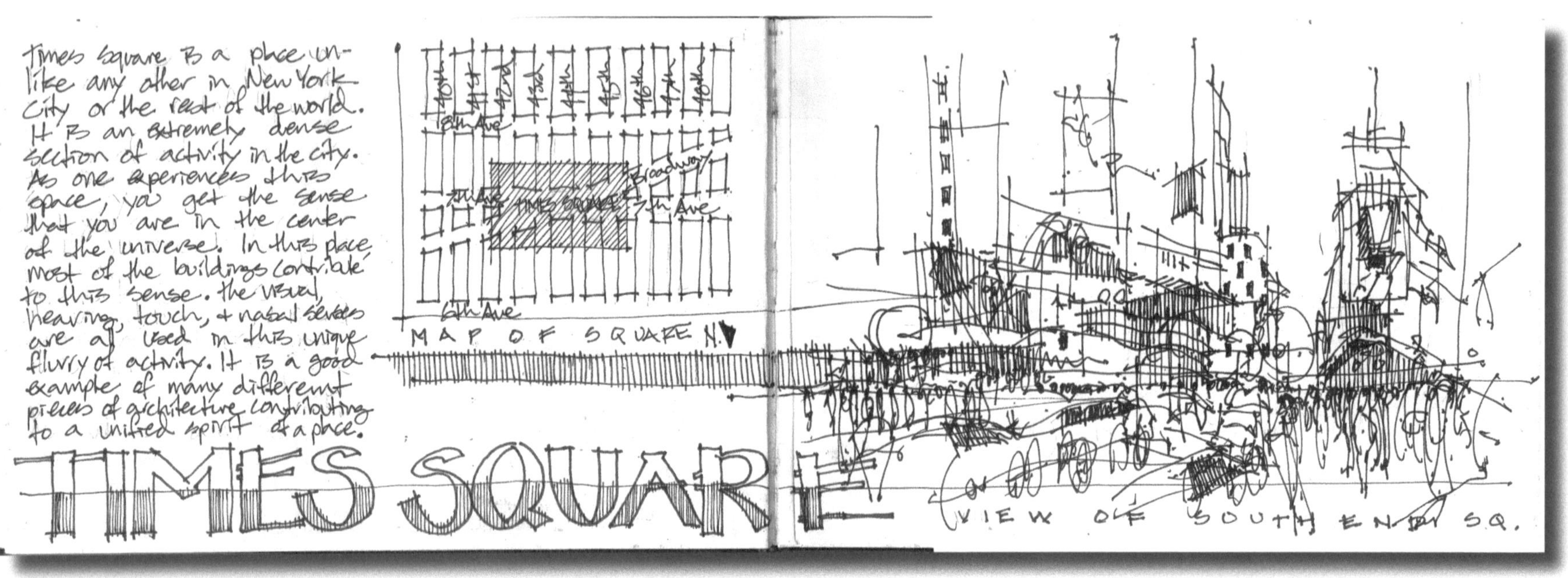

Fig. 09-47 Two-page journal entry, Nathan Richardson. Ink on paper. New York, New York.

This journal entry is divided equally between the supporting text and diagram (1/4 each), and the principal sketch (1/2). The sketch has a strong perspectival direction that forces the viewer to stay involved with the page. Vertical hatching and loose strokes convey the intensity of the atmosphere. The bottom of the layout is bound by the title.

EGJ-13.3

N. RICHARDSON

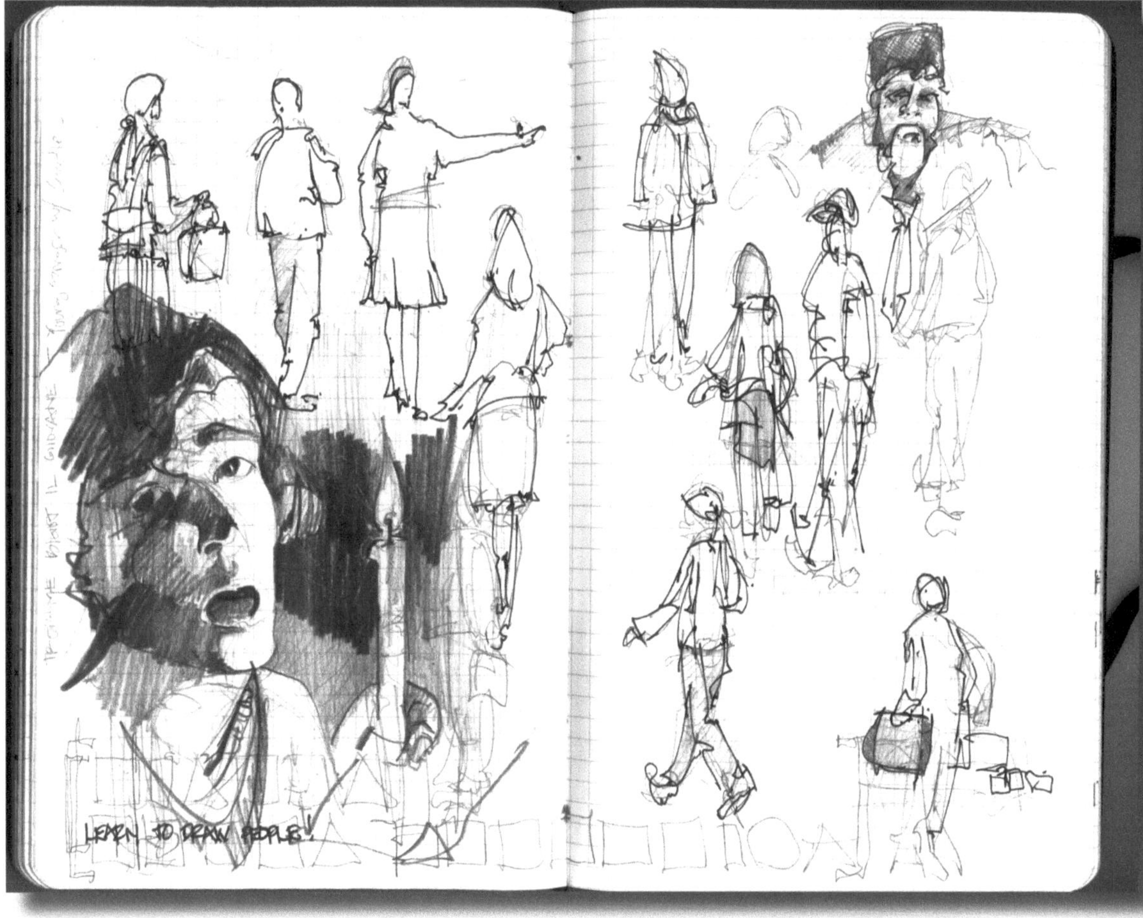

Fig. 09-48 Two-page journal entry, Nathan Richardson. Ink and pencil on paper.

The layout in this journal entry appears arbitrary; however, the inclusion of the heavily shaded figure at the bottom left of the composition conveys the message: the closer the object, the more detail. Even though the intent is simply to practice drawing people, the journal entry is well composed and titled appropriately.

EGJ-13.4

N. RICHARDSON

This journal entry is limited to a sketch and a title. The sketch has a strong sense of movement due to the location of the vanishing point at the one third point on the page. This technique stops the viewer's eye from leaving the composition. The sketch is rather complex and the graphic value is achieved through hatching and high contrast placement of solid areas of black.

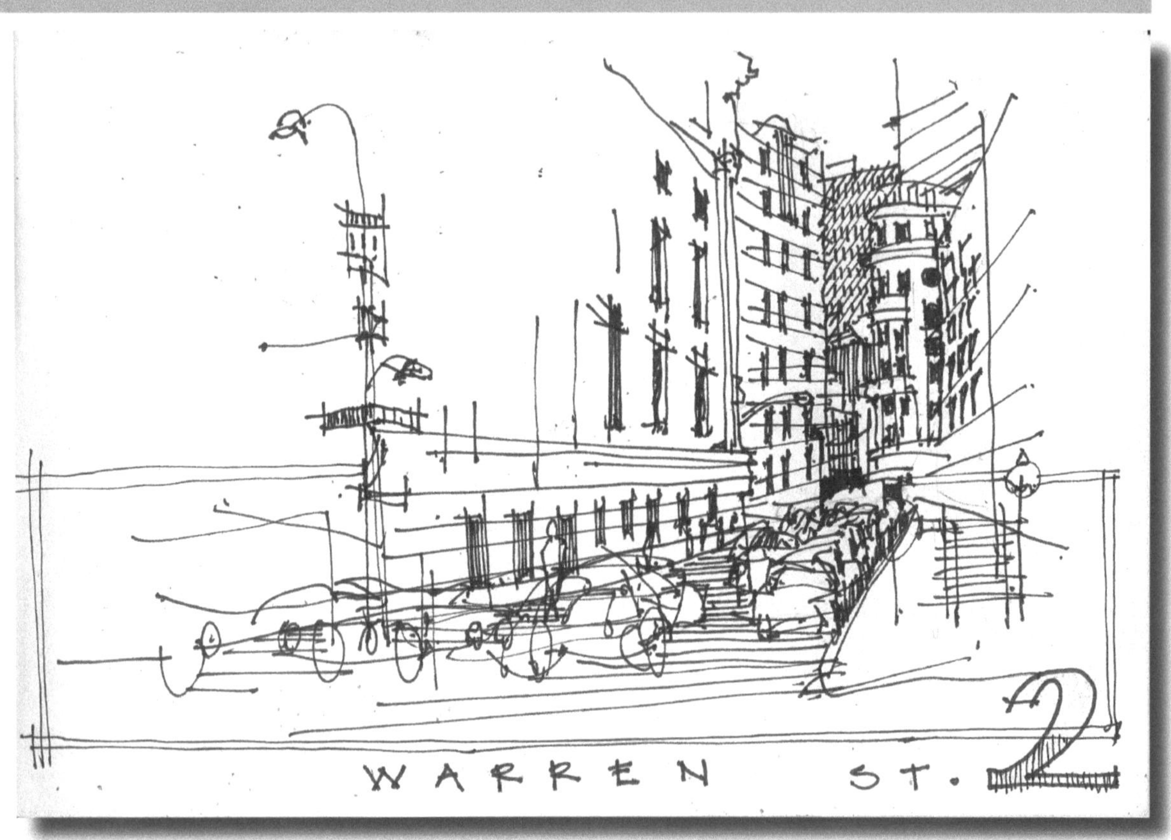

Fig. 09-49 One page journal entry, Nathan Richardson. Ink on paper. New York, New York.

EGJ-13.5

N. RICHARDSON

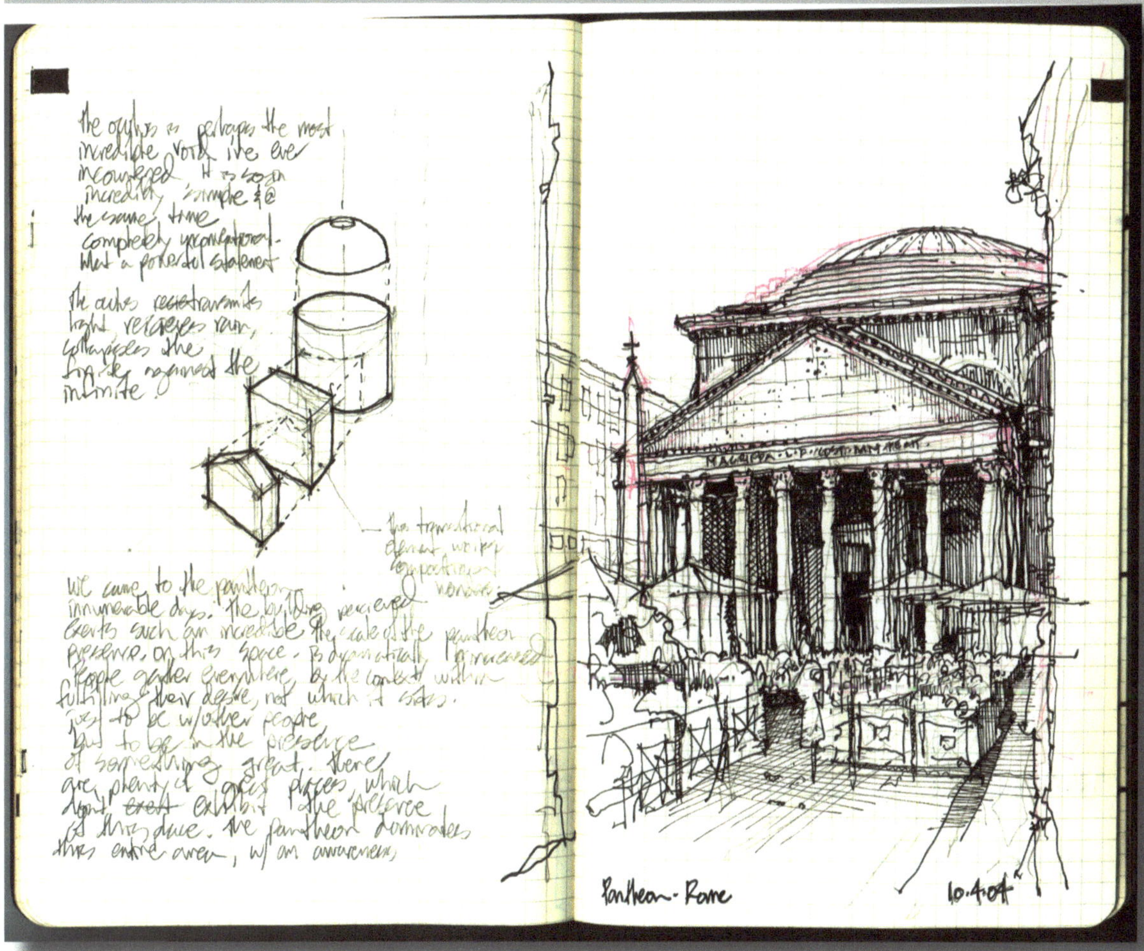

The layout is divided equally between the supporting text/diagrams and the principal sketch. The perspective sketch is very intense, and very expressive in nature. It is contained by the edges of buildings on either side of the actual view. The sketch is directional, facing the left side, which creates an immediate relationship between the text/diagram and the sketch. Hatching and cross hatching is used to develop graphic value within the composition.

Fig. 09-50 Two-page journal entry, Nathan Richardson. Ink and pencil on paper. Rome, Italy.

EGJ-13.6

N. RICHARDSON

This single page layout is divided vertically into thirds with the sketches occupying the right two thirds. The sketches are laid-out initially in pencil and later finished in ink. The plan sketch is partially superimposed on the elevation sketch to foster interaction. The supporting text is rather large and tends to overwhelm the journal entry. The title is very modest and situated at the bottom of the page to anchor the entire composition.

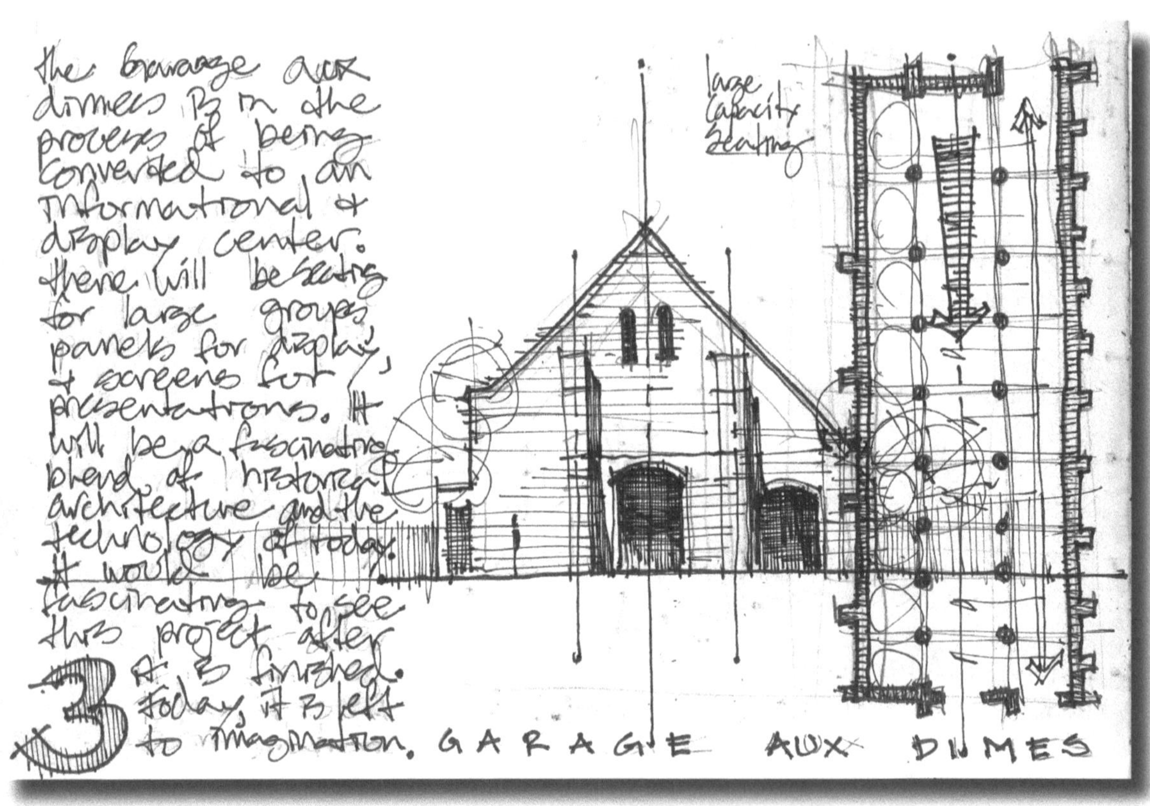

Fig. 09-51 One page journal entry, Nathan Richardson. Ink and pencil on paper. France.

EGJ-13.7

N. RICHARDSON

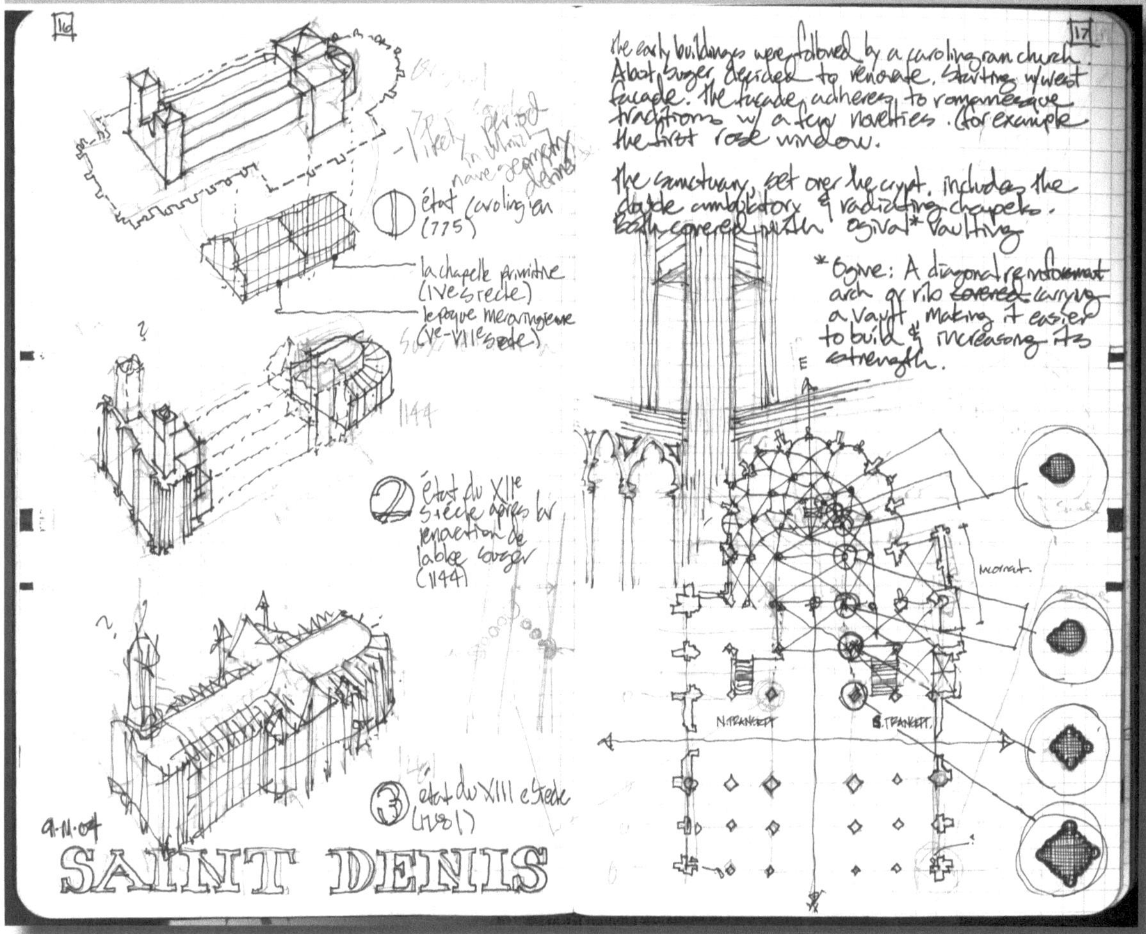

This journal page exhibits an analytical, yet casual (spontaneous) dialogue between the sketch and the supporting text. This relationship is facilitated through the use of graphic leaders. The views are artificial (non-experiential) to illustrate the analysis. The two-page composition is titled with a serif font to accentuate the historical feel of the journal entry.

Fig. 09-52 Two-page journal entry, Nathan Richardson. Ink and pencil on paper. St. Denis, France.

EGJ-13.8

N. RICHARDSON

This layout is composed of two major sketches, one per page - a gestural sketch to the right and an orthographic sketch to the left. The directional orientation and addition of shading give the perspectival sketch a sense of dominance, even though being paired with a fairly detailed floor plan. The lack of space on the pages forces the supporting text to be placed where needed, as needed, and sometimes at a different orientation. Graphic value is achieved through hatching and cross hatching.

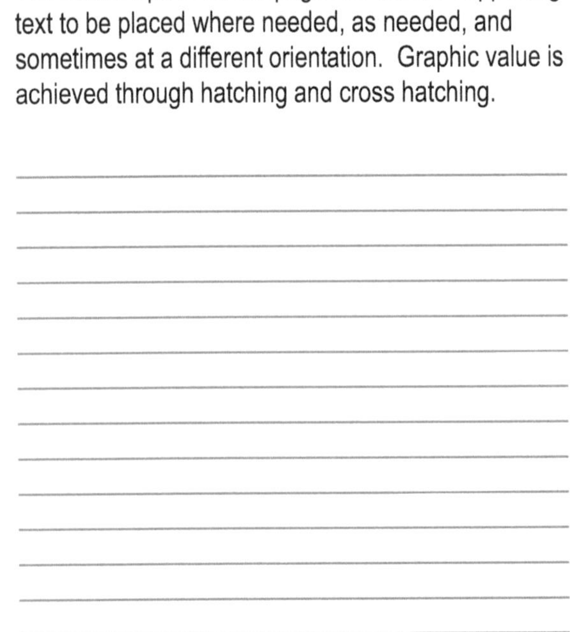

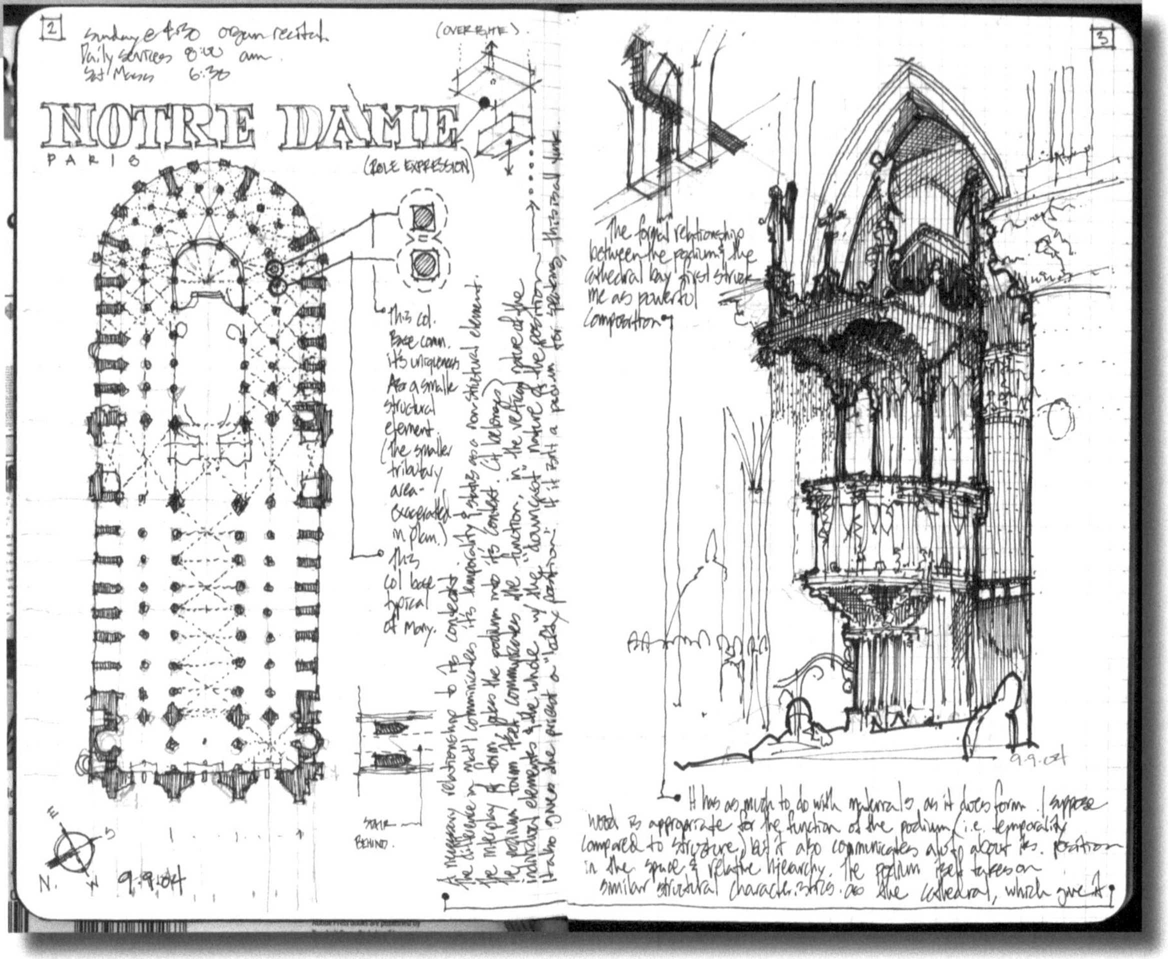

Fig. 09-53 Two-page journal entry, Nathan Richardson. Ink and pencil on paper. Paris, France.

EGJ-13.9

N. RICHARDSON

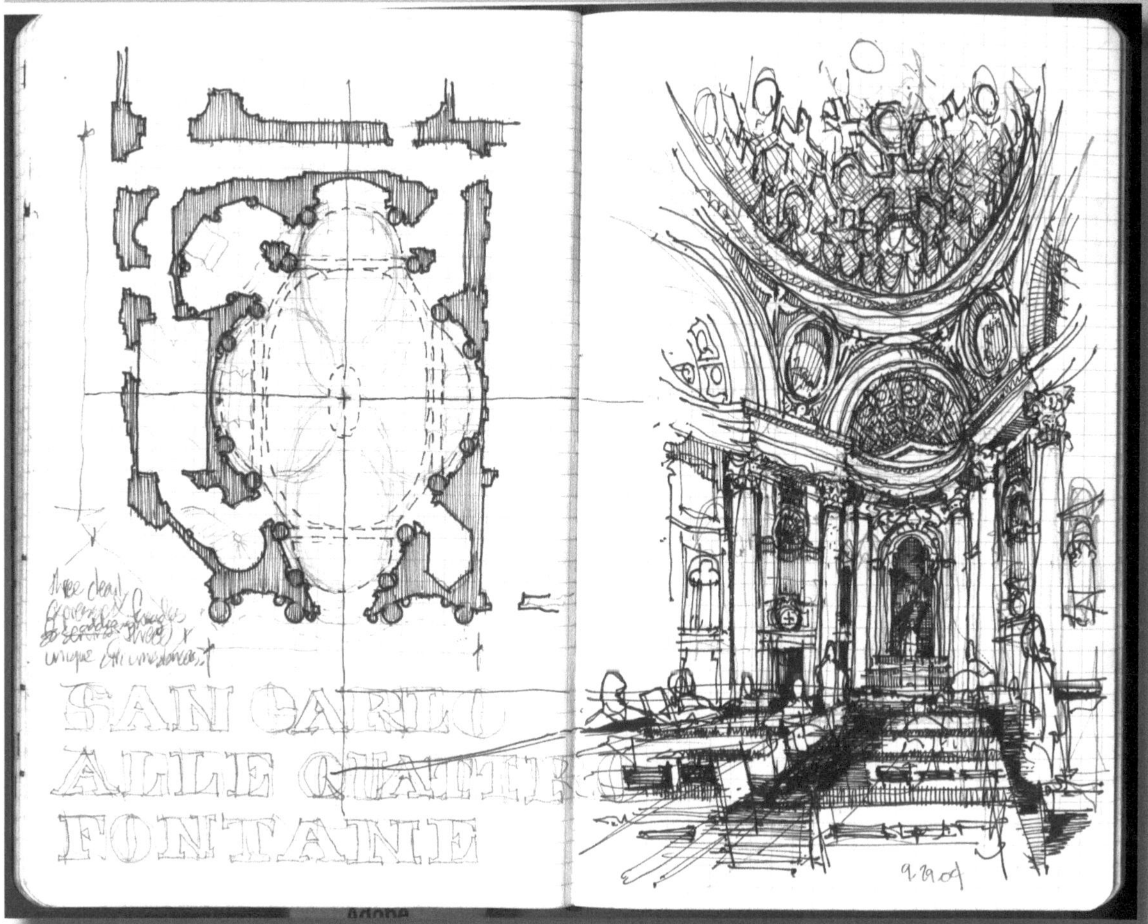

Fig. 09-54 Two-page journal entry, Nathan Richardson. Ink and pencil on paper. Italy.

This entry is composed as two separate pages on a common topic. The only item joining the two pages is the title. Though the plan diagram to the left is fairly detailed, the emphasis remains on the perspective sketch because of the intensity of linework. The placement of the vanishing point at the intersection of the lower right third of the sheet adds to the sense of drama of the overall composition.

EGJ-13.10

N. RICHARDSON

The two pages of the journal are combined to form a tableau, a single sheet with the main sketch facing the left and the amount of detail fading towards the edges of the pages. The title is very faintly added to the left as a graphic edge element. Graphic value is achieved through modulated hatching and cross hatching that decreases in value as it recedes into the picture plane.

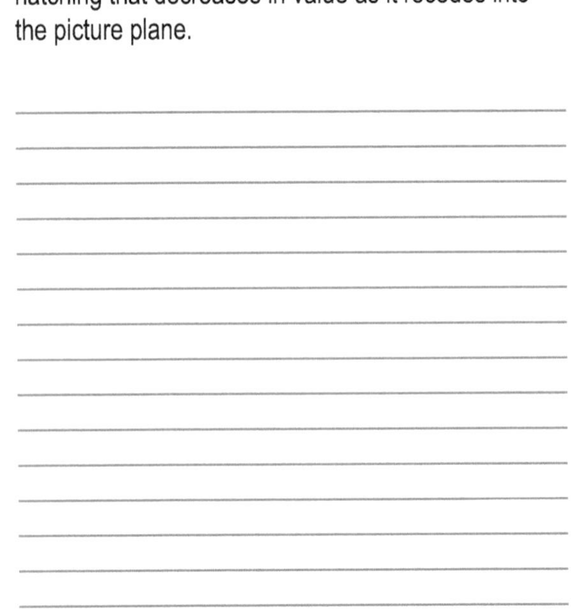

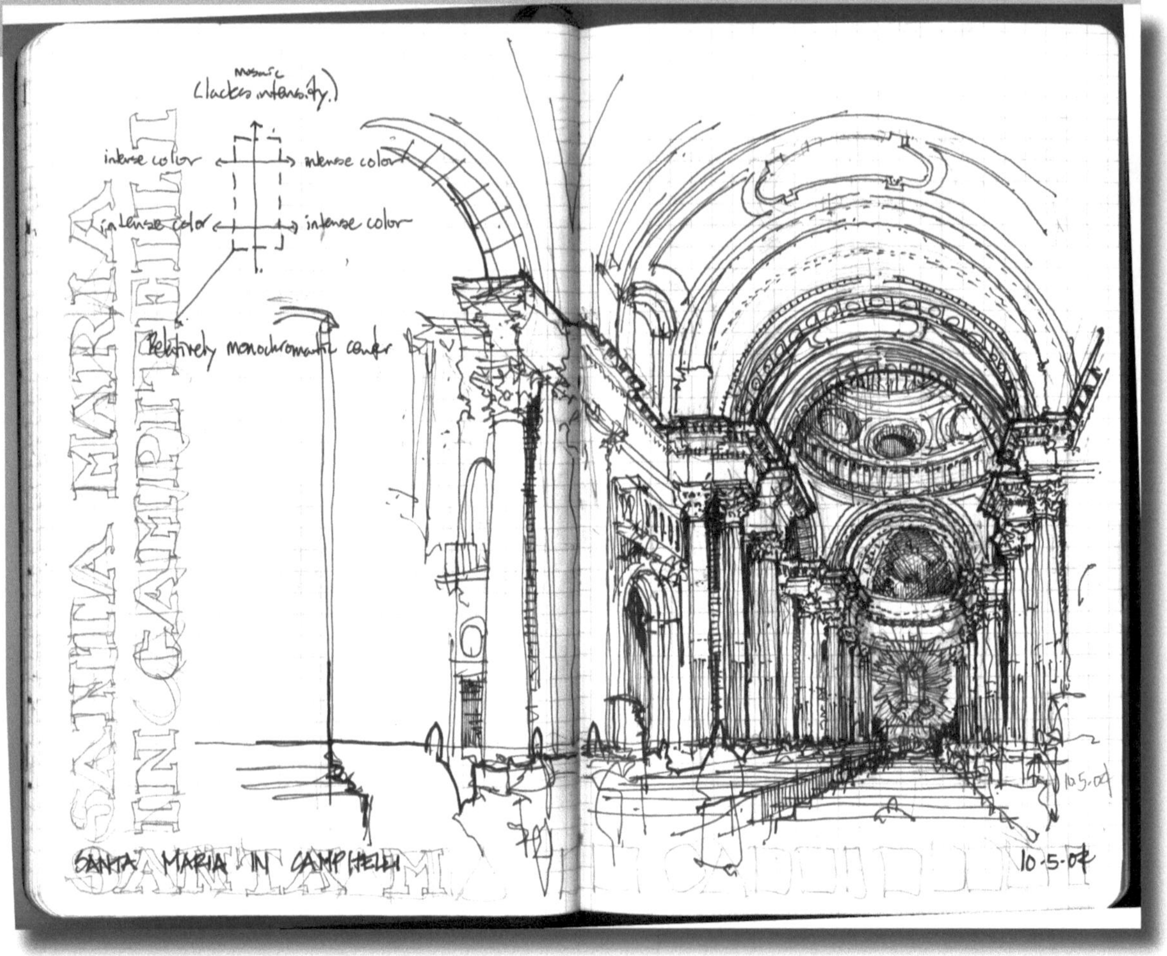

Fig. 09-55 Two-page journal entry, Nathan Richardson. Ink and pencil on paper. Italy.

EGJ-14.1

J. SALMONS

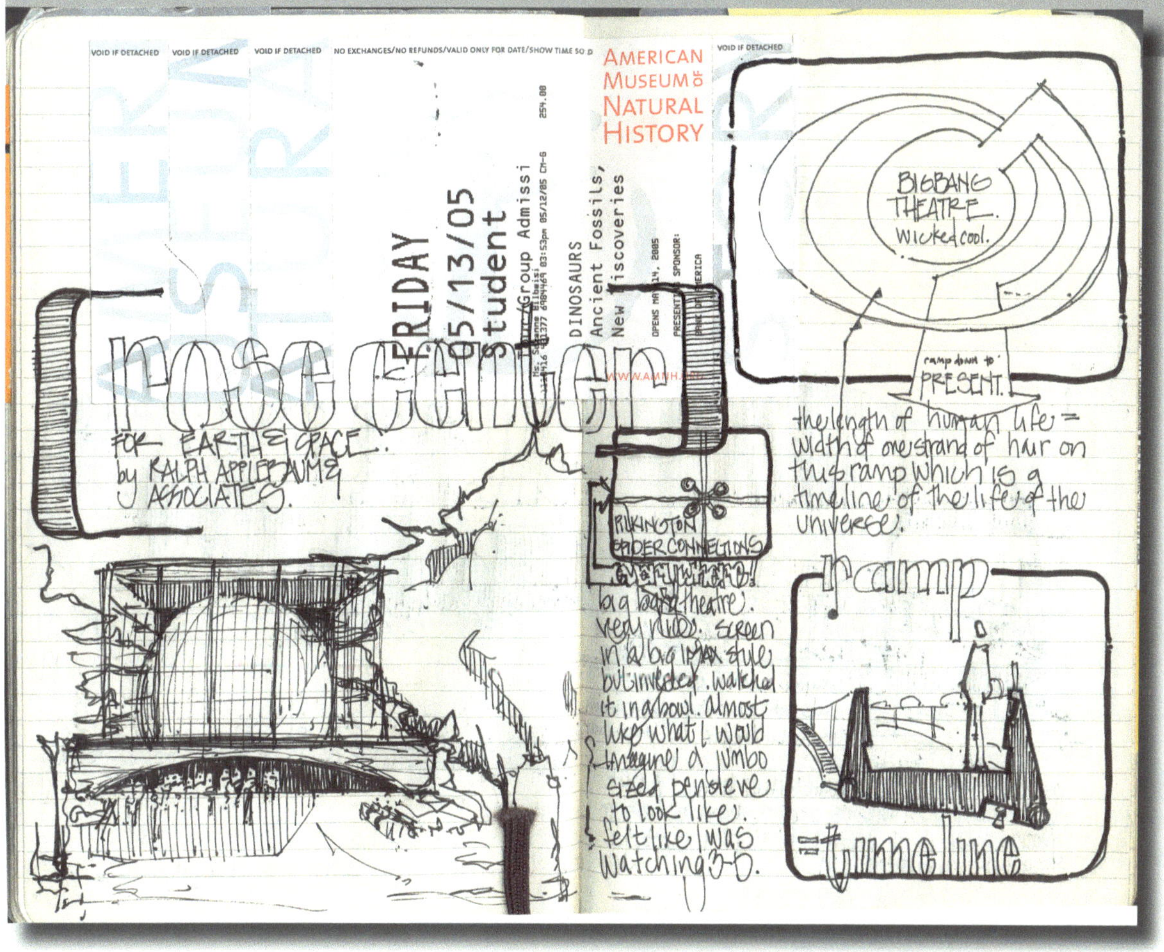

In this two-page layout, the prominent sketch occupies the bottom left area. Two secondary diagram sketches are included as vignettes. The use of line modulation, thin and thick, is very effective in giving depth to the journal entry. The title is highly stylized, reaching across the two pages and bracketed. Supporting text is nestled between the sketches. The entry ticket is added to the composition to personalize the experience.

Fig. 09-56 Two-page journal entry, Jacque Salmons. Ink on paper. New York, New York.

EGJ-14.2

J. SALMONS

The pages with their frames of graphic information are almost independent, only connected by a low value title spanning across the bottom of the two page spread. There is a consistent intensity of the linework throughout the journal entry; the entry ticket is included as an element of color to add drama. Bracketing and line modulation are used successfully to add depth and graphic value to the journal entry.

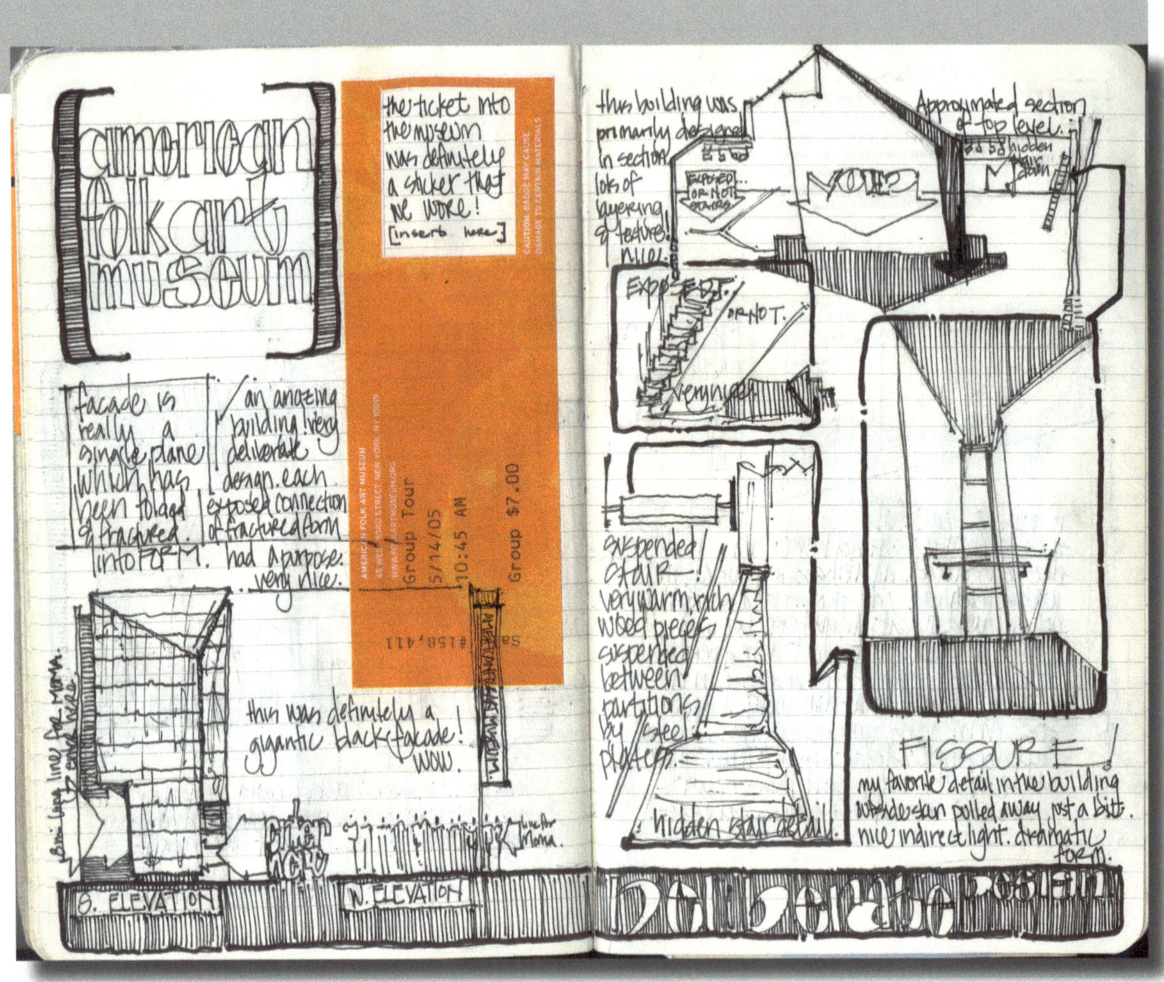

Fig. 09-57 Two-page journal entry, Jacque Salmons. Ink on paper. New York, New York.

EGJ-15.1

SCOTT SMARDO

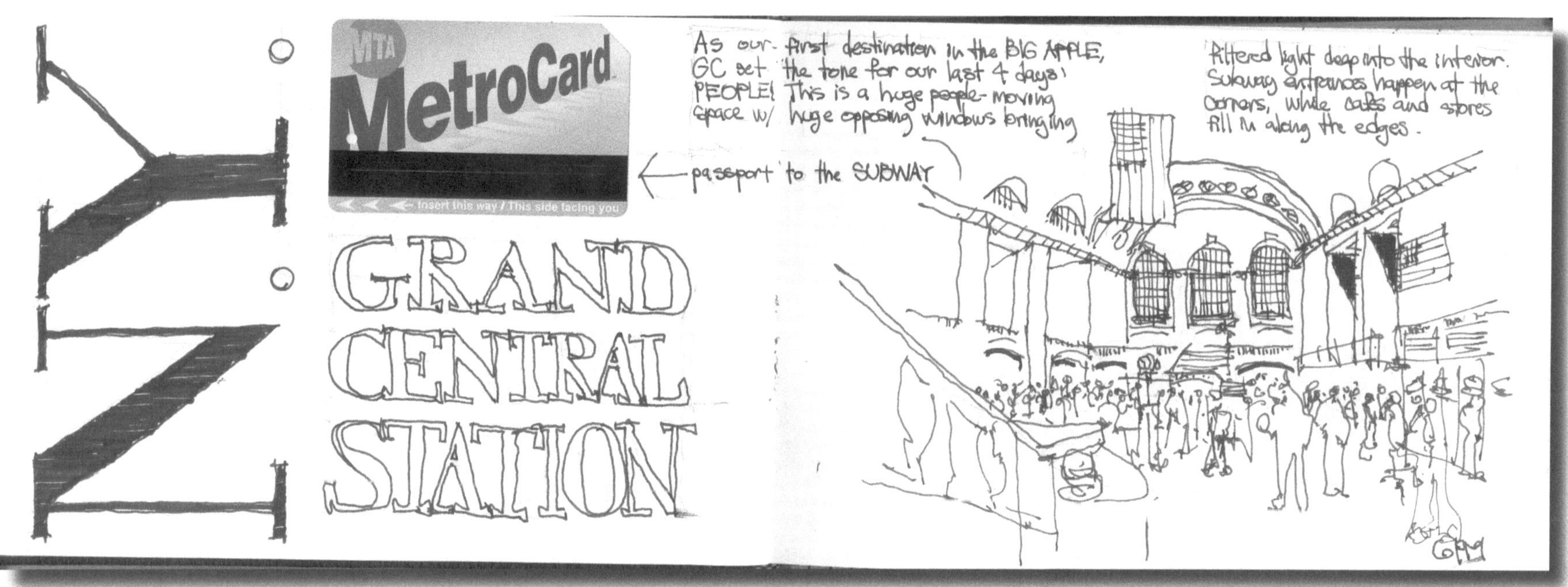

Fig. 09-58 Two-page journal entry, Scott Smardo. Ink on paper. New York, New York.

This journal entry uses two pages to communicate a single topic. The main sketch is located on the right side with the large title occupying the left page. The supporting text atop the sketch is used as a unifying element to join the two pages and add graphic value to the composition.

EGJ-15.2

SCOTT SMARDO

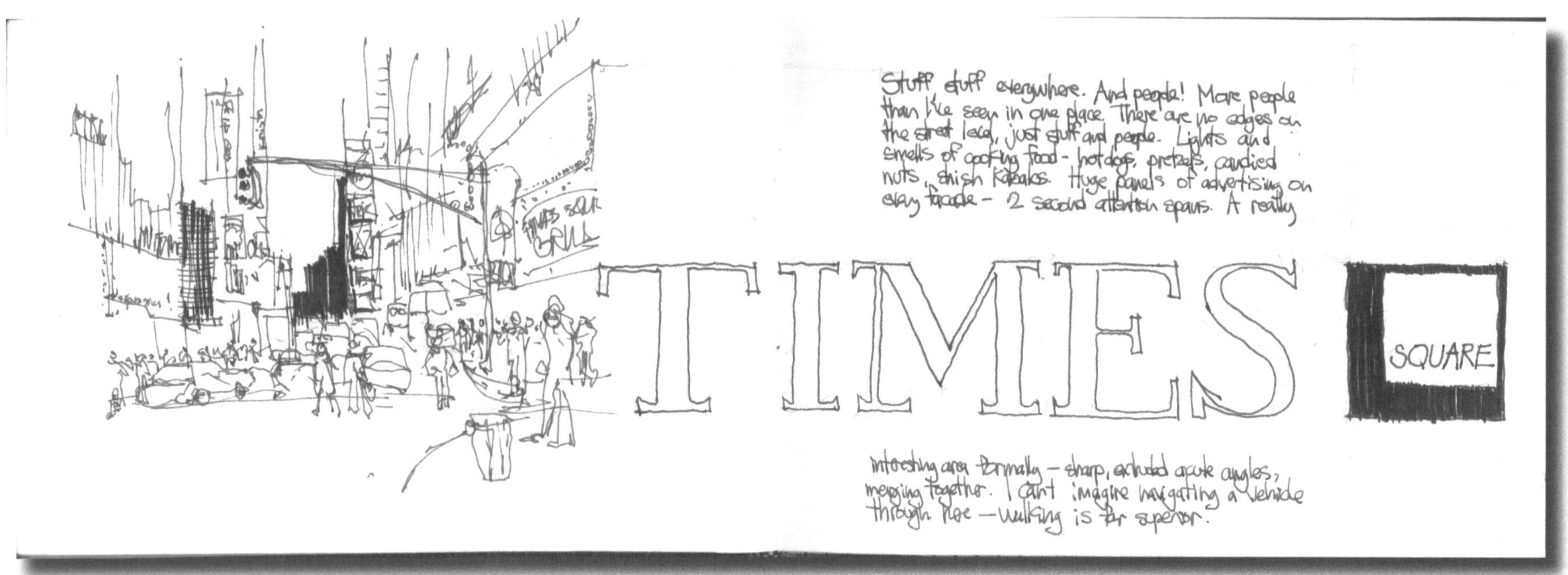

Fig. 09-59 Two-page journal entry, Scott Smardo. Ink on paper. New York, New York.

This journal entry uses a a single eye-level contour sketch with some low graphic values to achieve focus. The two-page spread is minimally composed, which aids in achieving clarity. The page titles are highly articulated and work compositionally to unify the lengthy landscape format.

EGJ-15.3

SCOTT SMARDO

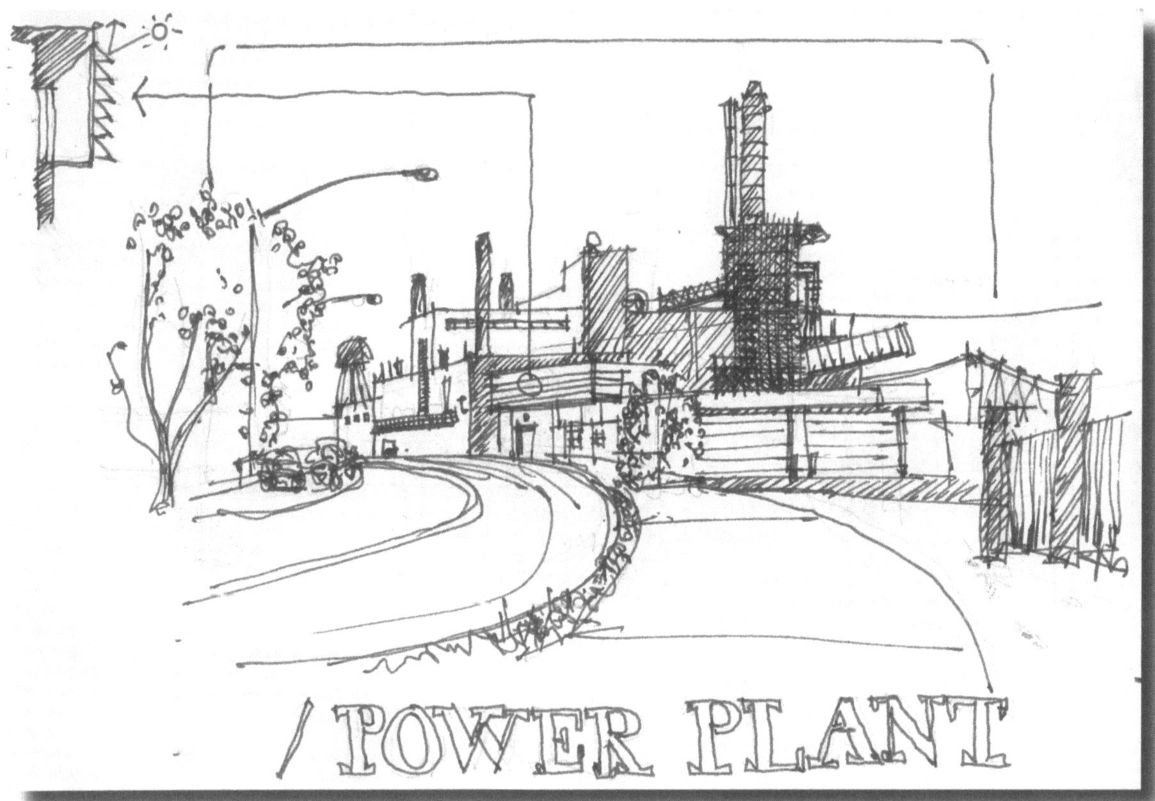

Fig. 09-60 One page journal entry, Scott Smardo. Ink on paper. Alaska.

This single page composition contains a single sketch situated at the center of the page. The sketch exhibits strong perspectival tendencies through the convergence of the edges of the road at the left one third point of the page. This adds a dynamic quality to the entry, which is balanced by the large area of cross hatching at the right one third point. A section detail is included towards the top left side of the page with the exact location indicated by a graphic leader. Graphic value is achieved through hatching and cross hatching.

EGJ-15.4

SCOTT SMARDO

In this single page layout, the sketch is situated in the center, though being a bit partial to the top two thirds of the page. A graphic frame is integrated with the pictorial elements within the sketch to graphically detach it from the page. Notation and graphic leaders are added to explain and communicate the experience. The placement of the notes is not confined to a particular location on the page.

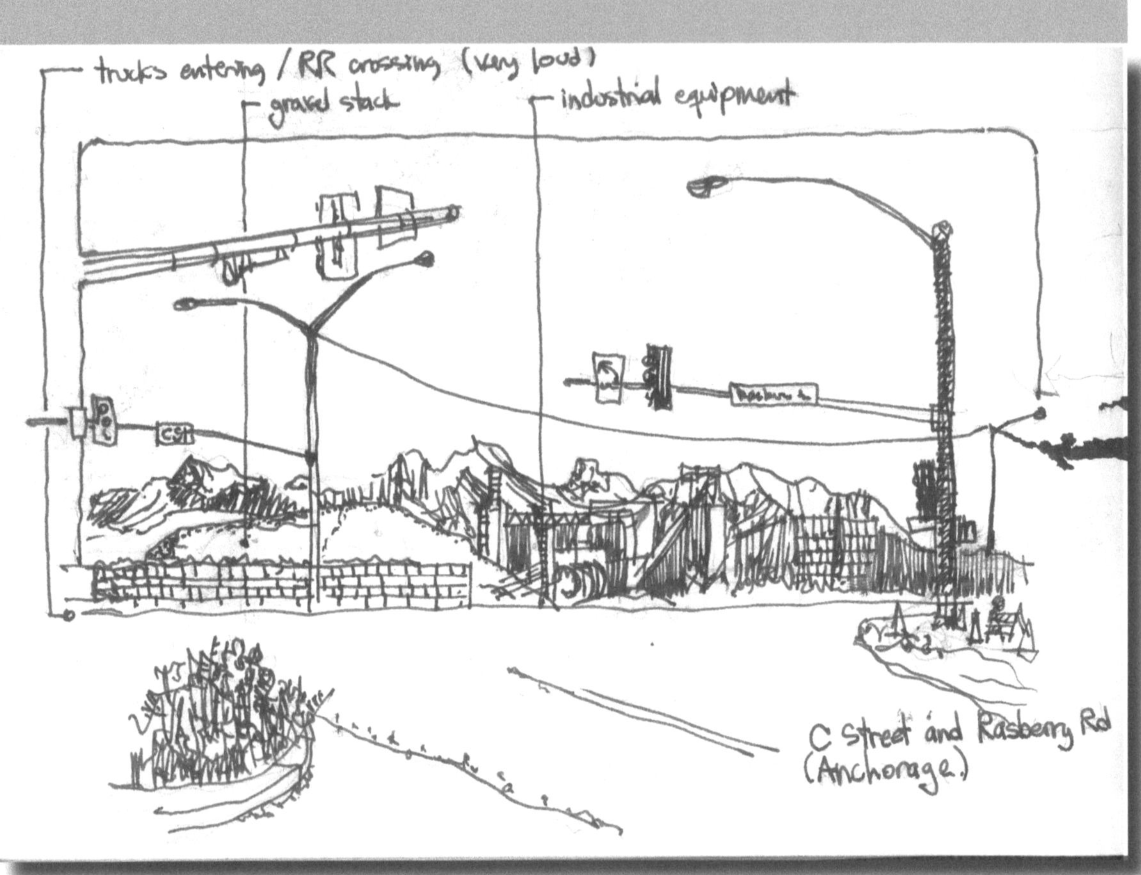

Fig. 09-61 One page journal entry, Scott Smardo. Ink on paper. Alaska.

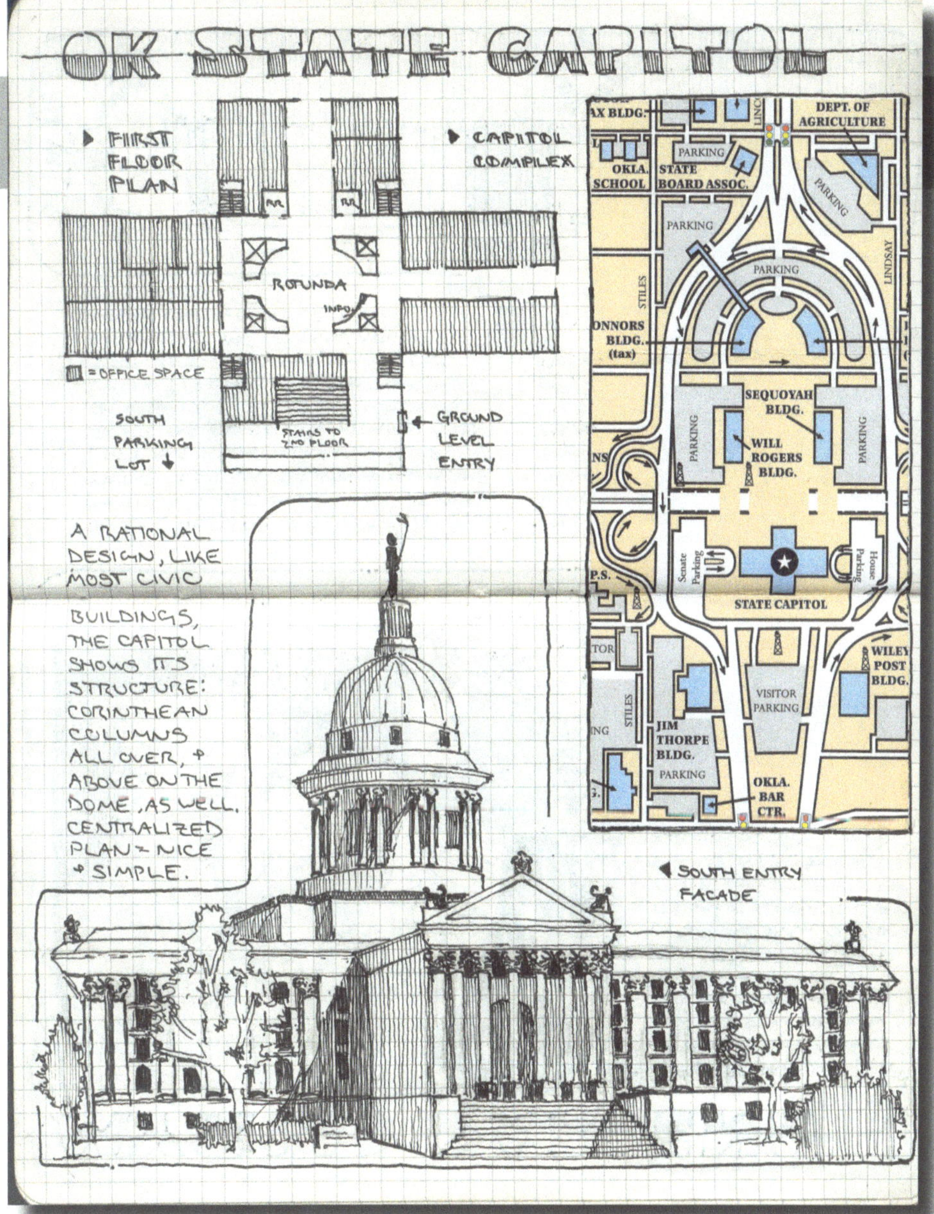

EGJ-16.1

J. SPLINTER

This two-page composition is oriented vertically with the primary sketch/lowest value anchoring the layout. This sketch is surrounded by a graphic frame to further detach it from the page. A secondary plan sketch is suspended above the main sketch and a printed location map is adhered to the right side. The supporting text is positioned in the space adjacent to the sketch frame, thus completing the overall rectangular geometry of the composition.

Fig. 09-62 Two-page journal entry, Janelle Splinter. Ink on paper. Washington, D.C.

EGJ-17.1

FLYNN THOMAS

These pages are consistently ordered in a one-third/ two-third composition in landscape format. Color photography is utilized in lieu of the hand drawn sketch. Since the photograph has the lowest graphic value, it was situated to the right side to form the edge of the layout. Extensive supporting text is keyed to the image via graphic leaders. Journal titles are also placed consistently at the same location. Such an approach to journaling is possible due to advances in digital photography and printing. Spontaneous notation is a challenge when journaling through photography.

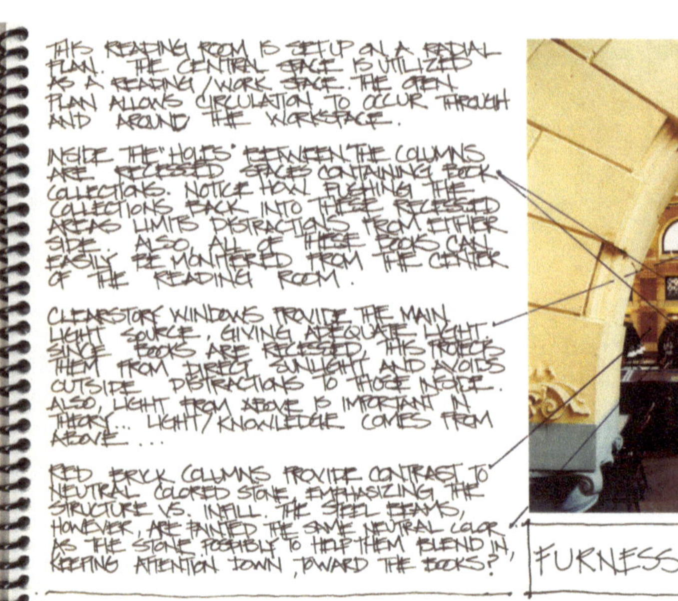

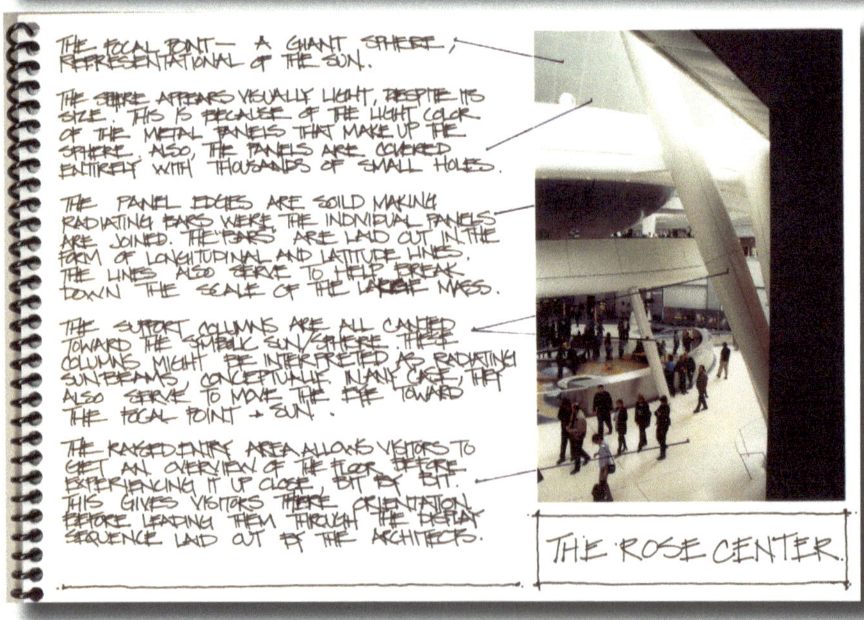

Fig. 09-63 One page journal entries, Flynn Thomas. Ink and photography on paper. Philadelphia, Pennsylvania, and Washington, D.C.

EGJ-18.1

ERIC VOGT

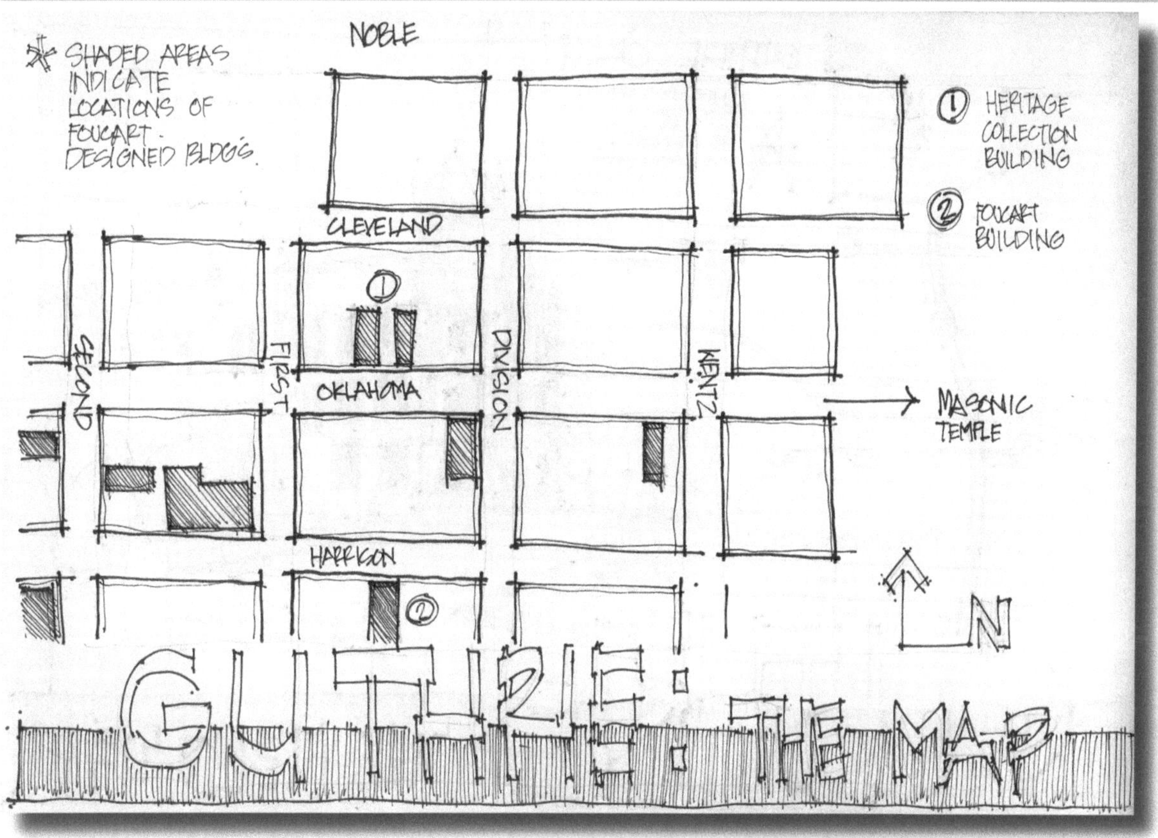

Fig. 09-64 One page journal entry, Eric Vogt. Ink on paper. Guthrie, Oklahoma.

This layout was created as the title page for a series of analytical sketches, and is composed of a location map and a large title. The page is anchored by a stylized title superimposed over a low value hatched graphic strip. The various graphic elements, including the supporting text, are composed to occupy an implied overall rectangular geometry.

EGJ-18.2

ERIC VOGT

This analytical study is composed with an orthogonal high contrast sketch forming a horizontal strip across the page. The page itself is anchored by a low value journal entry title across the entire width of the page. The notation and the supporting text are tied to the sketch through graphic leaders. Graphic value is achieved through hatching and high contrast shading.

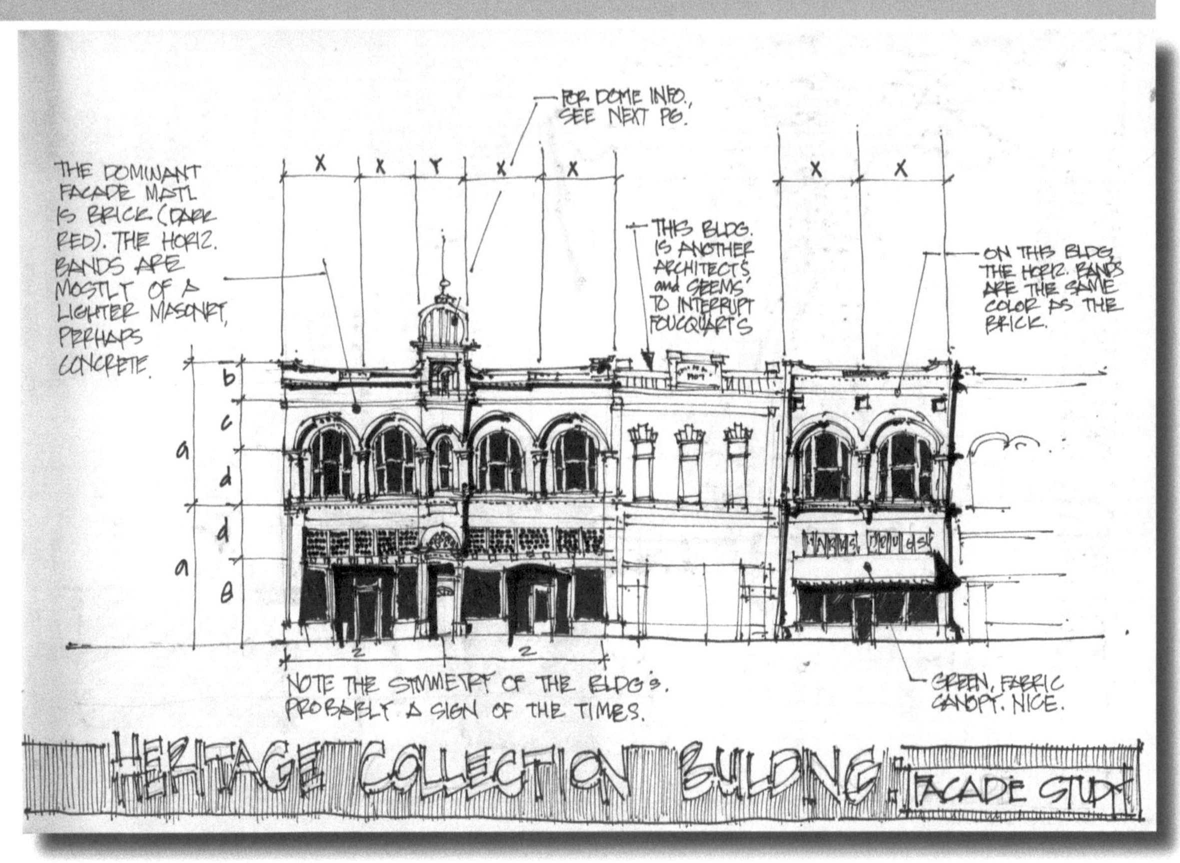

Fig. 09-65 One page journal entry, Eric Vogt. Ink on paper. Guthrie, Oklahoma.

EGJ-18.3

ERIC VOGT

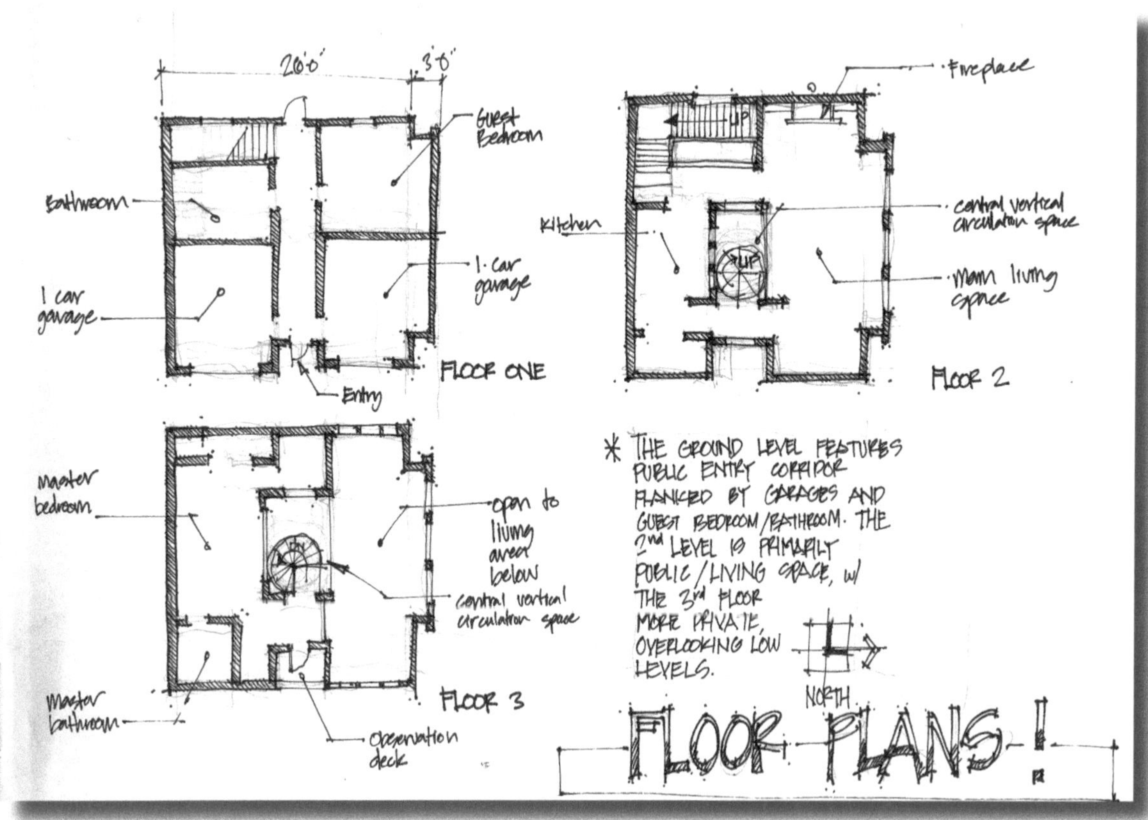

Fig. 09-66 One page journal entry, Eric Vogt. Ink on paper. Stillwater, Oklahoma.

This single page composition is arranged in quadrants; three orthographic projections and the supporting text. Secondary notation is keyed to the sketches via graphic leaders. A casual entry title is added and incorporated with the supporting text.

EGJ-18.4

ERIC VOGT

The single page composition is divided into halves. Each half is occupied by an axonometric (paraline) sketch. The sketch to the right is an explodometric, an artificial view of the structure with roof detached and the walls removed. Notations form a circular pattern surrounding each sketch and are keyed to the sketches via graphic leaders.

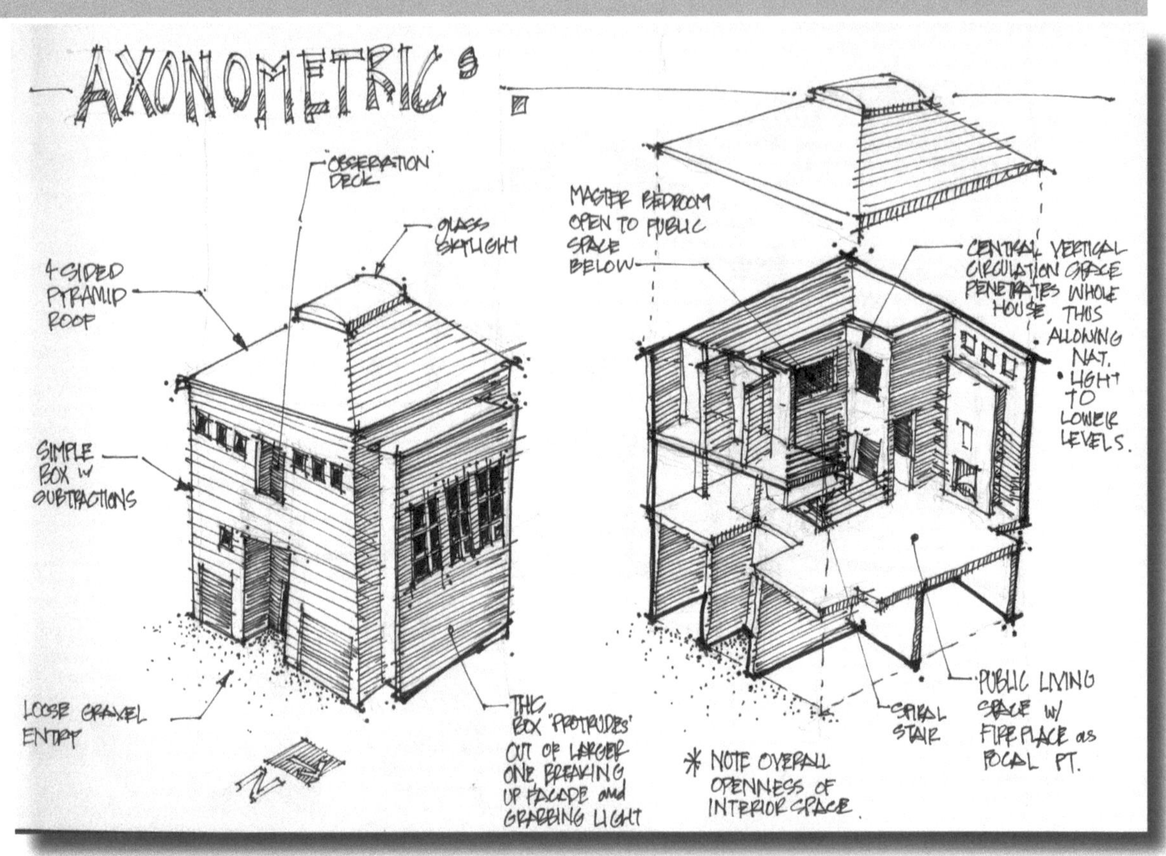

Fig. 09-67 One page journal entry, Eric Vogt. Ink on paper. Stillwater, Oklahoma.

EGJ-18.5

ERIC VOGT

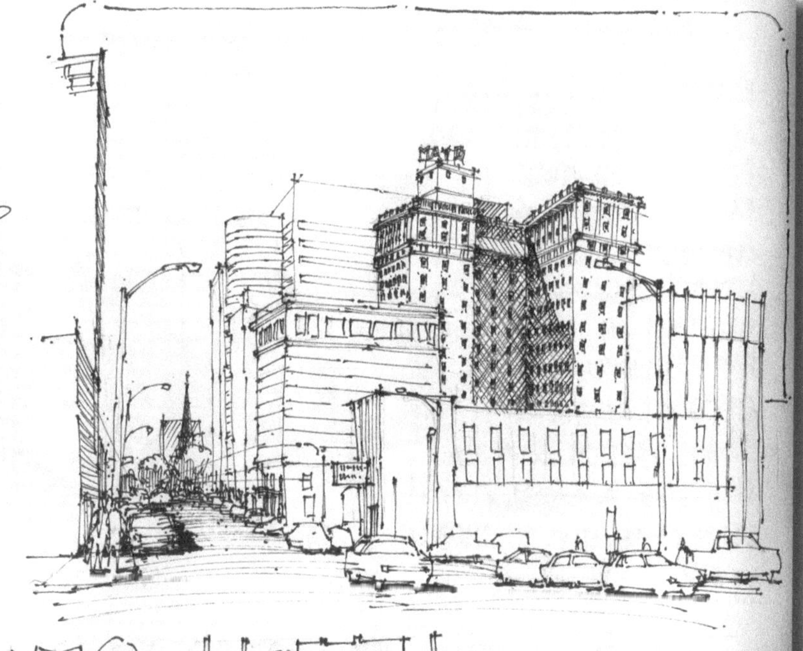

Fig. 09-68 One page journal entry, Eric Vogt. Ink on paper. Tulsa, Oklahoma.

This single page layout has a classic one-third/ two-third composition, with an eye-level sketch occupying the right two thirds. Graphic value modulation is achieved through hatching and cross hatching. A graphic frame is used to detach the sketch from the page. The supporting text is organized within an implied column with the page entry title informally located at the bottom to graphically anchor the page.

EGJ-18.6

ERIC VOGT

The single page journal entry is focused upon an analytical orthographic sketch. The sketch occupies the right two thirds of the sheet, with white space in the remaining one third. Low value hatching is applied to the background to provide better contrast, while the sketch sits on a thick line. Notation is kept to a minimum and the title is scripted in an informal font towards the top of the page.

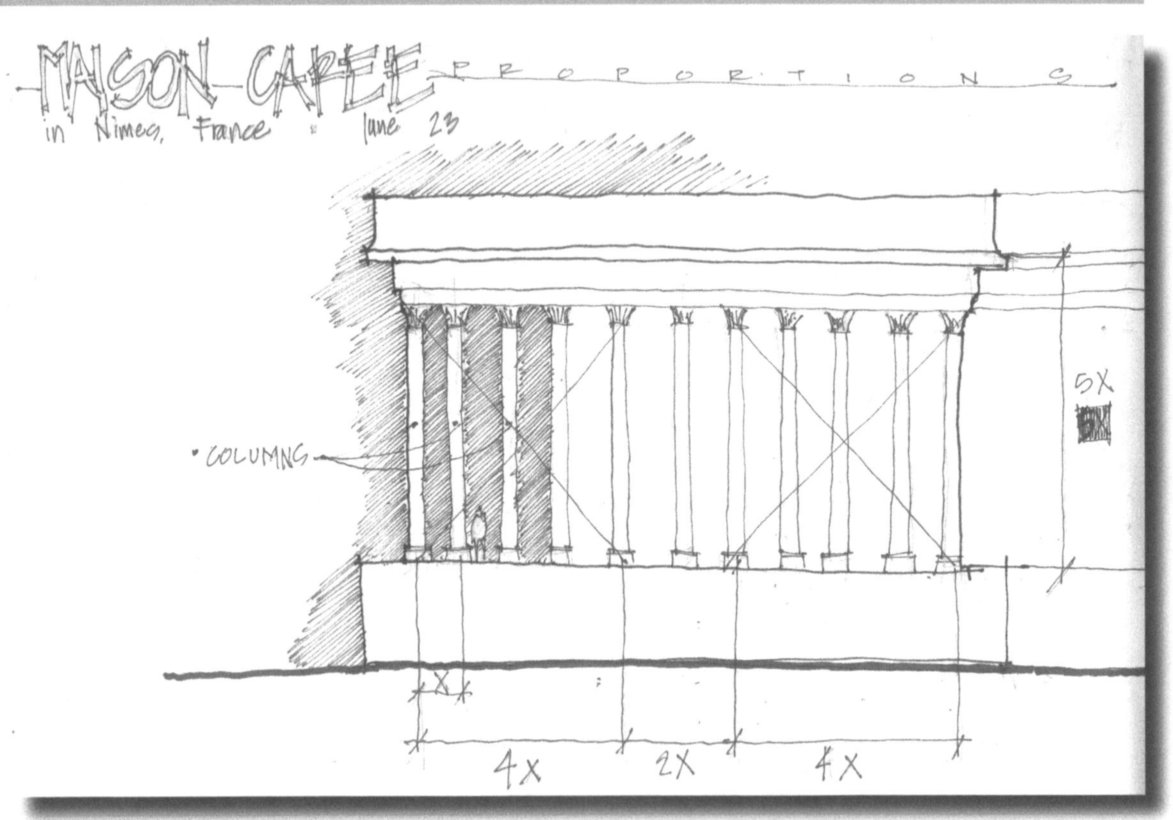

Fig. 09-69 One page journal entry, Eric Vogt. Ink on paper. Nimes, France.

EGJ-18.7

ERIC VOGT

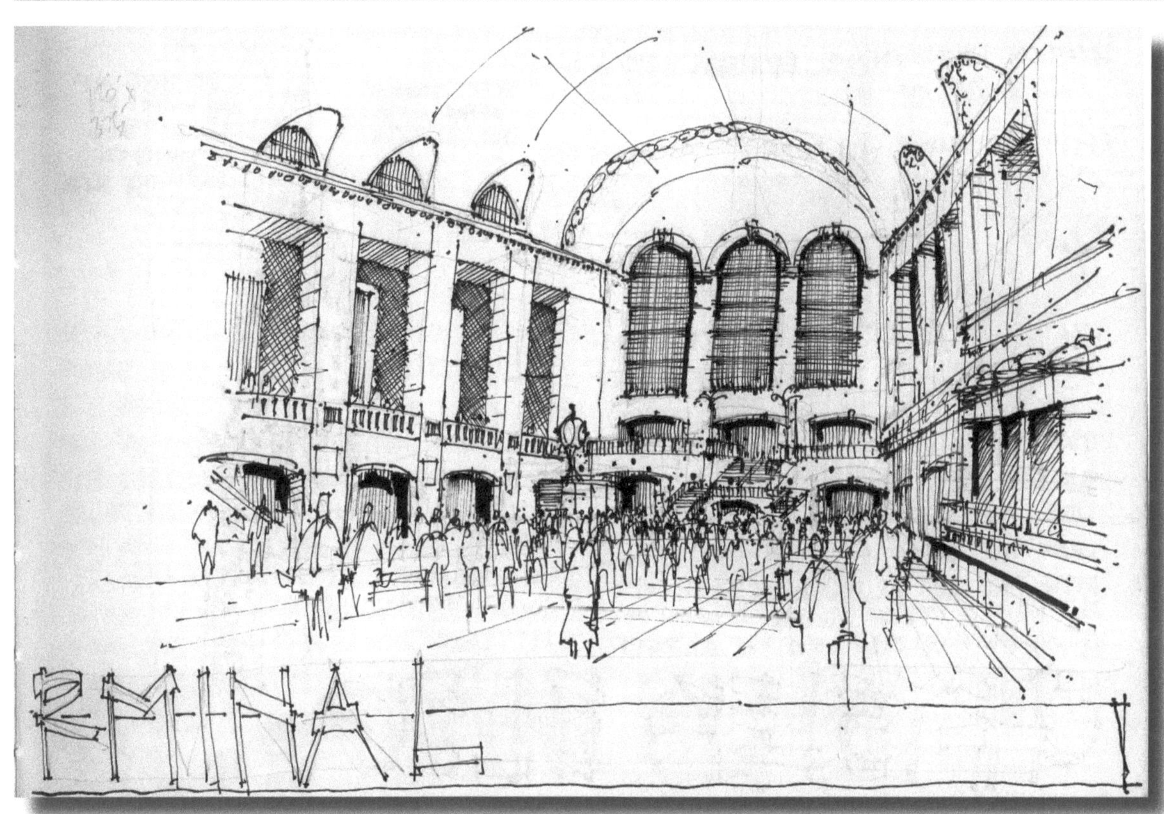

Fig. 09-70 One page journal entry, Eric Vogt. Ink on paper. New York, New York.

The single page layout is composed of an eye-level perspectival sketch. The vanishing point was located at the right one-third line, to add a dynamic quality to the view. Hatching is skillfully used to modulate value and indicate depth within the sketch. Note that the graphic value decreases as objects recede from the picture plane. The human figures add character and scale to the sketch. Graphic stipple (disease) adds intensity. A framed title is situated towards the bottom of the page to anchor the page.

EGJ-19.1

SHANNON WEST

The hand sketches in this journal entry were made during lecture class while the images were projected upon the screen, and then these sketches were scanned and imported into a desktop publishing software program. This method allowed printed text to be added. A consistent graphic band (of course title and date) forms the foundation of the consistent page layout, situated along the outer edge of every page to form an edge for the overall composition.

GREAT MOSQUE OF DAMASCUS

- Built on the site of the Roman TEMPLE OF JUPITER DAMASCENUS
- It has 3 Minarets and 3 Entrances
- Built on the Remains of the CHURCH OF ST. JOHN THE BAPTIST
    - This means that the church was originally Built by Christian Artisans, not Muslims
- Built from Salvaged Materials
    - Salvaged Stone, NOT Sun Dried Brick
    - Salvaged Columns, etc.
- The Mosque had NO Calligraphy Originally
- It is approximately 157m x 130m in Plan

february 24, 1999

ISLAMIC ARCHITECTURE

Fig. 09-71 One page class notes journal entry, Shannon West. Ink on paper, composed digitally.

EGJ-19.2

SHANNON WEST

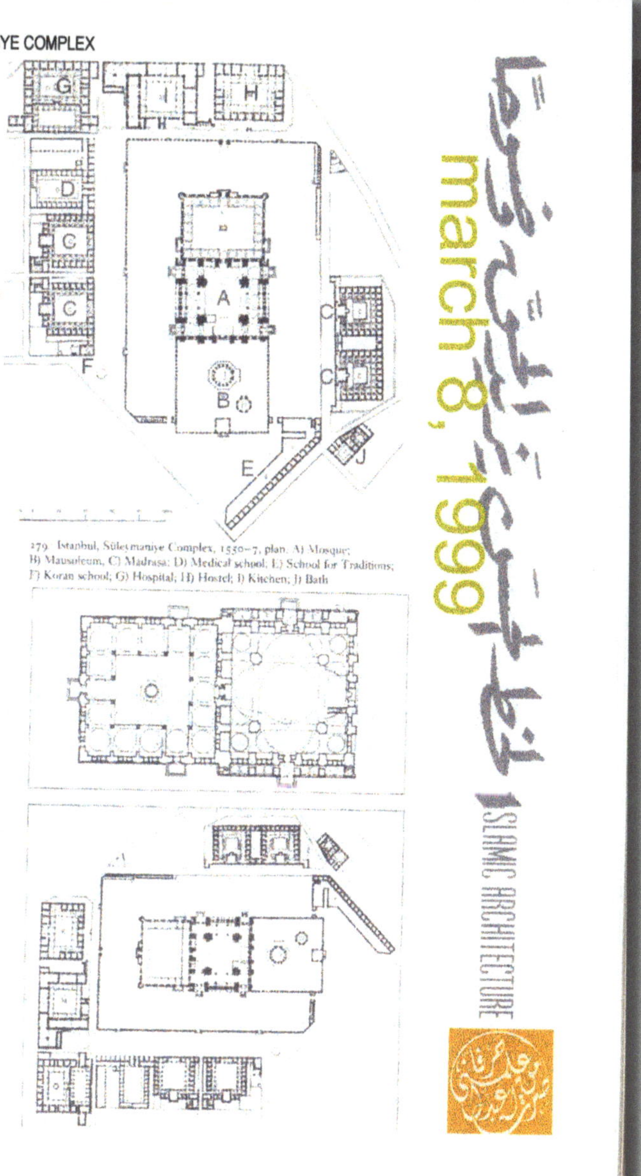

Using desktop publishing software, these graphic journal lecture notes are interspersed with scanned images where detailed information was necessary. The course title and lecture date were composed as a band and situated along the outer edge of every page.

Fig. 09-72 One page class notes journal entry, Shannon West. Ink on paper, composed digitally.

EGJ-19.3

SHANNON WEST

This single page lecture course journal entry combines hand sketching and printed text within a consistent page layout. In this particular journal entry, the hand sketches were drawn directly on the printed sheet, after the lecture occurred. The student used this process as a study tool for the exams.

GREAT MOSQUE OF CORDOBA (785)

- Turned into a Cathedral
  - Obvious because the Flying Buttresses are visually distinguishable

SAHN

NEW CATHEDRAL

MIHRAB

NORTH

march 1, 1999

ISLAMIC ARCHITECTURE

EXPANSIONS

- The Mosque was expanded 4 times, each mathematically based on the use of the GOLDEN SECTION

SECOND EXPANSION

129 M

FIRST EXPANSION

NORTH

HYPOSTYLE

179 M

PHASE ONE

PHASE TWO

PHASE THREE

PHASE FOUR

STRUCTURAL SYSTEM

- Taken from the Aquaduct
- Hypostyle System

Fig. 09-73 One page class notes journal entry, Shannon West. Ink on paper, composed digitally.

EGJ-20.1

RYAN WILLIAMS

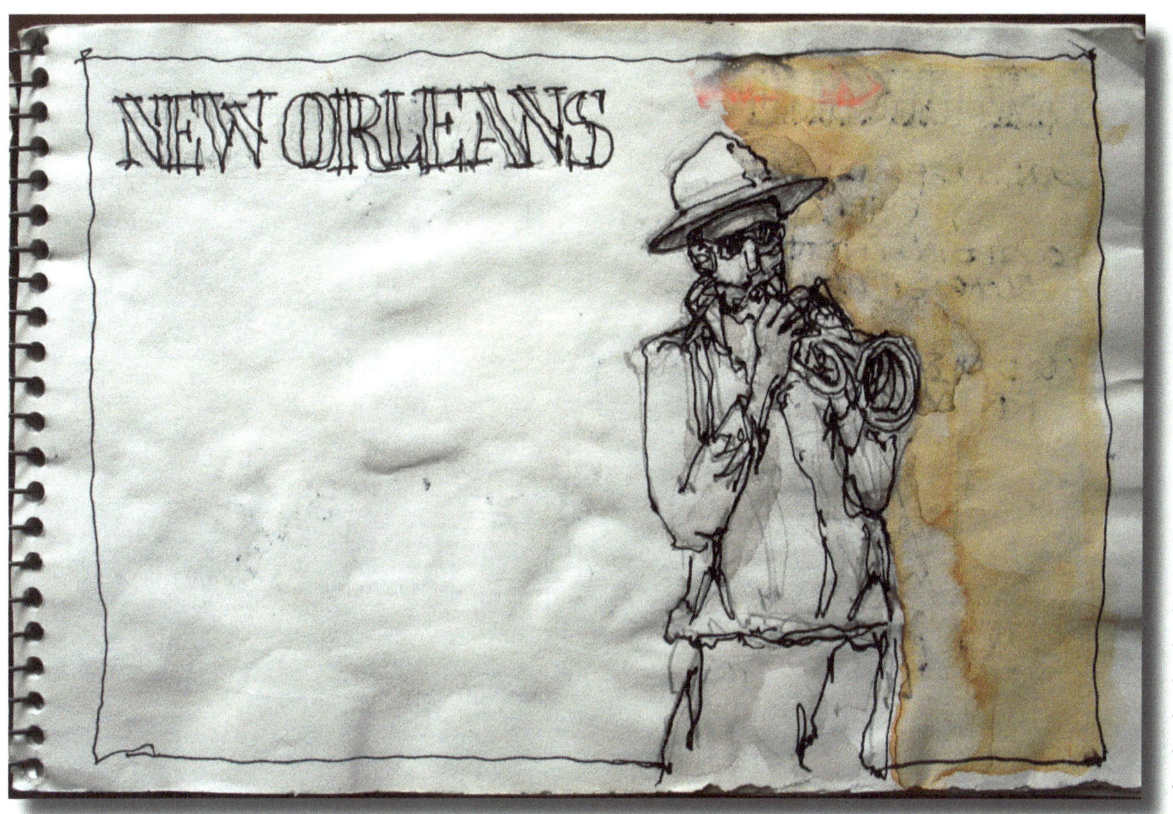

Fig. 09-74 One page journal entry, Ryan Williams. Ink and watercolors on paper. New Orleans, Louisiana.

The single page layout contains an overly expressive contour sketch highlighted with an ochre watercolor wash on the right side of the page. The low-quality of the sketchbook paper caused some serious wrinkles because of the wash. In the end, however, the wrinkles added a nice effect that complemented the informality of the sketch. The white space serves to add focus and impact to the message of the sketch. The entire composition is graphically framed and titled by a single line to define its edges.

EGJ-20.2

RYAN WILLIAMS

This single page layout contains a large contour sketch occupying the entire page. Watercolor washes are added to certain areas of the sketch to add depth and graphic value to the subject matter. A simple title forms the bottom edge of the page.

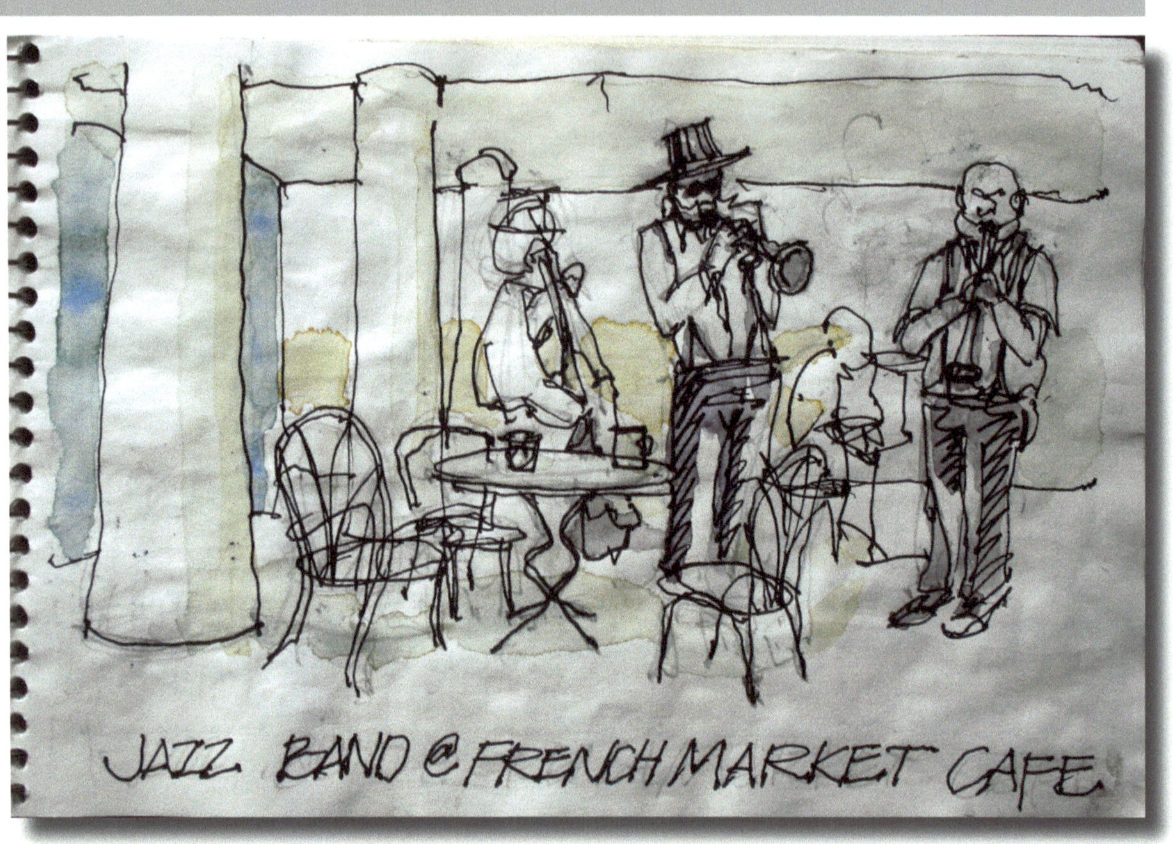

Fig. 09-75 One page journal entry, Ryan Williams. Ink, pencil, and watercolors on paper. New Orleans, Louisiana.

EGJ-20.3

RYAN WILLIAMS

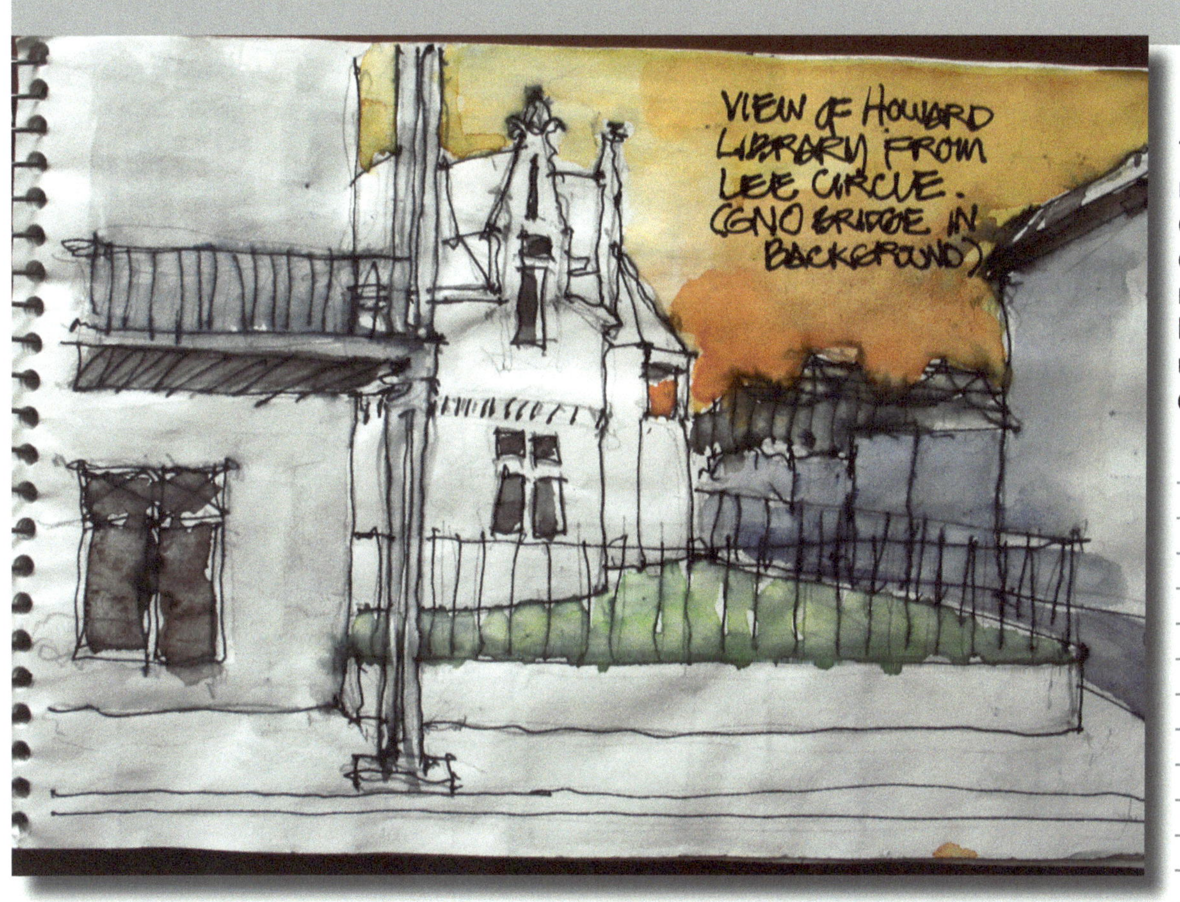

Fig. 09-76 One page journal entry, Ryan Williams. Ink and watercolors on paper. New Orleans, Louisiana.

This eye-level perspective sketch placed the area of most complexity along the one-third line of the page composition. The intensity of the watercolors adds a certain implied temperature to the sketch. There is no attempt to contain the sketch on the page so the lines and the watercolor wash extend their impact up to the edge of the page. The supporting text is casually floating in the background.

EGJ-20.4

RYAN WILLIAMS

The eye-level perspective sketch forms a strip of information across the center of the page layout. A simple floor plan sketch is floating within the composition to act as a vehicle for further communication of the subject matter. The page title is situated opposite the supporting sketch to create a balanced composition.

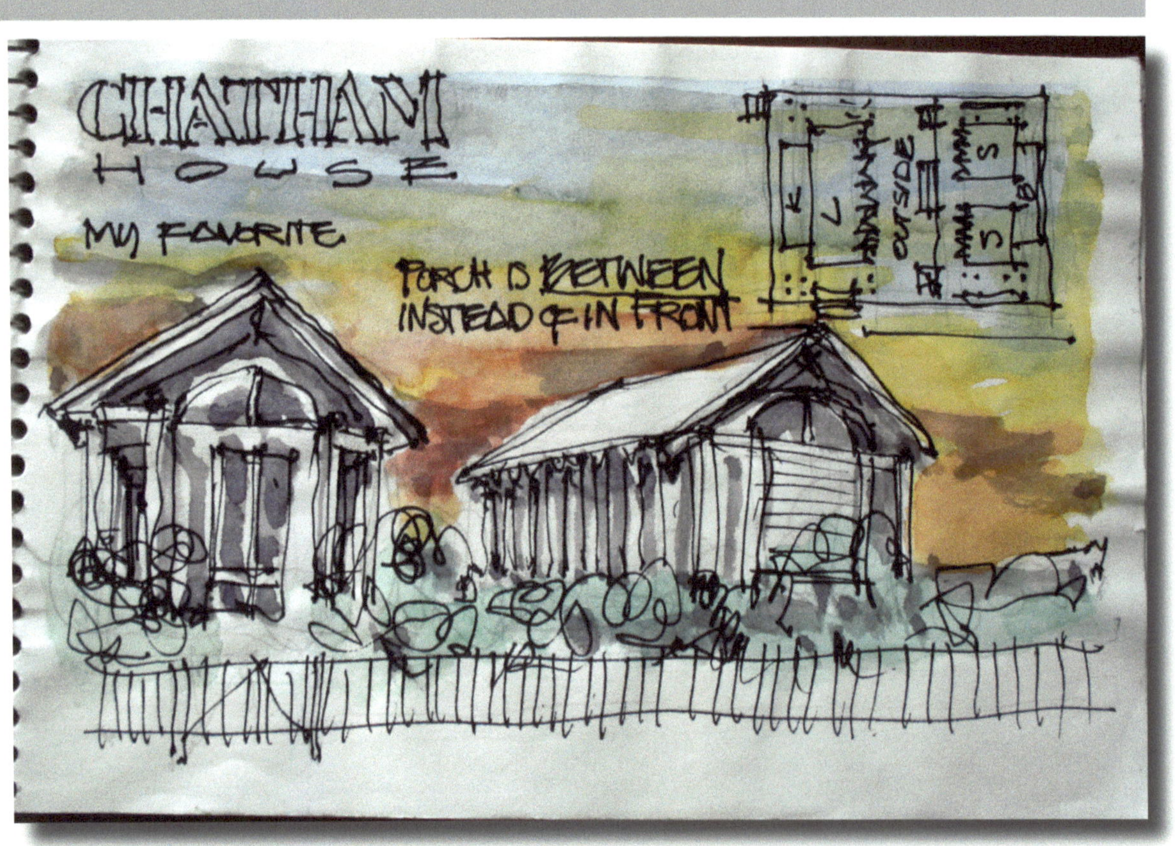

Fig. 09-77 One page journal entry, Ryan Williams. Ink, pencil, and watercolors on paper. New Orleans, Louisiana.

EGJ-20.5

RYAN WILLIAMS

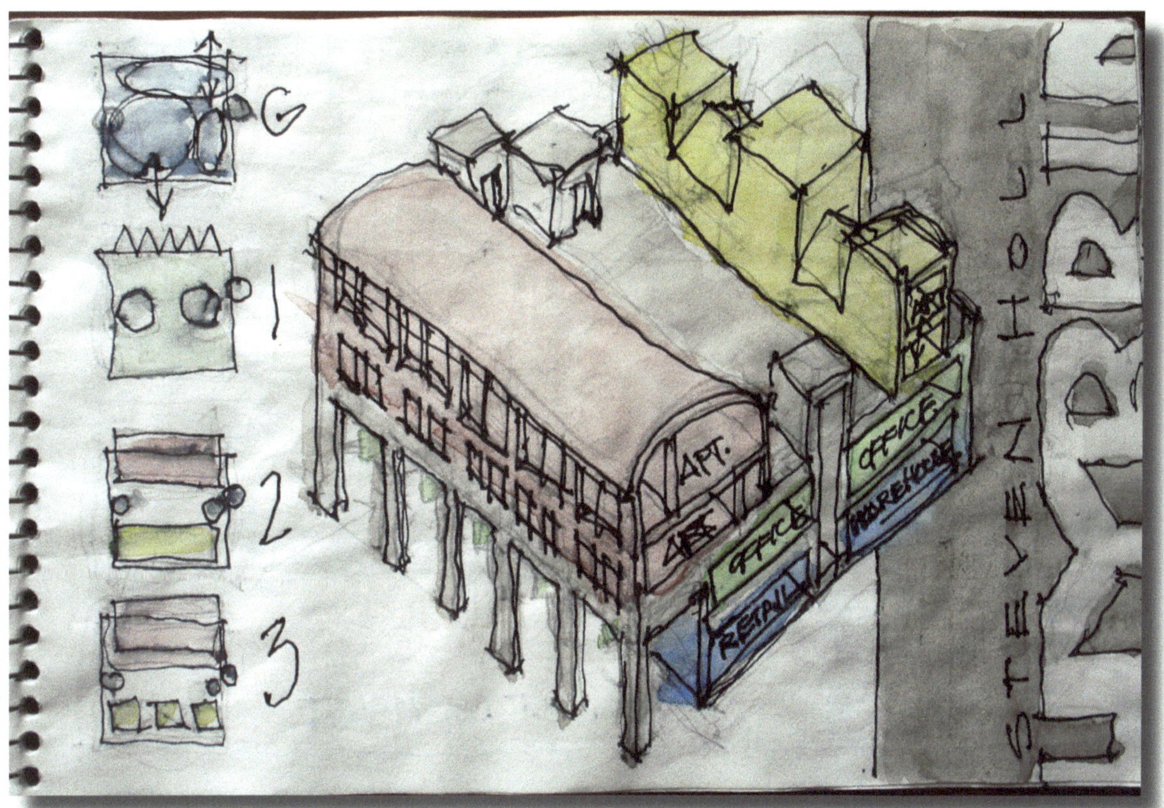

Fig. 09-78 One page journal entry, Ryan Williams. Ink, pencil, and watercolors on paper. Seaside, Florida.

This single page layout is divided vertically into fourths with a contour axonometric drawing occupying the exact center of the page. The right one-quarter of the page is dedicated to a prominent title with a low value watercolor wash. The left one-quarter of the page is occupied by four colorful supporting diagrams. Color is applied to the main sketch as an analytical aid.

EGJ-20.6

RYAN WILLIAMS

This analytical journal page presents three case studies, not situated in context. The axonometric drawings form the base of the page with the corresponding floor plans floating above. The watercolor wash provides an interesting background for the entire composition, placing emphasis on the form study rather than on the plan view. A simple page title is located at the bottom of the page.

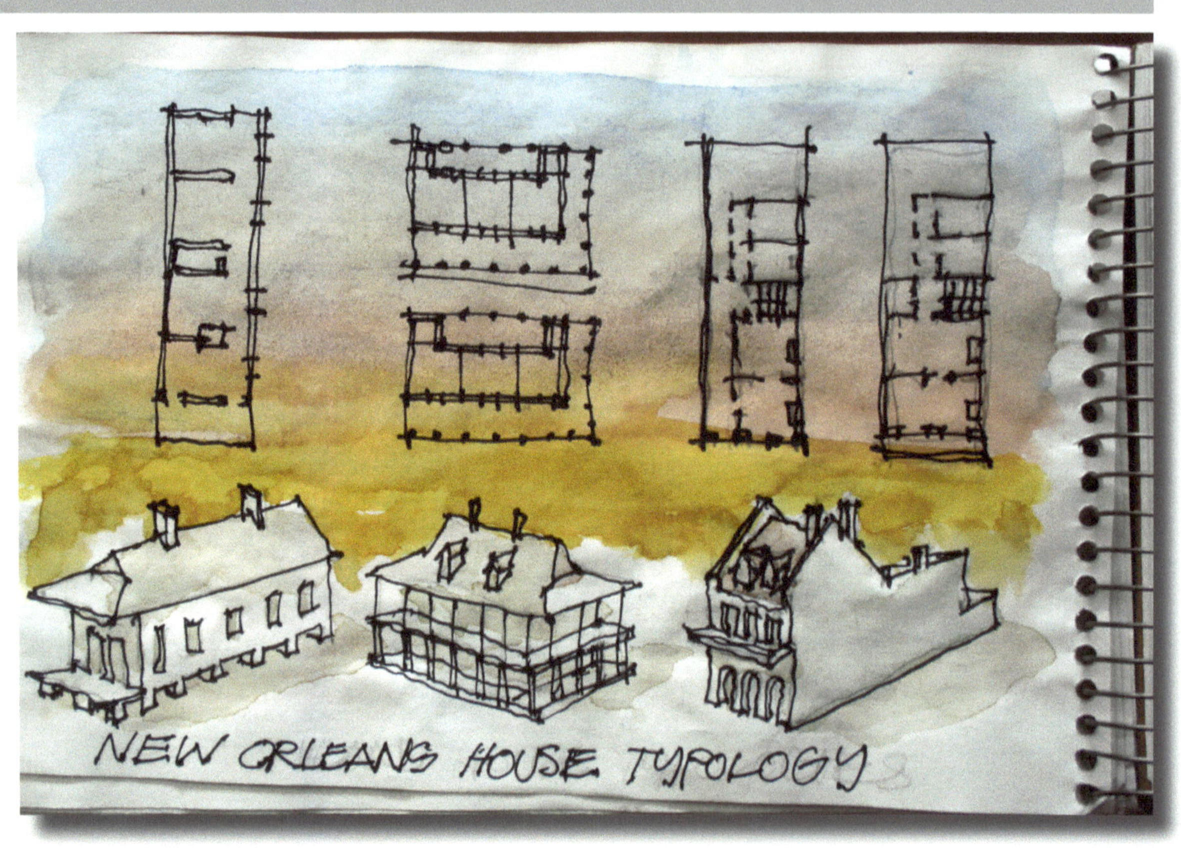

Fig. 09-79 One page journal entry by Ryan Williams. Ink, pencil, and watercolors on paper. New Orleans, Louisiana.

EGJ-21.1

JOHN WOMACK

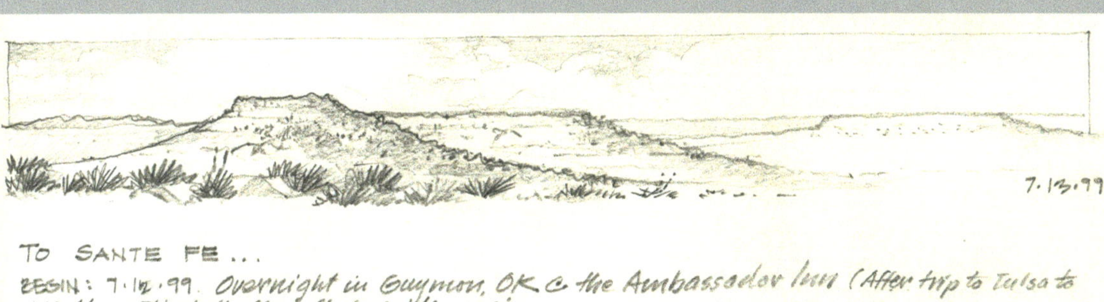

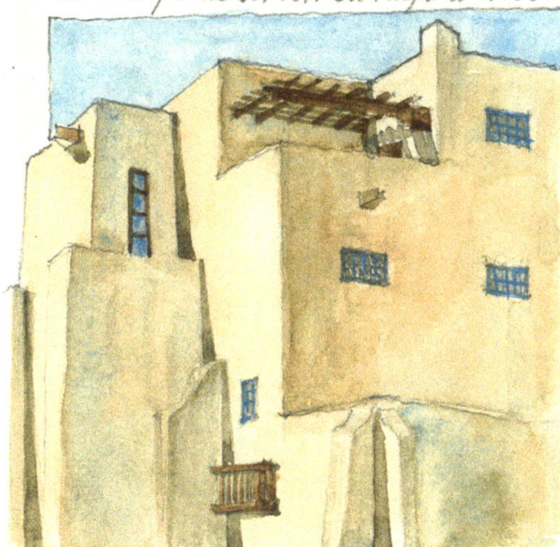

Fig. 09-80 One page journal entry, John Womack. Pencil, and watercolors on paper. Guymon, Oklahoma and Santa Fe, New Mexico.

A single page layout that is divided vertically into halves and horizontally into thirds. The top one-third is a panoramic gesture drawing, and the left half of the bottom two thirds is a detail view rendered in watercolors. There is an extensive area of supporting text with the entry title discreetly included at the beginning of the text.

EGJ-21.2

JOHN WOMACK

This single page layout is simply divided horizontally into halves. The upper half is occupied by a gesture sketch rendered in watercolors and framed with a graphic edge. The white space of the lower half anchors the composition, with the supporting text floating in the center of the area.

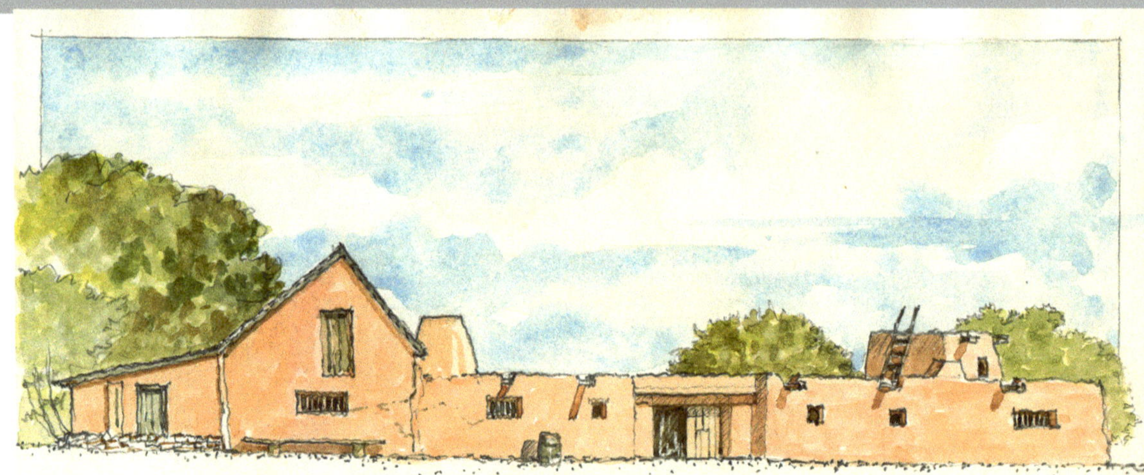

"Ranch of the Swallows"
El Rancho de las Golondrinas 7.16.99 - This "ranch" is a refurbished and reconstructed group of various buildings that originally dated from the 18th century. It served in addition to being a homeplace, as a reststop on the route from Santa Fe to Mexico City. Today it serves as a living history museum and, on occasion, as a movie set for various film productions. It is a most compelling place—a place to return to again and again.

Fig. 09-81 One page journal entry, John Womack. Pencil, and watercolors on paper. New Mexico.

EGJ-22.1

KYLE ZERBEY

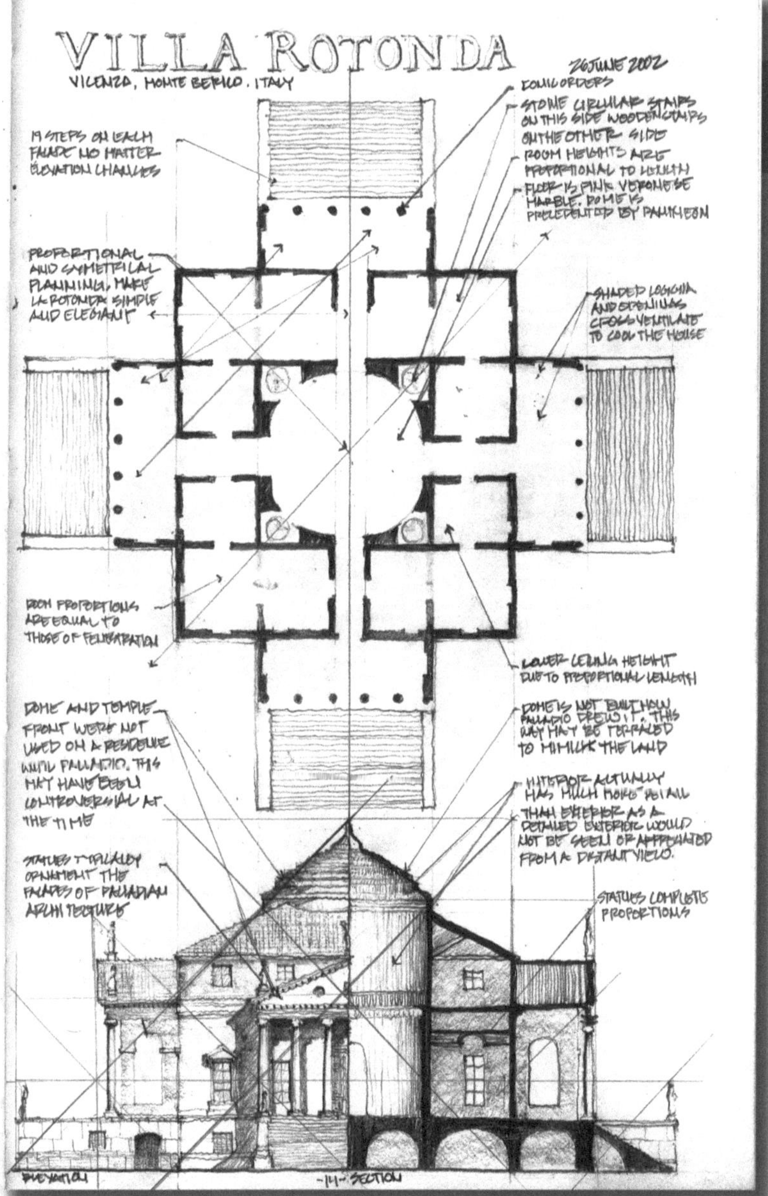

This single page layout in portrait format is divided into a two-thirds/ one-third composition. The top two thirds is dedicated to a floor plan sketch, while the bottom third is occupied by an orthographic sketch of a corresponding section/ elevation. The page is axially symmetrical to reflect the subject matter. The sketches are highly detailed with the graphic value modulated by the versatility of the drawing medium. The notation is extensive and organized in two columns on the sides of the page. The entry is titled with a classic font, again, to match the subject matter.

Fig. 09-82 One page journal entry, Kyle Zerbey. Pencil on paper. Vicenza, Italy.

EGJ-22.2

KYLE ZERBEY

This single page layout in portrait format is divided into three horizontal strips of information. The top strip is dedicated to the supporting text. The middle band is dedicated to the sketch consisting of a floor plan and its corresponding section. The lower band is a strip that is divided equally between an elevation sketch and a supporting text. The sketches are gestural in nature with a skillful manipulation of graphic value through the drawing medium.

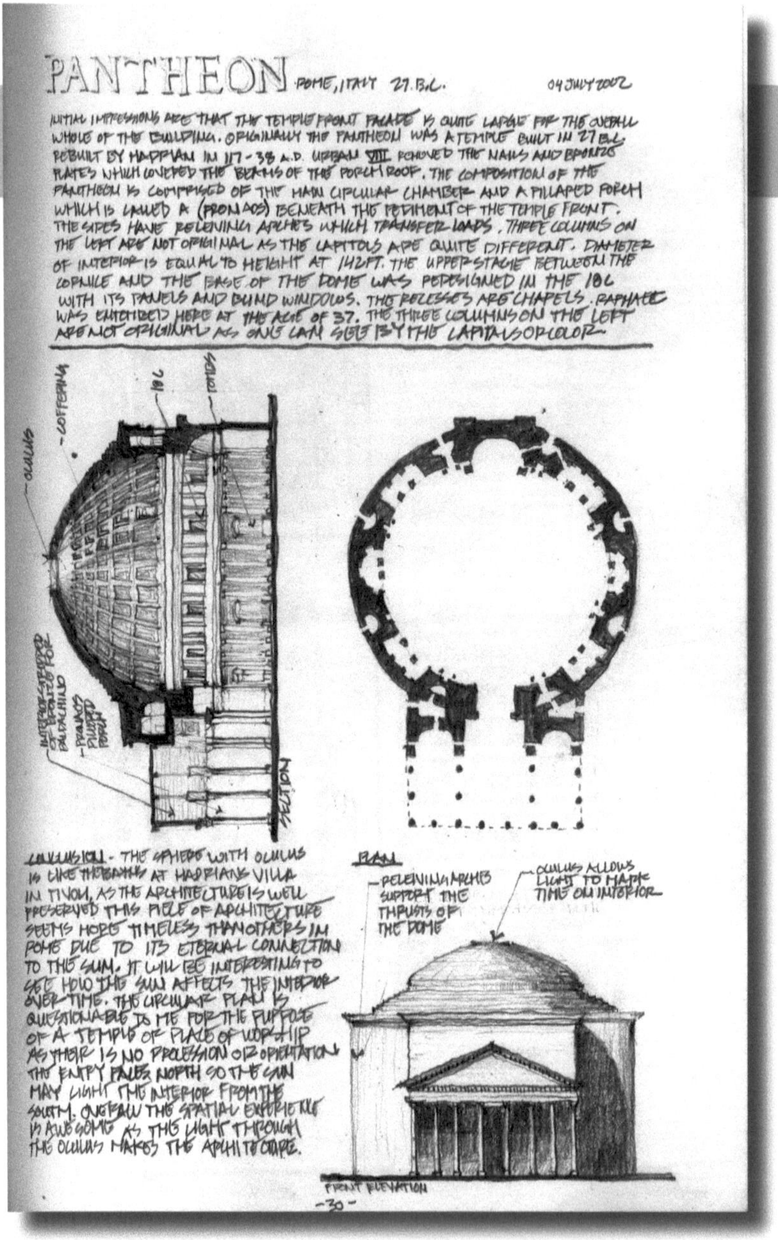

Fig. 09-83 One page journal entry, Kyle Zerbey. Pencil on paper. Rome, Italy.

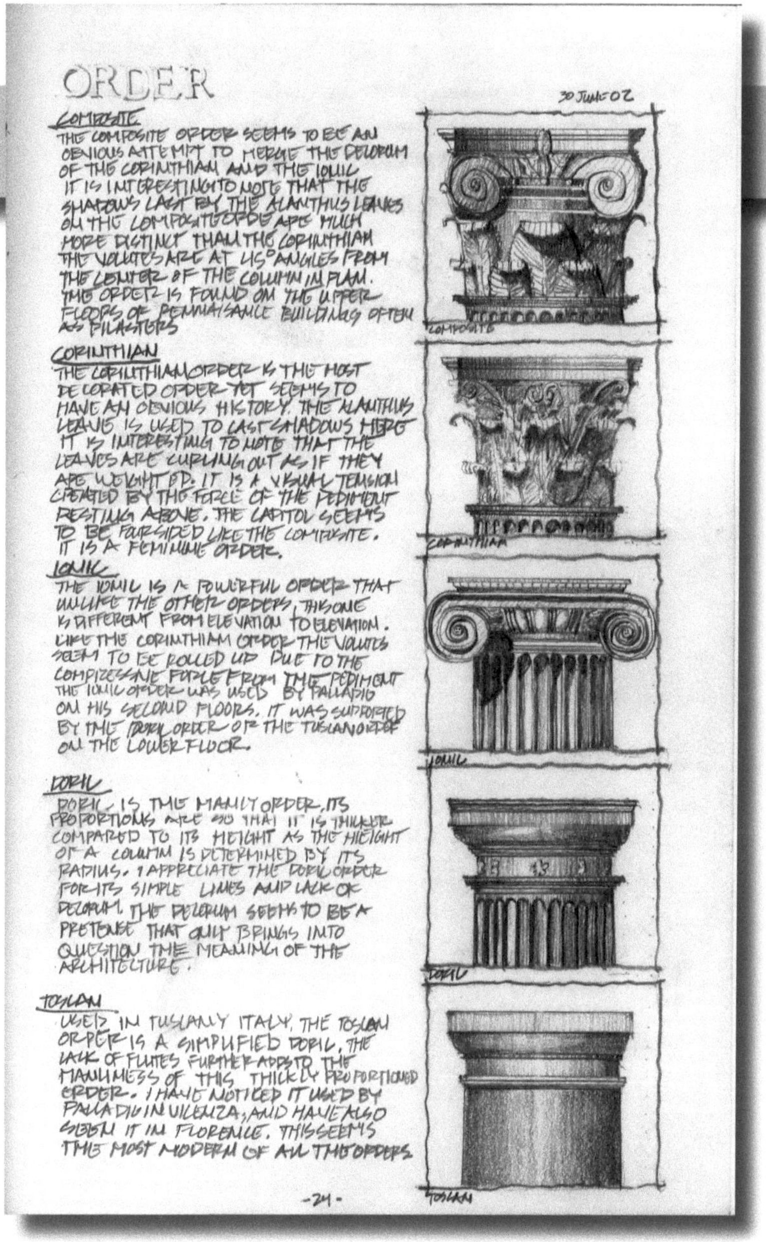

EGJ-22.3

KYLE ZERBEY

In this composition, the page is divided vertically into thirds and horizontally into fifths. The right third is occupied by a series of gestural sketches that are contained within graphic frames. The left two thirds is dedicated to the supporting text. The ability of the pencil to produce an endless array of values gives this journal entry an almost photographic feel.

Fig. 09-84 One page journal entry, Kyle Zerbey. Pencil on paper. Italy.

EGJ-22.4

KYLE ZERBEY

The single page layout in portrait format is divided vertically into halves. The right half contains a sketch and the left half contains the supporting text. The sketch is gestural in nature, and towards the bottom it indicates certain sectional properties for illustrative purposes. There is some notation that is keyed to the sketch via graphic leaders. Text also forms the base of the overall page composition, joining the two halves in the same fashion as the title across the top edge of the page.

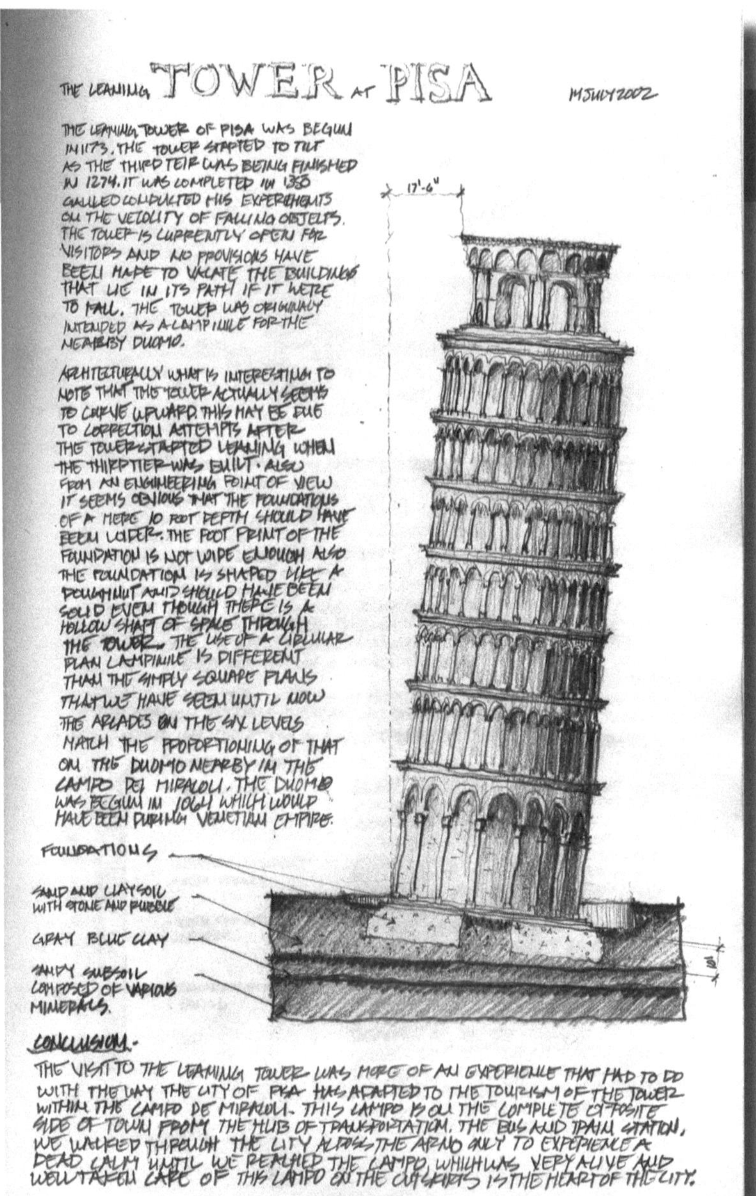

Fig. 09-85 One page journal entry, Kyle Zerbey. Pencil on paper. Pisa, Italy.

IGJ-1.1

RASEM BADRAN

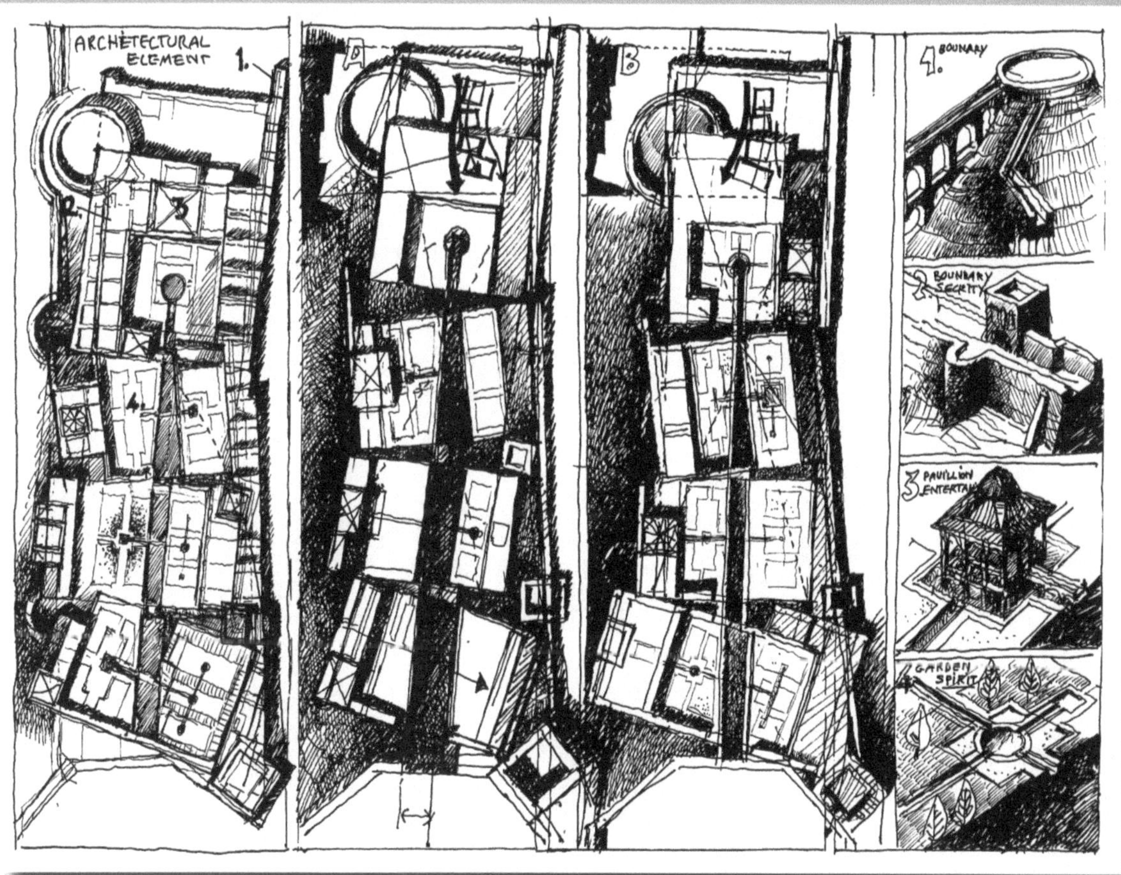

Fig. 09-86 One page journal entry, Rasem Badran. Pen on paper.

In this large format single page journal entry, the page is divided into four vertical strips. Each strip contains architectural studies that are rendered through modulated hatching. The left strip of information is further subdivided into four vignettes. The studies are bound by a graphic frame that attempts to detach the sketches from the page.

IGJ-1.2

RASEM BADRAN

The aerial architectural sketches on this large format single page journal entry achieve a dynamic quality due to the angle of view. The sketches are executed in pen with the graphic value achieved through carefully modulated hatching.

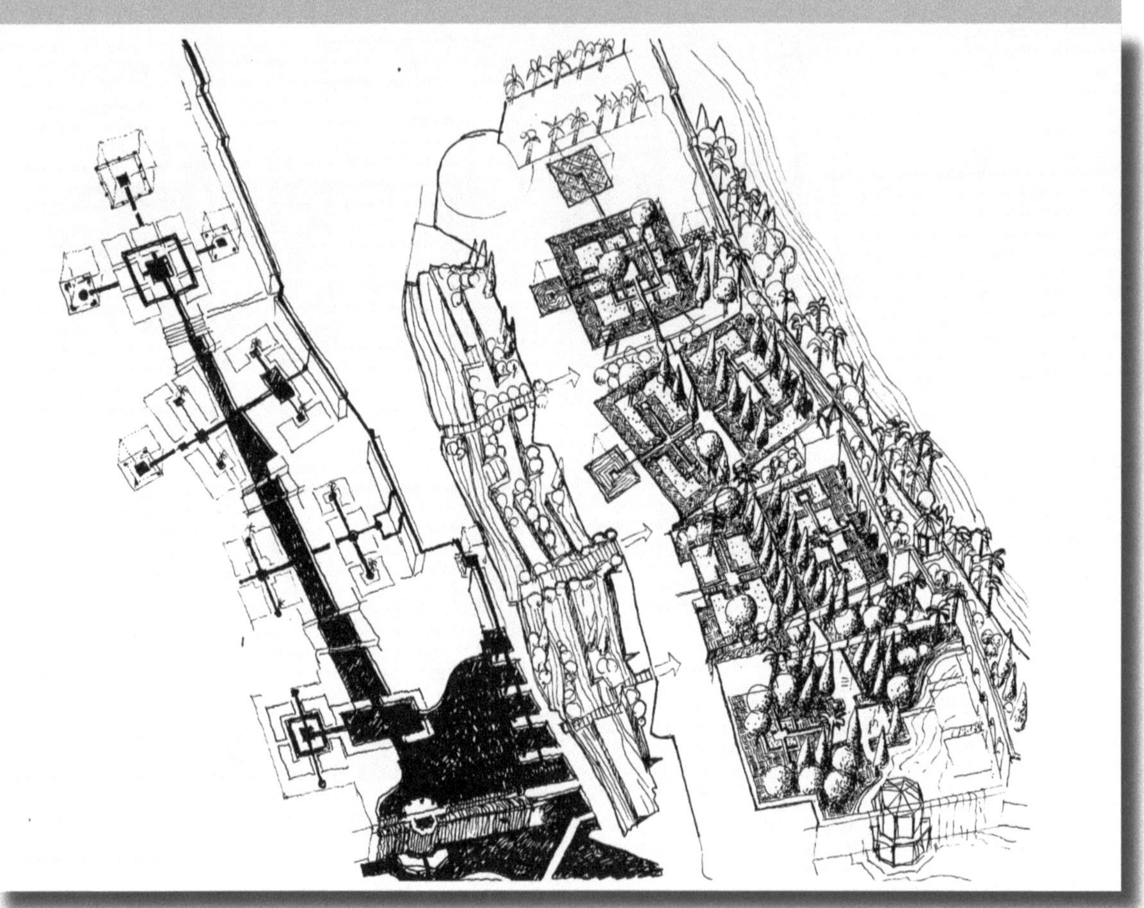

Fig. 09-87 One page journal entry, Rasem Badran. Pen on paper.

IGJ-1.3

RASEM BADRAN

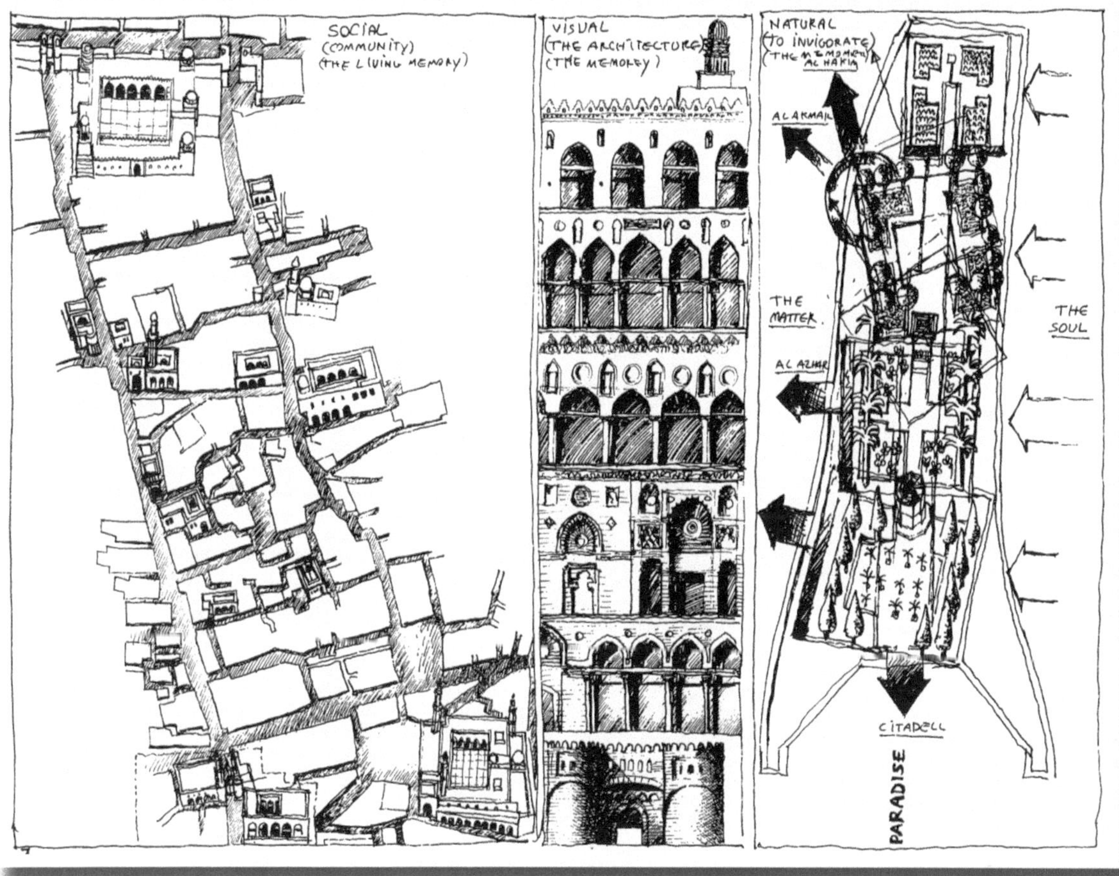

Fig. 09-88 One page journal entry, Rasem Badran. Pen on paper.

The three graphic vertical strips on this large format single page journal entry are arranged to convey different kinds of information. The architectural drawings are supplemented with supporting graphic elements such as arrows and bubbles. Shades and shadows are indicated through modulated hatching. The drawings are informally titled; however, notation and supporting text are kept to a minimum.

IGJ-1.4

RASEM BADRAN

This large format single page composition is divided vertically into two strips that are framed and loaded with graphic information. A thinner strip is squeezed in between acting as a graphic connector between the two, and also containing the minimal notation.

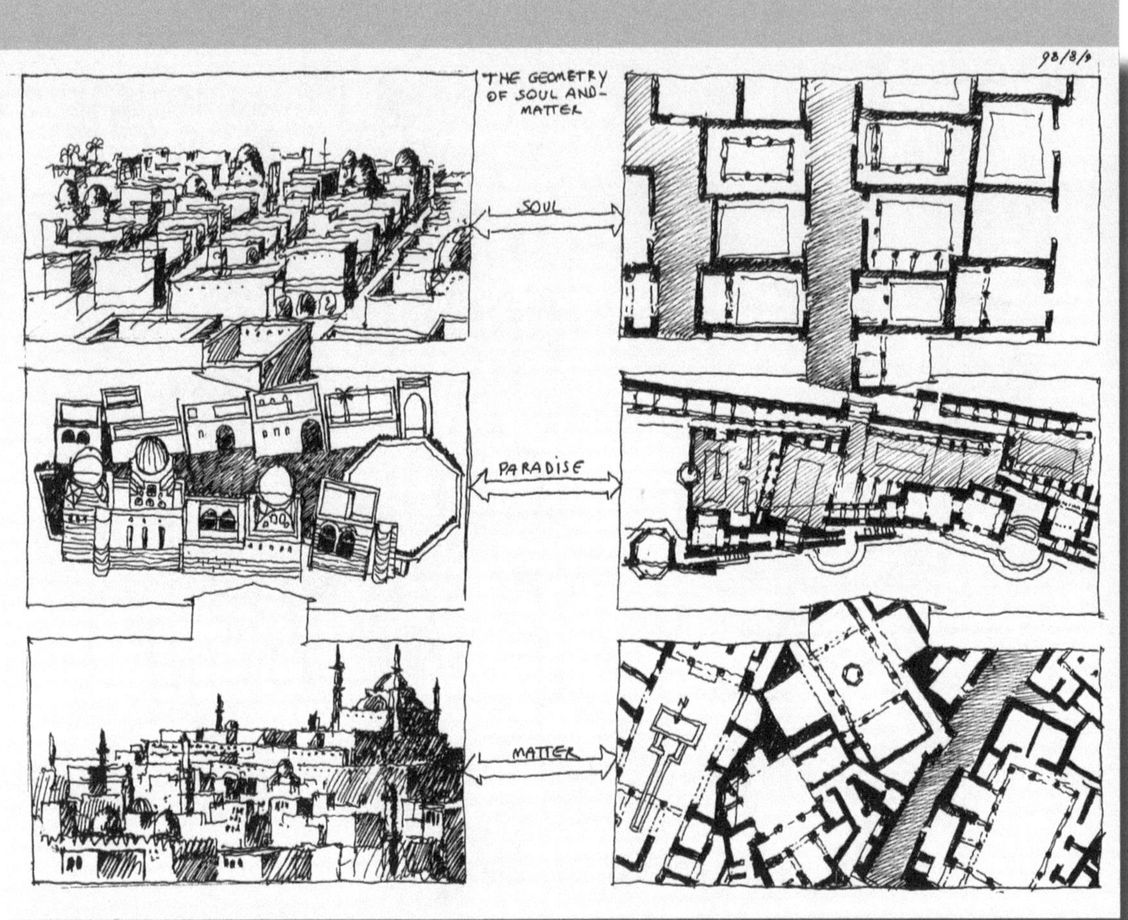

Fig. 09-89 One page journal entry, Rasem Badran. Pen on paper.

IGJ-1.5

RASEM BADRAN

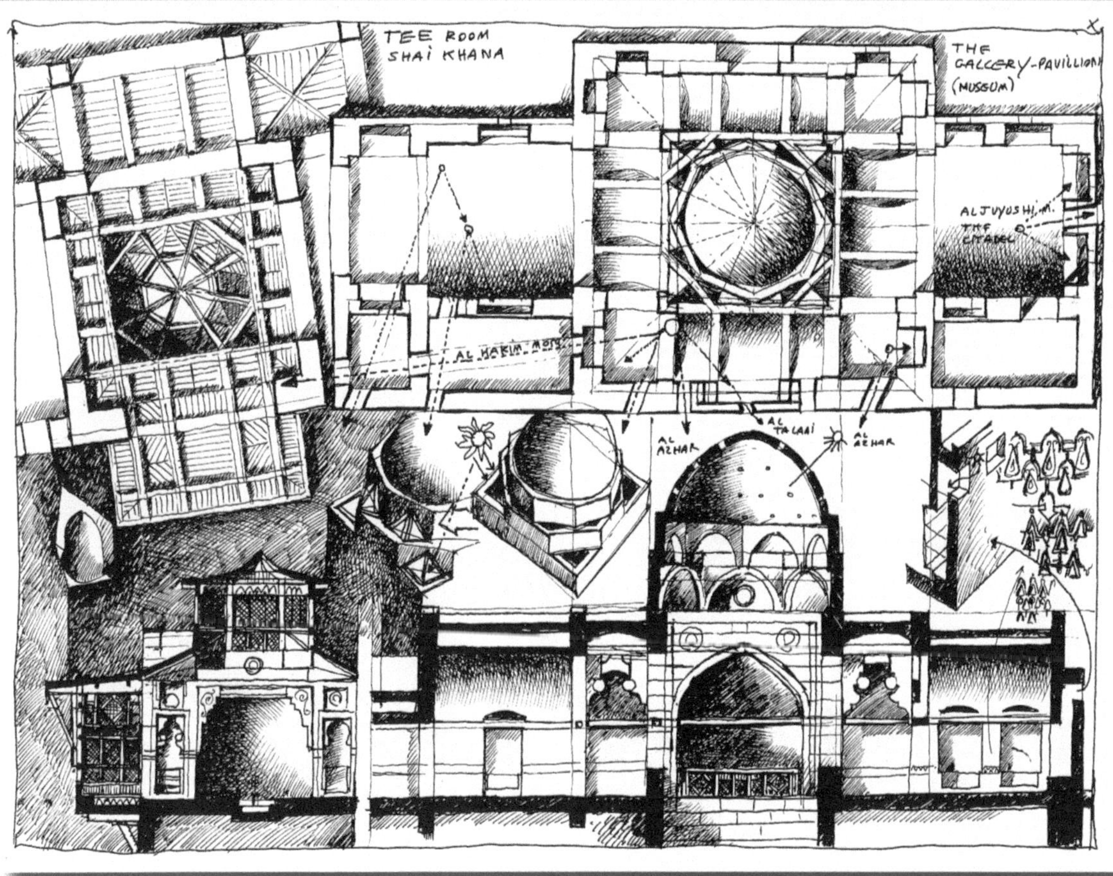

Fig. 09-90 One page journal entry, Rasem Badran. Pen on paper.

This large format single page layout contains more than ten interconnected architectural gesture sketches. Graphic superimposition and direct projection are used to further explain the design intent. Shades and shadows are indicated through carefully modulated hatching. The section sketch has the lowest graphic value. There is a minimal amount of notation and the entire composition is framed by a thin line to graphically detach it from the page.

IGJ-1.6

RASEM BADRAN

The large format single page composition is divided vertically into four equal strips of graphic information. Each strip is packed with a multitude of drawings that are shaded through modulated hatching. The sketches are related to each other by graphic arrows, leaders, and projection lines. There is little text notation; however, the strips are titled and their sequence is numerically indicated.

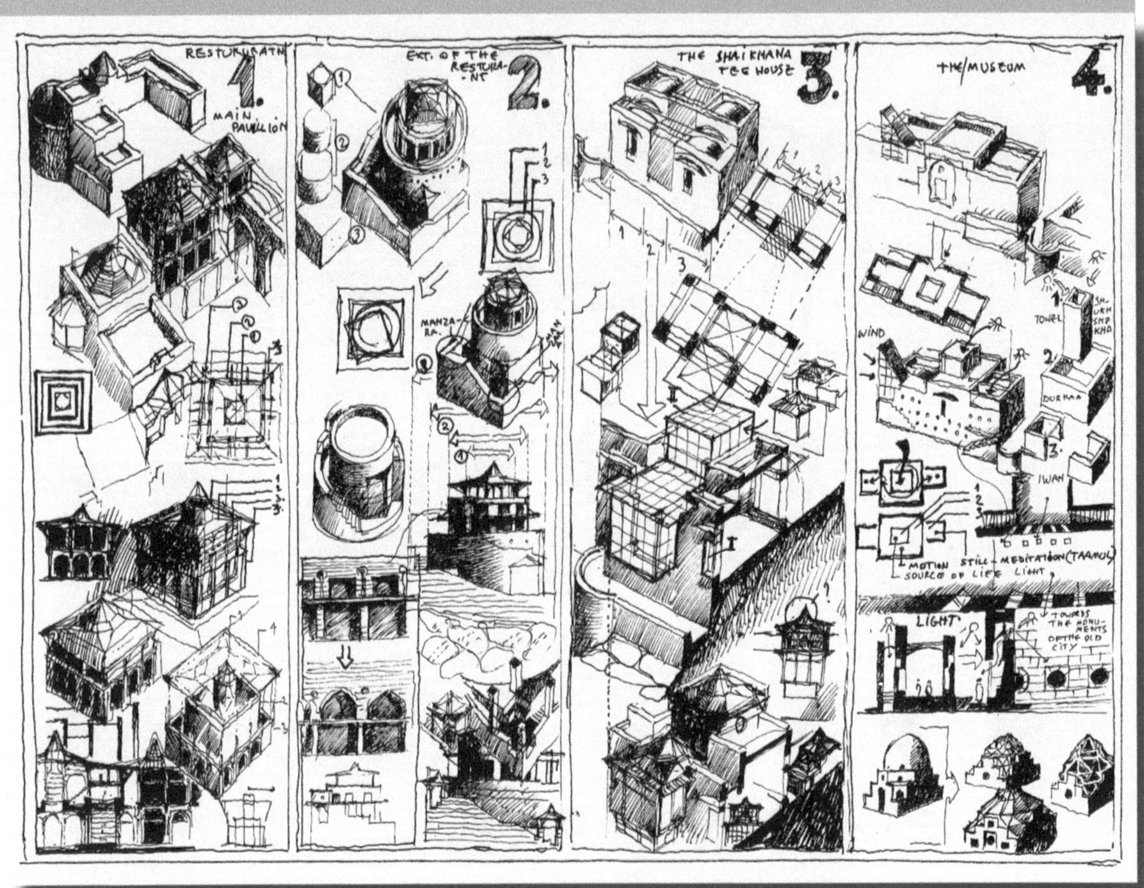

Fig. 09-91 One page journal entry, Rasem Badran. Pen on paper.

IGJ-1.7

RASEM BADRAN

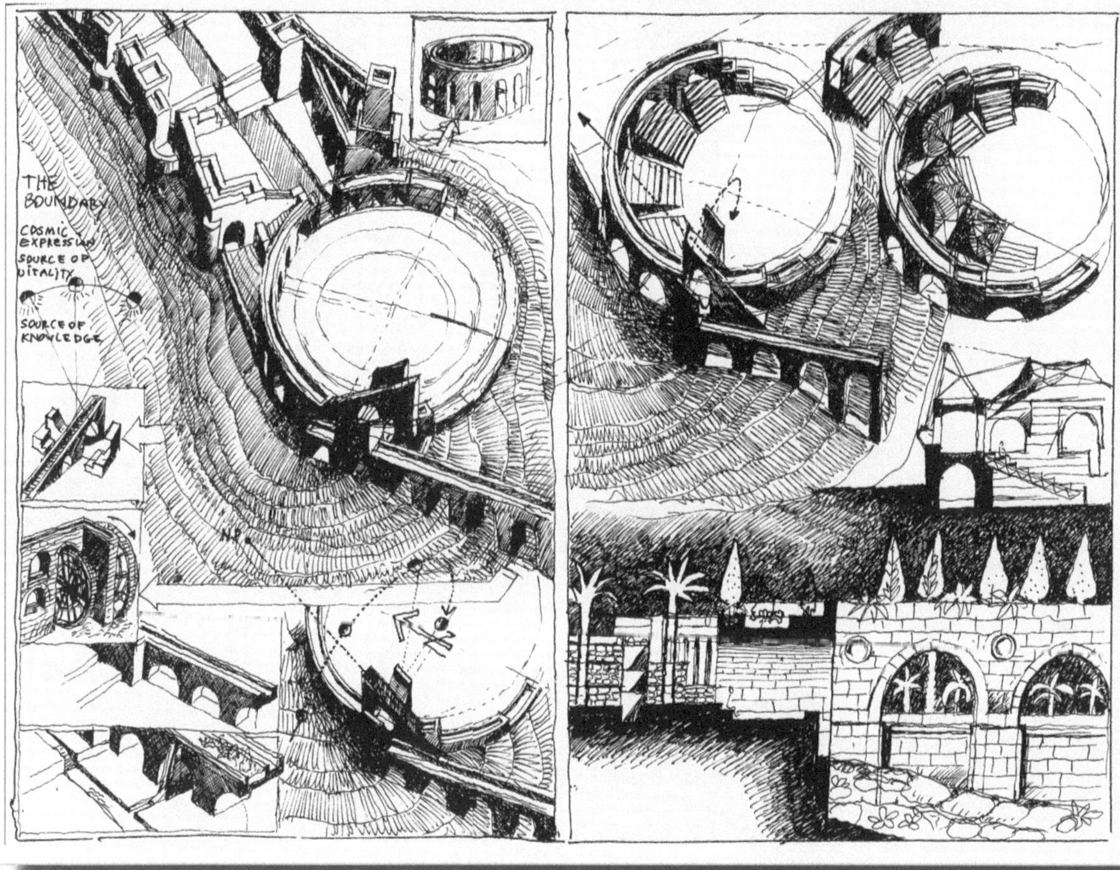

Fig. 09-92 One page journal entry, Rasem Badran. Pen on paper.

This large format single page layout is divided into two vertical strips. Each strip contains a major aerial gestural sketch with several supporting sketches. Graphic value is achieved through carefully modulated hatching of varying intensities. The sketches are contained graphically through frames.

IGJ-1.8

RASEM BADRAN

The large format single page composition is focused upon one major plan view sketch occupying the center band of the page. There is a corresponding sketch at the bottom of the page. Other sketches are graphically framed and skillfully tagged to the central sketch by graphic arrows projection lines. Graphic value is achieved through hatching and the entire composition is framed without any notation.

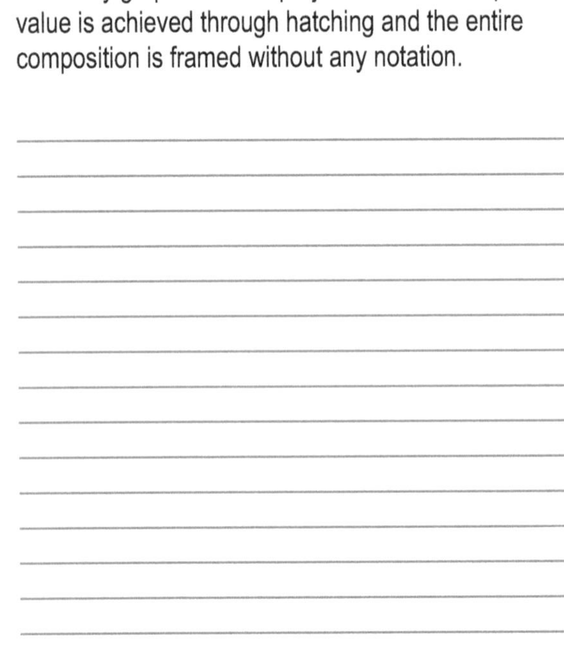

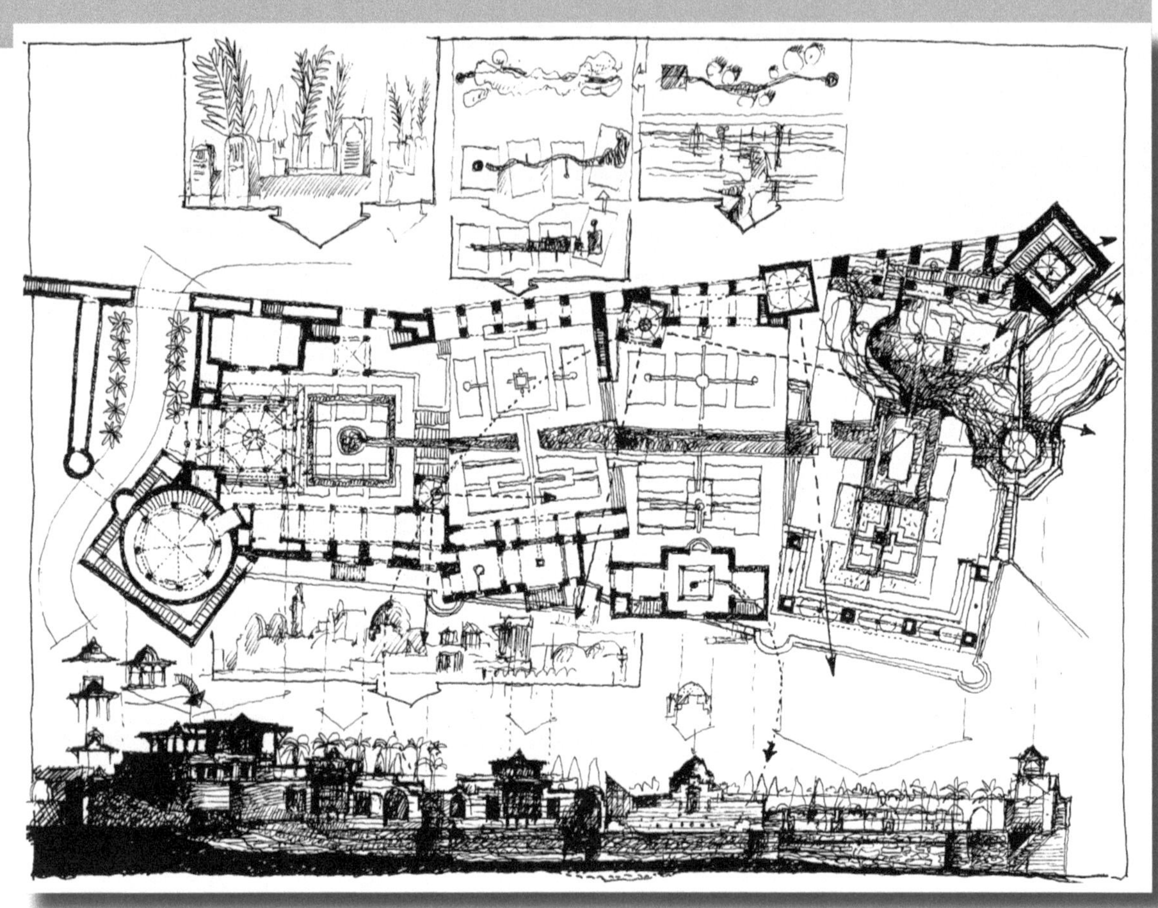

Fig. 09-93 One page journal entry, Rasem Badran. Pen on paper.

IGJ-1.9

RASEM BADRAN

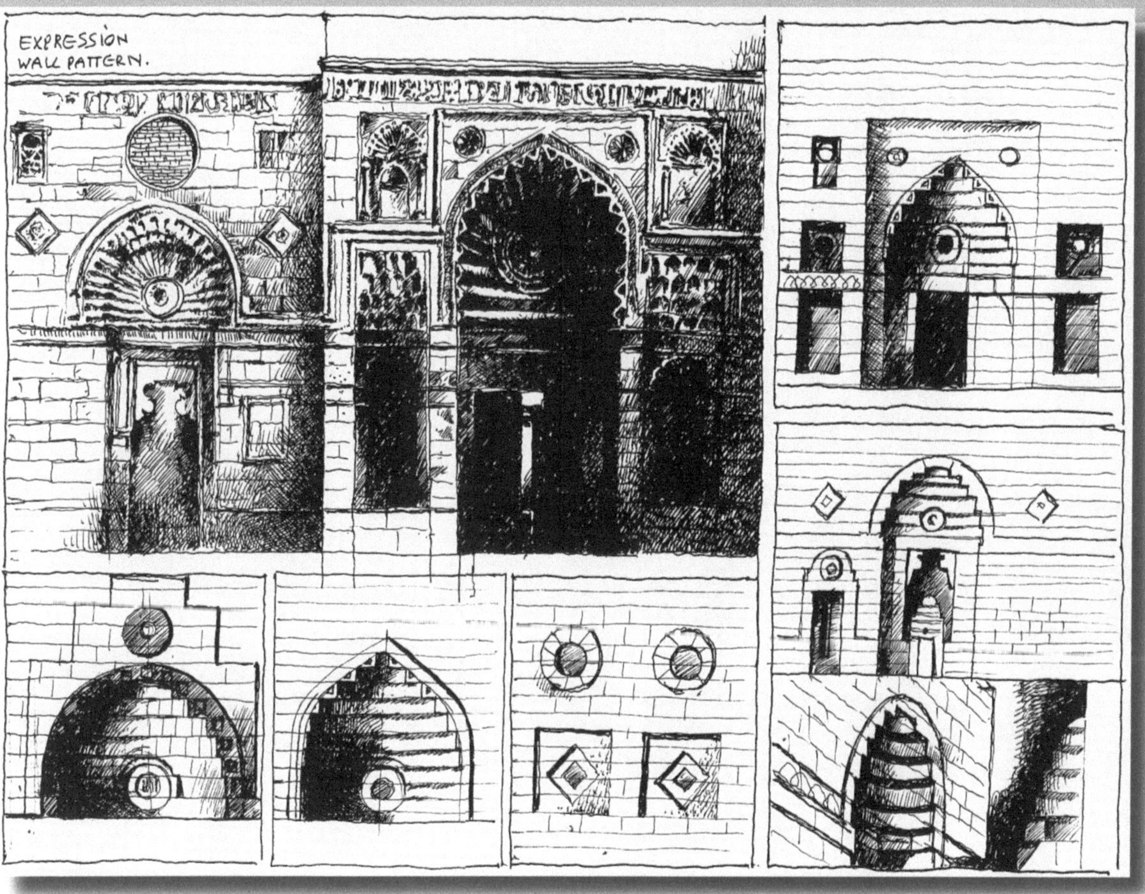

Fig. 09-94 One page journal entry, Rasem Badran. Pen on paper.

The large format single page composition consists of several graphic frames of varying sizes. Each frame is occupied by an elevation orthographic projection sketch. Graphic value is achieved through modulated hatching. There is a single informal journal entry title at the top left corner of the page.

IGJ-1.10

RASEM BADRAN

The large format single page journal entry is composed of four major graphic frames, roughly occupying the quadrants of the sheet. These frames are subsequently divided into two or more smaller graphic frames. The gestural sketches are diagrammatic in nature with the graphic value indicated through hatching. Graphic arrows and graphic codes are used to help facilitate the graphic thinking process.

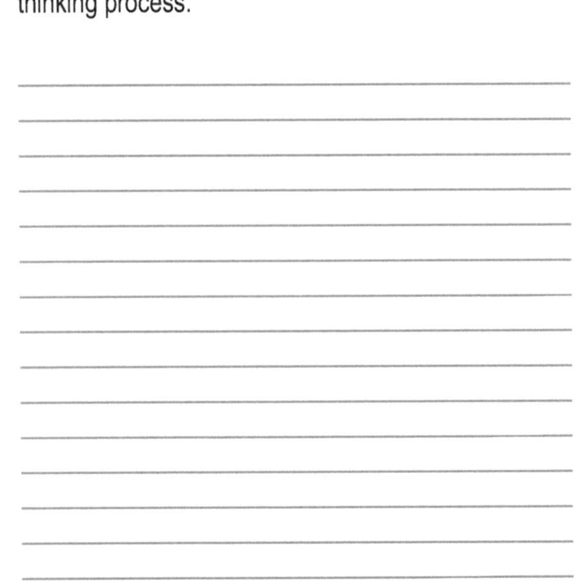

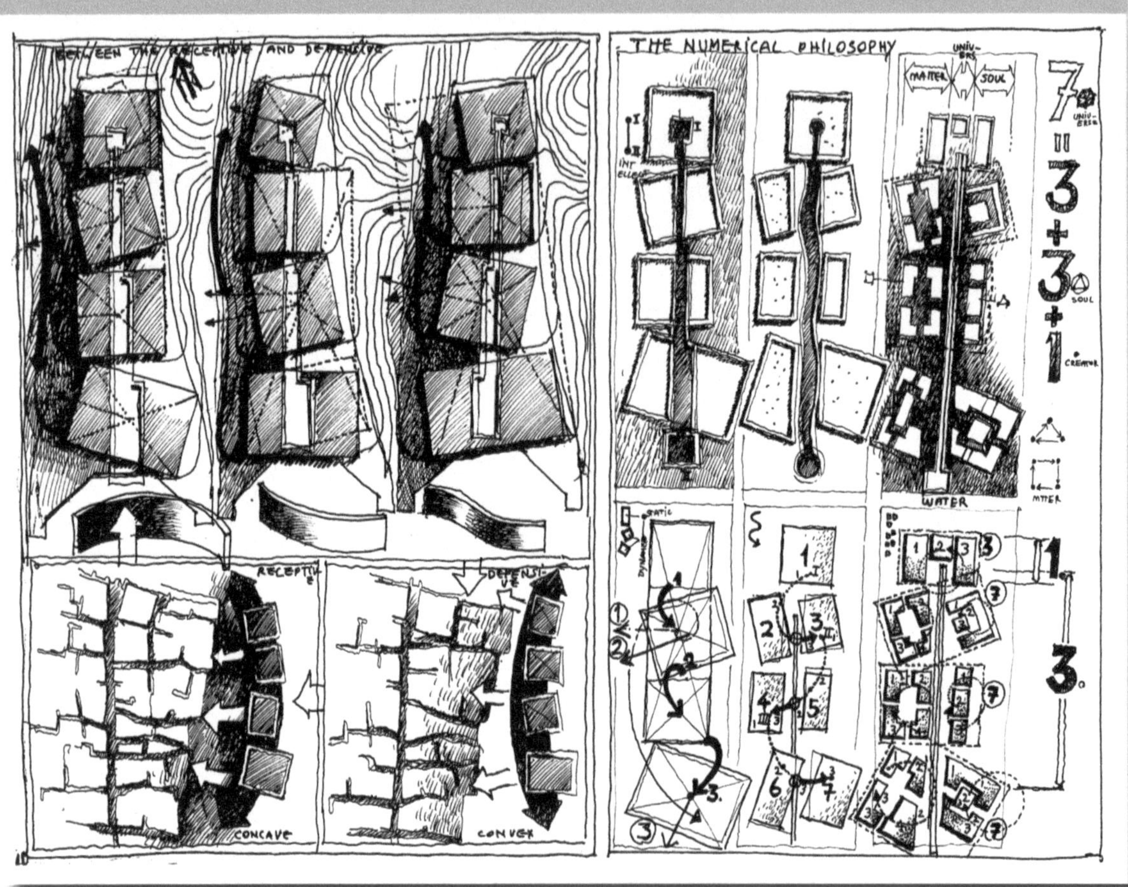

Fig. 09-95 One page journal entry, Rasem Badran. Pen on paper.

IGJ-2.1

INAD BILBEISI

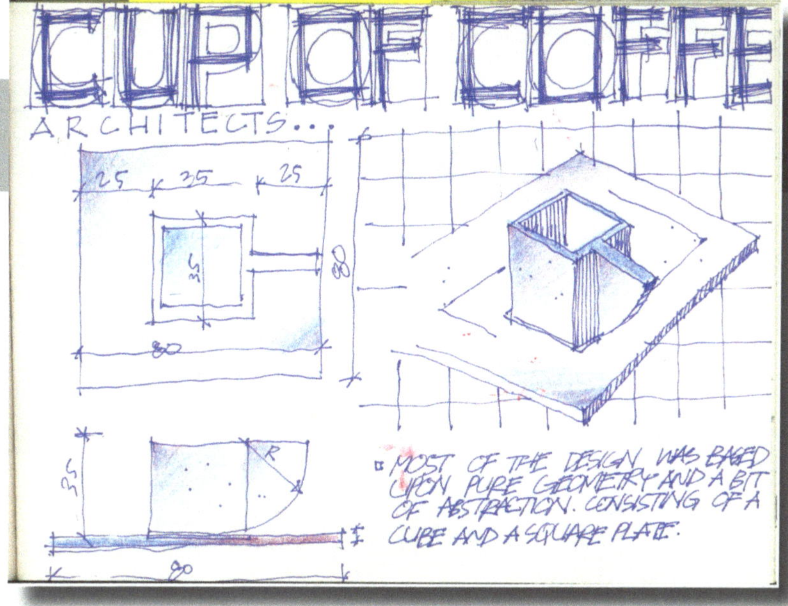

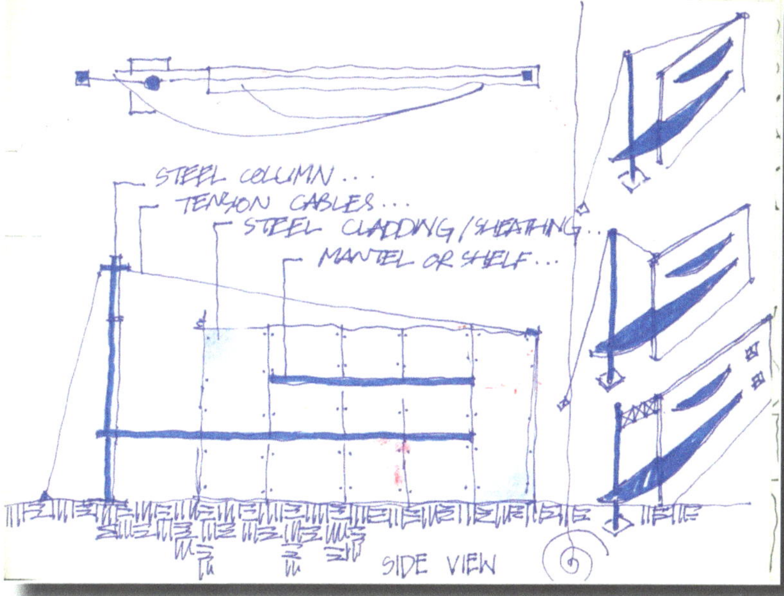

These two examples of single page layouts offer sketches and supporting text to communicate the design intent. The pages are compositionally balanced with a larger image as the focus, supported by smaller sketches and text. The sketches are rendered through hatching in pen and color pencil. The lowest graphic value occurs towards the bottom of the pages and the entry titles are stylized to match the aesthetic intent.

Fig. 09-96 One page journal entries, Inad Bilbeisi. Pen and colored pencils on paper.

IGJ-2.2

INAD BILBEISI

This informal single page layout is divided into halves. The left half contains the sketch and the right half contains the supporting text. The sketch is rendered and its graphic value highlighted via quick hatching and colored pencil. The composition as a whole is anchored by an informal page title located at the bottom of the page.

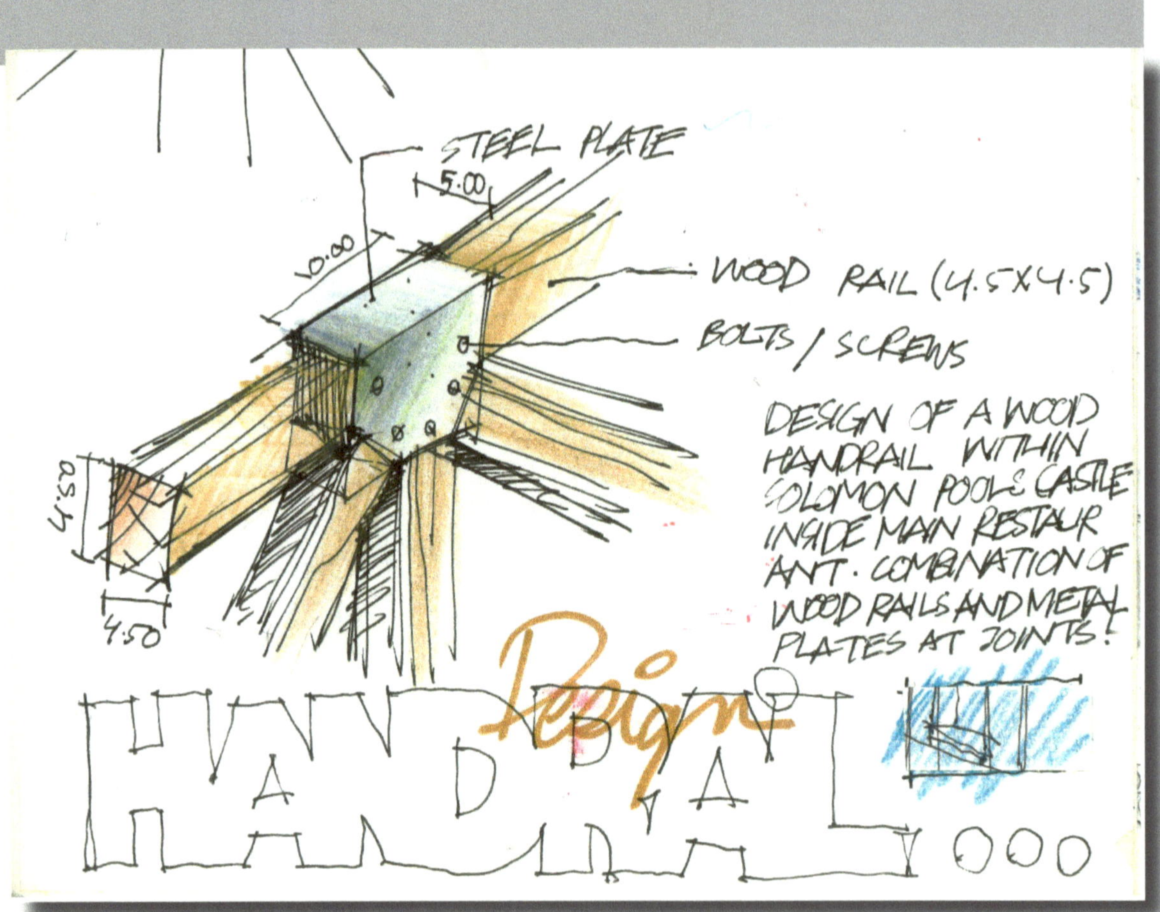

Fig. 09-97 One page journal entry, Inad Bilbeisi. Pen and colored pencils on paper.

IGJ-3.1
MOH'D BILBEISI

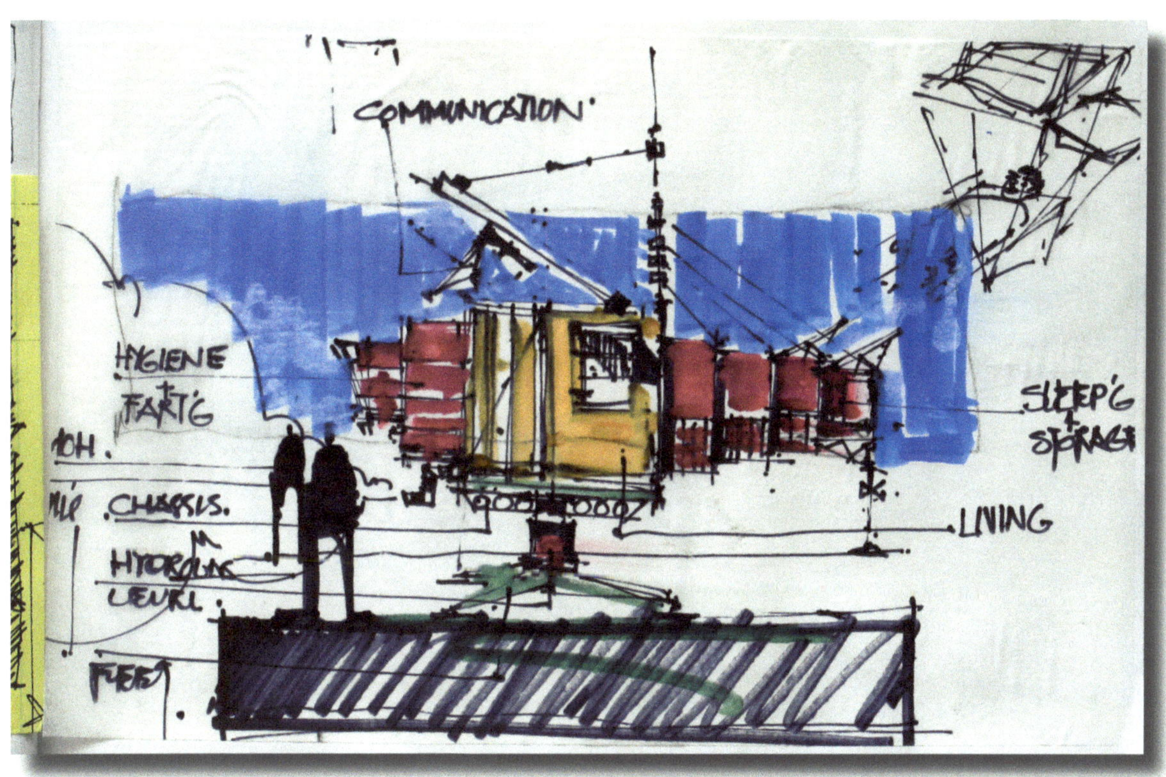

Fig. 09-98 One page journal entry, Moh'd Bilbeisi. Pen and marker on paper.

The single page layout in landscape format accommodates the horizontal geometry of the subject matter. The sketch is loosely drawn, superimposed on a blue graphic background, and anchored by a low value base at the bottom of the page. There is little supporting text and notation is tied to the sketch through graphic leaders.

IGJ-3.2

MOH'D BILBEISI

This single page entry is a collage - the sketch and the supporting text were drawn on a separate sheet of paper and then trimmed and glued within the journal. Graphic value is achieved through high contrast hatching and the application of colored pencils. The page is titled with a vertical text on the left side of the page.

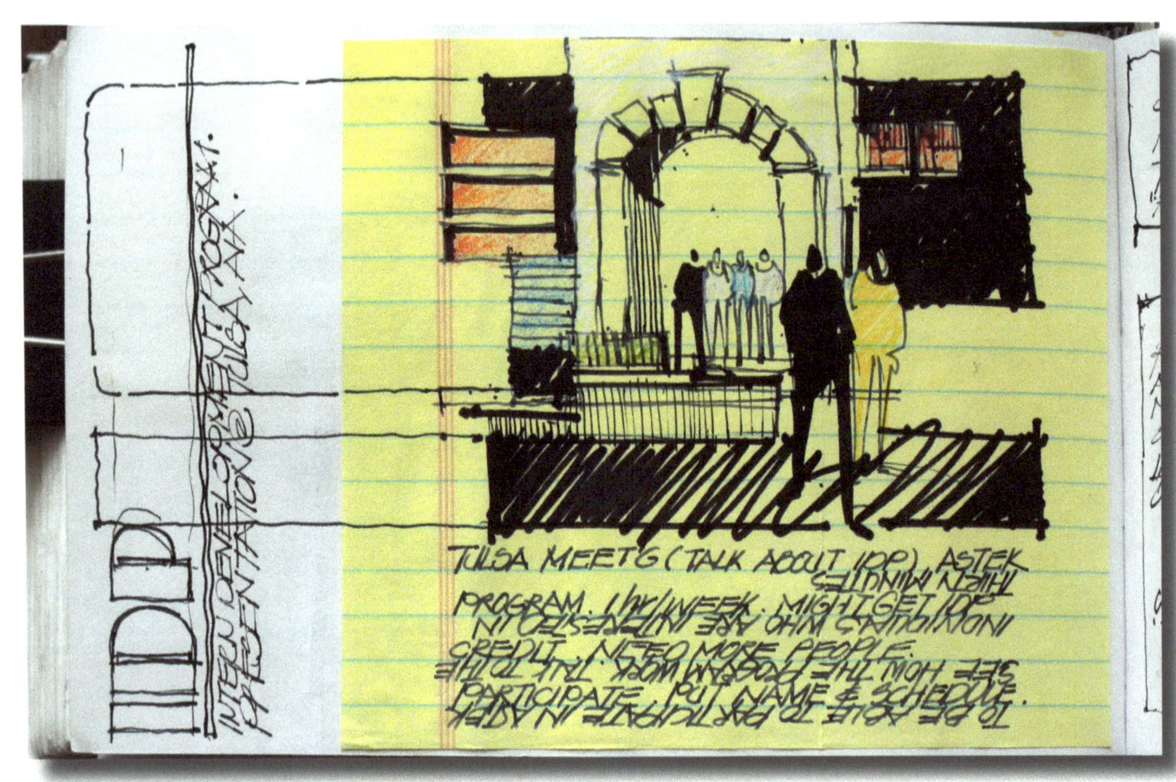

Fig. 09-99 One page journal entry, Moh'd Bilbeisi. Pen, colored pencils, and marker on paper.

IGJ-3.3

MOH'D BILBEISI

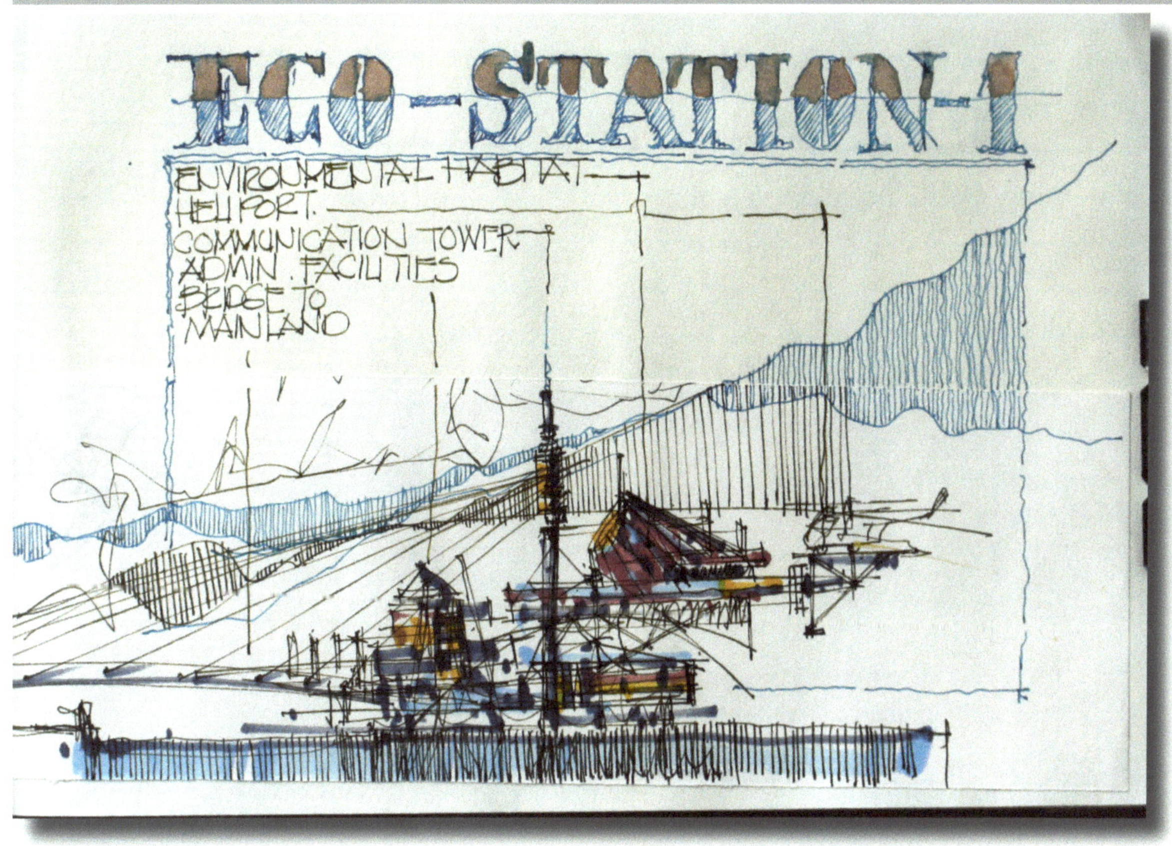

Fig. 09-100 One page journal entry, Moh'd Bilbeisi. Pen and marker on paper.

A single orthographic sketch is the focus of this single page layout. A low-value base anchors the page. The sketch is loosely drawn and superimposed on a dynamic undulating shape that is vertically hatched. This directional shape is added to graphically detach the sketch from the page. The journal entry sketch, title, and the justified notation form an implied rectangle of graphic information.

IGJ-3.4

MOH'D BILBEISI

This entire journal entry is drawn on notepad paper and later glued to a page inside the graphic journal. The text is composed in two vertical columns hovering over the sketch spanning both sides of the page. An area of hatching is used as a graphic background for the sketch. Watercolors are used to add drama to the composition.

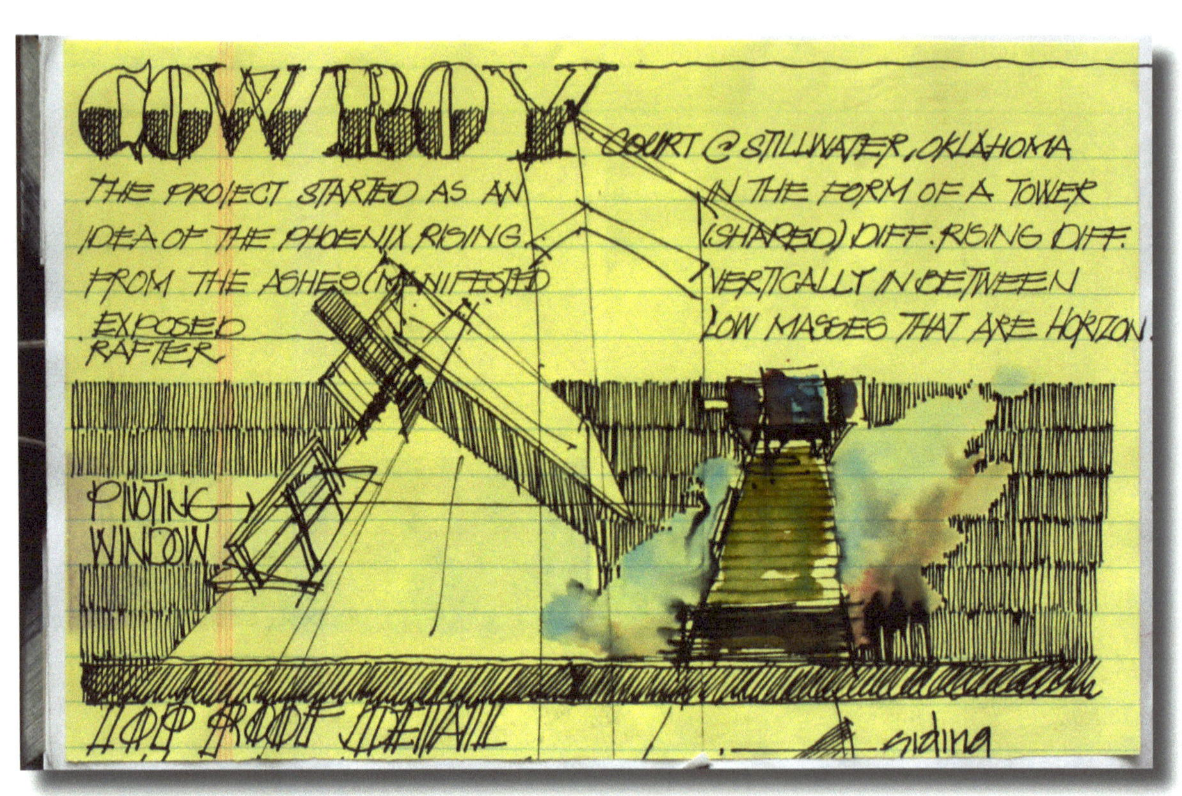

Fig. 09-101 One page journal entry, Moh'd Bilbeisi. Pen and watercolors on paper.

IGJ-3.5

MOH'D BILBEISI

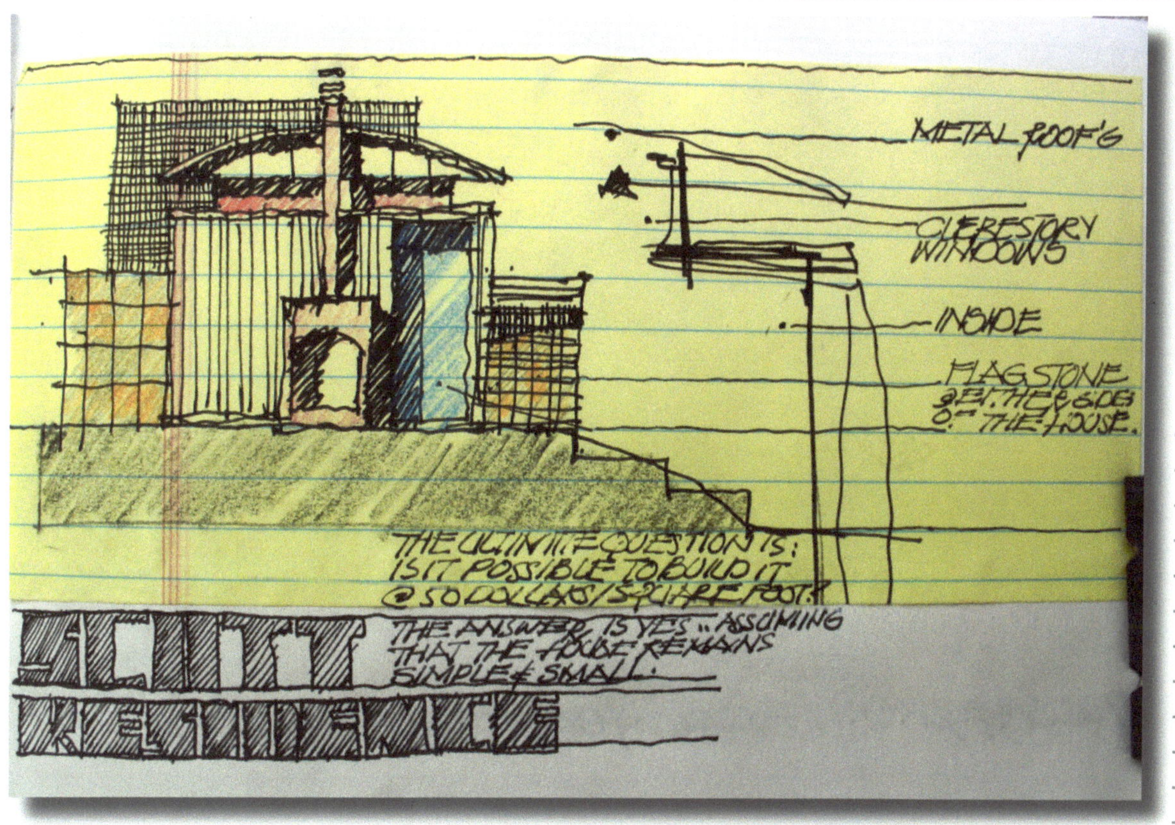

Fig. 09-102 One page journal entry, Moh'd Bilbeisi. Pen and colored pencils on paper.

The title and supporting text occupy the bottom third of the page in this single page layout. The major orthographic sketch is rendered in color with an annotated secondary sketch that is intentionally left unrendered to communicate hierarchy. Graphic value is achieved through careful hatching and the addition of color. The guidelines for the page title are done in ink without any attempt to conceal them.

IGJ-3.6

MOH'D BILBEISI

The sketch was executed on a yellow notepad and later trimmed and glued to the journal page. The page is divided horizontally into thirds with the top two thirds dedicated to an experiential sketch with a strong sense of perspective. Graphic value is achieved through modulated random lines. Color is applied with the warmer shades located at the vanishing point. The addition of human figures helps identify scale. The page title and the supporting text are added as a high contrast strip towards the bottom to graphically anchor the composition.

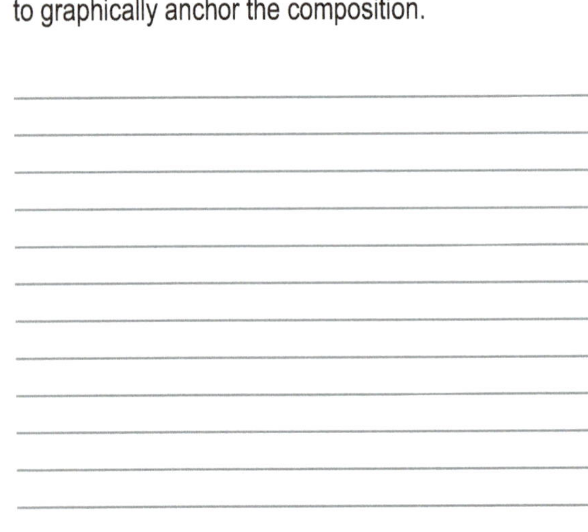

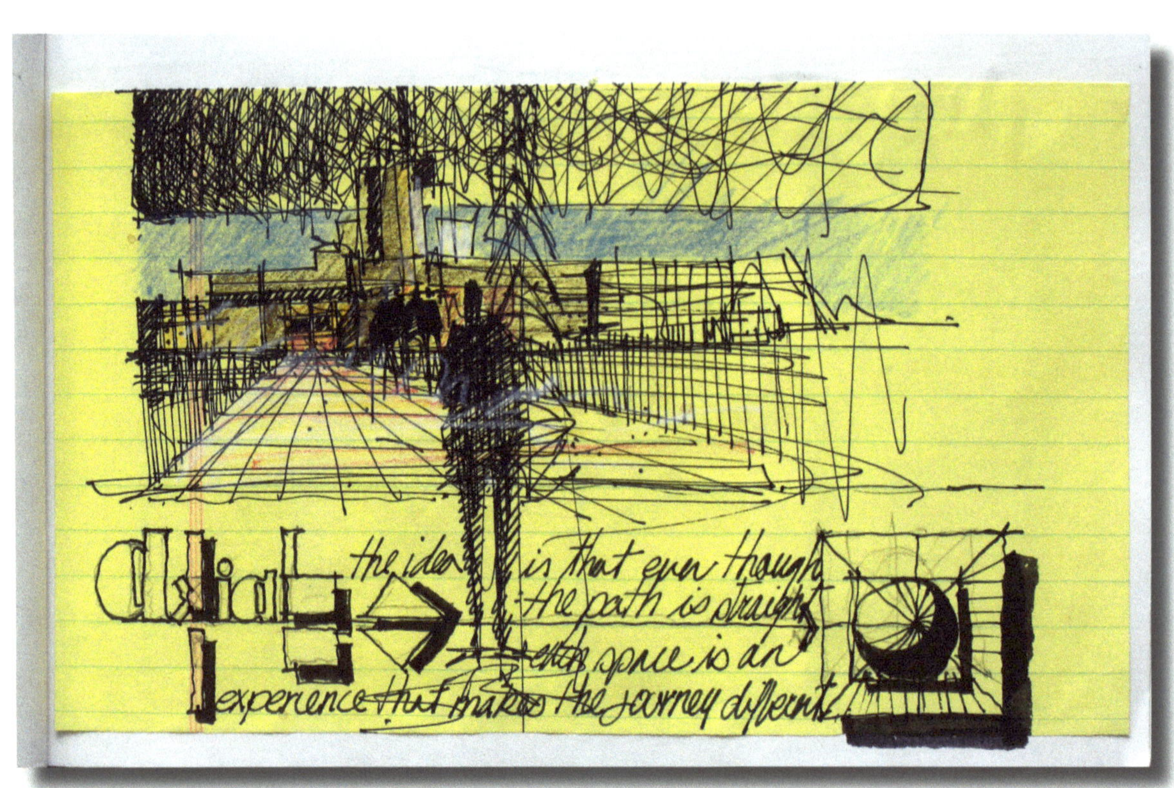

Fig. 09-103 One page journal entry, Moh'd Bilbeisi. Pen, marker, and colored pencil on paper.

IGJ-3.7

MOH'D BILBEISI

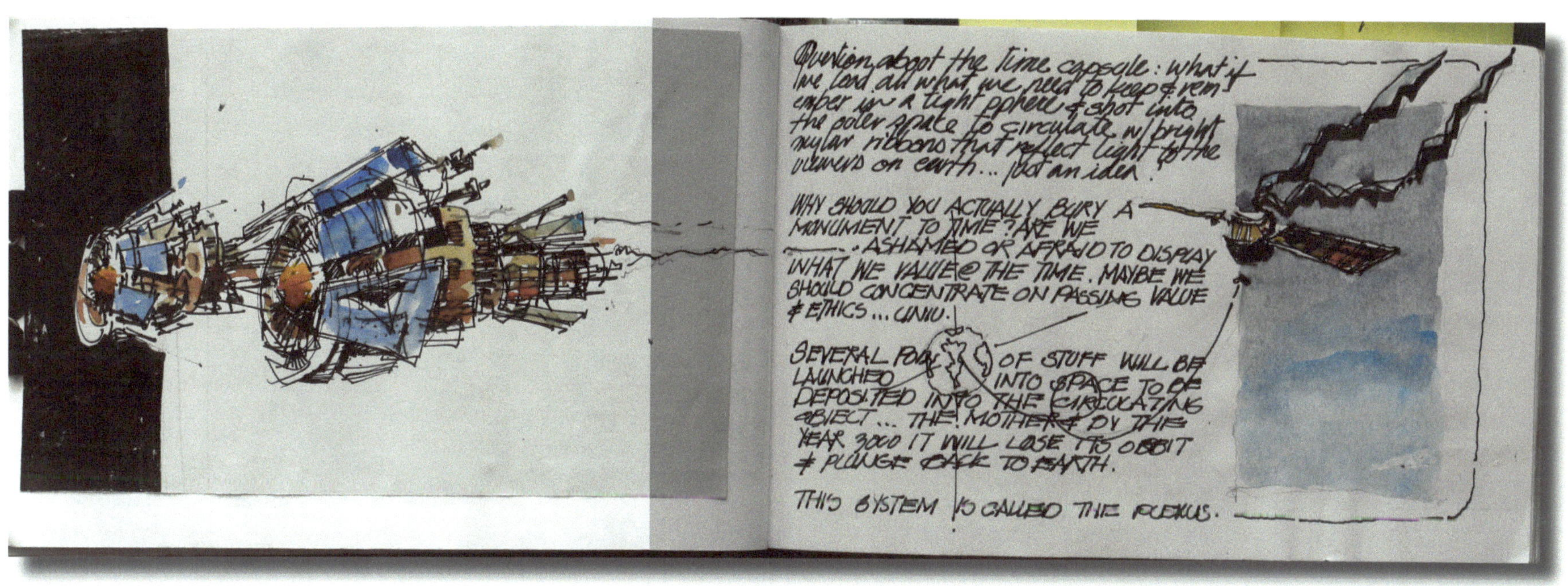

Fig. 09-104 Two-page journal entry, Moh'd Bilbeisi. Pen, marker, and watercolors on paper.

This journal entry is composed with a single sketch on one page and the supporting text on the second. High contrast graphic values are used to produce a modulated wash. Graphic bracketing is used to contain the sketches and a graphic background is used to detach the sketches from the pages.

IGJ-3.8

MOH'D BILBEISI

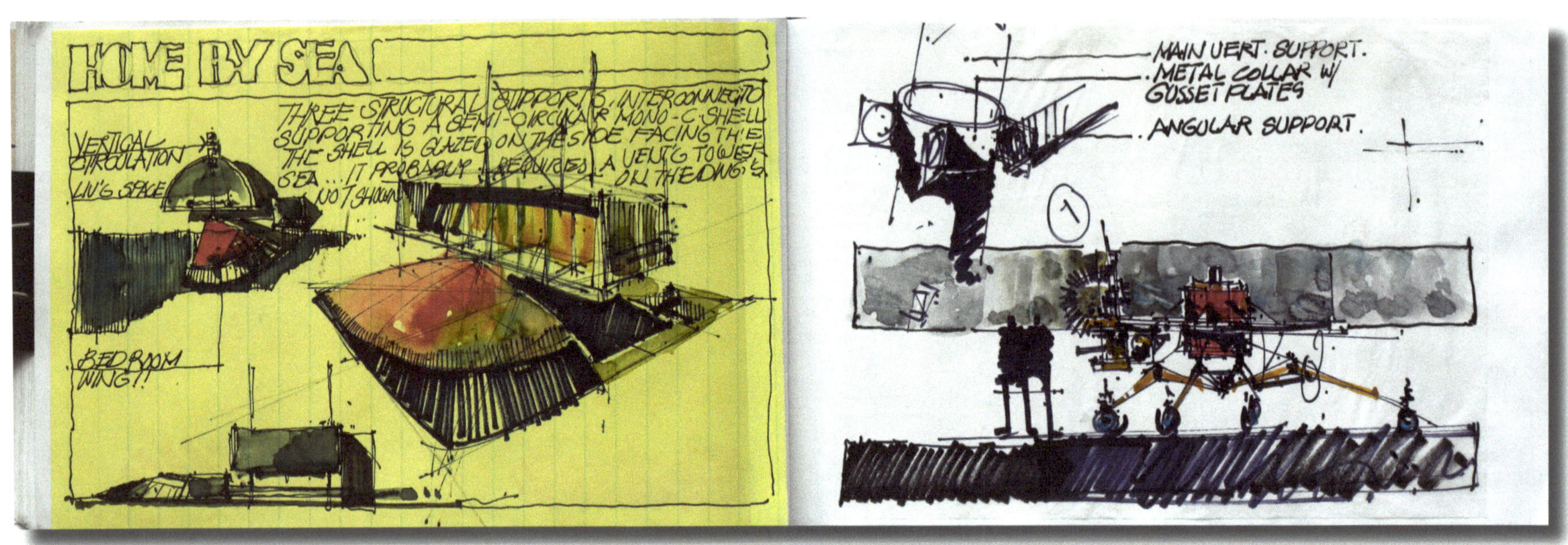

The sketches on the left were executed on a yellow notepad, and later trimmed and glued onto the pages of the journal. The sketch in the middle is the hierarchical element, as it is the largest and supported with text. Graphic value is achieved through hatching and application of color.

Fig. 09-105 Two-page journal entry, Moh'd Bilbeisi. Pen, marker, and watercolors on paper.

IGJ-3.9

MOH'D BILBEISI

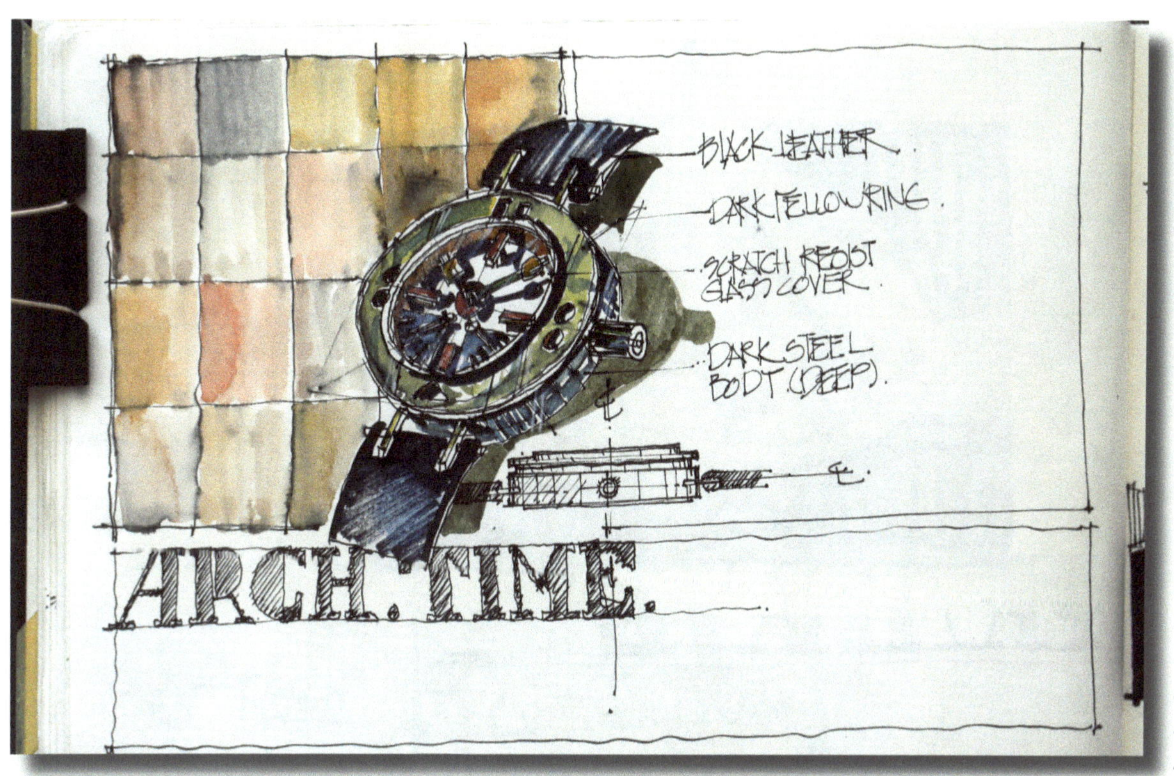

Fig. 09-106 One page journal entry, Moh'd Bilbeisi. Pen, and watercolors on paper.

This single page composition is divided horizontally into thirds. The divisions of the page are stroked with a thin line, and the sketch and its annotation are overlaid upon the left half of the page. The sketch is rendered in watercolors that reacted positively with the fountain pen ink. A colorful graphic background is used to detach the sketch from the page. A hatched title is aligned with the sketch and located at the bottom of the page.

IGJ-3.10

MOH'D BILBEISI

The layout is divided into compositional graphic rectangles that relate in different ways to constitute the page. A plan sketch, a perspective sketch, and the page title are situated on the outer edges of the page, focusing attention on the notation. Watercolors are used to highlight the sketches and the backgrounds.

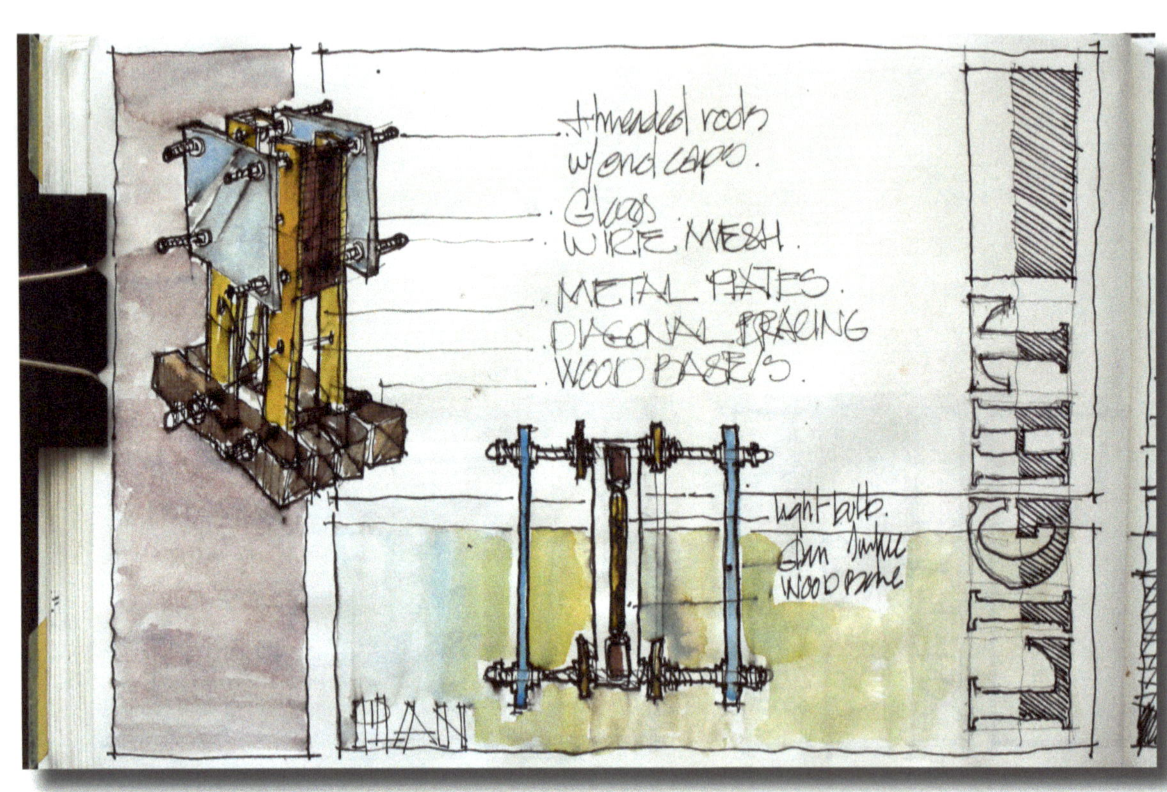

Fig. 09-107 One page journal entry, Moh'd Bilbeisi. Pen, and watercolors on paper.

IGJ-3.11

MOH'D BILBEISI

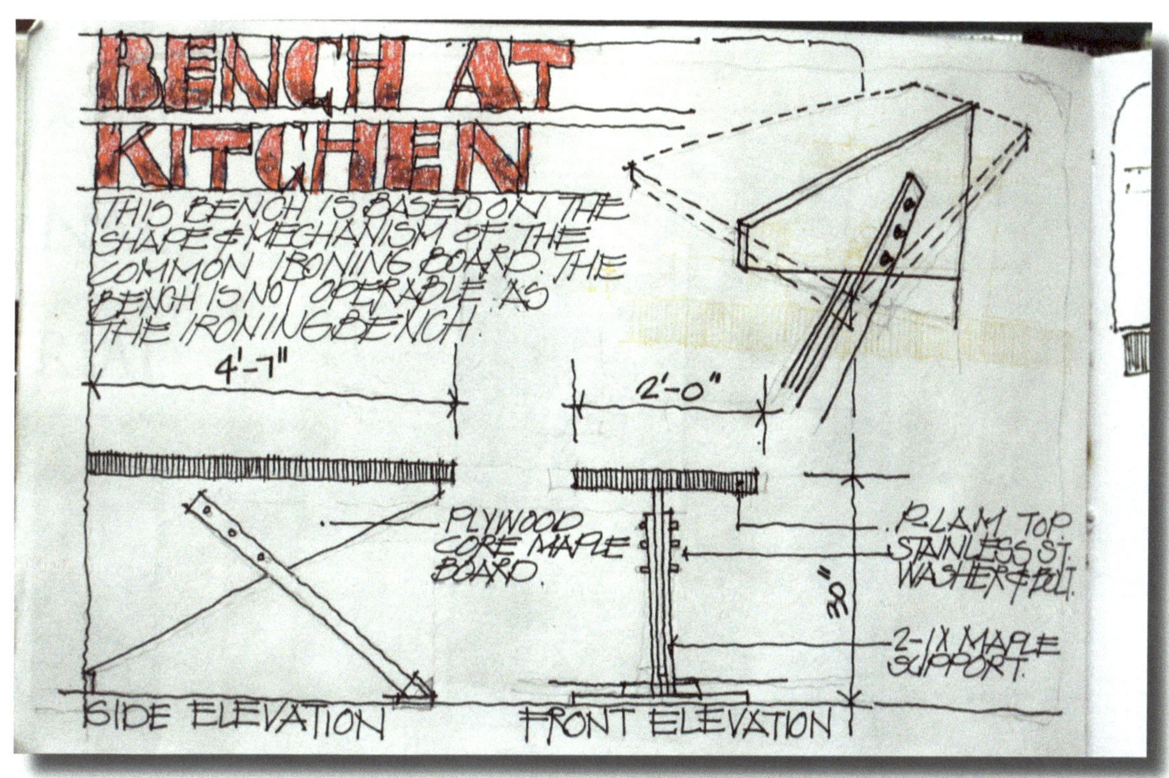

Fig. 09-108 One page journal entry, Moh'd Bilbeisi. Pen, and colored pencils on paper.

The single page composition is divided into four quadrants. Three of the quadrants are occupied by technical sketches and the fourth quadrant is occupied by the title and the supporting text. The sketches are drawn with clarity and without any shading to obscure the design intent.

IGJ-3.12

MOH'D BILBEISI

This page is divided into two halves with a thick dark line acting as a base and a graphic connector. The sketches are gestural in nature with their graphic value expressed through watercolors and hatching. The sketch on the left employs a graphic frame to detach it from the page while the other sketch employs a shadowed area. The journal entry title adheres to the rectangular nature of the composition.

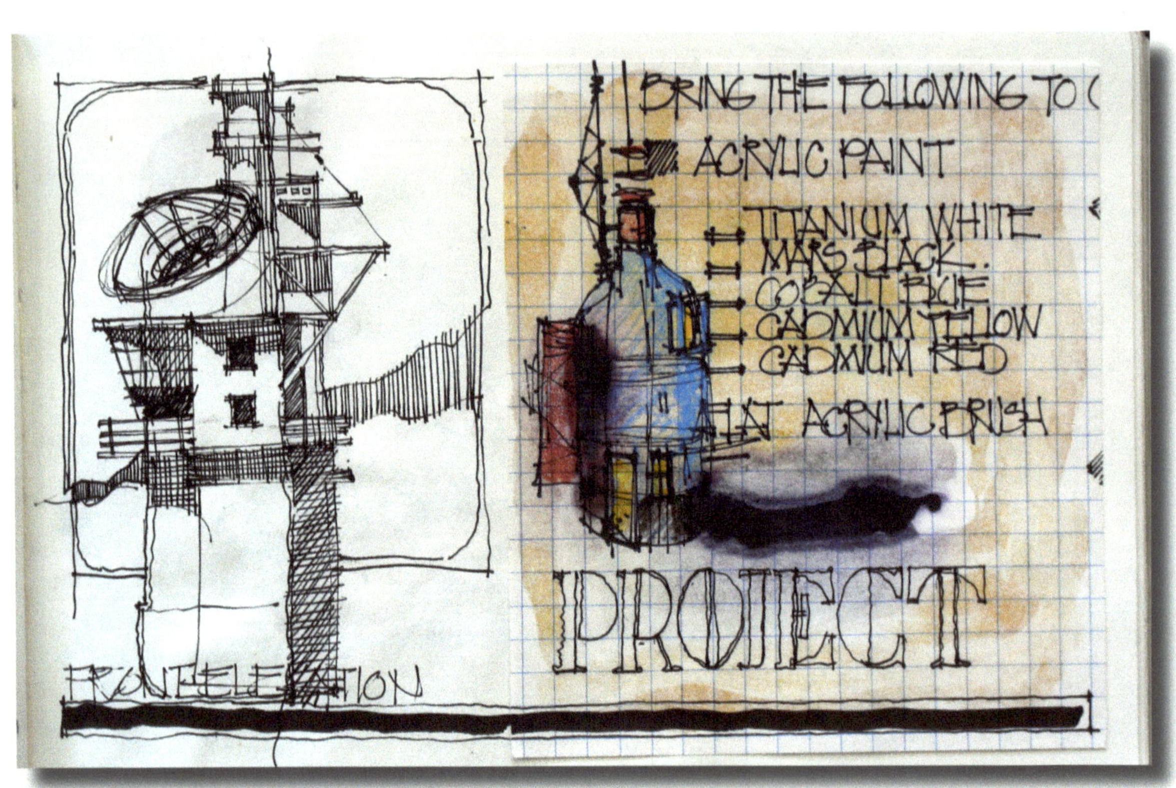

Fig. 09-109 One page journal entry, Moh'd Bilbeisi. Pen, colored pencils, and watercolors on paper.

IGJ-3.13

MOH'D BILBEISI

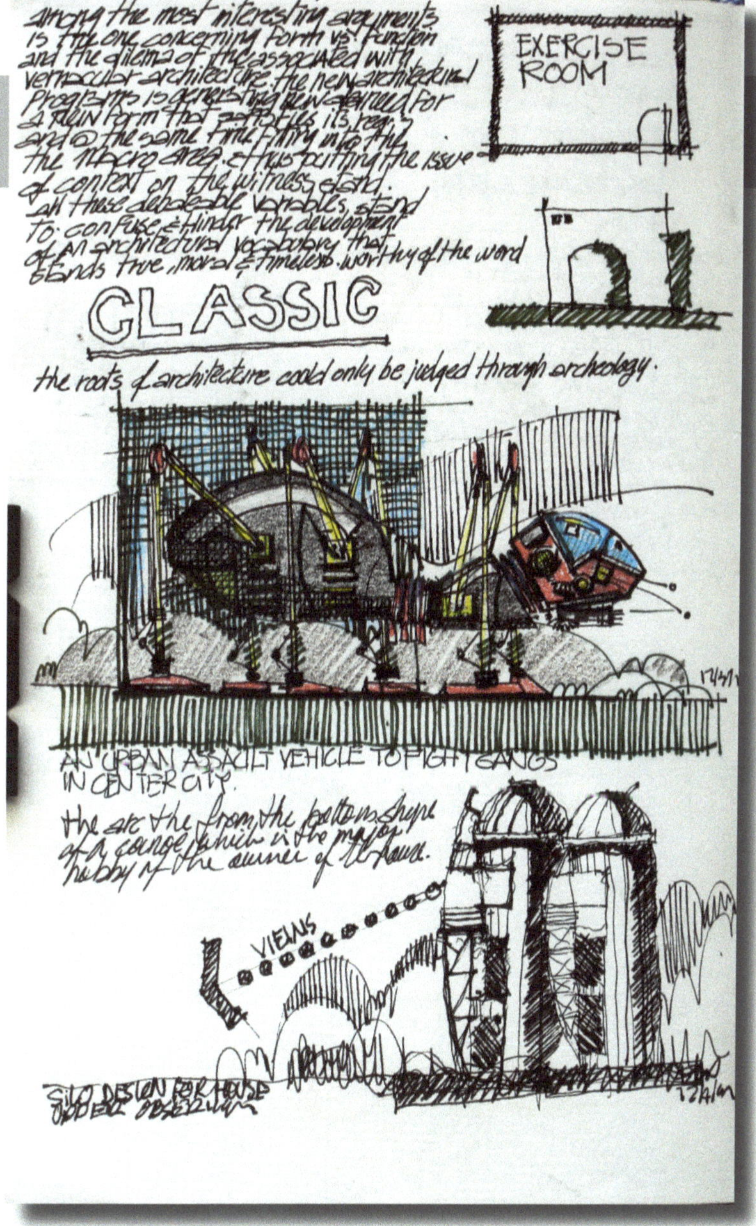

The single page composition is divided into three horizontal strips. The bottom two strips contain the sketches and the top strip contains the supporting text. All the sketches use hatching or cross hatching to achieve graphic value, and all of the sketches employ a dark base as an anchor.

Fig. 09-110 One page journal entry, Moh'd Bilbeisi. Pen and colored pencils on paper.

IGJ-3.14

MOH'D BILBEISI

This single page journal entry utilizes collage as a medium to enhance graphic communication. The "to go" menu cover of a local restaurant is used as a starting point for this entry to communicate the design intent. Graphic value is achieved through hatching. The existing graphics on the restaurant's preprinted sketch set the scale for the drawing.

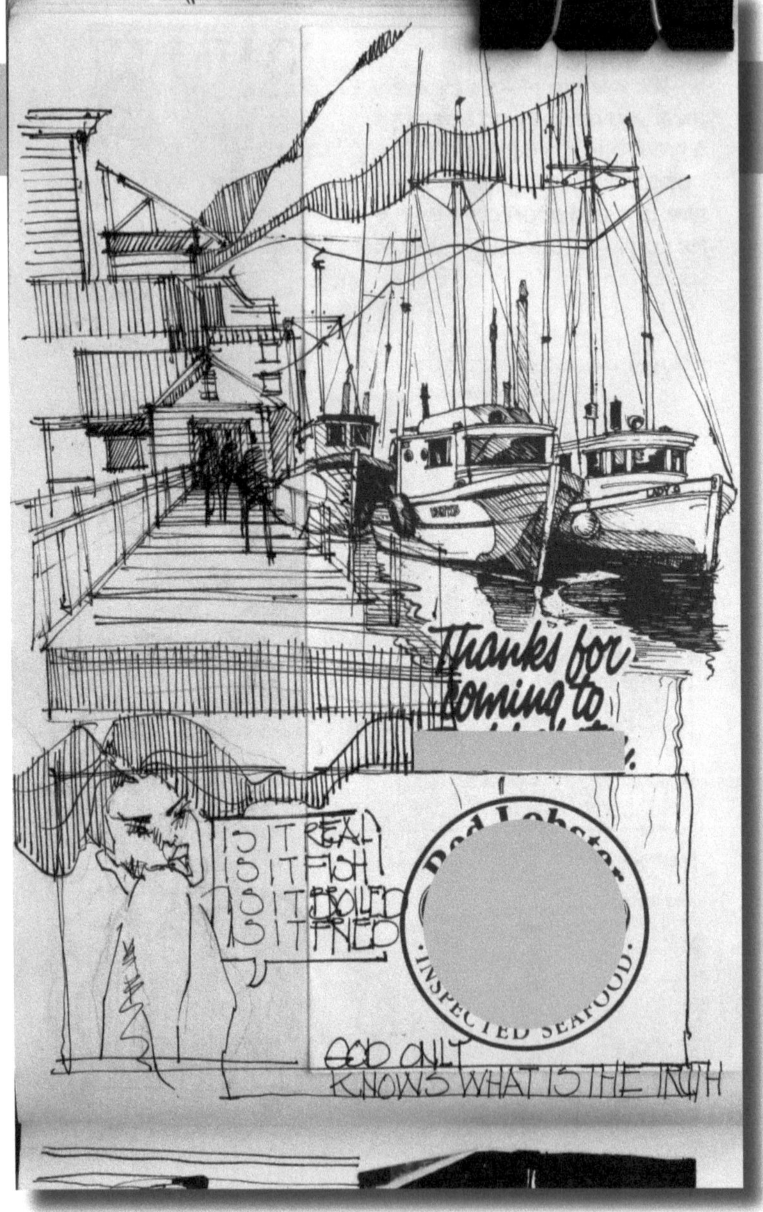

Fig. 09-111 One page journal entry, Moh'd Bilbeisi. Pen on paper.

IGJ-3.15

MOH'D BILBEISI

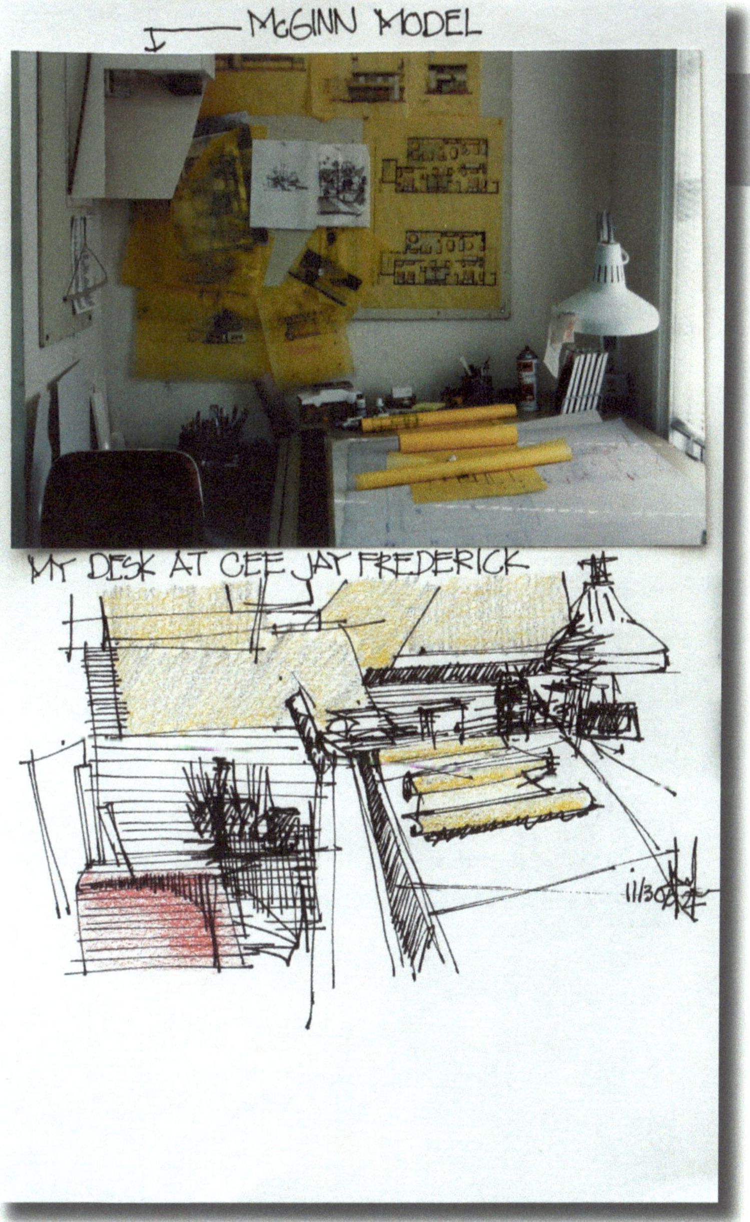

Photography is included within the composition of this single page journal entry. The photograph occupies the top one half of the page, and a sketch is used to anchor the other half. Graphic value is achieved though hatching and the use of color.

Fig. 09-112 One page journal entry, Moh'd Bilbeisi. Pen, colored pencils, and photography on paper.

IGJ-3.16

MOH'D BILBEISI

This page is divided into two halves. The top half was executed on a yellow notepad, and later trimmed, glued, and composed onto the page of the journal. Hatching, watercolors, and high contrast shading are employed to detach the sketch from the pages of the journal to give it a more three dimensional aspect. The supporting text and a graphic frame are applied to both halves so as to tie them together compositionally.

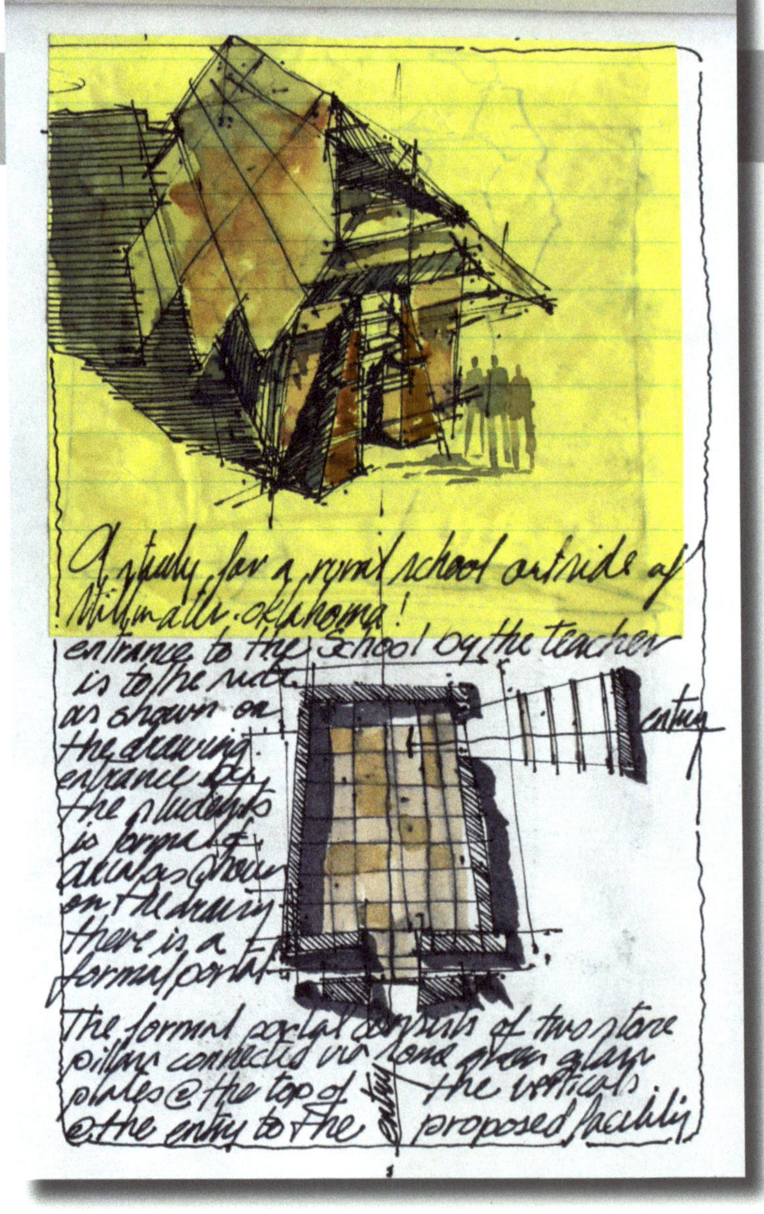

Fig. 09-113 One page journal entry, Moh'd Bilbeisi. Pen, marker, and newsprint on paper.

IGJ-3.17

MOH'D BILBEISI

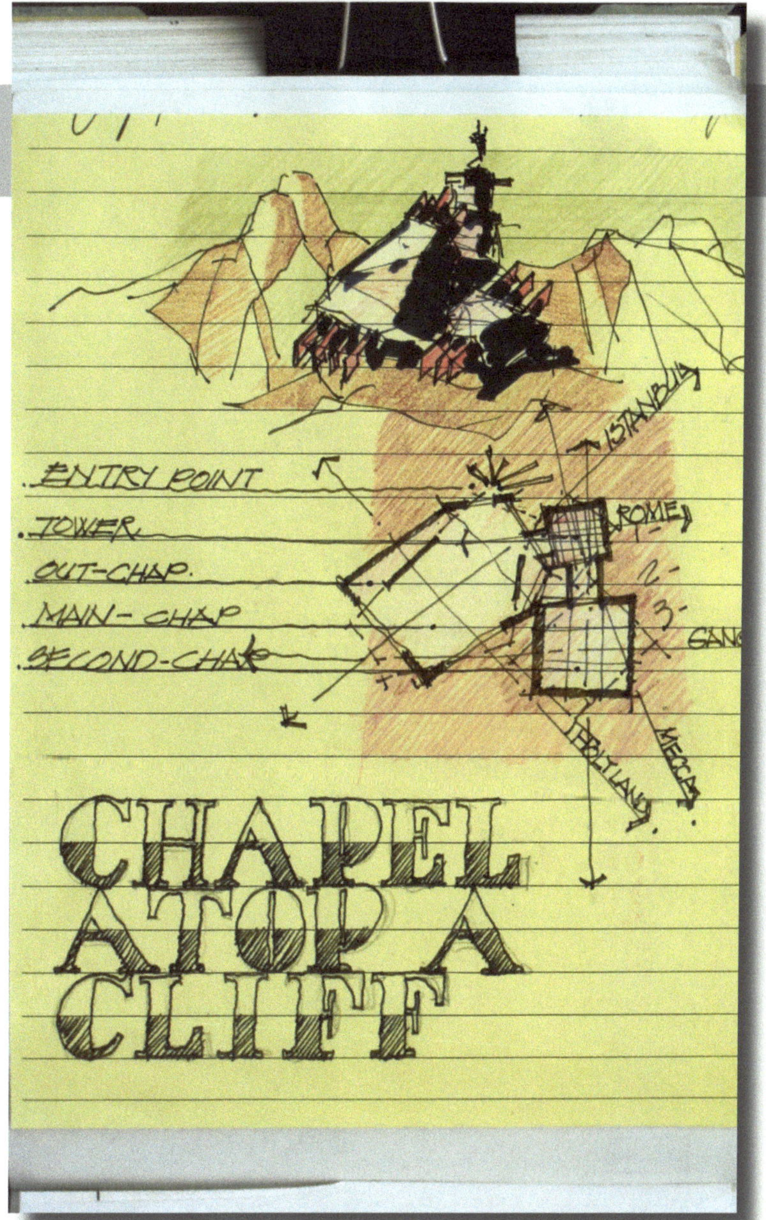

This graphic information was executed on a separate sheet of yellow notepad paper, and later trimmed and glued to the journal page. The page is horizontally divided into thirds with the top two thirds dedicated to the sketch and the annotation. The main sketch itself is informal and includes a secondary sketch, a floor plan, that is superimposed to show hierarchy. The title and the supporting text occupy the lower part of the page in an attempt to anchor the composition.

Fig. 09-114 One page journal entry, Moh'd Bilbeisi. Pen, colored pencils, and marker on paper.

IGJ-3.18

MOH'D BILBEISI

The beginnings of this primary sketch were drawn on another piece of paper, and then trimmed and glued to the journal page to start a composition. Graphic bracketing, text, and other graphic elements were drawn on both pages, the original sheet and the journal page. The major vertical sketch was located to the right of the page to contain the view. Two secondary sketches are included to communicate the design intent. A band of vertical hatching anchors the composition.

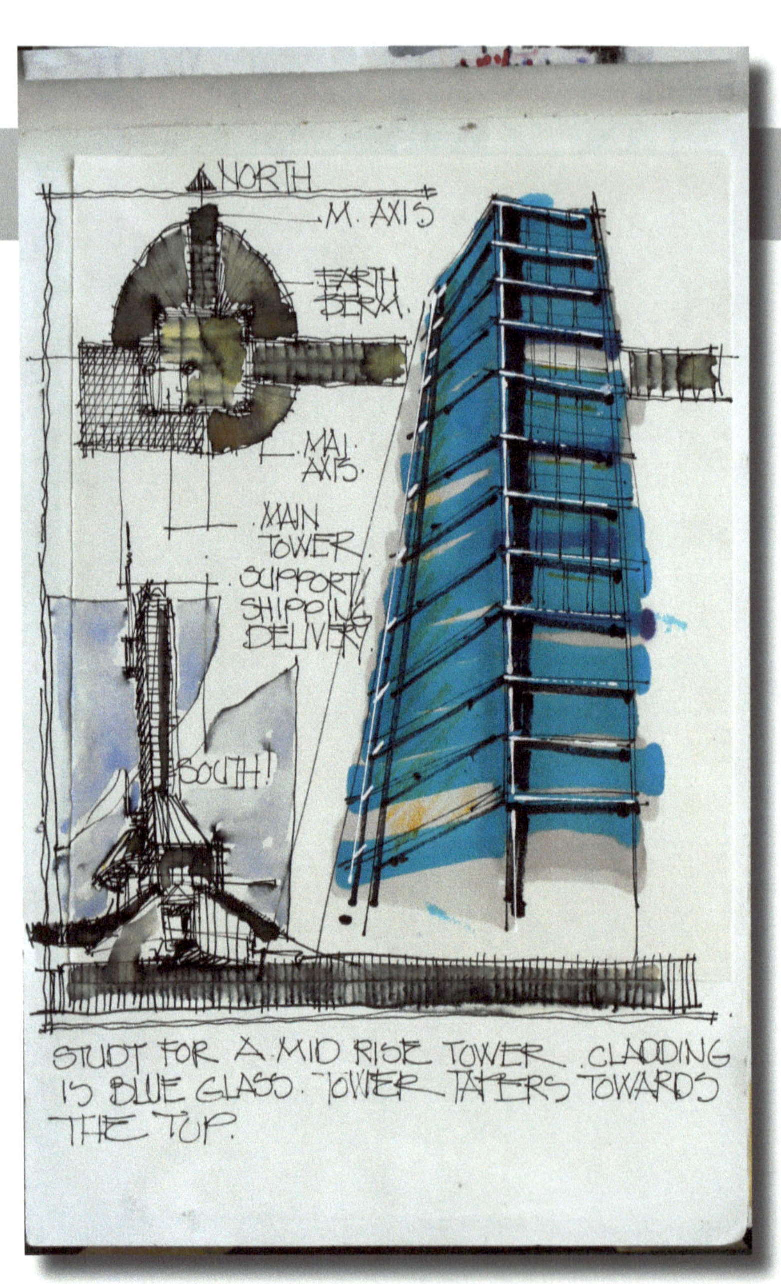

Fig. 09-115 One page journal entry, Moh'd Bilbeisi. Pen, marker, colored pencils, and watercolors on paper.

IGJ-3.19

MOH'D BILBEISI

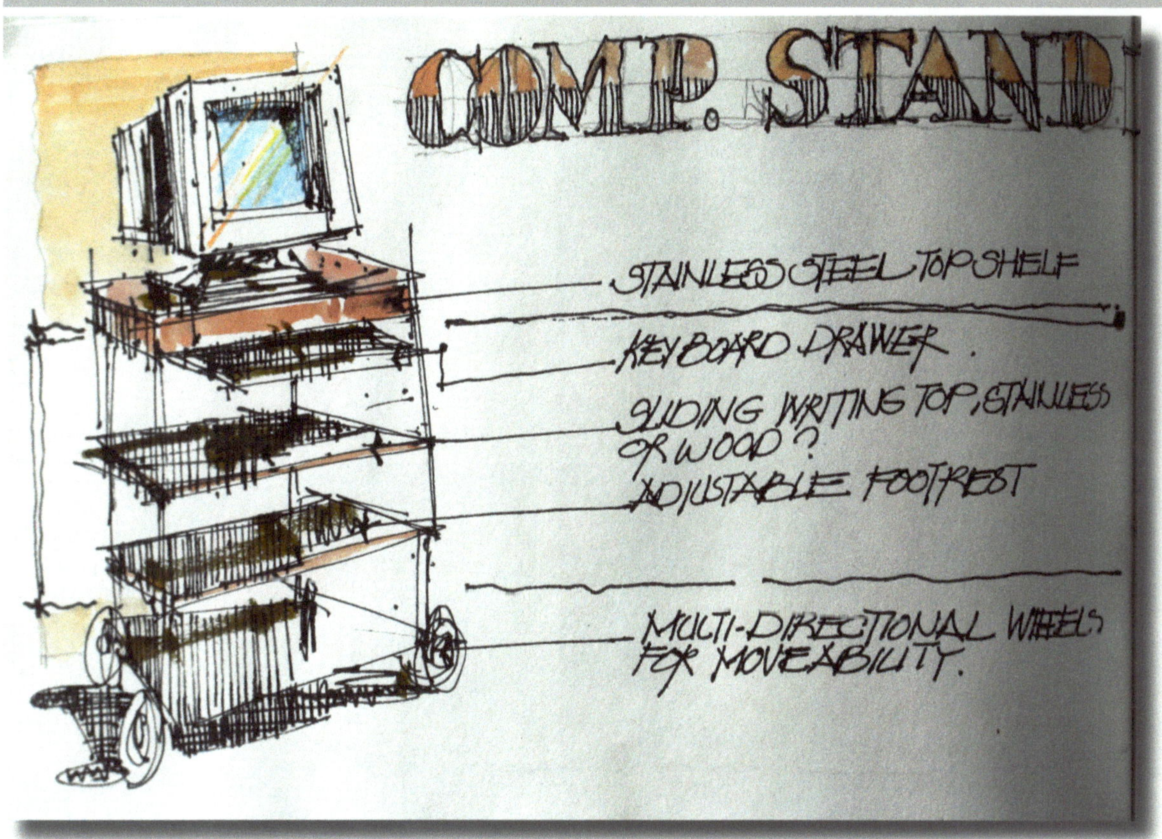

Fig. 09-116 One page journal entry, Moh'd Bilbeisi. Pen, colored pencils, and watercolors on paper.

The single page composition is divided vertically into thirds. The directional sketch is occupying the left third, while facing the right to contain the journal entry. Notation is keyed to the sketch by graphic leaders and the title is situated atop the right two-thirds of the sheet. Hatching, cross hatching, and watercolors are used to add graphic value.

IGJ-3.20

MOH'D BILBEISI

The single sketch journal entry is supported by annotation keyed to the sketch by graphic leaders. The sketch is rendered in watercolors, which have interacted with fountain pen ink to produce an interesting color range in the washes. Graphic value is achieved through loose manipulation of hue. The title is extended via a graphic frame to form the base for the sketch.

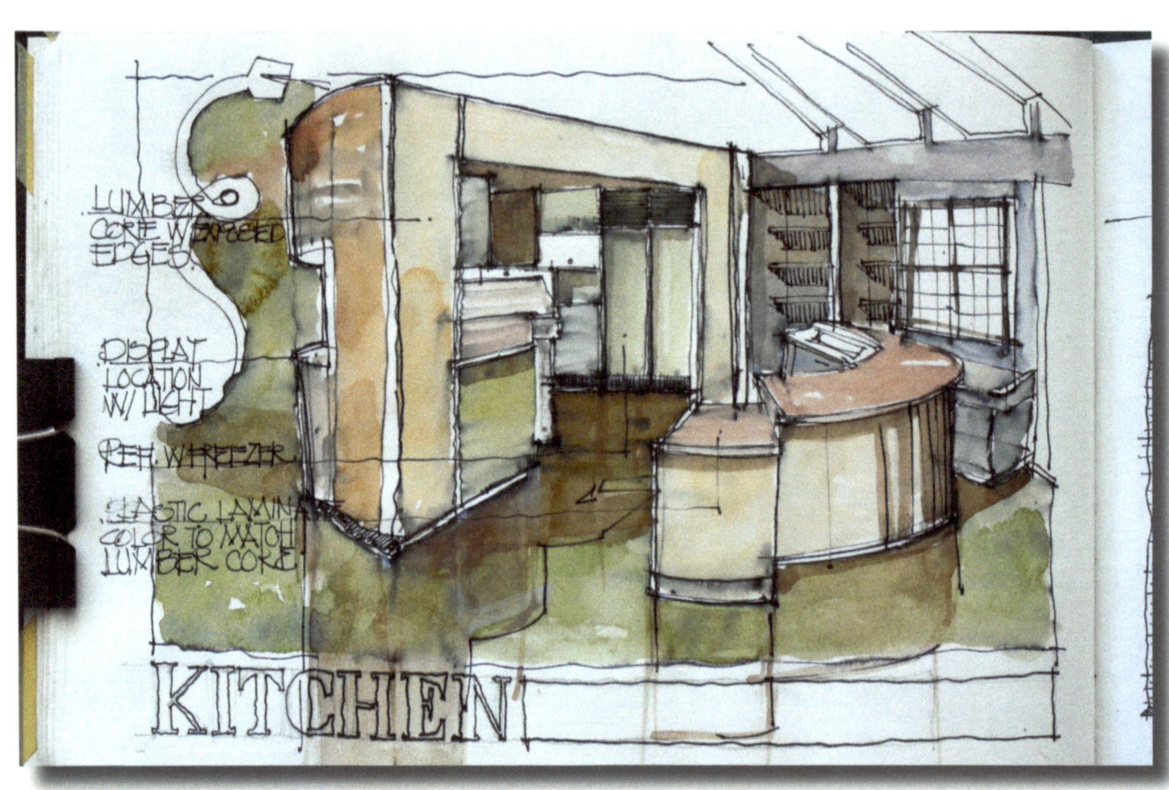

Fig. 09-117 One page journal entry, Moh'd Bilbeisi. Pen and watercolors on paper.

IGJ-3.21

MOH'D BILBEISI

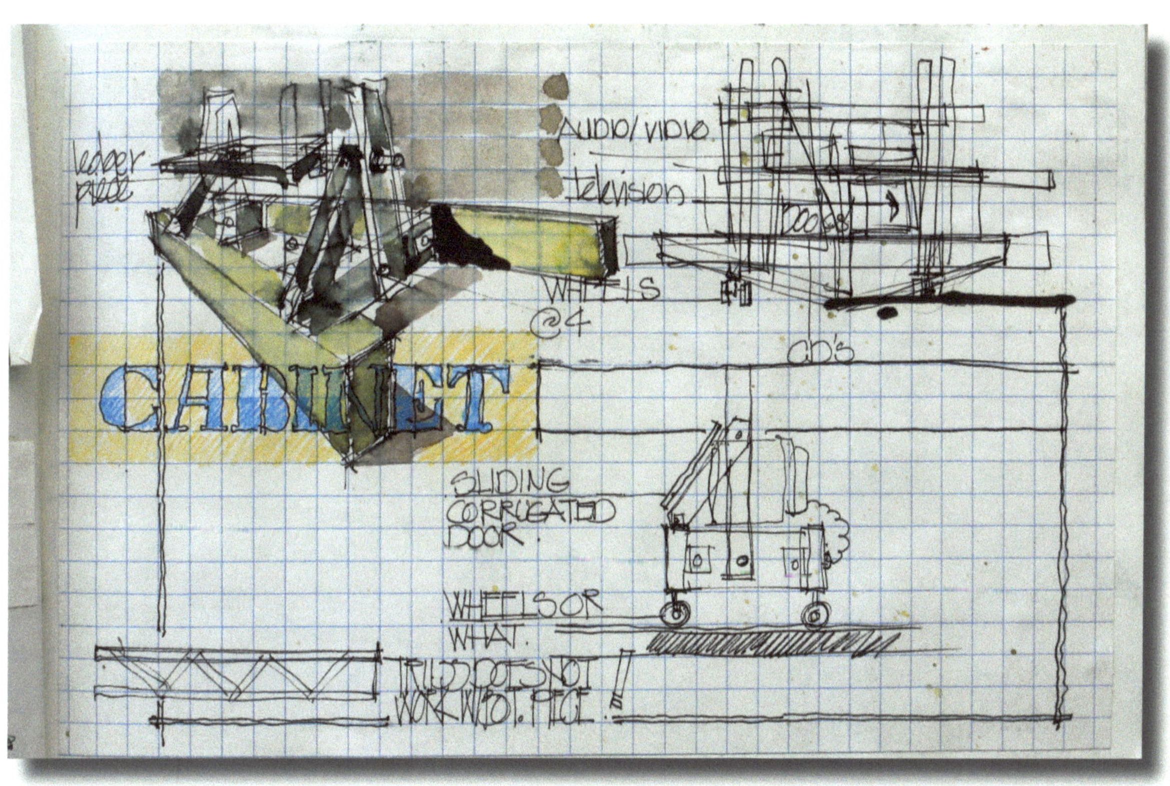

Fig. 09-118 One page journal entry, Moh'd Bilbeisi. Pen, colored pencils, and watercolors on paper.

The single page composition is divided into four quadrants. The main perspectival sketch is occupying the first quadrant and the remaining quadrants are occupied by three secondary sketches. The major sketch is the only one that is rendered in watercolors and the remaining sketches are rather diagrammatic in nature to illustrate the design intent. The title is treated as a transparent strip that is superimposed on the composition.

IGJ-3.22

MOH'D BILBEISI

The single page composition uses a large sketch to set the mood for the journal entry. A second high contrast sketch is added to further communicate the design intent. A large title and the supporting text are located towards the bottom of the page to balance the black graphic background behind the secondary sketch. A single line is added at the top of the page to connect the two sketches.

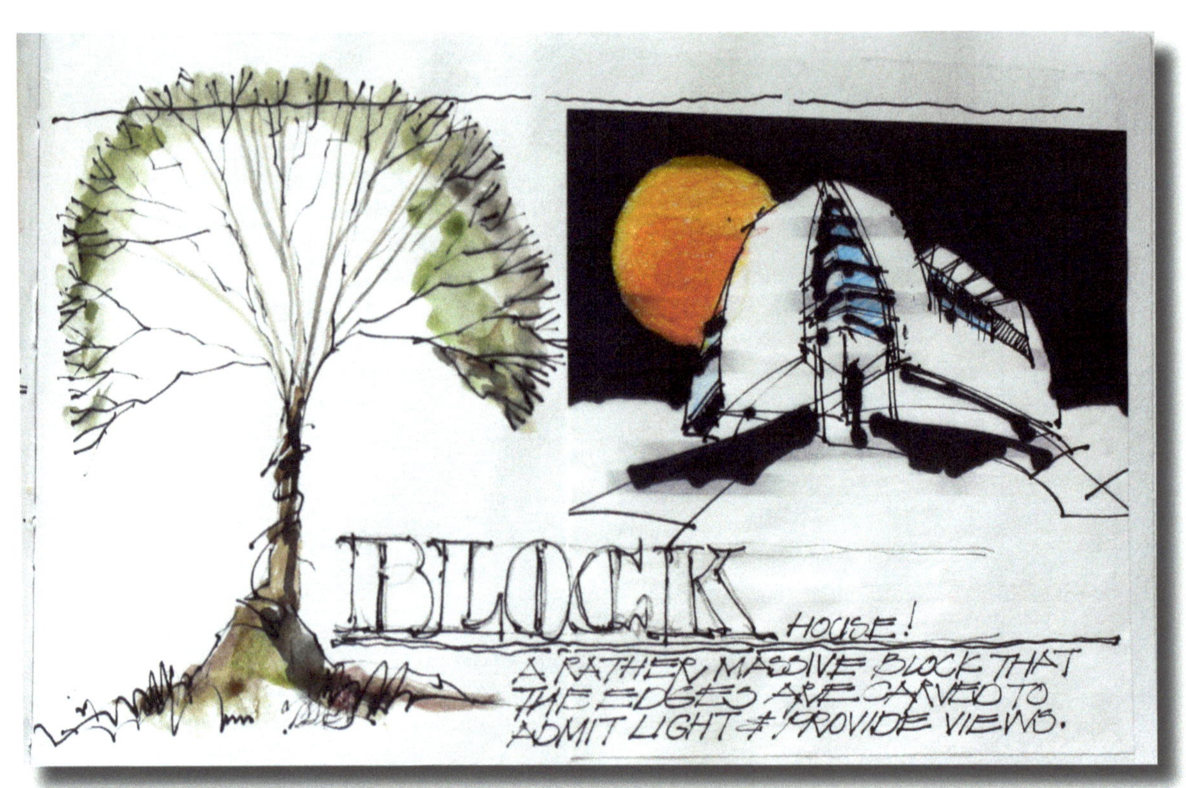

Fig. 09-119 One page journal entry, Moh'd Bilbeisi. Pen and marker on newsprint paper.

IGJ-3.23

MOH'D BILBEISI

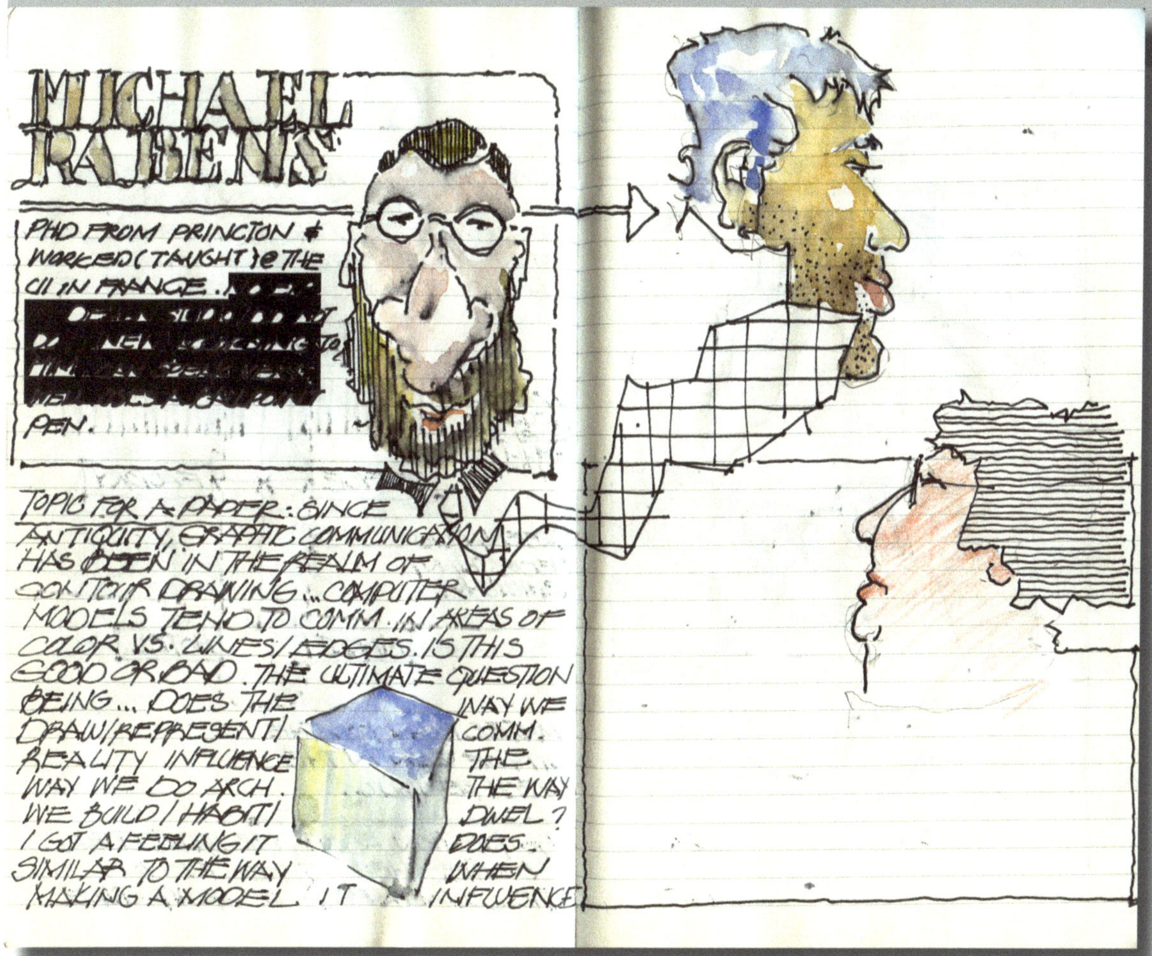

This two-page composition carries the bulk of the information on one page. The sketches on the second page are graphically connected to the first page via graphic tools such as arrows, connectors, and line frames. The page title is located on the first page towards the top, to establish hierarchy. The sketches are rendered through watercolors, colored pencils, and hatching.

Fig. 09-120 Two-page journal entry, Moh'd Bilbeisi. Pen, colored pencils, and watercolors on paper.

IGJ-3.24

MOH'D BILBEISI

This journal entry began with a logo on a restaurant napkin, which was later glued onto a journal page. The sketch is attempting to detach itself from the surface through a graphic frame. The effect of watercolors is enhanced by the interaction with the fountain pen ink. The logo serves as a title for the journal entry.

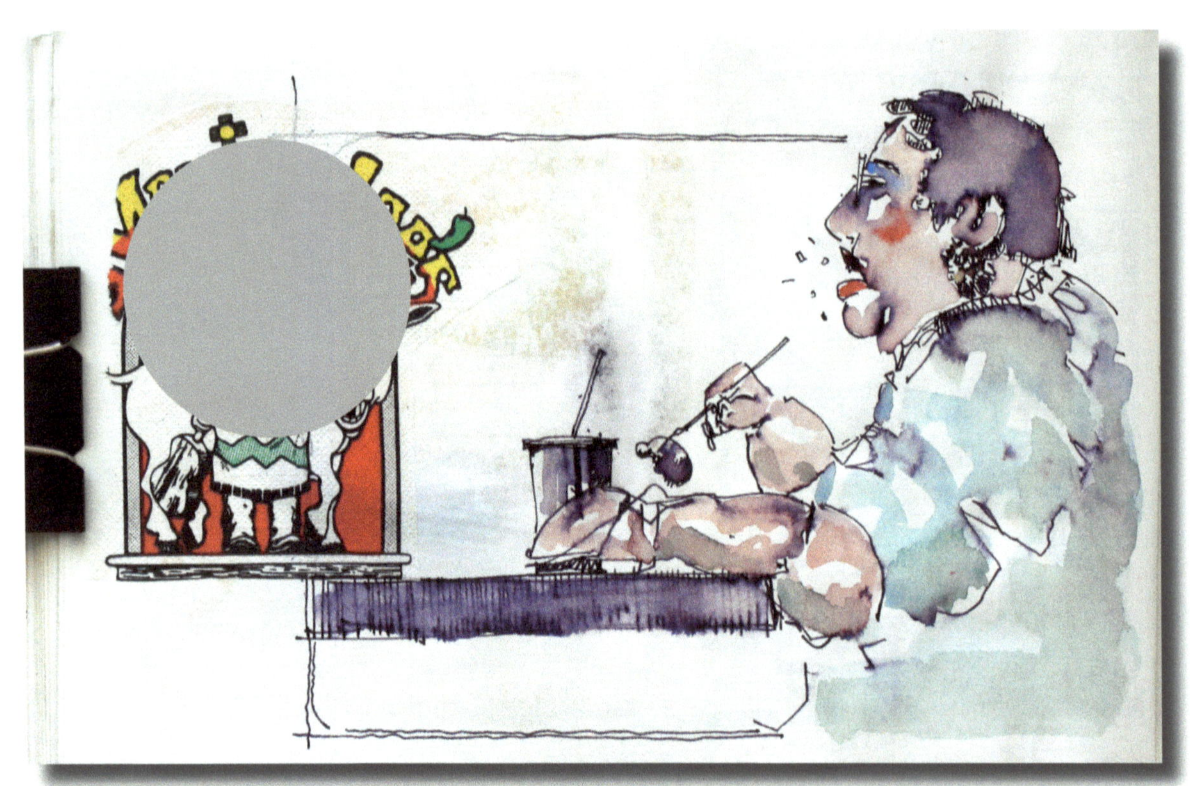

Fig. 09-121 One page journal entry, Moh'd Bilbeisi. Pen and watercolors on paper.

IGJ-3.25

MOH'D BILBEISI

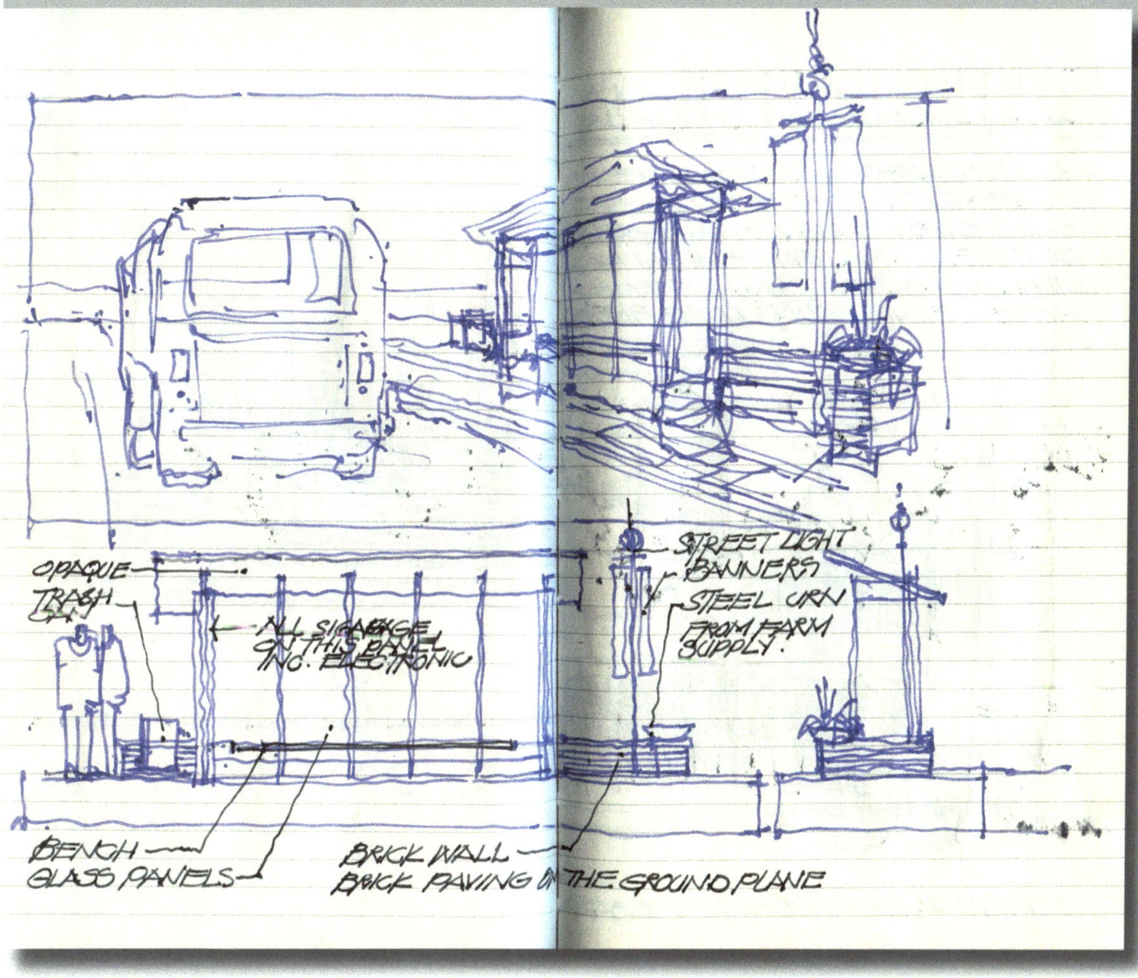

This two-page composition is divided into two horizontal strips of graphic information. The top sketch is perspectival in nature with a graphic frame to detach it from the page and the bottom one is orthographic with annotation interspersed throughout, keyed to the sketch by graphic leaders.

Fig. 09-122 Two-page journal entry, Moh'd Bilbeisi. Pen on paper.

IGJ-3.26

MOH'D BILBEISI

This two-page composition is divided into two horizontal graphic strips. The bottom strip contains the diagrams and the top strip is dedicated to the supporting text. The title is incorporated with the supporting text and a portrait sketch engages the text and adds a degree of integration and dynamism to the composition. Watercolors are used to highlight the sketches and diagrams.

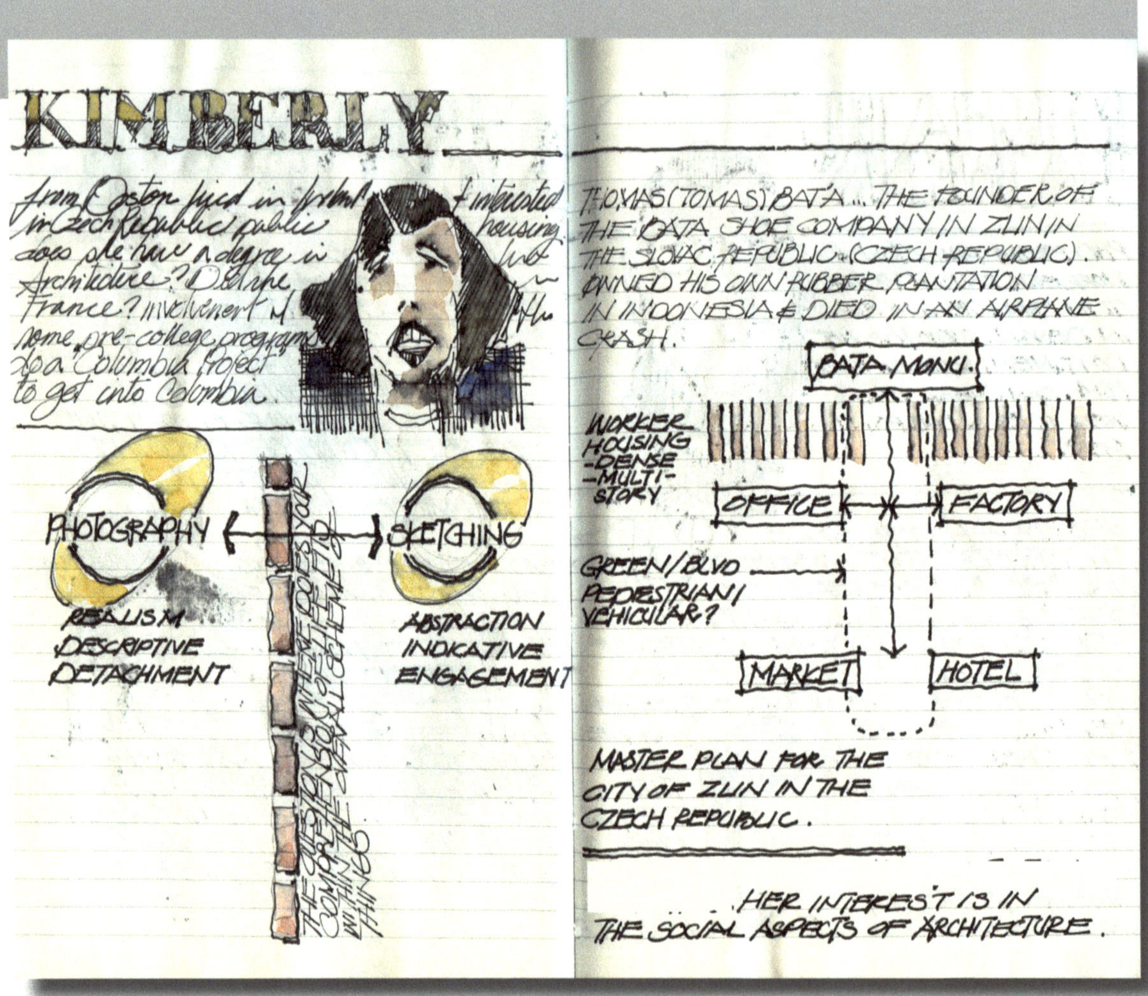

Fig. 09-123 Two-page journal entry, Moh'd Bilbeisi. Pen and watercolors on paper.

IGJ-4.1

BOB CONDIA

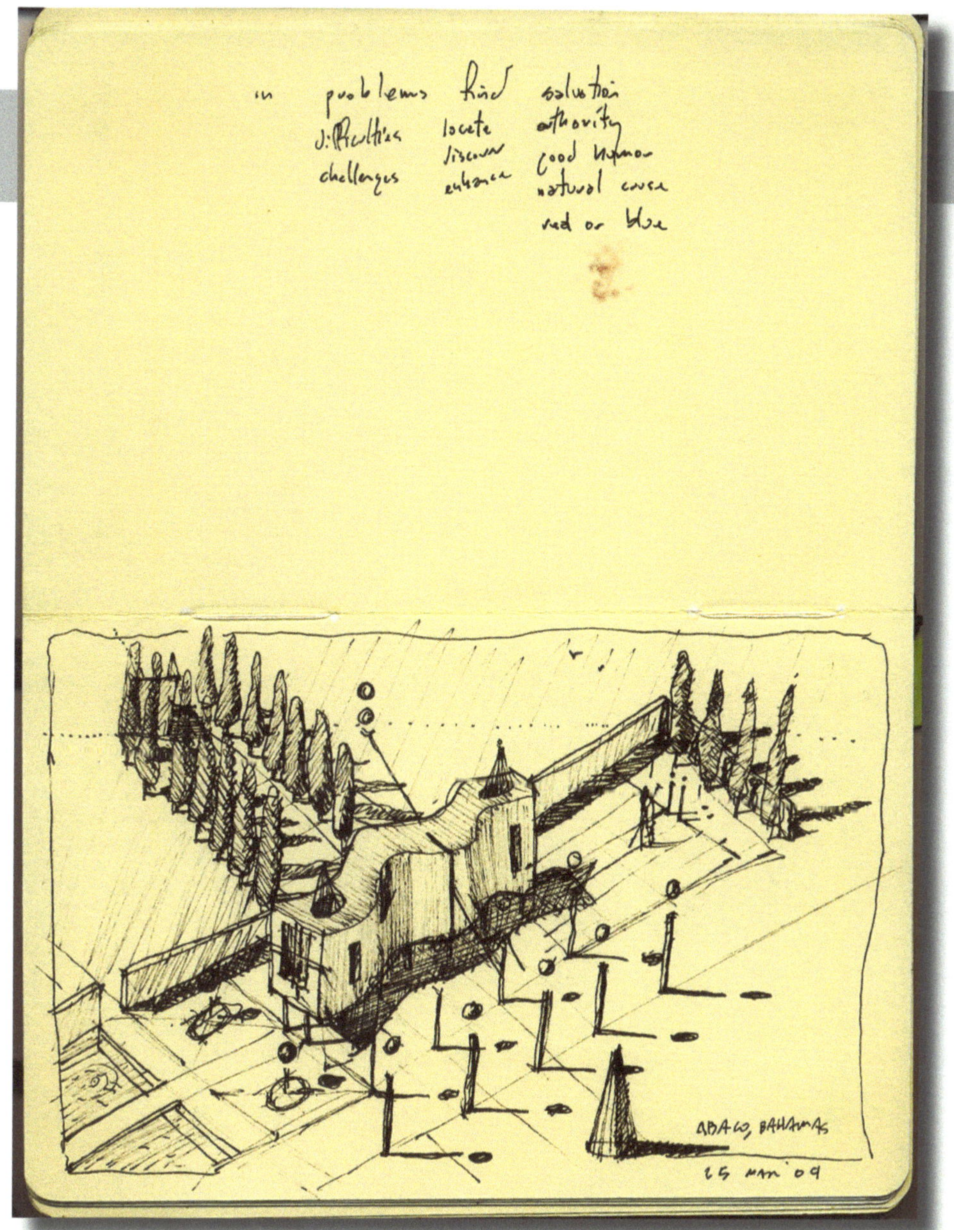

In this two-page composition, the lower page is occupied by the sketch while the top page is dedicated to the sparse enigmatic supporting text. The aerial sketch is graphically framed, although it opens along the bottom edge to allow the eye to escape from the view. It is rendered with hatching and cross hatching. The entire composition is dated and titled modestly at the lower right side.

Fig. 09-124 Two-page journal entry, Bob Condia. Pen on paper.

IGJ-4.2

BOB CONDIA

The two-page composition is divided into equal halves; the sketch is located on the right page and the supporting text is located on the left page. The sketch is rotated to acknowledge the longitudinal nature of the sketch as it best fits on a landscape format. Graphic value is achieved through the manipulation of the width and the darkness of the linework.

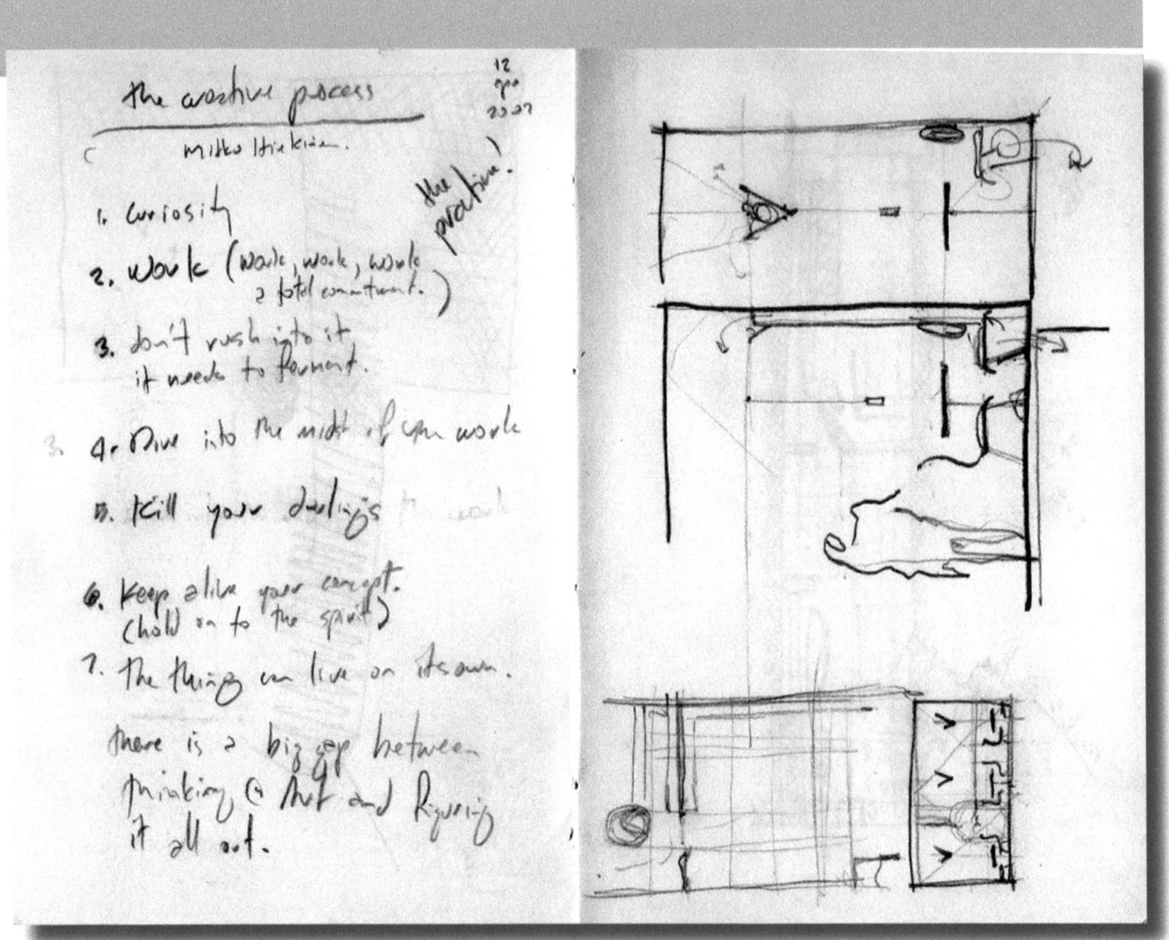

Fig. 09-125 Two-page journal entry, Bob Condia. Pencil on paper.

IGJ-5.1

ADAM LANMAN

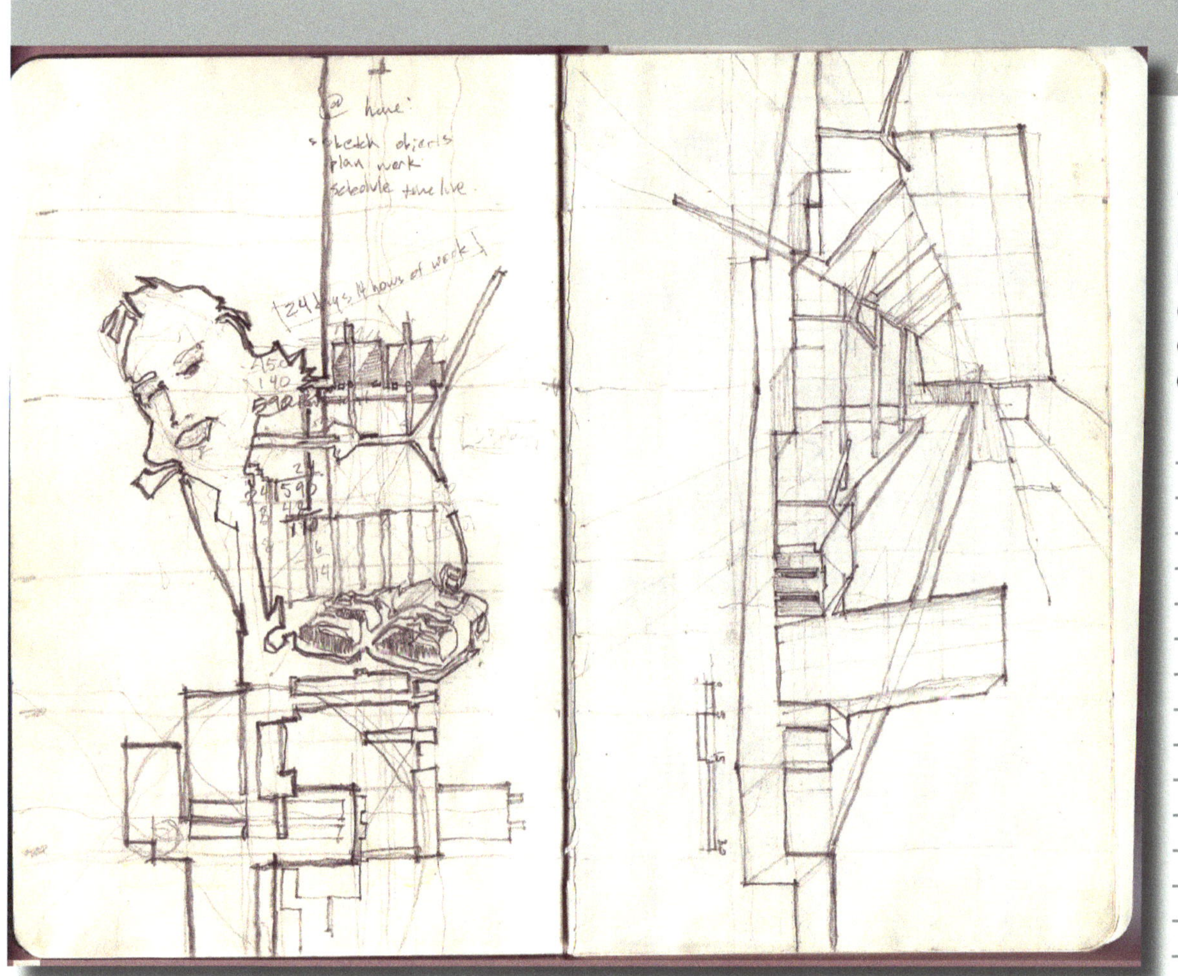

Fig. 09-126 Two-page journal entry, Adam Lanman. Pencil on paper.

This two-page composition offers a single sketch located at the center of each page. The left page has multiple sketches and text superimposed upon one another. There is little containment for the composition. Graphic value is expressed through the careful manipulation of the line thickness.

IGJ-5.2

ADAM LANMAN

This two-page composition displays hierarchy and intensity, though it is a balanced layout of equal halves. The page on the left is dominated by a single sketch with supporting text at the top and bottom. The right page holds a series of seven stacked bands of graphic information. Graphic value is expressed through the careful manipulation of the line thickness.

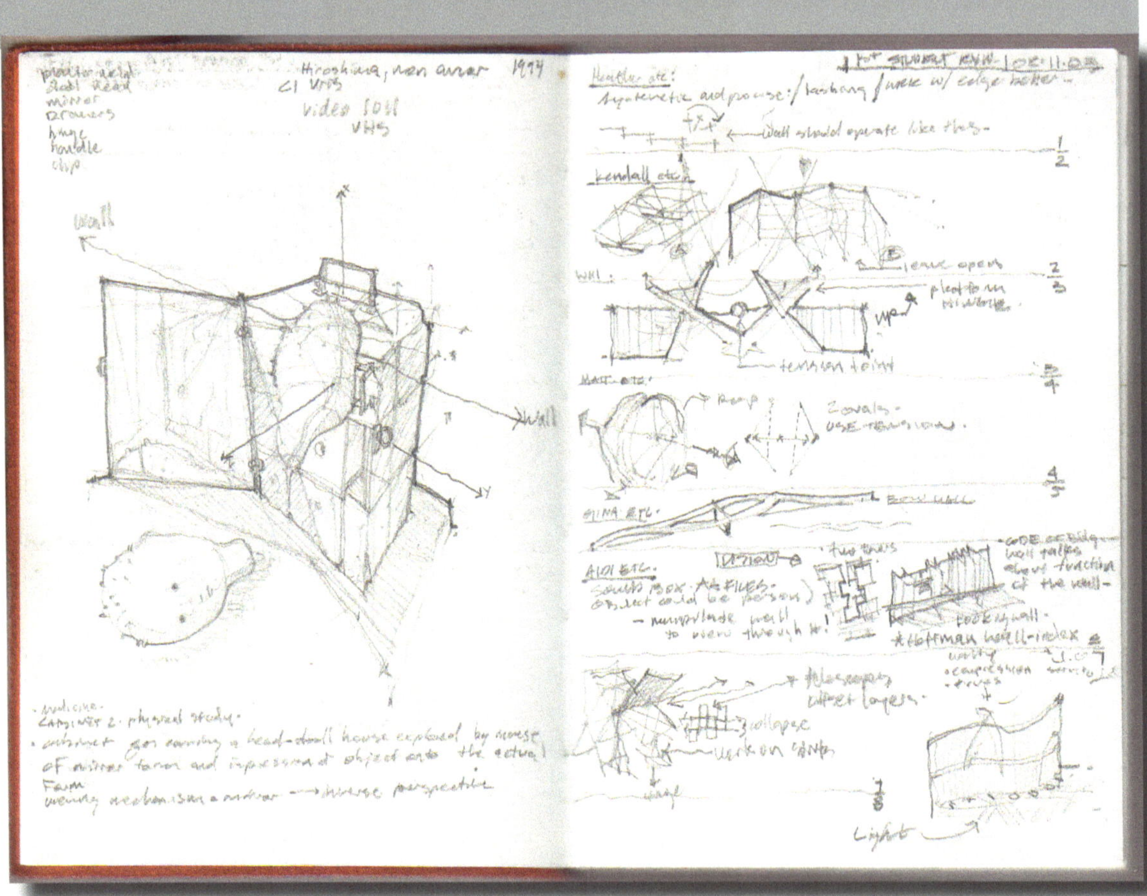

Fig. 09-127 Two-page journal entry, Adam Lanman. Pencil on paper.

IGJ-5.3

ADAM LANMAN

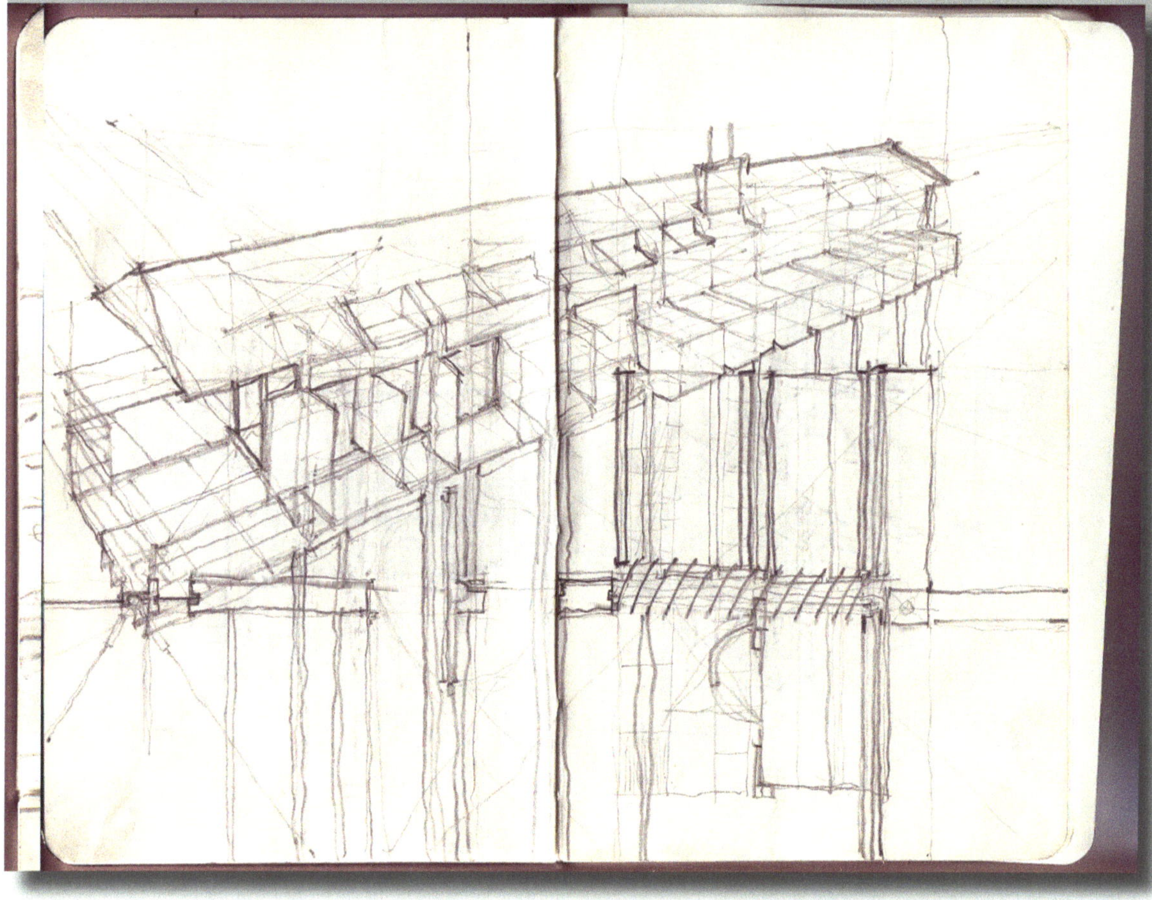

A single image spans the entire width of this two-page journal composition. The image consists of a perspectival sketch superimposed upon an orthogonal view. The primary sketch creates a diagonal line that adds a sense of dynamism to the overall composition. The underlying sketch is very static. The sketches extend beyond the margins of the page.

Fig. 09-128 Two-page journal entry, Adam Lanman. Pencil on paper.

IGJ-5.4

ADAM LANMAN

This two-page journal entry contains separate subject matters that are supported by text. The sketch on the left is highly informal and executed in pencil, with text surrounding the image in an informal manner. The sketch on the right is heavy on the text, and rather formal in ink lines including its graphic frame. The graphic value is indicated by manipulating the thickness of the lines.

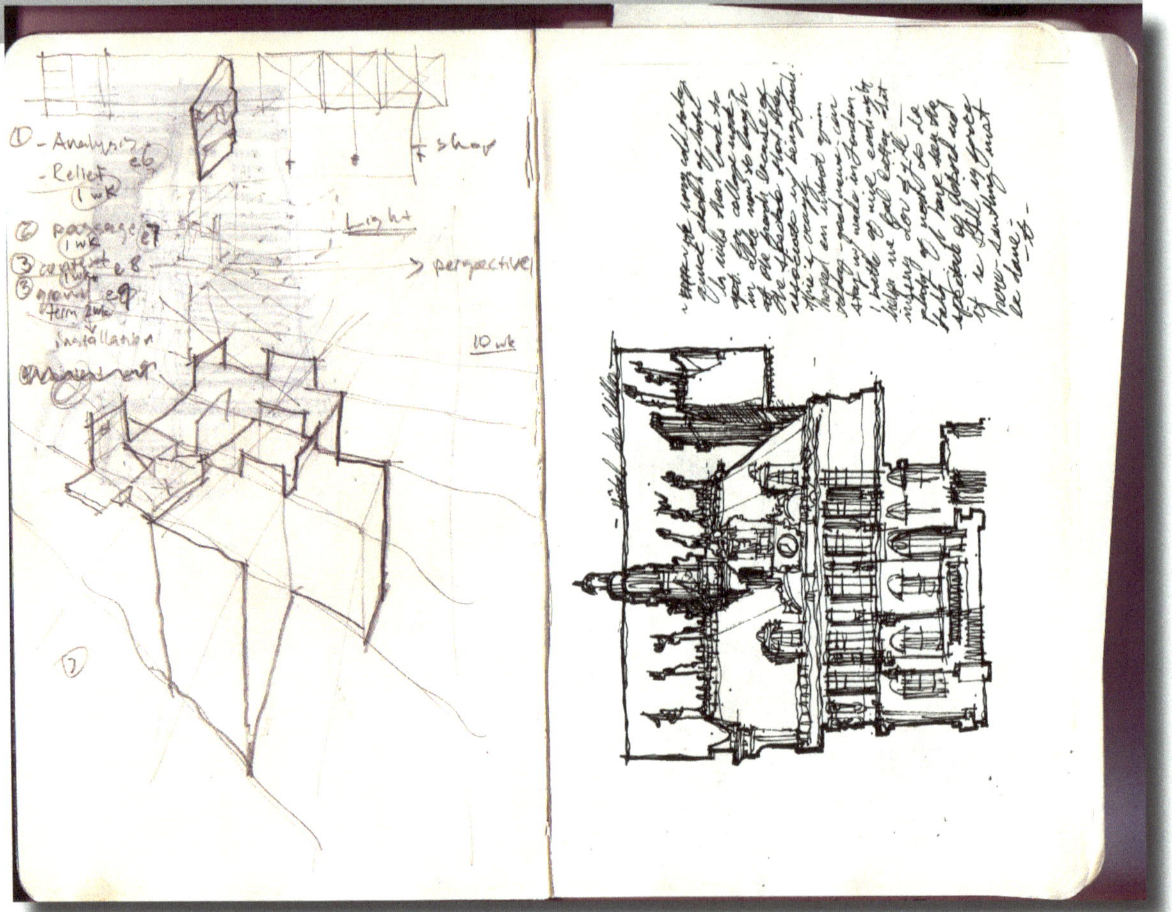

Fig. 09-129 Two-page journal entry, Adam Lanman. Pen and pencil on paper.

IGJ-6.1

PAUL LASEAU

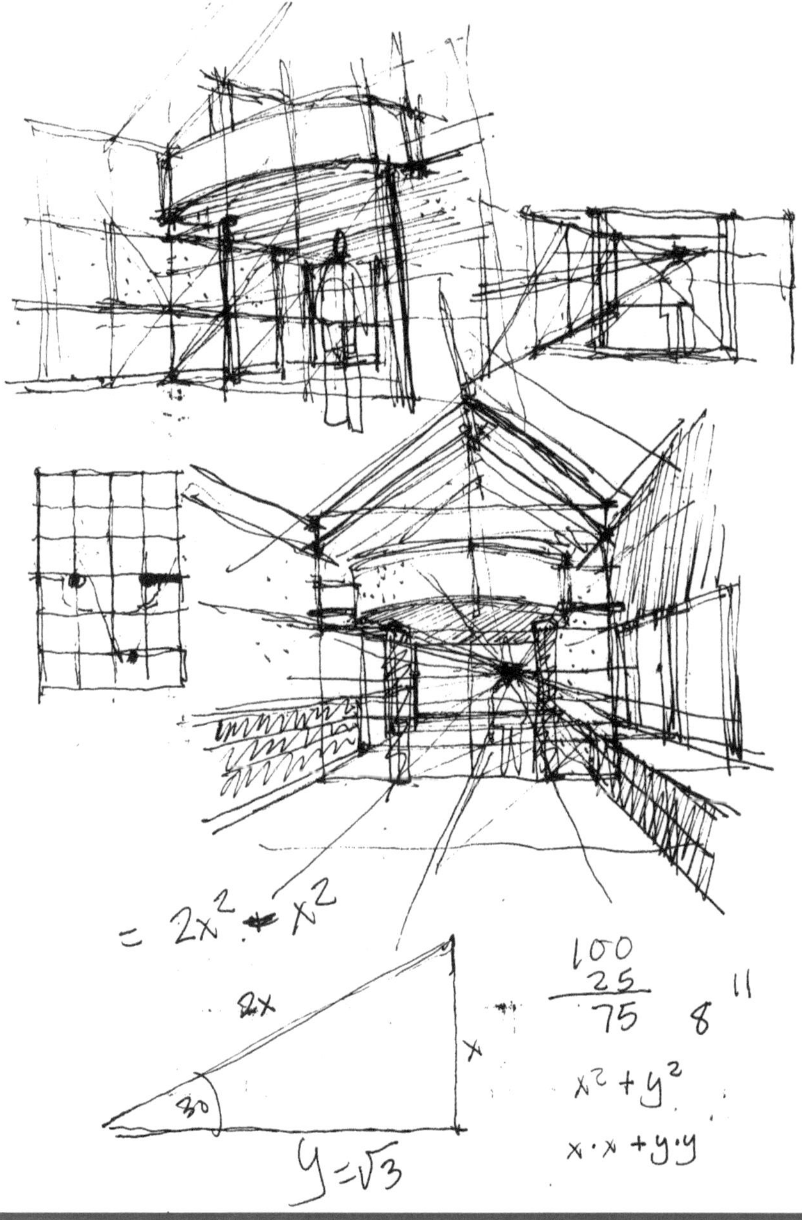

This single page journal entry communicates the subject matter through a series of informal perspectival sketches arranged radially. The major sketch occurs at the center. Human figures are used to communicate scale and graphic value is expressed through modulated hatching.

Fig. 09-130 One page journal entry, Paul Laseau. Pen on paper.

IGJ-6.2

PAUL LASEAU

The single page composition exhibits a central idea that is studied and communicated through several contour sketches. These sketches are arranged in an informal matrix with the graphic value achieved through hatching. A few lines of supporting text are added to further communicate the design intent.

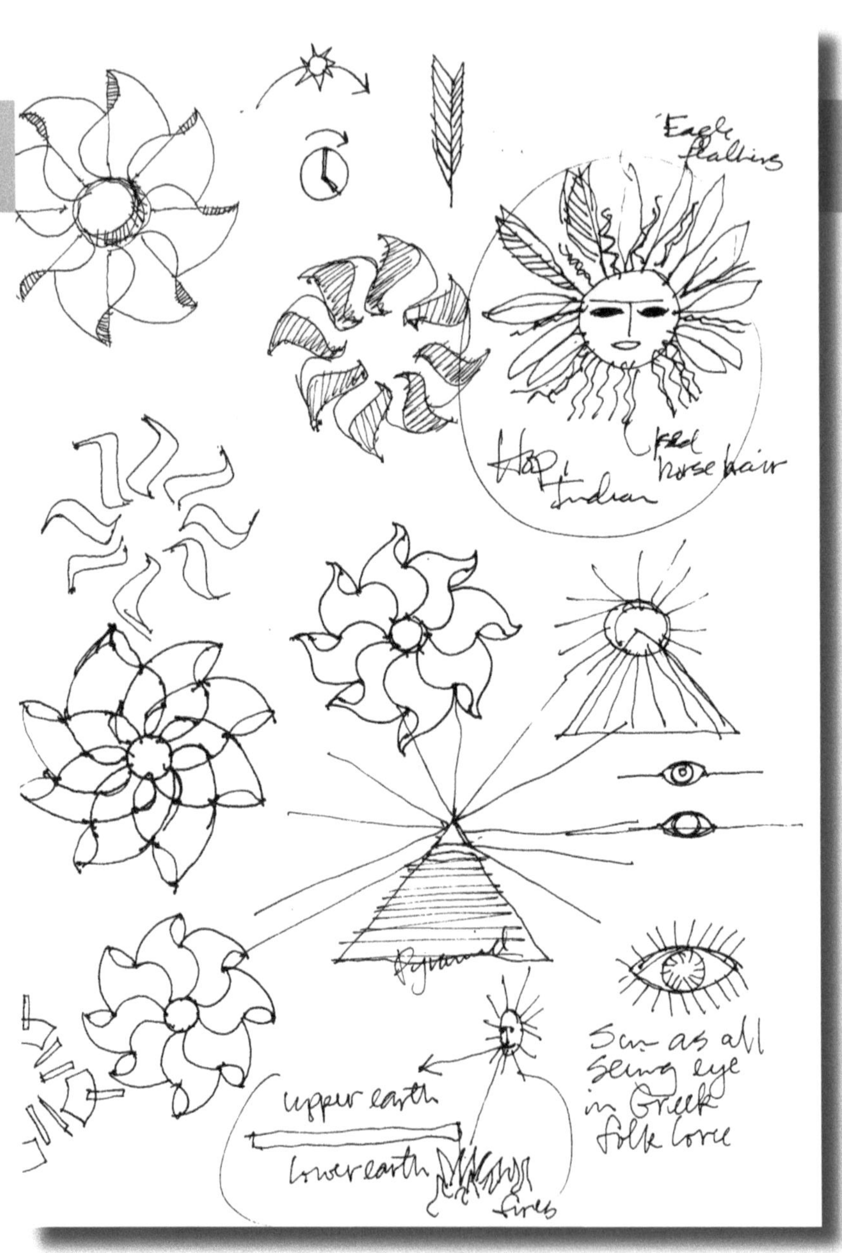

Fig. 09-131 One page journal entry, Paul Laseau. Pen on paper.

IGJ-6.3

PAUL LASEAU

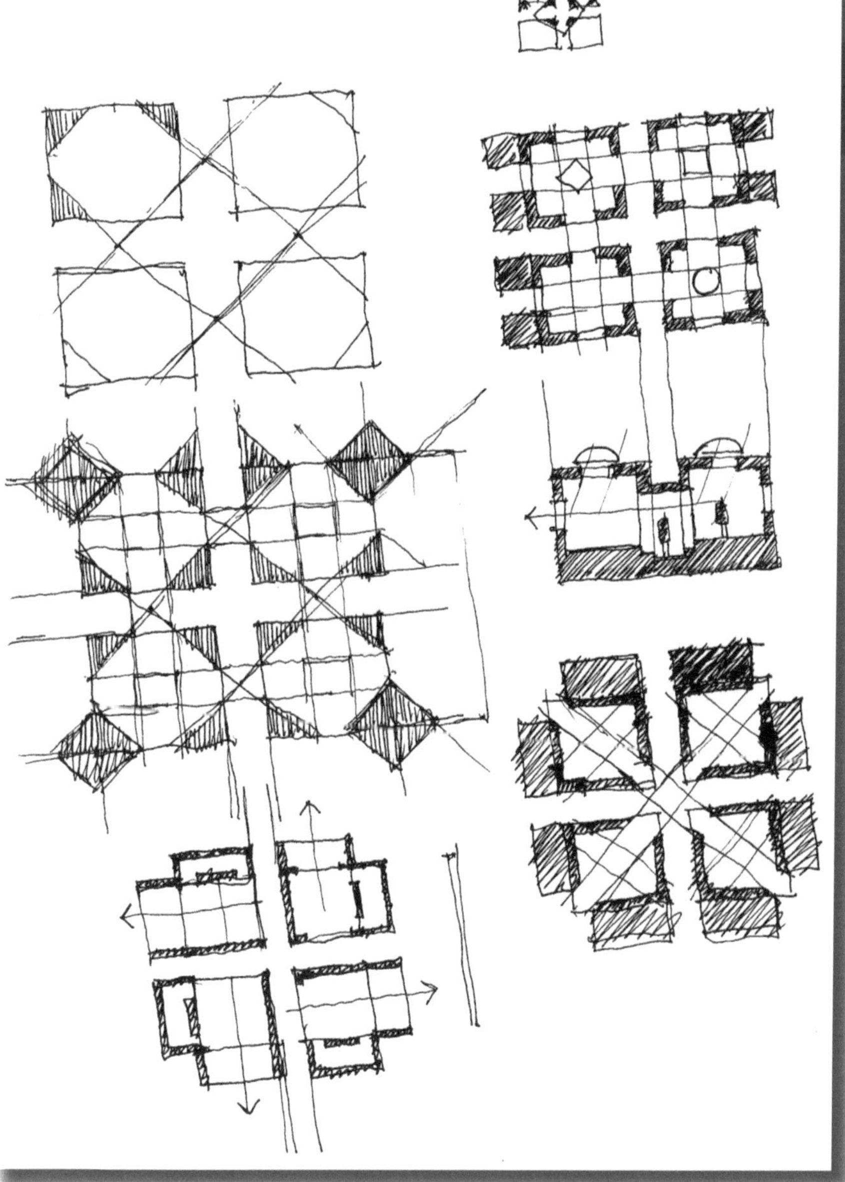

A matrix forms the basis of this single page composition. The development of an idea is communicated in a series of non-perspectival sketches. Relationships are sometimes expressed as projection lines or arrows. Graphic value is achieved through modulated hatching.

Fig. 09-132 One page journal entry, Paul Laseau. Pen on paper.

IGJ-6.4

PAUL LASEAU

This single page composition is focused upon a single informal sketch. The sketch is graphically framed to detach it from the page. Modulated hatching is used to communicate graphic value.

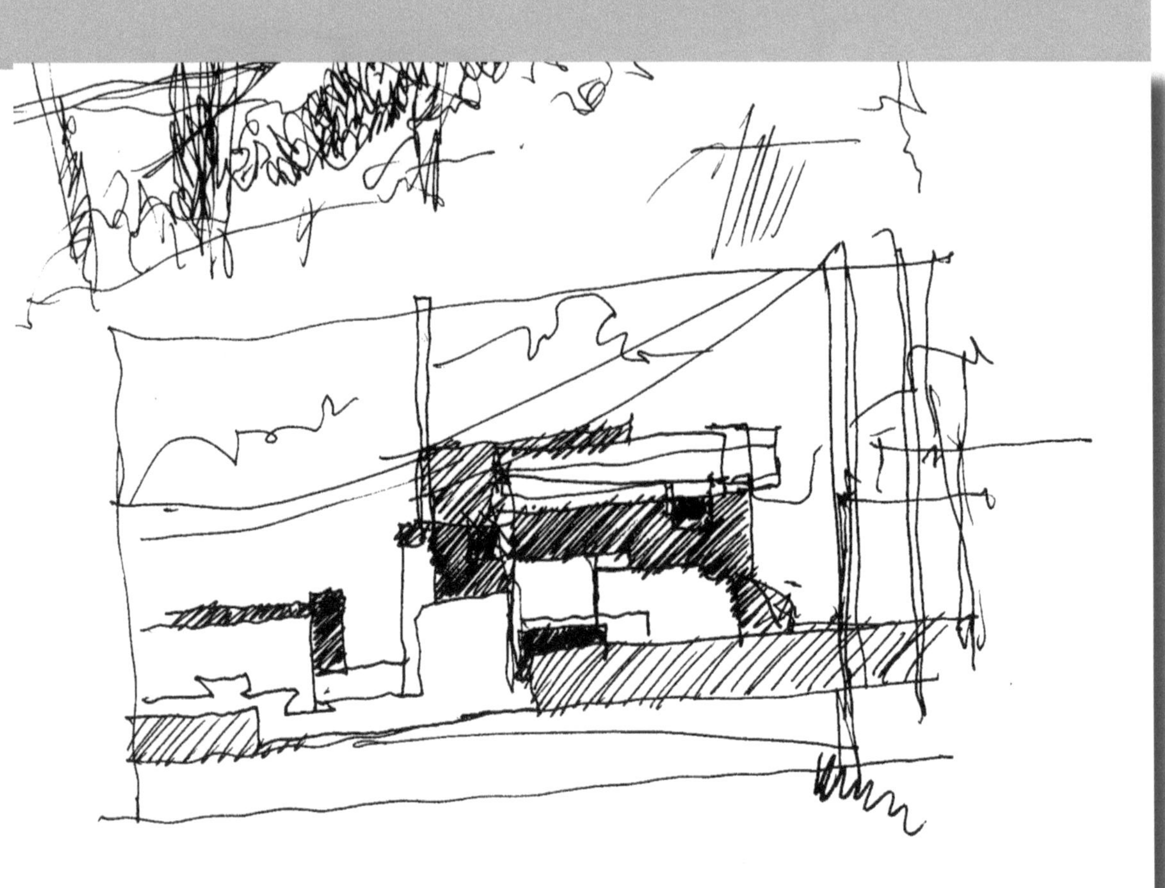

Fig. 09-133 One page journal entry, Paul Laseau. Pen on paper.

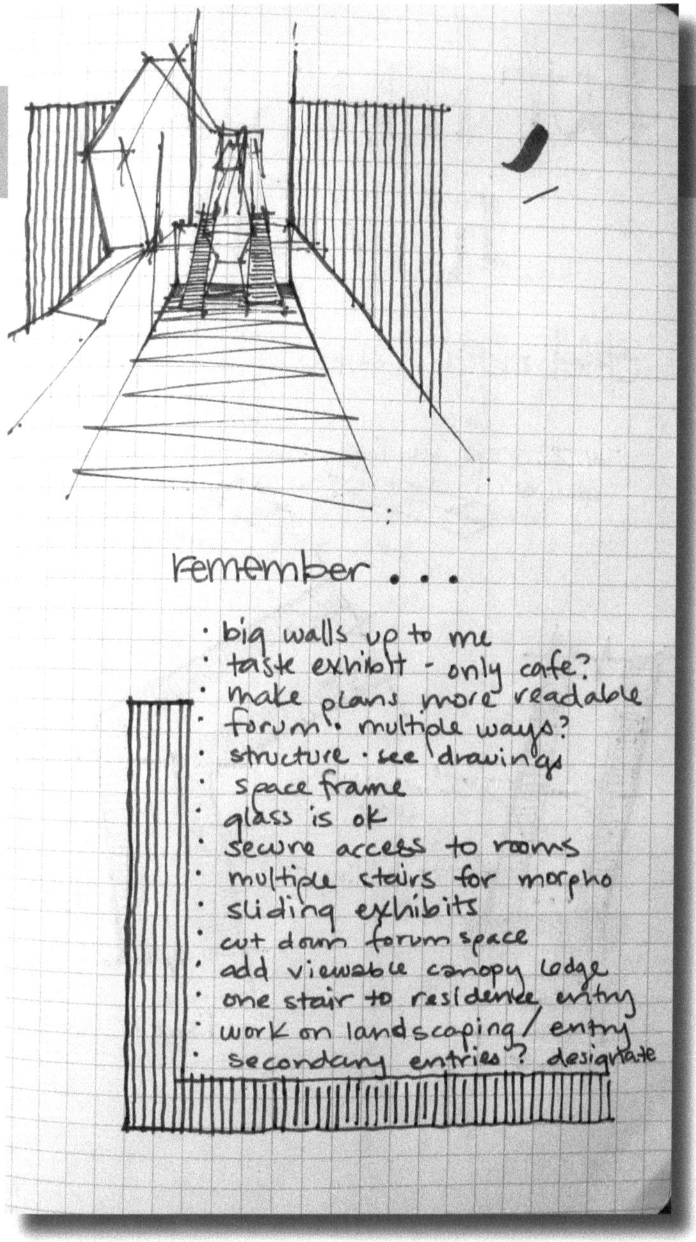

IGJ-7.1

ALEX MAJKOWSKI

This single page composition is divided horizontally into halves. The top half is the sketch and the bottom half is the supporting text. A graphic angle with a low value is added to provide a starter edge and to anchor the delicate text.

Fig. 09-134 One page journal entry, Alex Majkowski. Pen on paper.

IGJ-7.2

ALEX MAJKOWSKI

This single page composition is executed on a grid paper journal. The page includes a wealth of information depicted spatially, graphically, and organized in a grid format. The sketches are both perspectival and diagrammatic and use hatching to modulate the graphic value. The page title is rotated to be able to fit on a page that is very crowded with information.

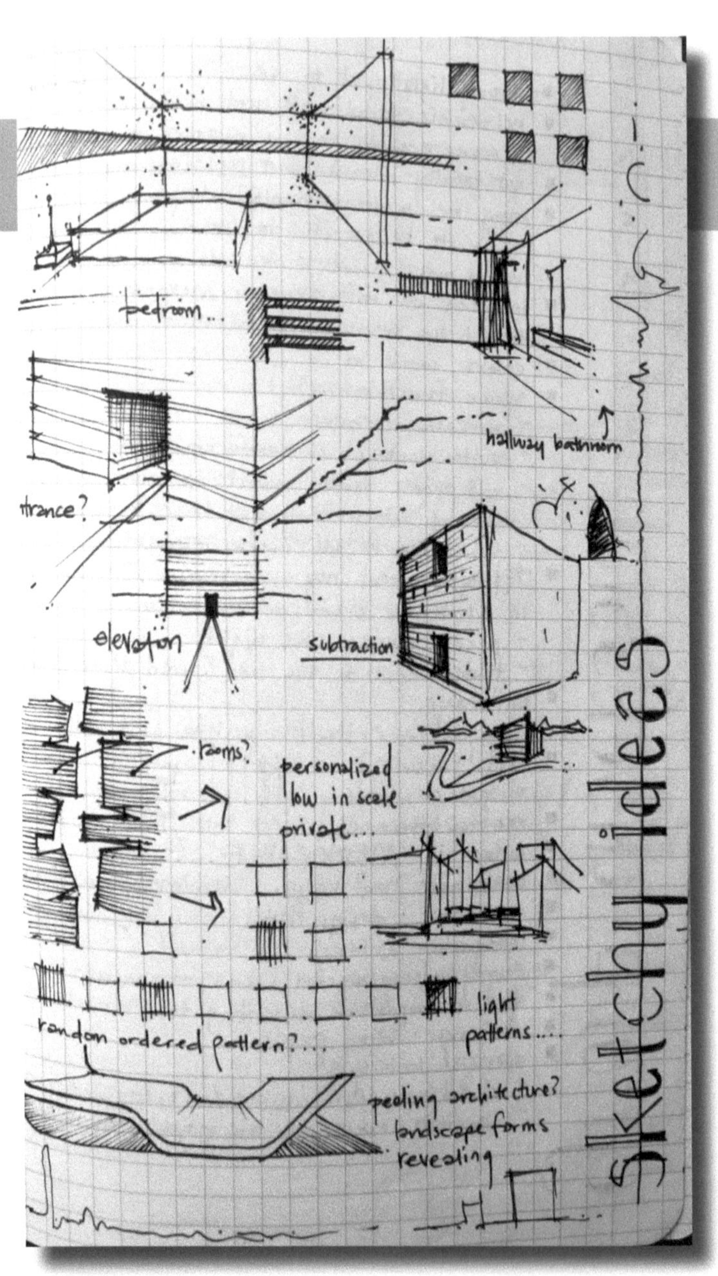

Fig. 09-135 One page journal entry, Alex Majkowski. Pen on paper.

IGJ-8.1

MITCH PRIDE

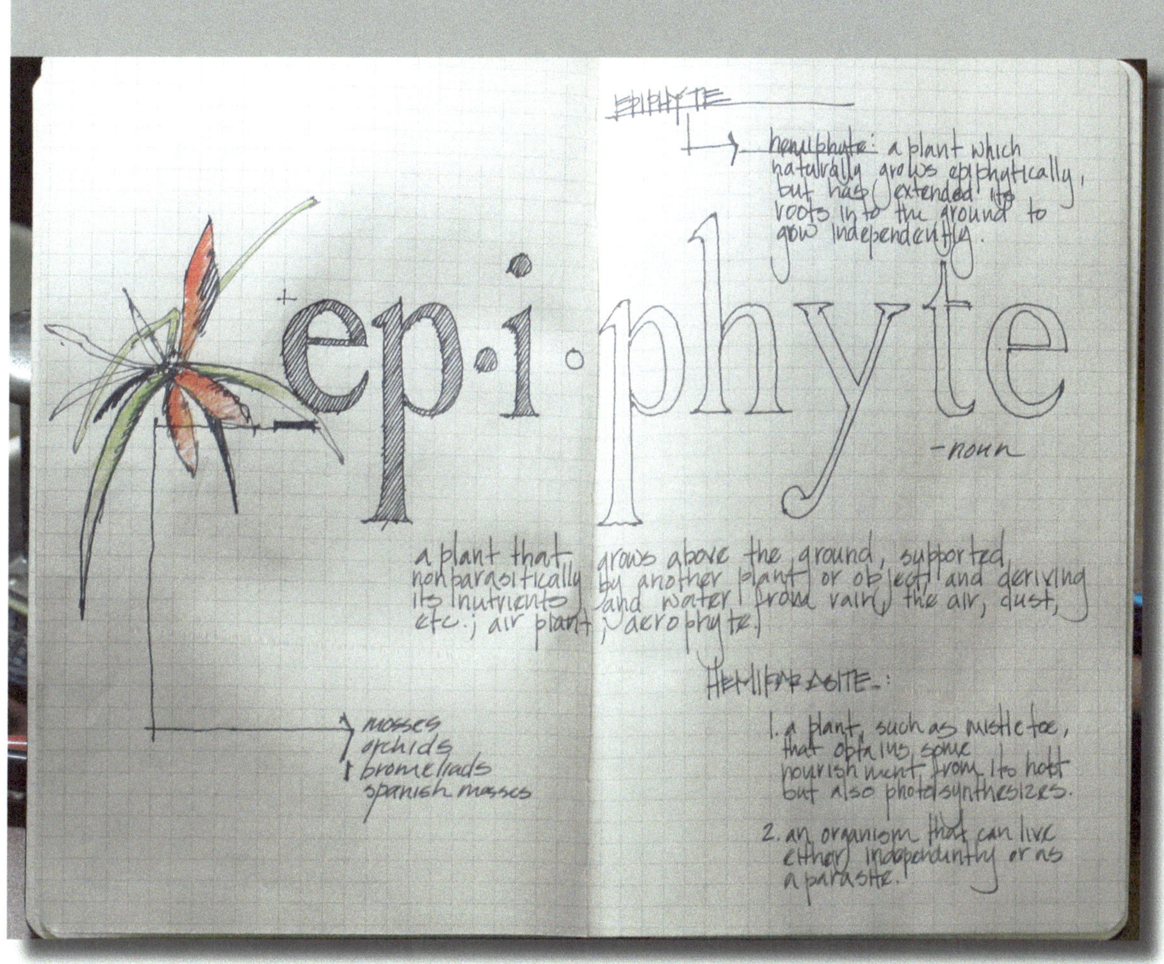

Fig. 09-136 Two-page journal entry, Mitch Pride. Pen and colored pencils on paper.

In this dramatic two-page composition, less is more. The graphic information and the page title are articulated hierarchically as they interact with the supporting text. The journal entry is executed asymmetrically to add dynamism and excitement. Selective hatching and cross hatching are used to add graphic value to the text and the sketches.

IGJ-8.2

MITCH PRIDE

There is an overwhelming amount of text in this two-page composition. The graphic information, with its immediate notation and supporting text, is framed and added as a series of vignettes to establish hierarchy. Graphic value is achieved through hatching. The composition is titled informally at the top of the page.

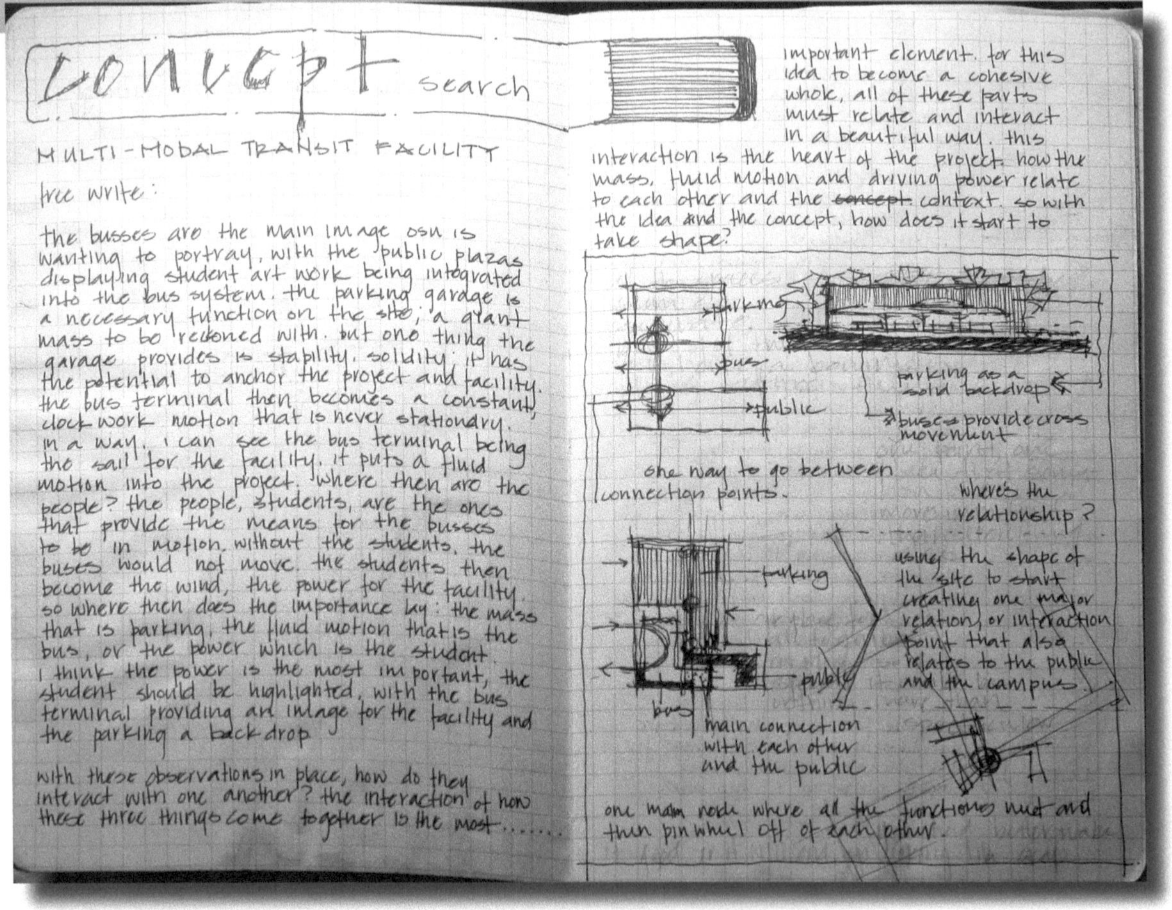

Fig. 09-137 Two-page journal entry, Mitch Pride. Pen on paper.

IGJ-8.3

MITCH PRIDE

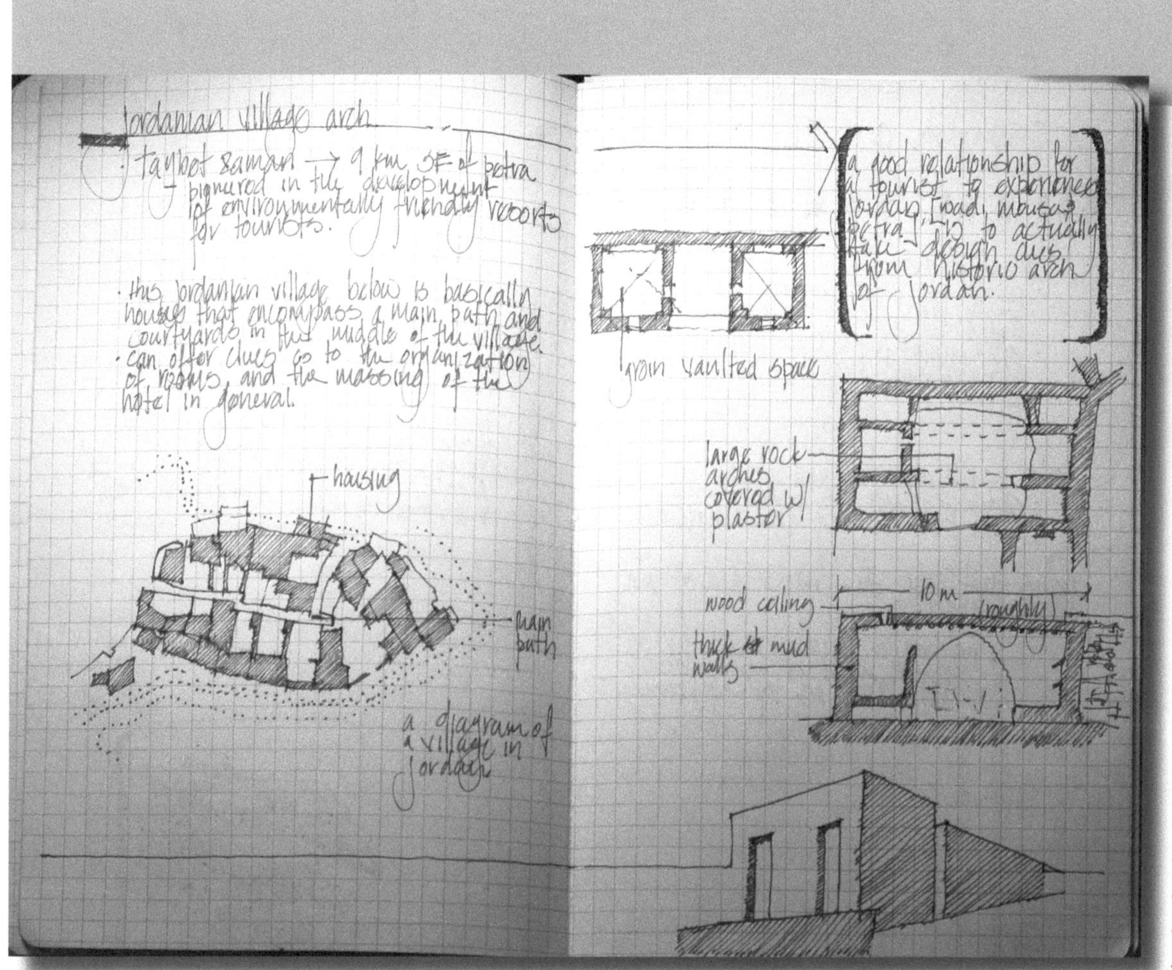

Fig. 09-138 Two-page journal entry, Mitch Pride. Pen on paper.

This two-page composition contains a collection of five sketches related to a single idea that are either orthographic, perspectival, or pictorial. The corner perspectival sketch employs an extended edge to anchor the composition while allowing the rest of the orthographic sketches and their notation to alternate.

IGJ-8.4

MITCH PRIDE

In this two-page composition the sketches and the supporting text are organized in columns in different widths. The primary sketch, with its low value base, is located towards the bottom right corner to anchor the overall composition. The entry title is articulated, rendered, and integrated as part of the information that is being communicated.

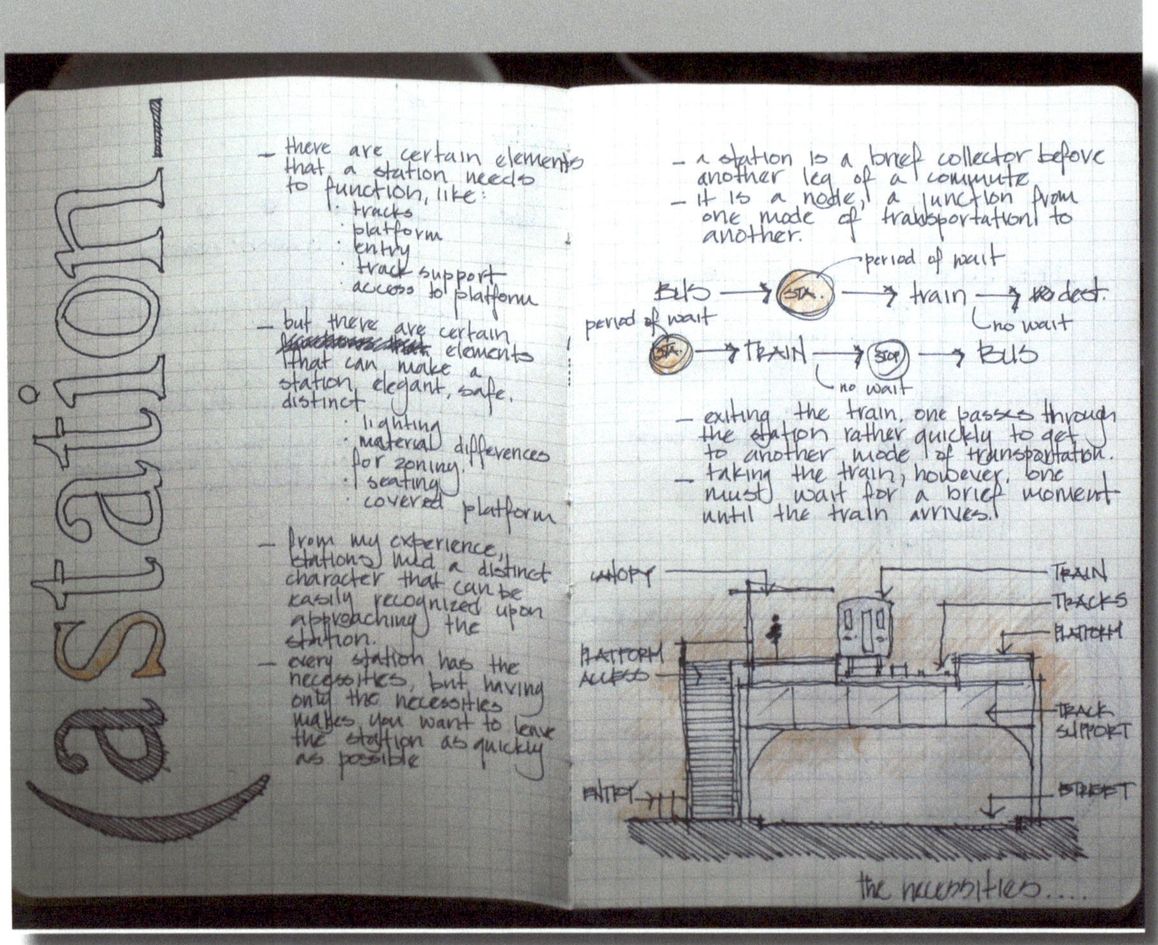

Fig. 09-139 Two-page journal entry, Mitch Pride. Pen and colored pencils on paper.

IGJ-9.1

SHANNON WEST

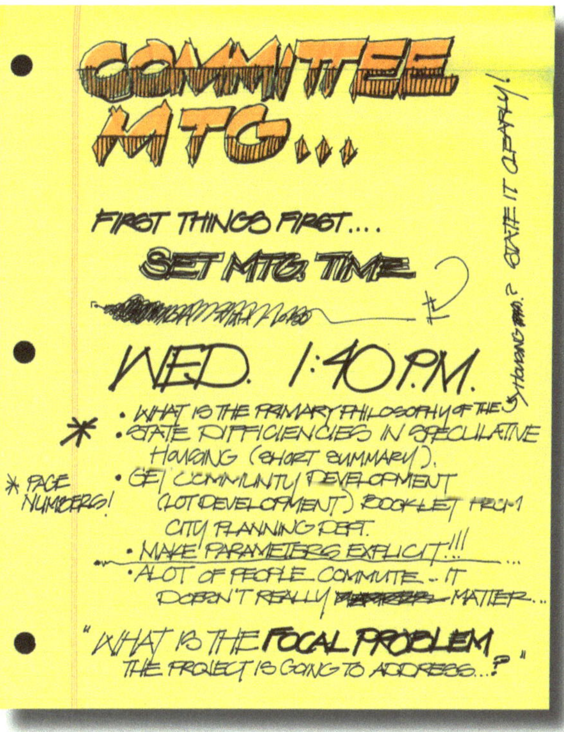

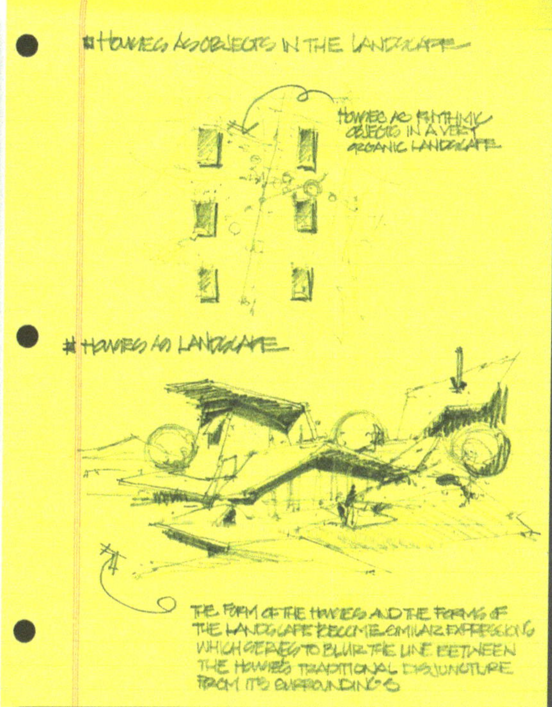

Fig. 09-140 Journal entries, Shannon West. Pen, pencil, and marker on paper.

These single page compositions were executed on the pages of a yellow tablet. The left entry is completely textual with the title rendered and situated in a position of prominence. The width of the lines are manipulated to achieve hierarchical emphasis. The right page is divided horizontally into halves with the sketches and diagrams centrally located. Graphic value is achieved through hatching. The use of block lettering adds an architectural flavor to the journal entry.

IGJ-9.2

SHANNON WEST

The sketch is located at the center of the page in this composition. There is very little supporting text. Graphic value is achieved through hatching. The application of low values at certain locations adds to the graphic impact of the sketch. The addition of a human figure communicates the perception of scale.

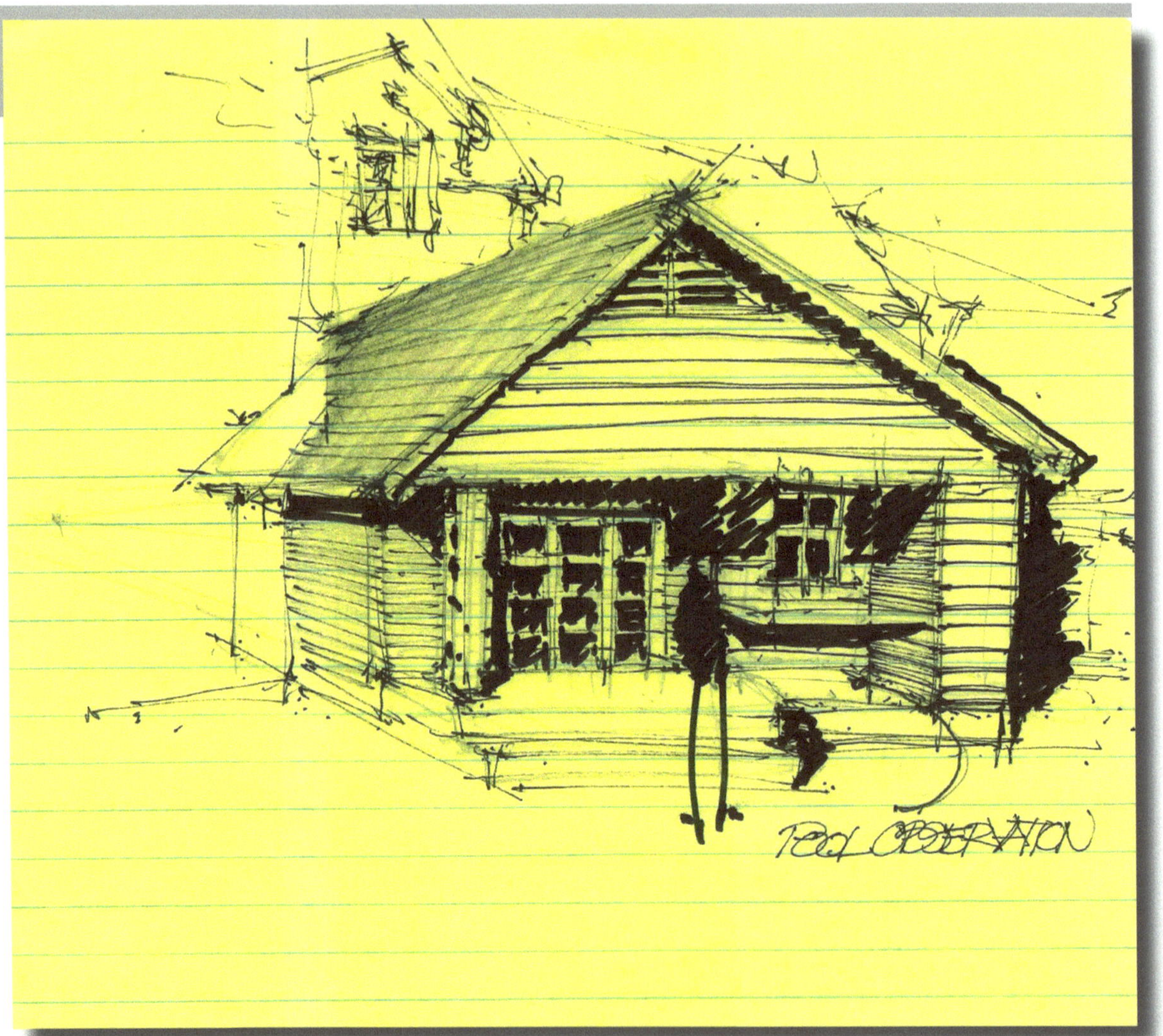

Fig. 09-141 One page journal entry, Shannon West. Pen and pencil on paper.

IGJ-9.3

SHANNON WEST

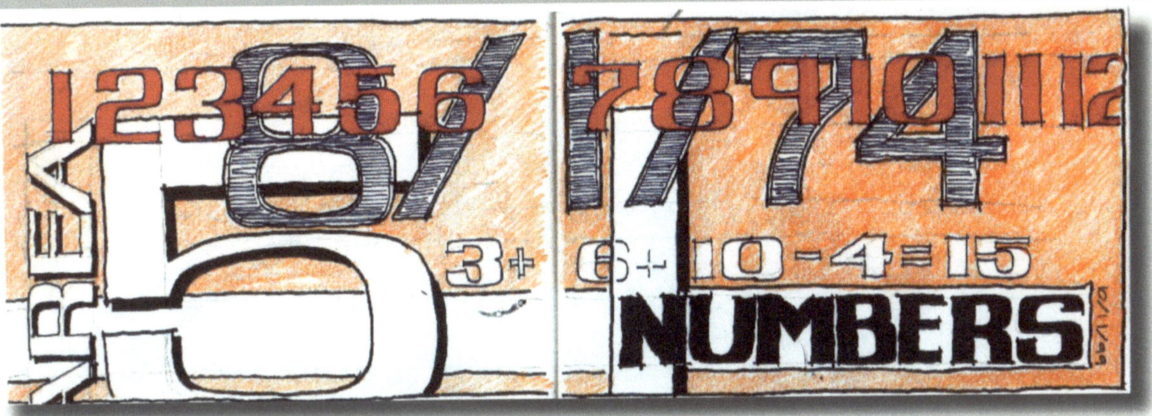

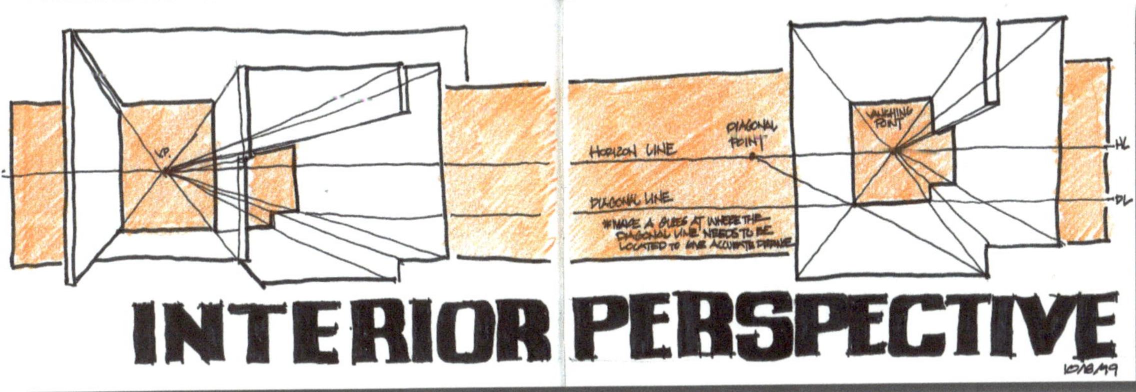

Fig. 09-142 Two-page journal entries, Shannon West. Pen, pencil, colored pencils, and marker on paper.

These two journal entries employ a graphic value that achieves maximum contrast. Superimposition and shadows are used to achieve depth within the pages. The inclusion of a graphic strip unites the two pages and establishes a strong connection. The page titles are graphically as strong as the sketches themselves.

IGJ-9.4

SHANNON WEST

These landscape format two-page compositions display two different approaches to graphic unity. The top journal entry uses a strong graphic title and frames to join the pages. Technical diagrams and their supporting text occupy the right page while leaving the left page open for the text. The lower journal entry allows the three related architectural sketches to float across the white space of the pages, while explaining the design intent through adjacent notation linked by graphic leaders.

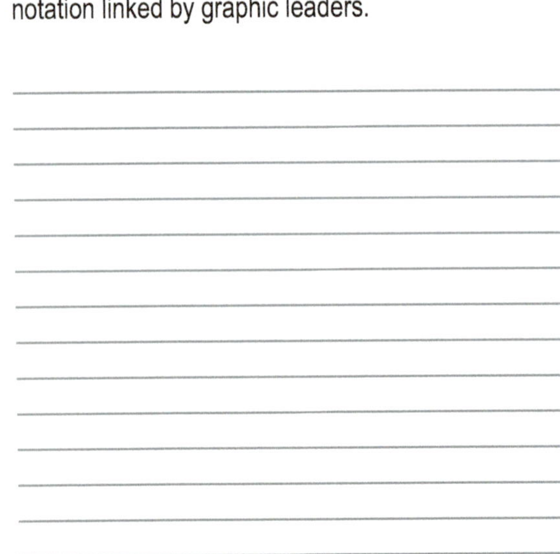

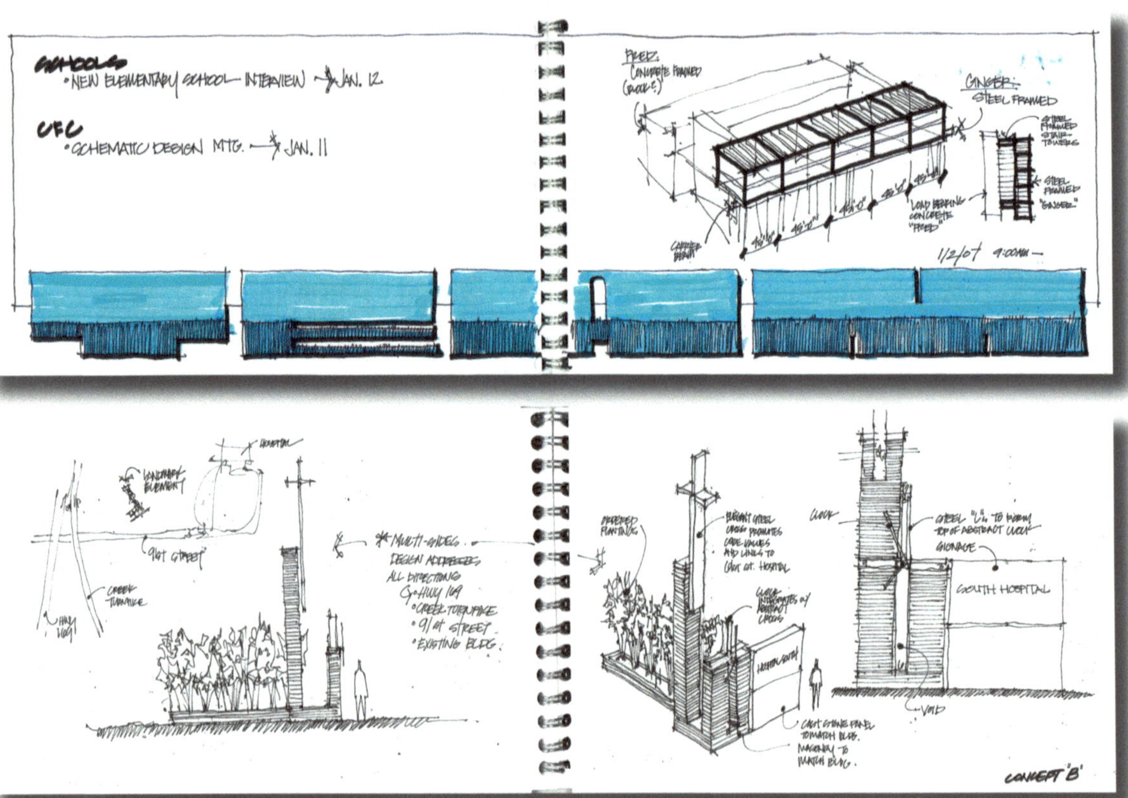

Fig. 09-143 Two-page journal entries, Shannon West. Pen and marker on paper.

IGJ-9.5

SHANNON WEST

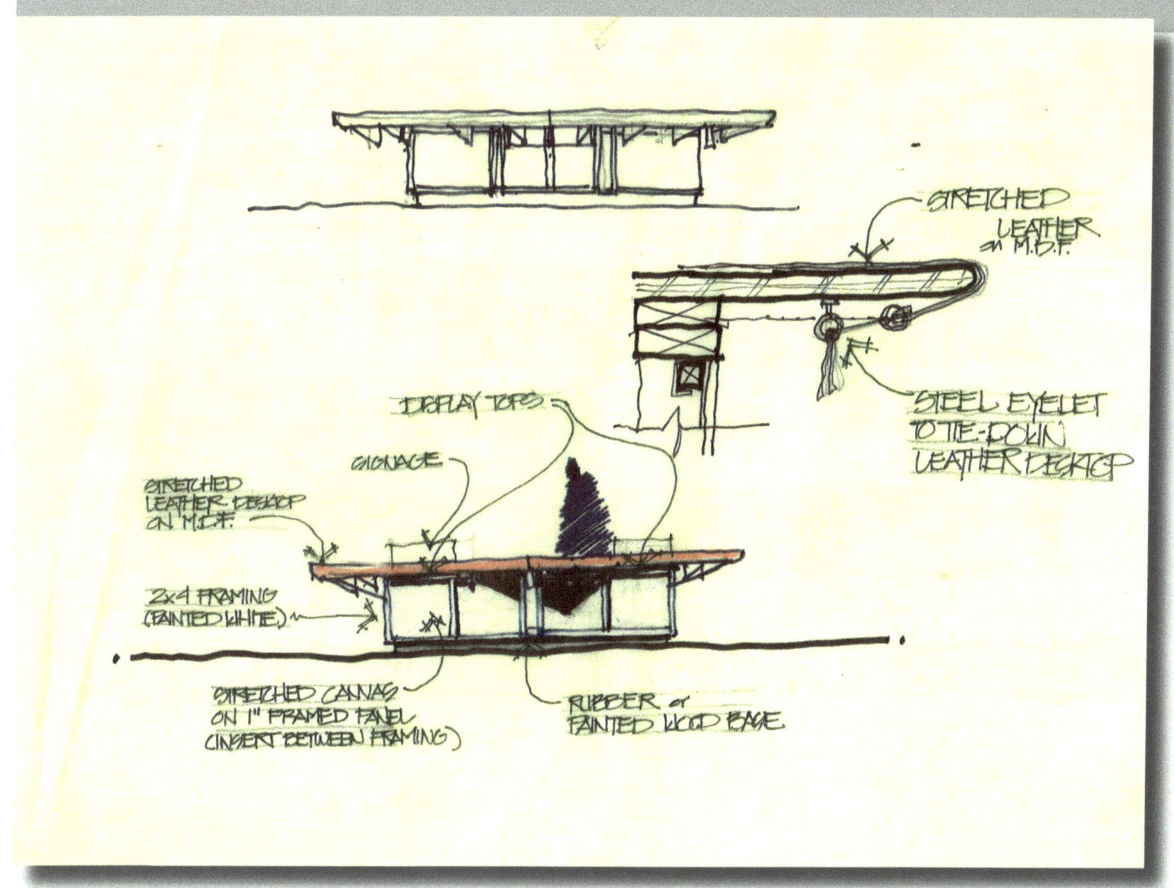

Fig. 09-144 One page journal entry, Shannon West. Pen, pencil, and colored pencils on paper.

In this single page journal entry, the information is presented in alternating horizontal bands of sketches. The development of the idea is sequential, from the top sketch through iterations leading to the bottom of the page. Text surrounds the final sketch.

IGJ-9.6

SHANNON WEST

These two-page compositions exhibit isolated sketches, one per page, that relate to one another through the common subject matter. The top journal entry sketches were drawn directly on the page, and utilize thick lines to anchor the drawings in the overall composition. The bottom two sketches were executed on yellow tracing paper and later trimmed, adhered, and composed onto the journal pages. Graphic value is achieved through hatching and high contrast highlights.

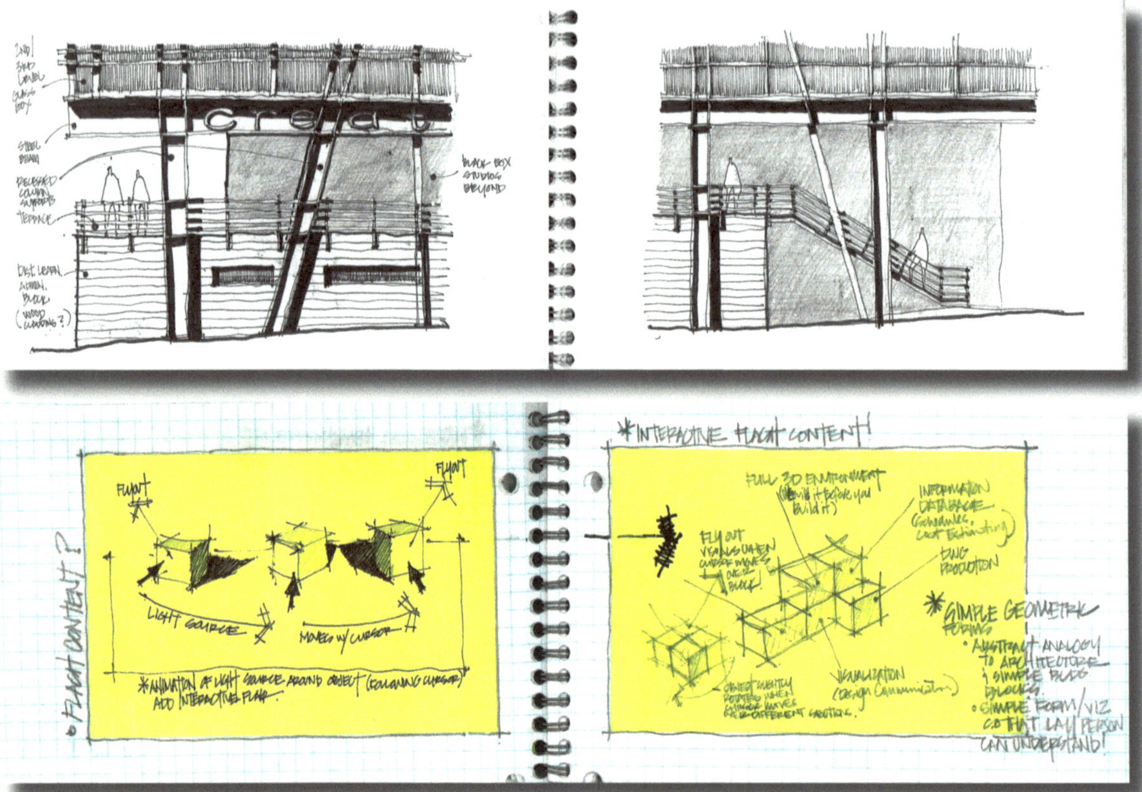

Fig. 09-145 Two-page journal entries, Shannon West. Pen and marker on paper.

paradigms

10 - BIBLIOGRAPHY

excellent resources about drawing, sketching, and journaling

Ching, Francis. *Architectural Graphics.*
New York: Van Nostrand Reinhold Company, 1975.

Ching, Francis. *Drawing: A Creative Process.*
New York: Van Nostrand Reinhold Company, 1975.

Couch, Tony. *Watercolor.*
Cincinnati: North Light, 1987.

Doyle, Michael. *Color Drawing.*
New York: Van Nostrand Reinhold Company, 1981.

Edwards, Betty. *Drawing on the Right Side of the Brain.*
Los Angeles, CA: J. Van Nostrand Reinhold Company. Tarcher, 1979.

Frank, Frederick. *The Zen of Seeing.*
New York: Random House, 1973.

Hale, Robert. *Drawing Lessons from the Great Masters.*
New York: Watson-Guptill Publications, 1964.

Hogarth, Paul. *Creative Ink Drawing.*
New York: Watson-Guptill Publications, 1968.

Itten, Johannes. *The Elements of Color.*
New York: Van Nostrand Reinhold, 1970.

Kautzky, Theodore. *Pencil Book.*
New York: Van Nostrand Reinhold Company, 1920.

Laseau, Paul. *Architectural Drawing: Options for Design.*
New York: Design Press, 1991.

Lin, Mike. *Drawing and Designing with Confidence.*
New York: Van Nostrand Reinhold Company, 1993.

Lockard, William Kirby. *Design Drawing.*
Tucson, AZ: Pepper Publishing, 1975.

Lorenz, Albert and Salzman, Stanley. *Drawing in Color.*
New York: Watson-Guptill Publications, 1991.

Martin, Judy. *Sketching School.*
New York: The Reader's Digest Association, Inc., 1991.

Oliver, Robert. *The Complete Sketch.*
New York: Van Nostrand Reinhold Company, 1989.

Petroski, Henry. *The Pencil.*
New York: Alfred A. Knopf, Inc., 1989.

Porter, Tom and Greenstreet, Bob. *Manual of Graphic Techniques 1.*
New York: Charles Scribner's Sons, 1980.

Porter, Tom and Goodman, Sue. *Manual of Graphic Techniques 2.*
New York: Charles Scribner's Sons, 1982.

Porter, Tom and Goodman, Sue. *Manual of Graphic Techniques 3.*
New York: Charles Scribner's Sons, 1983.

Reid, Charles. *Painting What You Want to See.*
New York: Watson-Guptill Publications, 1983.

Reid, Charles. *Charles Reid's Watercolor Secrets.*
Cincinnati: North Light Books, 2004.

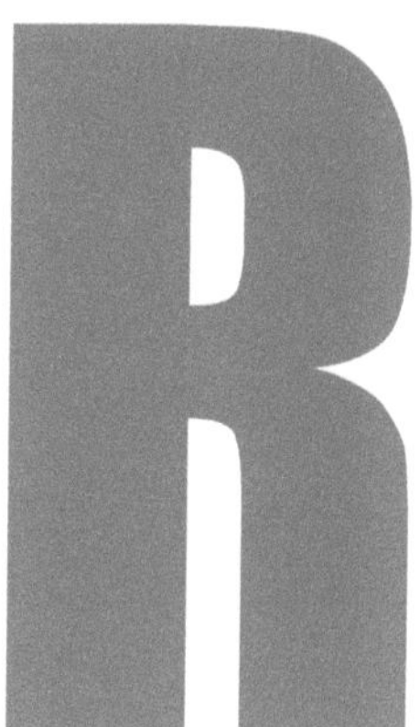

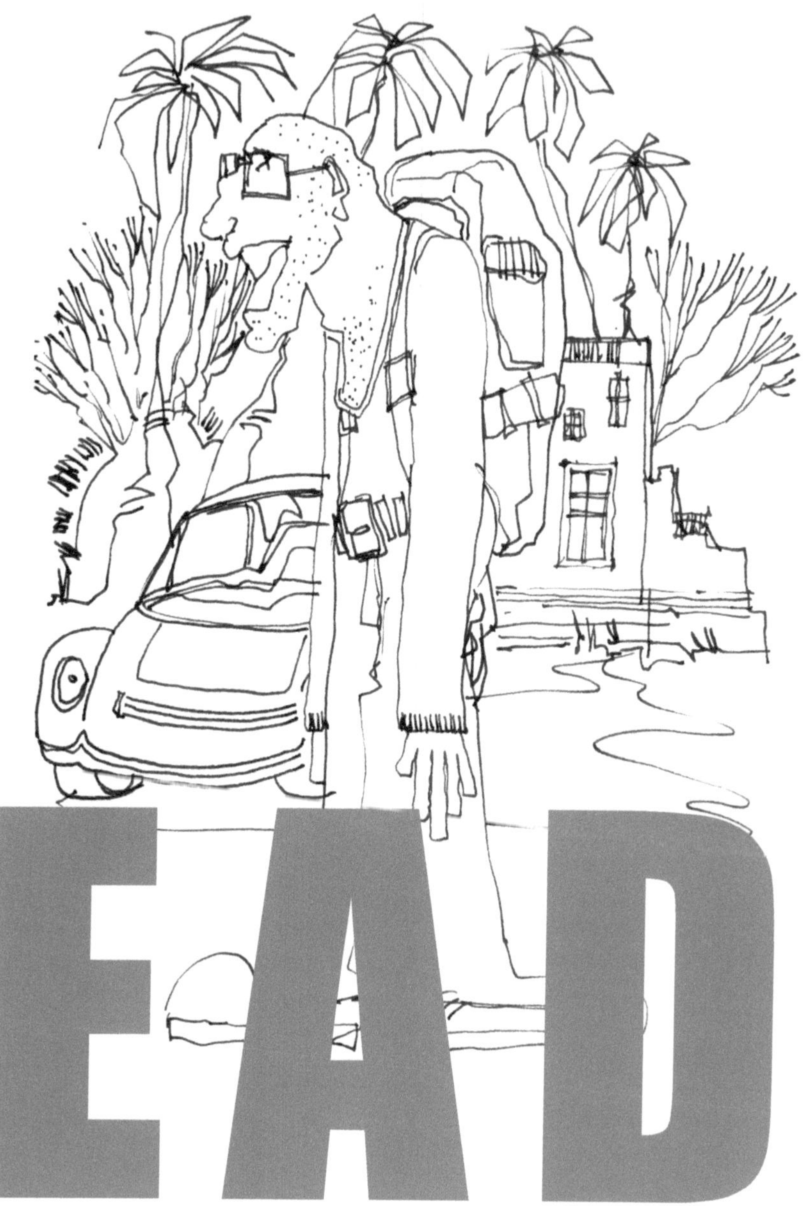

visual thinking/ graphic communication

Blaser, Werner. *Norman Foster Sketchbook.*
Basel: Birkhauser Verlag, 1993.

Eisner, Will. *Graphic Storytelling.*
Tamarac, FL: Poorhouse Press, 1996.

Hanks, Kurt and Belliston, Larry. *Rapid Viz: A New Method for the Rapid Visualization of Ideas.*
Los Altos, CA: William Kaufmann, Inc., 1980.

Hanks, Kurt and Belliston, Larry. *Draw! A Visual Approach to Thinking.*
Los Altos, CA: William Kaufmann, Inc., 1977.

Laseau, Paul. *Graphic Thinking for Architects and Designers.*
New York: John Wiley and Sons, Inc., 2001.

Laseau, Paul. *Graphic Problem Solving for Architects and Designers.*
New York: Van Nostrand Reinhold Company, 1987.

McCloud, Scott. *Understanding Comics: The Invisible Art.*
New York: Harper Collins Publishers, Inc., 1993.

McKim, Robert H. *Experiences in Visual Thinking.*
Belmont, CA: Wadsworth Publishing Company, Inc., 1972.

Porter, Tom. *How Architects Visualize.*
New York: Van Nostrand Reinhold Company, 1979.

Porter, Tom and Goodman, Sue. *Designer Primer.*
New York: Charles Scribner's Sons, 1988.

Robbins, Edward. Why Architects Draw.
Cambridge, MA: The MIT Press, 1994.

White, Jan. *Graphic Idea Notebook.*
New York: Watson-Guptill Publications, 1980.

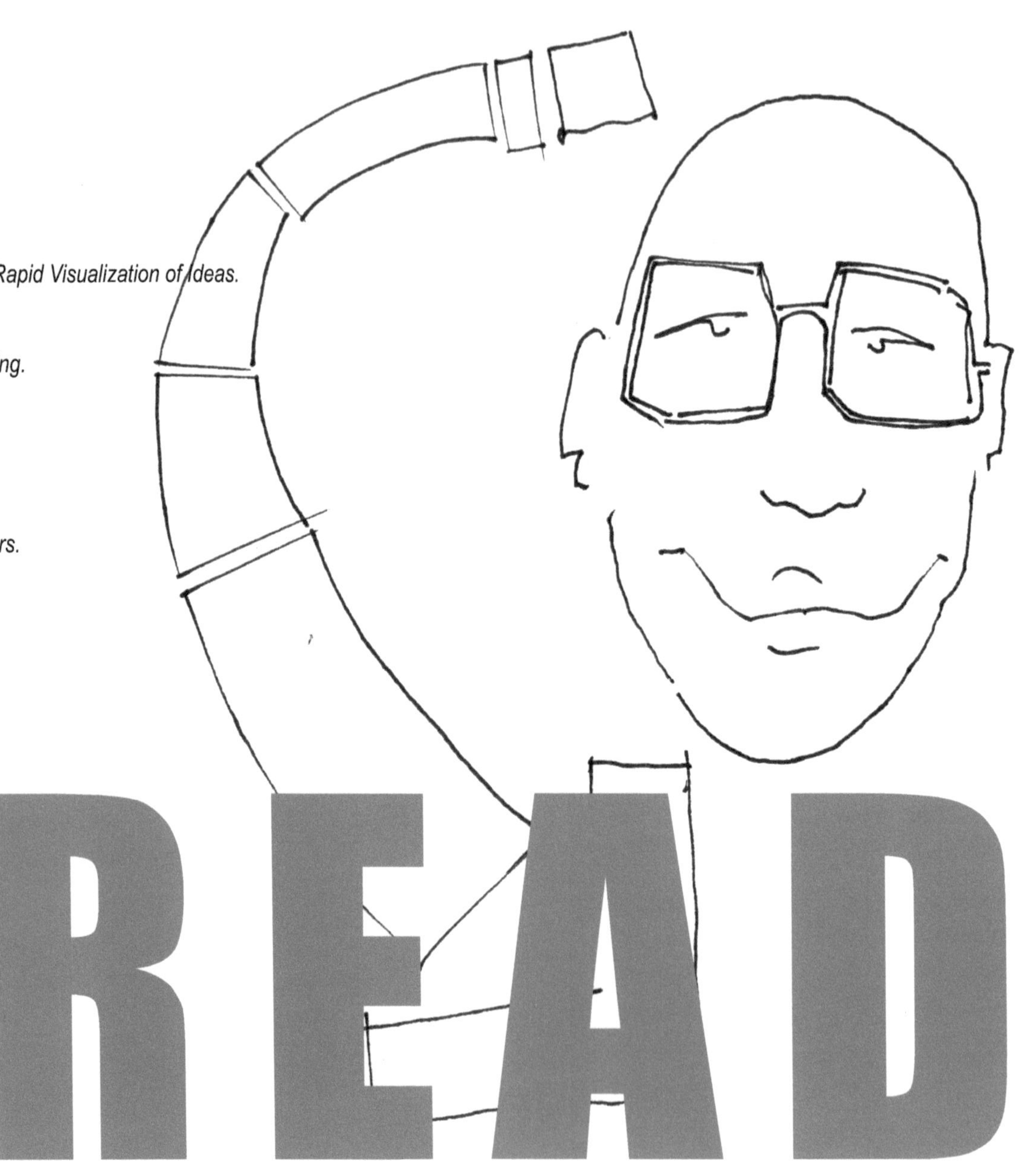

journaling/ sketchbooks

Carlson-Reddig, Thomas. *An Architect's Paris.*
Toronto: Little, Brown and Company, 1993.

Jeanneret, Charles-Edouard (Le Corbusier). *Journey to the East.*
Cambridge, MA: The MIT Press, 1989.

McLoughlin, Marlene. *Road to Rome.*
San Francisco: Chronicle Books, 1995.

Moireau, Fabrice, and Kelly, Mary. *Paris Sketchbook.*
New York: St Martin's Press, 2001.

Moireau, Fabrice, and Pigeat, Paul. *Loire Valley Sketchbook.*
New York: St Martin's Press, 2003.

New, Jennifer. *Drawing from Life: The Journal as Art.*
New York: Princeton Architectural Press, 2005.

Nice, Claudia. *How to Keep a Sketchbook Journal.*
Cincinnati: North Light Books, 2001.

Portoghesi, Paolo. Aldo Rossi: *The Sketchbooks 1990-1997.*
New York: Thames and Hudson Ltd., 2000.

Watson, Lucy. *The Artist's Sketchbook.*
Cincinnati: North Light Books, 2001.

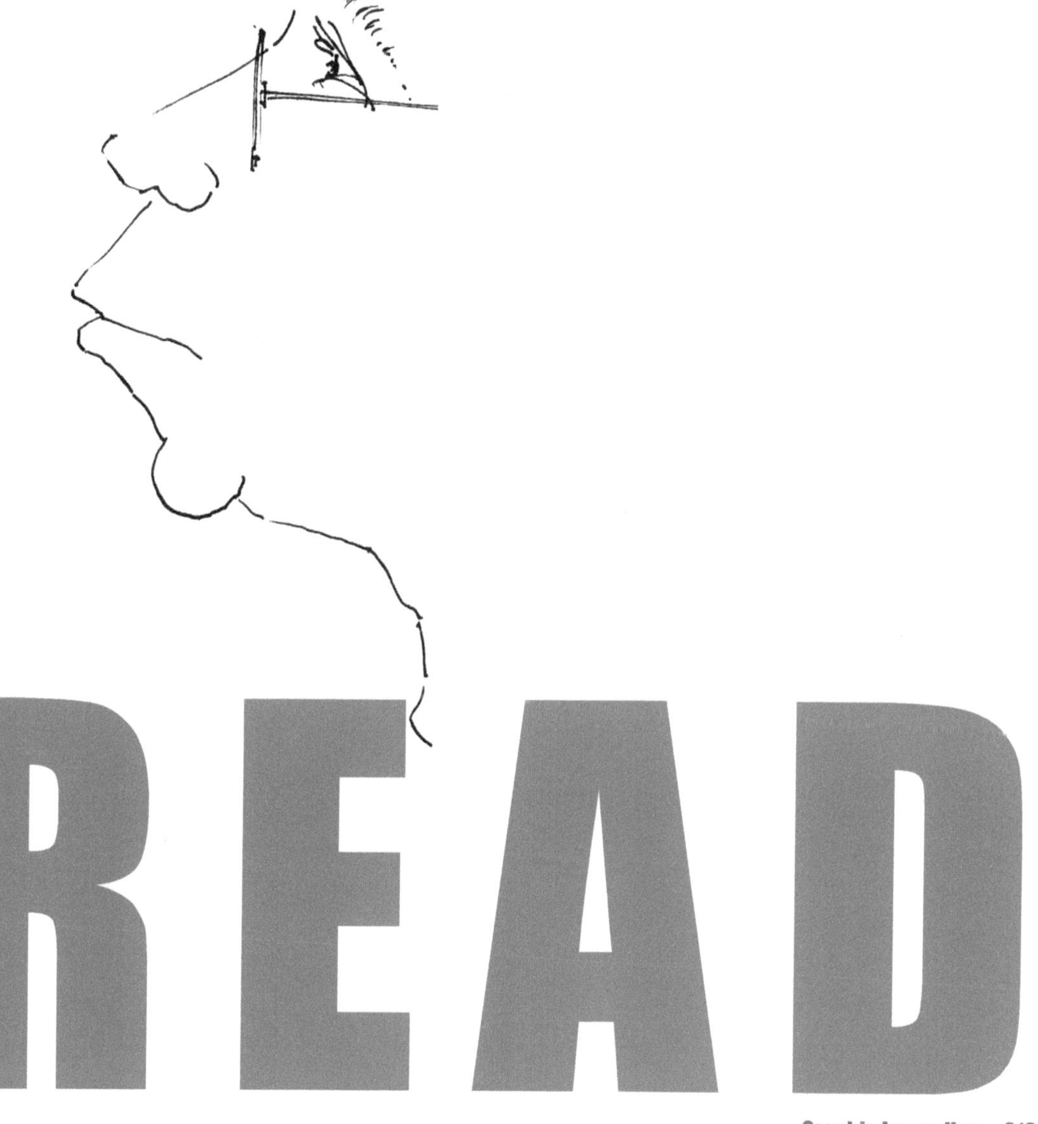